Developing Connections

Short Readings for Writers
Second Edition

Judith A. Stanford
Rivier College

Mayfield Publishing Company
Mountain View, California
London • Toronto

For Lorraine Lordi, an understanding teacher, writer, friend

Copyright © 2000, 1995 by Mayfield Publishing Company

All rights reserved. No portion of this book may be reproduced in any form or by any means without written permission of the publisher.

Library of Congress Cataloging-in-Publication Data
Stanford, Judith Dupras
    Developing connections : short readings for writers / Judith A.
Stanford. — 2nd ed.
      p. cm.
    Includes index.
    ISBN 0-7674-1127-7
    1. English language—Rhetoric. 2. Report writing Problems,
exercises, etc. 3. College readers. I. Title.
PE1408.S674 1999
808'.042—dc21   99-38705
                                       CIP

Manufactured in the United States of America
10 9 8 7 6 5 4 3

Mayfield Publishing Company
1280 Villa Street
Mountain View, California 94041

Sponsoring editor, Renée Deljon; production, Publishing Support Services; developmental editor, Rick Roehrich; manuscript editor, Loralee Windsor; design manager, Glenda King; text and cover designer, Linda M. Robertson; illustrator, Robin Mouat; manufacturing manager, Randy Hurst. The text was set in 11/12 Bembo by Thompson Type and printed on 50# Finch Opaque by Malloy Lithographing, Inc.

Cover image: Equinox, Hans Hofmann. Courtesy University of California, Berkeley Art Museum, gift of the artist. Cover art © Estate of Hans Hofmann/Licensed by VAGA, New York, NY.

Text and photo credits continue at the back of the book on pages 335–338, which constitute an extension of the copyright page.

Preface

"Only connect!" E. M. Forster's widely quoted injunction urges us. The passage from *Howards End* continues: "Only connect the prose and the passion, and both will be exalted, and human love will be seen at its height. Live in fragments no longer." This book takes its title and its philosophy from Forster's vision.

The structure, the apparatus, and the selections in *Developing Connections* encourage student writers to seek relationships: among the processes of reading, writing, and thinking; among the ideas and emotions expressed by the reading selections; among and within the cultural contexts represented by these diverse pieces; and, most of all, between the reading, writing, and thinking students are doing and the process of their own lives.

Developing Connections does much more than simply provide a collection of short readings that represents the diversity of the United States today. Because this book's audience is students who are in the process of developing reading and writing skills, Part 1 provides five introductory sections encouraging step-by-step progress in strategies essential for college-level reading, writing, and thinking. The first four sections demonstrate three key reading-to-write strategies: responding, understanding, and evaluating. Integrated with the reading strategies in these sections are carefully planned prompts that introduce various aspects of the writing process through short one- or two-paragraph assignments. The fifth section shows how these strategies lead to conceiving and writing longer essays, including approaches to the discovery, drafting, and revising of longer essays. Throughout the first five sections abundant student responses—sample discussions, journal entries, summaries, and a paper in various stages of the writing process—exemplify possible ways of reading, writing, and thinking, both individually and collaboratively.

Following Sections 1–5 on the reading and writing process, Part 2 provides seven sections of thematically arranged reading selections: Arrivals, Roots, and Memories; Families; Questions of Language; Ways of Learning; Health: Mind and Body; Men and Women; and Choices, Actions, and the

Future. Readings have been carefully chosen to challenge and interest students while not overwhelming them with ornate organization or arcane vocabulary.

The writing apparatus that accompanies each selection involves students in a variety of roles and rhetorical situations. Each selection is introduced by a brief note on the author and the circumstances of the original publication, followed by a series of prereading prompts designed especially for journal writing, brief informal class writing, or discussion that will lead to thoughtful reading. Following each selection is a series of topics for writing and discussion as well as suggestions for longer papers related to the reading. At the end of each thematic section, "Suggestions for Making Connections" asks students to stretch their responses beyond a single selection. Every writing suggestion encourages students to read closely, carefully, and with an open mind and seeks to engage students in meaningful writing that raises questions and does not just simply answer them.

Preceding each thematic section is a pair of photographs related to the theme, as well as prompts for discussion and writing. The instructor's guide provides additional questions that give students the opportunity to respond to these photographs as a further means of introduction to the theme. The instructor's guide also includes detailed discussion of each selection and innovative and flexible suggestions for using the text with various semester or quarter schedules.

Selections have been carefully chosen to provide diversity in terms of both the voices and the types of discourse represented. Readers will find an intriguing mix of letters, essays, newspaper columns, speeches, short stories, and poems. Again, the emphasis is on connection; selections represent an extraordinarily wide range of cultures that extends *multicultural* to include accounts of immigrants, first-generation sons and daughters, the educated and the uneducated, the poor and the middle-class, white, gay, handicapped, male, young, and old.

NEW TO THE SECOND EDITION

The second edition of **Developing Connections** differs from the first edition in several significant ways that make this book even more accessible and relevant to today's student writers.

This revision offers two entirely new themes—"Health: Mind and Body" (Section 10) and "Choices, Actions, and the Future" (Section 12)—and one refocused theme, "Families" (Section 7), replacing "Parents and Children" to provide an expanded, more inclusive focus. Altogether, 31 of the reading selections in the seven thematic sections are new to this edition; among these new readings are a few additional longer selections, as well as a greater number of contemporary issues-oriented selections.

Developing Connections, Second Edition, also offers two new kinds of apparatus. To further enhance the connections students make between the book's verbal and visual texts, discussion and writing prompts now accompany the photographs that open each thematic section. Finally, vocabulary activities, called "Word Check," now complete the apparatus set that follows each reading selection. These vocabulary activities complement the instruction provided in Section 3, "Reading to Understand," and guide students through the process of defining terms and making meaning within the context of each reading.

ACKNOWLEDGMENTS

Once again, I wish to thank the Writing Center faculty as well as the English Department faculty at Rivier College for creating a working atmosphere that promotes sharing ideas, exploring new possibilities, and taking risks. I am especially grateful to colleagues who have used *Connections* in their classes and who have generously offered suggestions for approaches to this related textbook.

My colleague Lorraine Lordi deserves special mention for her astute advice on selections and, particularly, for her creative and wise contributions to the apparatus accompanying selections. Once again, she has also planned and written the main sections of the detailed instructor's guide. I appreciate her support, her humor, and most of all her constant devotion to the true purpose of education: enabling students to learn through joy as well as through hard work.

My husband, Don, as always, has provided a listening ear, a sympathetic heart, and the wisdom of his constant wide reading to help me through the project. My mother, Arline Dupras, continues to give me her full and generous support. Her editing, word processing, and proofreading are valued; but more important are the love of reading, the dedication to teaching, and the optimistic view of life that she has passed on to me.

The reviewers of the second edition offered helpful and wise suggestions, which I greatly appreciate: Kirk Adams, Tarrant County Junior College Southeast; Cathryn Amdahl, Harrisburg Area Community College; Thomas P. Barber, Diablo Valley College; Constance Eggers, Western Washington University; William B. Lalicker, West Chester University; Robert S. Mann, Des Moines Area Community College; Julie Nichols, Okaloosa-Walton Community College; Mark Picus, Houston Community College–Central; Billie Theriot, Southeastern Louisiana University. I wish to thank again the reviewers of the first edition: Cathryn Amdahl, Harrisburg Area Community College; Leslie O. Bradley, Pennsylvania State University; Ann George, Pennsylvania State University; Scott Oates, Salt Lake Community College; Mary Sauer, Indiana University, Indianapolis; Marti

Singer, Georgia State University; Alison Smith, Western Washington University; and Beckey Stamm, Columbus State Community College.

Vicki Moran of Publishing Support Services skillfully guided the book through production, while Loralee Windsor offered excellent suggestions for fine-tuning as she copyedited the manuscript. Catherine New of Mayfield provided valuable assistance researching headnotes.

I thank Jan Beatty, the editor whose vision shaped the first edition of *Developing Connections*. Jan, I will always be grateful for the energy and creativity you brought to our work together and for our friendship. I would also like to thank Renée Deljon, my editor for this edition. Renée, you have definitely accompanied me on this journey to the second edition with wit, wisdom, faith, and a great willingness to provide the help I needed at so many points along the way. The shaping of the new thematic sections, in particular, benefited from your insights as well as from your ability to discover intriguing new selections. I also appreciate the time you took to travel great distances so that we could have "working time" together. Finally, thanks for shared meals and conversations and for understanding that developing connections means more than putting a book together.

Contents

The Promised Land, MARY ANTIN 62
A Russian immigrant recalls the wondrous and magical first weeks of life in America during the late 1800s. The novelty of even the most basic objects, from rocking chairs to street lamps, instills in this writer an early sense that freedom, above all the riches her family left behind, is the most valuable gift a person can possess.

The Woman Who Makes Swell Doughnuts, TOSHIO MORI 68
Memories of Mama's homemade fried doughnuts form the center of one man's peace.

The Education of Berenice Belizaire, JOE KLEIN 72
In this piece, Berenice Belizaire, a young immigrant from Haiti, proves that despite cultural struggles, she, like so many other hard-working and ambitious immigrants, can rise to the top in New York City's public school system—often with greater speed and height than her apathetic American peers.

Readings Arranged By Rhetorical Strategy

Process Analysis

Illustration/Examples

Fiction and Poetry

What Does It Mean to Think in Cultural Contexts? A Letter to the Reader

This text asks readers to think, read, and write with cultural contexts in mind. While Section 1 includes a definition of culture and provides options for considering the impact of cultural contexts on the way we see ourselves and others, I want to explore with you, the instructors and students who use *Developing Connections*, my personal reasons for writing this book.

I find that I—and many people—think and learn best through storytelling. So, as I thought about writing this letter, stories about my own life came to mind. My first story takes place in 1962, when, as a senior in college, I thought seriously about what I wanted to do for the rest of my life. I arrived as a freshman intending to become a high school English teacher, yet as I settled more and more fully into campus life, I fell in love with the energy and the exhaustion, the order and the chaos, the elation and the frustration that comprise academia. Now I was puzzled: How could I reach my goal of high school teaching, yet stay part of the college world I loved so much? I solved my dilemma by fantasizing that I might someday meet and marry a man who would be a college professor! It simply did not occur to me that I myself might fill that role. In 1962 I believed that only unusual, extraordinarily brilliant women—who were willing to sacrifice a "normal" family life for a very long time—could pursue the paths to graduate school, law school, medical school. Not until the late 1970s did I start to think about gender-based assumptions. Only then did I see myself as a member of the culture group "women." Only then did I recognize that I had been profoundly affected by what I perceived to be the expected roles and behaviors of that culture group. I began reading works written by and about women with the "culture group" idea in mind, and my life began to change. One of those changes led me to graduate school and thus to work I love and a world that has opened to me in ways I never believed possible.

I began to be aware of the impact of cultural contexts when my interest in gender issues led me to recognize that there were many other culture groups I had previously not recognized or, more often, simply ignored. As I sought out and read works by African American, Asian American, Latino, Jewish, Catholic, homosexual, teenaged, and elderly authors (among many others), I was forced to confront my own narrowness of thinking. I learned new ways of looking at the world in which I live, and I discovered ambiguities, questions, and paradoxes that still intrigue, delight, and, often, disturb me. Rarely do I find answers in what I read, yet somehow I feel a great hopefulness from learning about everyday heroism, survival, and growth, not simply in the dominant culture in which I grew up but also in hundreds of hidden cultures I never knew about or acknowledged.

My final story provides an example of what I mean by hidden cultures. During my childhood years, I knew in a vague sort of way that my father's family was French Canadian. He told wonderful tales, passed down from his grandparents; his characters were sharp-witted ghosts, animals with uncanny wiles, and, most of all, heroes who were "short and small, but very smart and clever." Except for these stories, I knew nothing about the French Canadian side of my family and definitely did not consider myself part of that culture group. When my father dragged my sister and me to yet another funeral of a distant friend or previously unknown relative, we rolled our eyes at each other as he spoke a few words of French to the bereaved and then, in English, offered his comforting opinion of the corpse's appearance: "looks just like himself" or "looks like she's asleep." He always stayed away from the groups of people conversing in rapid French and told us, disparagingly, that those people were "old-fashioned." He never spoke French to us, and we were not surprised when he said he knew only "two or three words," remembered from childhood visits with his grandparents.

During his final years, my father suffered from a brain disease that led him to be confused, angry, suspicious, and mean-spirited. Whenever he was in a hospital or rehab facility he ranted and raved, telling us how awful everything was. Finally, exhausted and unable to care for him at home, my mother, my sister, and I found a nursing home willing to accept him. Fearfully we anticipated his usual anger and outbursts. But on my first visit, I was astonished to hear, "They are nice people here" and "They take good care of me." My father lived for a month, and each visit found him calm, able to recognize us, at peace. At the funeral, we wondered what had brought about the change. In my heart, I will always believe the answer came from the French Canadian Sister of Mercy, who worked at the nursing home and who came to tell us that she had visited Gilbert (she gave it the French pronunciation, Jil–ber) often. "He told me such stories, and all in French, too." Astonished, we asked, "In French? But he only spoke a few words." She looked surprised, "Ah, no! He was fluent! He told me of his mother. Sometimes, he was a very naughty boy, Gilbert!" I felt at that moment as if a key piece to a puzzle suddenly fell into place. My father had found a grace-filled way to die because he had quite literally found a way home to the language of his childhood, which he had denied but never lost. Even when much of his mind was gone, he knew those words "by heart."

Since then, I've started to read and think about the French Canadians who emigrated in such large numbers to New England. As I read, I discover things I never knew about the place where I grew up and about the people who were and are part of my "hidden culture." I've begun to find collections of French Canadian narratives, and I am not at all surprised to find that their heroes are often "short and small but very smart and clever."

Judith A. Stanford

PART 1

Critical Reading and Writing

1

Critical Reading and Thinking: Recognizing Cultural Contexts

Every day, each of us encounters customs, actions, beliefs, or values that seem different from our own. On a city street, in an international airport, on nightly television news programs, we see people who dress, talk, and act in unfamiliar ways. As the population of our country—small towns as well as large cities—grows increasingly diverse, thinking about the ways we respond to difference becomes increasingly important.

As a way to begin, consider your responses as you read the following sections of anthropologist Horace Miner's essay "Body Ritual among the Nacirema." Miner offers a look at a people he describes as obsessed with the idea "that the human body is ugly and that its natural tendency is to debility and disease."

BODY RITUAL AMONG THE NACIREMA
Horace Miner

The anthropologist has become so familiar with the diversity of ways in which different peoples behave in similar situations that he is not apt to be surprised by even the most exotic customs. In fact, if all of the logically possible combinations of behavior have not been found somewhere in the world, he is apt to suspect that they must be present in some yet undescribed tribe. . . . In this light, the magical beliefs and practices of the Nacirema present such unusual aspects that it seems desirable to describe them as an example of the extremes to which human behavior can go. . . .

Nacirema culture is characterized by a highly developed market economy which has evolved in a rich natural habitat. While much of the people's time is devoted to economic pursuits, a large part of the fruits of these labors and a considerable portion of the day are spent in ritual activity. The focus of this activity is the human body, the appearance and health of which loom as a dominant concern in the ethos of the people. While such a concern is certainly not unusual, its ceremonial aspects and associated philosophy are unique.

The fundamental belief underlying the whole system appears to be that the human body is ugly and that its natural tendency is to debility and disease. Incarcerated in such a body, man's only hope is to avert these characteristics through the use of the powerful influences of ritual and ceremony. Every household has one or more shrines devoted to this purpose. The more powerful individuals in the society have several shrines in their houses and, in fact, the opulence of a house is often referred to in terms of the number of such ritual centers it possesses. Most houses are of wattle and daub constructions, but the shrine rooms of the more wealthy are walled with stone. Poorer families imitate the rich by applying pottery plaques to their shrine walls.

Exercise 1

As you read these paragraphs, what is your initial response? Do the Nacirema seem similar to any group of people with whom you are familiar? Is your overall reaction to the Nacirema society negative or positive, so far?

After writing your response, continue to read the following passages from Miner's article.

The focal point of the shrine is a box or chest which is built into the wall. In this chest are kept the many charms and magical potions without which no native believes he could live. These preparations are secured from a variety of specialized practitioners. The most powerful of these are the medicine men, whose assistance must be rewarded with substantial gifts. However, the medicine men do not provide the curative potions for their clients, but decide what the ingredients should be and then write them down in an ancient and secret language. This writing is understood only by the medicine men and by the herbalists who, for another gift, provide the required charm. . . .

In the hierarchy of magical practitioners, and below the medicine men in prestige, are specialists whose designation is best translated as "holy-mouth-men." The Nacirema have an almost pathological horror of and fascination with the mouth, the condition of which is believed to have a supernatural influence on all social relationships. Were it not for the rituals of the mouth, they believe that their teeth would fall out, their gums bleed, their jaws shrink, their friends desert them, and their lovers reject them.

The daily body ritual performed by everyone includes a mouth-rite. Despite the fact that these people are so punctilious about care of the mouth, this rite involves a practice which strikes the uninitiated stranger as revolting. It was reported to me that the ritual consists of inserting a small bundle of hog hairs into the mouth, along with certain magical powders, and then moving the bundle in a highly formalized series of gestures.

Exercise 2

As you read the additional passages from Miner's essay, did your response to the Nacirema change? Do you see their practices and beliefs as entirely different from your own? Or do you see some similarities?

Could you explain the Nacirema practices, beliefs, and rituals in a way that would make them seem more familiar?

Most readers encountering Miner's essay for the first time agree with his observation that these practices "strike the uninitiated stranger as revolting." These initial responses change, however, as the reader continues reading. The essay goes on to describe such details as the twice-yearly visit to the "holy-mouth-man" who engages in "unbelievable ritual torture" by enlarging "any holes which decay may have created in the teeth" and inserting "magical materials" into these holes. It soon becomes clear that Miner has been pulling the reader's leg by describing aspects of modern American (*Nacirema* spelled backward) culture in unfamiliar ways. With his exaggerations and distorted viewpoints, he gently pokes fun at what he sees as the American obsession with health and cleanliness. Perhaps more importantly, he insists that we examine our tendency to judge different customs, actions, beliefs, and values as strange, odd, or even "revolting."

WHAT IS CULTURE?

The title of Miner's essay, "Body Ritual among the Nacirema," leads us to expect that we will be reading about a culture different from our own. To understand the responses often triggered by such an expectation, we need to know what the word *culture* means.

Culture may be defined as the ideas, customs, values, skills, and arts of a specific group of people. Most of us do live not in one cultural context but in several. For instance, our age places us in the culture of childhood, youth, middle age, and so on. We may be called "baby boomers," or "Generation X," and these phrases may trigger certain images or values in the minds of those who hear or read them. In addition, we are all either male or female, and various societies have traditionally created cultural distinctions between men and women. Another group we belong to relates to the country of our birth or to the country where our ancestors were born. We may be Norwegian, Japanese, or Native American, or we may be Irish American,

African American, or even more complex combinations of ethnic roots. The selections in this book all look at some aspect of the various cultures that make up the United States.

WHY READ AND THINK IN CULTURAL CONTEXTS?

Learning to read and think critically in the context of different cultures is essential, not only to read this book but also to fully appreciate many other college courses. You also need these skills to work effectively in an increasingly diverse environment and to live, not just with tolerance but with real understanding, among the many groups of people who comprise the citizens of the United States and the world.

In addition to the practical reasons for considering cultural contexts, many pleasures and joys reward those of us who take the risks and meet the challenges of considering new ways to view our own lives and the lives of others. It's often comfortable and comforting to stay within the boundaries we have always known—and nearly all readers of this text will find selections that offer such comfort. Yet it can be exhilarating to step outside those boundaries and see the world from a different standpoint.

You will study aspects of other cultures in many other courses, including history, sociology, psychology, business, science, literature, art, music, and religion. In the future you will almost certainly work with people from different cultural groups who are making significant contributions to your chosen field. Developing the patterns of thinking encouraged in this book will help you communicate—read, speak, and write—as a fully aware citizen of the multicultural world in which we live.

STRATEGIES FOR READING AND THINKING ACROSS CULTURES

Reading cross-cultural selections thoughtfully and productively calls for both skill and courage—the skill to understand and evaluate a complex idea or issue and the courage to approach each writer's work with a mind open to multiple possibilities and points of view. You need to be willing to see and acknowledge differences and at the same time look for similarities and connections. Most of all, you should avoid hasty judgments, discard standard responses, and tolerate apparent contradictions.

To help you begin developing strategies for reading and thinking across cultures, the following exercises ask you to write paragraphs exploring your responses to your own culture groups as well as to other cultural perspectives. Before you respond to the exercises, you may want to consult the boxed guidelines that review the definition of a paragraph. As you read the guidelines, use this paragraph as a model:

Americans are a rootless people. Each year one in six of us changes residences; one in four changes jobs. We see nothing troubling in these statistics. For most of us, they merely reflect the restless energy that made America great. A nation of immigrants, unsurprisingly, celebrates those willing to pick up stakes and move on: the frontiersman, the cowboy, the entrepreneur, the corporate raider.
(Morris, David. "Rootlessness." *Utne Reader* [May/June 1990].)

Guidelines: Writing a Paragraph

1. A paragraph is a group of sentences that deals with one main idea.
   (In the example, the main idea is that Americans tend not to remain attached to the comfortable and familiar.)
2. A paragraph usually has a *topic sentence* that states the main idea (most often, the first or last sentence).
   (In the example, the topic sentence is the first: "Americans are a rootless people.")
3. A paragraph usually has several sentences that support and develop the main idea.
   (Each of the sentences that follows the topic sentence provides one or more examples of American rootlessness.)
4. Each supporting sentence in a paragraph should be written so that its relationship to the main idea is clear.
   (Each sentence clearly follows the previous sentence. For instance, sentence 3 analyzes the author's perceptions of the American people's response to the statistics given in sentence 2. Sentence 4 begins with the transitional phrase "for most of us," which connects the readers' reactions to the statistics and analysis provided in sentences 2 and 3.)
5. A paragraph that is too short often fails to develop its idea sufficiently.
   (The five sentences in this paragraph clearly develop its main idea.)
6. A paragraph that is too long often combines several main ideas and becomes confusing; it should be rewritten as two or more shorter paragraphs.
7. Paragraphs vary in length, but if you have written a paragraph of fewer than four sentences or more than ten sentences, check to see if you have either omitted needed support (too short) or tried to deal with too many ideas (too long).
8. Longer pieces of writing (such as essays, newspaper articles, and books) are made up of paragraphs that relate to one another.

Exercise 3

Exercise 3

Read the following entry from a journal written by John Coleman during a 1973–74 sabbatical leave from his position as president of Haverford College. During this year, Coleman worked at a variety of blue-collar jobs. The people with whom he worked did not know about his academic or professional background. His experiences showed him how belonging to a particular culture group affected the way others treated him.

From BLUE-COLLAR JOURNAL
John Coleman

Tuesday, March 27

One of the waitresses I find hard to take asked me at one point today, "Are you the boy who cuts the lemons?"

"I'm the man who does," I replied.

"Well, there are none cut." There wasn't a hint that she heard my point.

Dana, who has cooked here for twelve years or so, heard that exchange.

"It's no use, Jack," he said when she was gone. "If she doesn't know now, she never will." There was a trace of a smile on his face, but it was a sad look all the same.

In that moment, I learned the full thrust of those billboard ads of a few years ago that said, "BOY. Drop out of school and that's what they'll call you the rest of your life." I had read those ads before with a certain feeling of pride; education matters, they said, and that gave a lift to my field. Today I saw them saying something else. They were untrue in part; it turns out that you'll get called "boy" if you do work that others don't respect even if you have a Ph.D. It isn't education that counts, but the job in which you land. And the ads spoke too of a sad resignation about the world. They assumed that some people just won't learn respect for others, so you should adapt yourself to them. Don't try to change them. Get the right job and they won't call *you* boy any more. They'll save it for the next man.

It isn't just people like this one waitress who learn slowly, if at all. Haverford College has prided itself on being a caring, considerate community in the Quaker tradition for many long years. Yet when I came there I soon learned that the cleaning women in the dormitories were called "wombats" by all the students. No one seemed to know where the name came from or what connection, if any, it had with the dictionary definition. *The American College Dictionary* says a wombat is "any of three species of burrowing marsupials of Australia . . . somewhat resembling ground hogs." The name was just one of Haverford's unexamined ways of doing things.

It didn't take much persuasion to get the name dropped. Today there are few students who remember it at all. But I imagine the cleaning women remember it well.

Certainly I won't forget being called a boy today.

Exercise 4

After reading Coleman's journal entry, do the following:

1. Make a list of as many cultural groups as possible to which you see yourself as belonging. These cultural groups may relate to your age, your ethnic background, your religious preference, your political beliefs, your current work status.

2. After making the list, choose one of the cultural groups to which you belong and write a paragraph describing the ideas, customs, values, skills, and arts of that group that you see as positive. When you write your paragraph, refer to the guidelines on page 7.

Here is one student's approach to the preceding exercise:

List of Culture Groups

age: "twenty-something"

Italian-American

waitress

student

daughter

Catholic

Democrat (but voted for Perot)

Paragraph: BEING A WAITRESS

I never thought of waitresses as a culture group until now. But after reading John Coleman's journal entry, I can see that I and the other women I work with have things in common that relate to what we do. We all value working hard to make good money. Serving food is not easy, but it gives you a good way to make more than minimum wage. We also have all come to appreciate good relationships with customers for more reasons than tips. If you exchange a pleasant word or two with the people you wait on, the evening goes faster and you feel less tired. You also feel as if you are making the customer's meal more enjoyable.

Even better than talking with customers, I like talking with the other waitresses. At the end of the evening, after we've cleaned our stations, we all sit together and have coffee or a Coke and talk about what happened. It's something we all look forward to because we can just be ourselves and not worry about keeping that happy smile on our faces.

Exercise 5

Write a paragraph or two responding to one of the following topics:

1. Describe something you read or heard in another class that gave you a view of a cultural perspective other than your own. What new ideas or possibilities did this perspective suggest?

2. Describe an incident from a television program or a film you have seen that showed you a cultural perspective different from your own. What new ideas or possibilities did this perspective suggest?

3. Describe an event from your work that showed you a cultural perspective different from your own. What new ideas or possibilities did this perspective suggest?

2

Reading to Respond

We read for many reasons. These students' responses to the question "Why do you read?" suggest just a few possibilities.

Mostly I read to get information. Maybe I want to know how to fix something or where I can buy something for the best price. *Janet Mathis (age 23)*

"Self-help" would sum up my main reason. I feel like I can get power over some parts of my life by reading about ways to solve problems and how other people have learned to solve their problems. *Amon Wilkuski (age 33)*

I read purely to escape the troubles I see. I want a book that will entertain me and sometimes make me cry, but always end with a smile. Because there's too much trouble in life. I like to read about something that gives me a dream to hope for. *Keren Pfirschbaum (age 18)*

Mostly I read what is assigned for school or what I have to read at work. I don't have time for a lot of reading, and it's not easy for me. So mostly I read only when I have to. *Tony Vladim (age 20)*

Exercise 1

Write a few sentences describing the main reason or reasons you read. If possible, discuss your reasons with other members of the class.

THE PROCESS OF RESPONDING

Sometimes—for instance when you read a daily newspaper to learn the main events of the day—you may read quickly, scanning the information once and not returning to reread. When you read for classes or in your personal search for deeper insights into your world, you use a more complex strategy. This process includes reading to respond, reading to understand, and reading to evaluate. This chapter, and the two that follow, discuss ways of developing these three ways of reading.

When you first read any fiction or nonfiction work, one of the best strategies is to skim through quickly. Be sure to pay attention to your responses as you move quickly from point to point. Being aware of your first responses is particularly important when you read across cultures. When you encounter unfamiliar ideas, images, and values, it's easy to feel overwhelmed by new vocabulary, unexpected examples, or different values.

During a first reading, try not to block out any of your responses, whether they be negative, positive, or neutral. On the other hand, no matter how much you may agree or disagree with what you are reading, try expressing some of your reactions in the form of questions or open-ended statements. Such questions and statements should lead to discussion rather than closing it off. By working with these structures, you'll keep an honest record of your thoughts and feelings. Better yet, you'll help yourself remain alert to many different possibilities and directions.

RESPONDING BY MAKING MARGINAL NOTES

As an example of initial responses, consider the notes one student, Alyssa Clark, wrote in the margins of her book as she read this excerpt. The passage comes from "What's American about America?" an essay by Ishmael Reed, a black American novelist, poet, and editor. The original version of this selection appeared in Reed's 1983 nonfiction book, *Writin' Is Fightin'*.

From WHAT'S AMERICAN ABOUT AMERICA?
Ishmael Reed

(1) An item from the *New York Times,* June 23, 1983: "At   1
the annual Lower East Side Jewish Festival yesterday, a Chinese woman ate a pizza slice in front of Ty Thuan Duc's Vietnamese grocery store. Beside her a Spanish-speaking family patronized a cart with two signs: 'Italian Ices' and 'Kosher by Rabbi Alper.' And after the pastrami ran out, everybody ate knishes."

(2) On the day before Memorial Day, 1983, a poet called me to describe a city he had just visited. He said that one section included mosques, built by the Islamic people who dwelled there. Attending his reading, he said, were large numbers of Hispanic people, 40,000 of whom lived in the

Were all these people U.S. citizens? Tourists? new immigrants?

Where do Islamic people usually live? (Not in Detroit?)

same city. He was not talking about a fabled city located in some mysterious region of the world. The city he'd visited was Detroit.

(3) A few months before, as I was visiting Texas, I heard the taped voice used to guide passengers to their connections at the Dallas Airport announcing items in both Spanish and English. This trend is likely to continue; after all, for some southwestern states like Texas, where the largest minority is now Mexican-American, Spanish was the first written language and the Spanish style lives on in the Western way of life.

[margin: Should Spanish be a second language in U.S.? Why?/Why not?]

[margin: Do other airports do this? Other languages?]

(4) Shortly after my Texas trip, I sat in a campus auditorium at the University of Wisconsin at Milwaukee as a Yale professor—whose original work on the influence of African cultures upon those of the Americas has led to his ostracism from some intellectual circles—walked up and down the aisle like an old-time Southern evangelist, dancing and drumming the top of the lectern, illustrating his points before some Afro-American intellectuals and artists who cheered and applauded his performance. The professor was "white." After his lecture, he conversed with a group of Milwaukeeans—all of whom spoke Yoruban, though only the professor had ever traveled to Africa.

[margin: Why is he ostracized for this?]

[margin: Why the quotes?]

(5) One of the artists there told me that his paintings, which included African and Afro-American mythological symbols and imagery, were hanging in the local McDonald's restaurant. The next day I went to McDonald's and snapped pictures of smiling youngsters eating hamburgers below paintings that could grace the walls of any of the country's leading museums. The manager of the local McDonald's said, "I don't know what you boys are doing, but I like it," as he commissioned the local painters to exhibit in his restaurant.

[margin: great idea!!]

[margin: What makes him think this?]

5

(6) Such blurring of cultural styles occurs in everyday life in the United States to a greater extent than anyone can imagine. The result is what the above-mentioned Yale professor, Robert Thompson, referred to as a cultural bouillabaisse. Yet members of the nation's present educational and cultural elect still cling to the notion that the United States belongs to some vaguely defined entity they refer to as "Western civilization," by which they mean presumably, a civilization created by people of Europe, as if Europe can even be viewed in monolithic terms.

[margin: Yes—Examples here on campus—students wear clothes from other cultures]

[margin: meaning?]

[margin: Who does he mean?]

[margin: meaning?]

Yes!
Because it's   Is Beethoven's Ninth Symphony, which includes Turkish
mostly   marches, a part of Western civilization? Or the late-
Western!   nineteenth- and twentieth-century French paintings, whose
creators were influenced by Japanese art? And what of
the cubists, through whom the influence of African art
changed modern painting? Or the surrealists, who were so
impressed with the art of the Pacific Northwest Indians
that, in their map of North America, Alaska dwarfs the
lower forty-eight states in size?

As Alyssa read this article, she jotted in the margin any question or
observation that came to mind. While most people don't stop to analyze
their responses, it may be helpful to look closely not only at the content of
Alyssa's notes but also at the types of comments and questions she wrote.
You'll notice that many of her marginal observations fall loosely into the
categories listed in the following guidelines.

Guidelines: Marginal Notes

As you make marginal notes when you read, keep in mind the
following possibilities:

1. Questions that ask about people (paragraph 1)
2. Questions that ask about places (paragraph 2)
3. Questions that ask about actions (paragraphs 3, 4)
4. Questions that ask about policies, laws, or customs (paragraph 4)
5. Questions that address the writer's style, including such things as
   choice of example, vocabulary, sentence structure, or even unusual
   punctuation (paragraphs 4, 6)
6. Questions or comments that challenge or call for closer examination of the writer's observations, judgments or evaluations, or inferences (paragraphs 5, 6)
7. Comments that affirm or expand on the writer's observations,
   judgments or evaluations, or inferences (paragraphs 5, 6)

While there are many more ways of responding to reading, this list suggests
the wide variety of ways readers react when they encounter a text. As you
form your first responses, never be afraid of these early reactions. Don't
worry that your ideas, feelings, or questions will be "wrong" or "silly" or
"simplistic." Of course it's true that you may later change your mind and

decide to revise or even reject one or more of your original reactions. You'll base these revisions on rereading, on writing in response to reading, and, perhaps, on discussions with your fellow classmates and your instructor. These changes do not indicate that your first responses were unworthy or embarrassing; they demonstrate your willingness to apply critical thinking and remain open to new possibilities.

Exercise 2

Read the following essay written by Gloria Bonilla, who left her native El Salvador in 1981 and came to the United States. This essay was originally published in 1988 in *You Can't Drown the Fire: Latin American Women Writing in Exile.*

As you read, make notes in the margins. When you finish making notes, reread the guidelines on page 14. Then evaluate your own notes to see whether any of them fit the categories described. Next, reread the article and make notes in the margins of any new questions, observations, or comments that come to mind.

LEAVING EL SALVADOR
Gloria Bonilla

January 4, 1988

    I saw my friend Alicia this afternoon while I was at the post office waiting in   1 *line. We began chatting of things, projects, etc. The book, her deadline. El Salvador. Incredible! It has been almost seven years since I left. I have not been back since.*

    —Write something, write about your feelings—

    It is so difficult to write, to think, to reflect on it. My experience. It is still painful to remember.

    I fled El Salvador, leaving behind my family and friends, my undergraduate studies, a job, and all short- and long-term personal goals, in April of 1981 to escape government persecution. In an effort to remain in the United States more than three months at one time, and map out bits and pieces of an unknown future, I was required to change my tourist visa to a student visa. Because the United States recognized then, and continues to recognize today, the government of El Salvador, I have been unable to enter the United States as a refugee, nor can I realistically expect to receive political asylum.

    My story does not differ very much from the stories that most Sal-   5 vadorans tell. I consider myself more fortunate because I did not have to cross the Mexican border and enter the United States illegally. I was also able to maintain a legal status which allows me to continue my education in the United States.

I think, like my parents, I have learned through life quite a bit. My father used to say that we never stop learning in life. He did not go to college. I remember him very much because most of what he knew he had learned on his own. My first recollections of the history of El Salvador were through my father and mother. That history was not in print.

My trip to the United States was sudden, precipitous. I, like many other Salvadorans, finally realized that El Salvador was no longer a safe place to live.

I arrived in Washington, D.C., in April of 1981. When I arrived, my good friend, John, was waiting for me at the airport, carrying a heavy coat, assuming I would have no winter clothing. I met John in El Salvador back in the seventies when he was a Peace Corps volunteer. After he came back to the United States, he kept in touch with me, until the political conditions in El Salvador reached serious and dangerous proportions. Then he invited me to come to the United States, an invitation which I did not decline, but which I postponed until I could no longer remain in El Salvador. One day, I called John from Guatemala to let him know I was on my way.

I knew no one in Washington except John, who sheltered me until I was able to support myself. John introduced me to his friends, some of whom are my friends still. As insiders, they helped me to become familiar with the United States. I am grateful for all their help.

A lot has happened since that moment on that spring day in 1981, 10 when I arrived in the United States.

I underwent a metamorphosis. I went from a period of mutiny, in which I encapsulated myself like a larva in a cocoon, to a period of awakening and rebirth. The process was painful and difficult. But I survived. Because I left El Salvador so quickly, I hardly had the chance to reflect on what was happening. When I came to the United States, I carried with me my past, which tied me to people and a land that I had to give up.

There is no medicine to take care of heartache and homesickness—not even here in the United States where there are drugs for almost everything, mostly for pain. I believe we unconsciously or consciously develop methods to cope with those ailments. So, I made up a prescription of my own to help me stay sane and survive in my new niche. I filled my hours, my days, without respite, so I had no time to think, cry or break.

I forced myself to learn English. I took intensive English courses from 9:00 A.M. to 2:00 P.M. I worked in the afternoons. Later, I got a full-time job and I enrolled at the university, finished college and went straight for a master's degree in sociology. I did it all in five and a half years.

I did not do it alone, but with the support of friends. I had moments of despair in which I felt lost, with little or no hope. My driving force was that I had no relatives in Washington to look after me. Therefore, I could not afford to lose my most precious commodity, my mind. Some call it pride; for others it is survival instinct. I experienced both.

The United States Immigration and Naturalization Service regulates, *15* controls, and restricts the free access of foreigners to society and subsequently to its benefits. For example, I had a legal status that allowed me to study and remain in the United States as long as I attended school full time. On the other hand, that same status forbade me to work and compete freely for jobs that I thought I was qualified for.

I maintained that legal status as long as I went to school full time. I paid my bills as long as I worked full time. I had no choice. My constant concerns were basic: food, shelter, education, legal status.

A legal status which allows an immigrant to work is an imperative. In my case, the choice was to apply for political asylum or for permanent residence. The best bet was permanent residence.

Political asylum, in the case of Salvadorans, becomes a dead end since U.S. immigration law requires the applicant to provide evidence of a well-founded fear of persecution. A subjective condition, when you think about it. For example, the army did not need any evidence to determine that I was a "suspicious individual," and to break into my home and my parents' home in 1981. Ironically, it is the same subjective reasoning used by a U.S. immigration judge that determines the non-eligibility of a Salvadoran for political asylum. Salvadorans in exile in the United States have been required to all but present a signed affidavit from their persecutors in order to prove their well-founded fear of persecution.

I believe I had good enough reasons to be granted political asylum back in 1981 if I had applied. But a U.S. judge might have disagreed with me, since I did not have concrete evidence of my fear of persecution. Worse, I came from a country whose government is friendly to the United States.

I eliminated the political asylum option from the very beginning. *20* Salvadorans had, back in the early 1980s, little or no chance of having a political asylum application approved; later, it became pointless, since the Reagan administration had invested so much money "democratizing" El Salvador.

I am only an example of what Salvadorans could do if given the chance. In my case, maintaining a student visa gave me access to education, something most Salvadorans have not been able to attain. That is why Salvadorans in the United States hold occupations that require little or no formal education.

I think Salvadorans have tried their best to prove their worth. Our future in the United States does not look promising. Lawmakers had an opportunity to offer better conditions to Salvadorans. The Immigration Reform and Control Act proves it. The United States had a chance to review the law and to review the Central American question, but did not. I believe Salvadorans in the United States have been sentenced without trial. When you think about it, it is not very different from the way our people are treated in El Salvador.

RESPONDING BY WRITING
JOURNAL ENTRIES

Another useful way of responding to reading is to keep a reading journal. Such journals take many different forms. You may keep a journal strictly as private writing that allows you to explore your responses. Or you may keep one as a course requirement. If you write a journal as a class assignment, the instructor may give you guidelines for the number of entries per week and their length. The instructor may also suggest topics or approaches to help you determine the focus of the entries.

Whether you are keeping a journal for yourself or as a requirement, writing entries in response to your initial readings can be a helpful way of thinking about the ideas and feelings the writer expresses. Here are several examples of journal entries that students wrote following their first quick reading of Ishmael Reed's "What's American about America?" (pp. 12–14):

1. I like the way the writer, I. Reed, looks at the positive side. His example of the quote from the *New York Times* in the first paragraph, for example, shows people from five different nationalities all getting along. On the other hand, this seems too ideal to me. From what I've seen and from what you see all the time on the television news, I think a situation like this festival would be a place for fights or at least name-calling. *Frank Pagiano*

2. He [Reed] just describes all these other people who live in these places, but he doesn't talk about the regular Americans. What I don't understand is why he keeps saying "Islamic," "Hispanic," and "Vietnamese." Aren't these people American? And why does he put quotes when he says "white"? Does he think only white people are real Americans? I can't really figure out his point, which he says in the title "What's American about America?" *Lee Ann Jamross*

3. When I read about hearing the announcements in Spanish and English, my reaction was Why should the announcements be in both languages? This is the United States and English is our language. Why should we have to have another language? I know in some places the ballots and other papers like that have to be printed in Spanish, and my question is Why? *Stan O'Brien*

4. The airport description made me think of traveling in other countries. My family is military, and we've lived in Germany, Italy, and Japan. At the civilian airports in major cities, the announcements are in many different languages. And English is always one that I am glad to hear when I am traveling. That's because I don't know the language of the country if it's not English. What I noticed was that in most other countries people know more than one language, and I think this is a good idea because it gives you more possibilities of ways to communicate. I think it would be a good idea in this country if we were more aware of other languages and maybe started to learn them in the early grades instead of one or two years in high school. *Danya Mielewski*

5. "Bouillabaisse." I circled this word as one I didn't know, and I had to look it up because it seemed to me to be important to what the paragraph was saying. Well, it means "a chowder made with several kinds of fish and shellfish, vegetables, and seasoning." At first I thought, well, this is like the "melting pot" that you hear used to describe this country. But then I thought, no, because in a melting pot everything just goes together and becomes one big mass and you can't tell the different parts. But in this "bouillabaisse," which Reed says Robert Thompson calls America, you would still see all the parts (like the different kind of fish and the different vegetables). So they would still be themselves, but they would be working together to make something different, too (the chowder). So I'm wondering if America is like this. Do all the different groups stay separate in some ways but work together in others? *William Ferguson*

As you can see from these journal entries, readers respond very differently to what they read. The following list briefly evaluates and comments on each of the entries:

1. Frank Pagiano identifies a detail that he admires in the essay and explains his reasons. However, he goes on to show some reservations he feels about the accuracy of this detail.

2. In her entry, Lee Ann Jamross asks many questions about the terms Reed uses to describe groups of people. Her final questions raise

points concerning definition: She wonders exactly how Reed defines *Americans*.

3. Stan O'Brien's initial response is to challenge an assumption that Reed makes. O'Brien doesn't flatly reject Reed's point about the Spanish language announcements, but the tone of his questions shows that he is not entirely convinced.

4. Taking a viewpoint quite different from Stan O'Brien's, Danya Mielewski addresses the same issue: the use of more than one language in the United States. Mielewski uses personal examples as a way of exploring the ideas inspired by Reed's essay.

5. William Ferguson focuses on one unfamiliar word in Reed's essay. Because this word seemed central to the meaning of the paragraph in which it occurred, and because he couldn't determine the meaning of the word from the context in which it was used, Ferguson used a dictionary to help him get started. After finding the dictionary definition, he spent time pondering the implications of the comparison Robert Thompson (cited by Reed) makes between the American culture and the chowder called bouillabaisse. By looking at language closely and refusing to be discouraged or put off by a word he didn't know, Ferguson discovered an idea he considered worth pursuing.

These five entries suggest ways of writing journal entries as initial responses to reading. Notice that many of the entries focus on questions and that most of them keep open many possibilities rather than seeking one simple, easy answer. These entries also reflect the way early responses often relate to the reader's own experiences and knowledge.

Two of the sample entries (3 and 4) disagree with each other, but each asks thoughtful questions and raises important issues. The point here is that there is no one "correct" way to respond to any piece of reading. In addition, when these students returned to Reed's essay to read it for a second or third time, many of them changed or modified their initial responses. Points that seemed puzzling during the first reading became clear during the second. Issues that seemed simple revealed complications that had not been noticed before. Some students even noticed that opinions they had believed to be true were not supported by evidence in the reading. The richness in reading—and particularly in reading across cultures—lies in the diversity and the possibilities it offers.

Exercise 3

Reread Gloria Bonilla's essay, "Leaving El Salvador" (p. 15), as well as the notes you made while reading it (Exercise 2, p. 15). Then choose three of those notes and develop each of them into a paragraph explaining and exploring your response.

As you plan to write, consult the guidelines for writing paragraphs (p. 7). In addition, keep in mind the following guidelines for writing journal entries in response to what you read.

Guidelines: Writing Journal Entries

As you think about topics for journal entries, consider the following possibilities:

1. *Write about a person.* (Perhaps you were struck by someone in the reading or the reading reminded you of someone.)
2. *Write about a place.* (Perhaps you find interesting, troubling, or pleasing a place the author described.)
3. *Write about an action.* (Perhaps the writer explains an action you find brave, cowardly, or strange.)
4. *Write about policies, laws, or customs.* (Maybe you can compare a custom the author talks about with a custom familiar to you.)
5. *Write to explain why you disagree with a particular point the author has made.* (Be sure to give specific reasons.)
6. *Write to explain why you agree with a particular point the author has made.* (Be sure to give specific reasons.)
7. *Write to ask the author a question.* (If you could speak directly to this writer, imagine what you'd ask, and explain why.)
8. *Write a personal example that relates in some way to something you have read.* (Perhaps the reading brought back an old memory.)
9. *Write to define a word in the reading that was unfamiliar.* (Give more than just a dictionary definition; choose a word with many possible implications to explore.)
10. *Write down an intriguing phrase or sentence from the reading, and explain why you found it interesting.*

3

Reading to Understand

After exploring your first responses to something you have read, the next step is to return to the selection and reread carefully. During the first reading, it is easy to skip over key points, miss important evidence, or be overwhelmed by the emotions the piece arouses. Second and third readings help you understand what the writer is saying and see how the author gets the message across to readers.

Writing down and talking about your first responses and then returning to the text before making firm evaluations are essential parts of critical thinking. While these steps are part of any careful, thoughtful reading, they are particularly important for reading across cultures. When we read something written from a different cultural viewpoint, it's easy to jump quickly to unwarranted conclusions or fail to see the author's point clearly.

UNDERSTANDING UNFAMILIAR WORDS

As you first read and make marginal notes, you'll almost certainly notice unfamiliar words. Readers have different responses when they encounter words they do not understand. Some become frustrated and stop reading. Others pause at every unknown word to use the dictionary. Many experienced readers, however, have learned three useful strategies: (1) to read through words they do not know if those words do not seem essential to the author's meaning; (2) to use context clues to identify the definitions of new words; and (3) after applying the other two strategies, to use the dictionary. This process saves both time and frustration.

To develop the skill of identifying meaning from context clues, consider the following guidelines:

Guidelines: Identifying Meaning from Context Clues

1. Discover definitions through examples.
   Example:
   Unfamiliar word: *affluence*
   Context: "In our days of *affluence* in Russia we had been accustomed to . . . embroidered linens, silver spoons and candlesticks, goblets of gold . . ."
   (from *The Promised Land* by Mary Antin, p. 62)
   Explanation: Because Antin provides the examples of the beautiful linens and the silver and gold tableware, the reader knows that *affluence* must mean great wealth and luxury.

2. Discover meaning through the author's definition.
   Example:
   Unfamiliar phrase: *Western civilization*
   Context: "[T]hey refer to . . . *Western civilization,* by which they mean, presumably, a civilization created by people of Europe."
   (from "What's American about America?" by Ishmael Reed, p. 12)
   Explanation: By providing the definition ("a civilization created by people of Europe"), Reed clearly identifies the concept he is challenging.

3. Discover meaning through a contrast.
   Example:
   Unfamiliar word: *hostility*
   Context: "Ultimately, I would grow to love him and appreciate how he dealt with becoming a single parent at the age of 56, but at first our relationship was . . . full of *hostility.*"
   (from "The Teacher Who Changed My Life" by Nicholas Gage, p. 186)
   Explanation: By providing the contrasting clue of the love and appreciation he later felt, Gage indicates that his first reaction opposed those positive emotions. So readers can easily infer that *hostile* can mean hateful and angry.

4. Discover meaning through a synonym.
   Example:
   Unfamiliar phrase: *tenement district*

(continued)

(continued)

Context: "They form a *tenement district,* or, in the newer phrase, the slums of Boston."

(from *The Promised Land* by Mary Antin, p. 62)

Explanation: The author explains what she means by *tenement district* by providing the synonym *slums,* which she believes might be more familiar to her readers than the older term her family used.

Exercise 1

Choose one of the following selections from Part 2: *The Promised Land* (p. 62); "Mothers, Sons, and the Gangs" (p. 123); "I Just Wanna Be Average" (p. 193); "The Discus Thrower" (p. 238), or "Illegal Motives" (p. 313). Then follow this process:

1. Read the first five paragraphs of the selection you chose.

2. Highlight or write down on a separate piece of paper any unfamiliar words.

3. Try to define as many of the words as you can from the context provided.

4. Look up the dictionary definitions of those words and compare your understanding with the dictionary definitions.

5. Write a paragraph or two using as many of the words as possible in your own context.

SUMMARIZING TO UNDERSTAND THE MAIN IDEA AND SUPPORTING IDEAS

As you identify and learn the meanings of unfamiliar words, you are also reading to discover the author's main idea. Look for the author's support for the main idea. At this point, you must work to understand fully what the writer is saying. Only then can you move from your first responses to a logical and carefully thought out evaluation of the writer's ideas.

To gain a clear sense of what the author is saying, try writing a summary of the selection. When you summarize, you move from your own first responses to an objective view of the writer's ideas. In a summary you briefly restate in your own words the author's main idea or ideas. You also restate the most important supporting points. You do not put your own responses into a summary. Useful summaries usually share the qualities listed in the following guidelines:

Guidelines: Writing a Summary

1. Identify the author's main point or points.
2. Identify the most important supporting points.
3. Make clear the relationship between the main point and the supporting points.
4. Condense these points without omitting important ideas.
5. *Use your own words!* If you do include a phrase or two of the author's words, enclose them in quotation marks and give credit to the author.
6. Do not include your own observations or evaluations; focus only on the author's ideas and feelings.

Here are sample paragraphs written by three different students who had read Gloria Bonilla's "Leaving El Salvador" (p. 15). Their instructor asked them to write a summary of what they had read. As you read these paragraphs, consider which one best demonstrates the qualities listed in the guidelines for writing a summary and note your reasons for making this judgment.

A. Gloria Bonilla left El Salvador to escape government persecution, and she had to change her tourist visa to a student visa. She learned the history of El Salvador from her parents. She came to Washington, DC, in April 1981, and she stayed with her friend John who she had called from Guatemala. She was homesick, but she forced herself to study and to get a job. She had the support of friends. She had trouble with the U.S. Immigration Service, and the army broke into her home in 1981. But she could not get political asylum. She explains why many Salvadorans have not done very well. Because they don't have the education. She also thinks immigration laws are unfair and that Salvadorans have been sentenced without trial.

B. The central idea of this essay is that the author came from El Salvador to the United States to try to find a better life. But all she does is complain about the different laws and problems. She got a college education here and even a master's degree, so I don't see what she is complaining about. It seems like she wants the United States to change the immigration laws, but she doesn't say why. Also, what does she mean by "it is not very different from the way our people are treated in El Salvador"?

C. In her essay "Leaving El Salvador," Gloria Bonilla describes the reasons she left El Salvador to come to the United States. She explains the problems and conditions in her native country, but the real central point of the essay is to describe the problems she encountered after she came here, to explain what caused the problems, and to tell how she tried to solve them. Although being homesick was a difficulty at first, the main obstacles Bonilla describes did not come from inside herself. They came from the regulations and rules established by the U.S. immigration service. She gives many examples of the many issues Salvadorans must face if they want to come to this country. For example, she argues that the only reason she was able to succeed was that she was able to go to college. To go to college she had to get a student visa, "something most Salvadorans have not been able to attain" (p. 18). She ends her essay with a statement that compares the way the U.S. Immigration Service treats Salvadoran immigrants to the way the government in El Salvador treated the same people when they were citizens of that country.

Example A does not fit the definition of a summary. First, this sample does not clearly identify the central point. Also it does not differentiate between main ideas and supporting ideas. Instead, it simply plows chronologically through the essay picking up details here and there. Some of the details are important points—for example, "Gloria Bonilla left El Salvador to escape government persecution." Yet in the same sentence, and given equal emphasis, is a much less important point: "she had to change her tourist visa to a student visa." In addition, several details in the summary, such as that included in the second sentence, "She learned the history of El Salvador from her parents," are not clearly related to Bonilla's main points.

Another problem with Example A shows up in this sentence: "She had trouble with the U.S. Immigration Service, and the army broke into her home in 1981." As written, the sentence implies that the U.S. army broke into her home. Careful reading shows, however, that Bonilla cites this detail as an example of her persecution by the government in El Salvador.

Finally, several sentences take words directly from the essay without enclosing them in quotation marks or providing correct documentation. Using sentences, phrases, or even ideas that are not your own without giving proper credit is a serious problem called *plagiarism*. In most colleges, plagiarism brings severe penalties, such as failure of the paper or even the course. In the professional world, plagiarism can result in costly lawsuits, as well as the loss of one's job and reputation.

This summary demonstrates problems that can arise from failing to read carefully to establish a clear overview of the author's ideas. It also shows that you must read closely to understand how the author uses details, reasons, and examples to support that idea.

Example B is not really a summary; it is a response. While responding freely to a text is a useful way to begin the reading process, a different process is required for summarizing. Without summarizing—or a similar clarifying strategy—the reader never moves from initial responses to carefully considered judgments.

The writer of Example B starts off with a sentence that might well start a summary since it does suggest Bonilla's main idea. The rest of Example B, however, expresses opinions and asks questions. While it's important to react and respond to what you read throughout the reading process, it's also essential to be able to set aside those responses at some point and look objectively at what the author is saying. You cannot evaluate the author's ideas—or your own responses to those ideas—until you understand the main and supporting points clearly.

Example C provides a useful summary of "Leaving El Salvador." In the opening sentence, the student provides a context by mentioning both the author's name and the title of the essay being summarized. The student also suggests one of the author's purposes. In the second sentence, the student moves from the initial purpose to the central idea of the essay. This sentence shows that he or she understands that the first section of the essay, which discusses leaving El Salvador and arriving in the United States, serves primarily as a long introduction to the author's main point: describing "the problems she encountered after she came here, [explaining] what caused the problems, and [telling] how she tried to solve them." Notice that this student has read through the entire essay and sees how the parts of the essay fit together. Rather than writing a summary that simply moves chronologically through the essay, the student provides an overview of what happens throughout (see sentence 2) and then offers examples that develop this overview.

This student correctly uses quotation marks and documentation to identify words taken directly from Bonilla's essay and refrains from making evaluations. The act of writing the summary, then, accomplishes at least two goals: It helps the student writer understand clearly what Bonilla is saying, and it provides time to think and thus avoid the rush to unconsidered judgments.

Exercise 2

Reread the excerpt from Ishmael Reed's "What's American about America?" (p. 12). Then read the following summaries of that excerpt. Consider the criteria given on page 25 and follow the process used in the evaluations on pages 26–27. Then state which summary you believe demonstrates the clearest understanding of Reed's observations. Explain the reasons for your choice.

A. In Ishmael Reed's article about "What's American about America?" he seems to wonder about all the different kinds of people in this country. He lists a lot of examples of the different kinds of people like Italian, Islamic, and Spanish. He is saying that announcements on speakers at airports should be in Spanish, too. He also wants professors to talk about other cultures even if they're white. But maybe if a professor was white, he wouldn't be as much of an expert on another culture, so I would say that this point is a problem.

B. In his article "What's American about America?" Ishmael Reed tells about an item he read in the *New York Times* that describes a festival attended by people of many different nationalities. He also talks about a poet who talked to Hispanic people in Detroit who were Islamic. While in Texas, Reed heard an airport announcement in both Spanish and English, and when he returned he listened to a Yale professor whose original work on African cultures has led to his ostracism from some intellectual circles. This professor was a white man.

Reed also went to a McDonald's and took pictures of kids eating hamburgers. Then he talks about a cultural bouillabaisse and about Beethoven's Ninth symphony, the cubists, and the surrealists.

C. In this excerpt from his essay "What's American about America?" Ishmael Reed gives a series of examples that illustrate the question he asks in the title. This question suggests that it is very hard to give a single definition of *American*. Instead, the examples show that America is made up of many different kinds of people from many different backgrounds. Some of the groups he mentions are religious, for example, Jewish and Islamic. Other groups relate to the country where these people or their ancestors came from, for example, Chinese, African, and Hispanic. All the examples lead to the final paragraph where Reed quotes the Yale professor Robert Thompson who calls the United States "a cultural bouillabaisse" (p. 13). This comparison reinforces the main idea by showing that the American culture is like a soup, made of many different ingredients. In this kind of soup each ingredient stays separate, but it also combines in an interesting way with the other ingredients.

Exercise 3

Choose one of the following essays: "The Education of Berenice Belizaire" (p. 72); "Spanglish" (p. 138); "Words That Hurt, Words That Heal: How to Choose Words Wisely and Well" (p. 155); "Give Us Jobs, Not Admiration" (p. 230); "'Real' Men and Women" (p. 279); "Unfair Game" (p. 282).

Write a summary of the article using the following process:

a. Read the essay and, in one or two sentences, explain the author's main idea: What is the primary point the author makes in this selection?

b. Look at each paragraph in the essay, identify the main point of that paragraph, and write one sentence explaining that point.

c. Combine the sentence you wrote explaining the main idea of the essay with the sentences you wrote explaining the main idea of each paragraph. As you put these sentences together, provide connecting words or phrases showing how the supporting ideas in each paragraph relate to the author's main idea.

READING TO UNDERSTAND INFERENCES

Writing a summary helps you understand the writer's main and supporting ideas. To understand the writer's meaning fully, however, you have to go further. You have to learn to "read between the lines" and make inferences. When you make inferences, you use hints or suggestions to understand more completely what a writer or speaker is saying. For example, if you show your uncle the hiking boots you have decided to buy, he might note that the high tops of the boot will be uncomfortable on summer hikes. While your uncle has not stated that you should reconsider your decision, you can infer that meaning from his comment. To understand his advice, you have to go beyond understanding the words he has said and recognize the implications of those words.

In a similar manner, to understand fully what you are reading, you need to go beyond recognizing the author's main and supporting points. You need to think more deeply so that you can see ideas, feelings, and values that are not directly stated but are implied.

When you make inferences, you use clues in what you read to understand more completely what the writer is saying. For instance, consider the excerpt from Ishmael Reed's essay "What's American about America?" (p. 12). He talks about listening to a Yale professor speak on "the influence of African cultures upon those of the Americas." Nowhere in that paragraph does Reed directly state his attitude toward the professor. Nor does he say how he feels about those he describes as disapproving of the professor. Yet the words and images he chooses allow the reader to infer that Reed admires the speaker and scorns those who fail to see the worth of his work. For example, he shows us the professor "dancing and drumming the top of the lectern." These activities would be interpreted by many readers as lively, energetic and, therefore, positive actions as opposed to the negative "ostracism" the professor encounters from some "intellectual circles." We can infer that these "intellectual circles" who shun the professor are probably white. Certainly they are not black, since in the next sentence Reed tells us that the professor is cheered and applauded by "Afro-American intellectuals and artists." From these details, the reader can infer Reed's disapproval of the white intellectuals' response, his affirmation of the Afro-American intellectuals', and his admiration for the professor.

When you read to make inferences, you dig deeply to learn what the writer suggests as well as what he or she actually states. As you develop your ability to make inferences, keep in mind the following guidelines:

Guidelines: Making Inferences

1. Note the writer's choice of words. Be aware of the connotation (the emotional associations of the words) as well as the denotation (the dictionary definition of the words).
2. Notice the examples the writer chooses to describe an individual or place or to explain a point. Consider the responses these examples evoke from readers.
3. Notice any value judgments the writer makes, and consider whether these stated judgments help you understand the writer's attitude toward other topics discussed in the selection.
4. Notice any preferences or prejudices the writer states, and consider how these views might relate to the topics discussed.

Exercise 4

Reread Gloria Bonilla's essay "Leaving El Salvador" (p. 15). Carefully note her choice of words as she describes her experiences in her native country and in the United States. Note also the examples she chooses to illustrate these experiences.

Then make a list of the inferences you can make about (1) Bonilla's attitude toward El Salvador and (2) Bonilla's attitude toward the United States. Does she seem to admire one country more than the other? Or does she dislike (or like) them equally? Explain your reasons.

Finally, write a brief paragraph discussing the inferences you can make about Bonilla's feelings concerning her fellow Salvadoran immigrants. Remember to go beyond what is actually stated and consider what is implied. For instance, what does she imply about the way she believes many U.S. citizens view Salvadoran immigrants?

4

Reading to Evaluate

While the process of reading is highly complex and varies widely from individual to individual, most effective critical reading moves through the two stages described in Sections 2 and 3—responding and understanding— to a third stage: evaluating.

UNDERSTANDING THE DISTINCTIONS: RESPONSE, SUMMARY, INFERENCE, AND EVALUATION

Before developing ways of making evaluations about what you read, it is important to understand the distinctions between responding, summarizing, inferring, and evaluating.

- **Responding** When you respond, you simply write down or think about any idea, feeling, or question that comes into your mind as you read. Responses begin with first impressions and are particularly important during the early stages of the reading process.

- **Summarizing** Summarizing is a strategy for understanding exactly what a writer says. When you make a summary, you briefly restate in your own words the author's main idea or ideas and, often, the most important supporting points. Unlike a response, a summary does not include your own opinions or reactions. When you are trying to understand objectively, you put your own feelings, thoughts, and questions aside.

- **Inferring** Sometimes you need to look beyond the stated facts and ideas for hints and suggestions that tell you more about what an author is saying. When you search for inferences, you study the evidence provided by the writer's words, but you also "read between the lines." Inferring, then, leads to more complete understanding. When you make inferences, you may find that you have new responses. It is important to be honest with yourself about the difference between what you truly believe the author is implying and your own feelings about the subject.

- **Evaluating** When you evaluate, you make judgments based on careful, fair-minded thinking. To evaluate what you read (and your responses), you need to think both about what the author states and about what the author implies. You also need to think about the way you first react to those statements and implications. When you are reading selections from a wide variety of cultural backgrounds, you have to work diligently to establish intelligent, fair criteria (standards) by which to evaluate what you have read and then use those criteria to make sensible, balanced judgments that you can successfully explain.

ESTABLISHING CRITERIA FOR EVALUATING

When you make judgments about anything, you begin by establishing your criteria. For example, think about the process of buying a new pair of shoes. Before you even begin looking, you have a list of criteria in your head. These criteria are, of course, affected by many circumstances and do not remain exactly the same for every pair of shoes you buy. For instance, what if you are buying shoes to wear to work at a job that requires standing on your feet for eight hours a day? In that situation your criteria might include comfortable fit, sturdy material, cushioned innersoles, and low cost. On the other hand, what if you are buying shoes to wear as part of a wedding party? Your criteria might change to include a formal style, a certain color, comfortable fit, and low cost. Notice that while some of the criteria change to suit the specific circumstances, others (comfortable fit and low cost) remain the same.

As you develop criteria to evaluate what you read, you'll find the process similar. Some criteria will remain important to you no matter what you are reading. Other criteria may need to be altered to fit the particular selection you are reading. For instance, consider the process of reading an essay written by someone from a culture very different from your own. To make a fair judgment, you may have to revise or even discard some of your standards. You may need to look at such writing in a new way.

As you develop criteria for evaluating what you read, keep the following guidelines in mind:

Guidelines: Developing Criteria for Evaluation

1. *Consider the author.* What do you know about the author? (In this book, the headnotes before each selection give some information

about the author.) Do the author's credentials give you confidence in his or her knowledge of the selection's topic? Do you have any reason to expect bias in the selection?

2. *Consider the audience.* For whom was the author originally writing? (In this book, the headnote often provides this information by telling you where the selection was first published.) How successful do you believe the author would have been in communicating with this audience? For instance, how well does he or she seem to know *who the readers are,* considering such things as

age	religious beliefs
sex	occupation
ethnic background	economic status
political philosophy	

How well does he or she consider *what the audience might already know?* Consider such things as

level of education
experience with the topic
prejudices about the topic

To what extent do you believe this author is successful in communicating with you and your fellow students as an audience? (Consider the aspects of audience analysis listed above.)

3. *Consider the author's purpose.* While it's usually not possible to neatly ascribe one specific reason for an author's writing any given selection, keep in mind three broad aims:

Writing to express emotions, ideas, incidents, and observations. When authors write expressively, they are usually describing something, often by telling a true story that they have experienced or observed. Their purpose is to create a word picture that will show the reader a new way of looking at life.

Writing to explain. When authors write to explain, they convey information to prove a point about the subjects they explore. To accomplish their purpose, they may analyze, evaluate, synthesize, describe a process, make a comparison, define an unfamiliar concept, or explain the causes and effects of an action or a decision, or they may use a combination of these strategies.

Writing to persuade. When authors write to persuade, they offer evidence or make emotional appeals designed to convince the reader to accept the idea they are promoting. Often they also hope

(continued)

(continued)

to move the audience to certain actions. Identifying the author's aim allows you to establish criteria to determine how well he or she has accomplished that aim.

4. *Consider the author's use of details, reasons, and examples.* After you have identified the author's intended audience and purpose, you need to look carefully at the way he or she works to accomplish the purpose. Depending on the audience and purpose you have identified, you may want to consider either or both of the following:

Use of evidence: Does the author provide evidence that convincingly supports the points he or she is making? For instance, if the author uses statistics, does he or she clearly explain them, and do they come from sources you believe to be reliable? If the author quotes experts, are these individuals' qualifications mentioned so that you can determine their reliability?

Use of emotional appeals: Does the author use examples, **anecdotes** (brief stories), or specific words that appeal particularly strongly to the readers' emotions? If so, do these emotional appeals help the writer communicate effectively or are they a hindrance? Many readers find that emotional appeals help a writer's efforts when they seem honest. When emotional appeals seem planned simply to play on people's emotions, many readers resent them. There are no easy tests to separate "honest" use of emotion from "dishonest" use of emotion. You'll need to establish your own ways of making such judgments.

5. *Consider the values represented.* In addition to evaluating how effectively the author communicates with the audience, you may also analyze the values suggested by what he or she has written. You might, for example, believe a selection that communicates strongly but disagree with what the author has to say.

When you make judgments about an author's values, you also think about and explore your own values, which serve as criteria for evaluating the writer. As you read selections written by writers who may share some, but not all, of your values, you'll often need to rethink both the author's views and your own. This rethinking is the most challenging, and often disturbing, part of reading critically. It is challenging because it requires you to examine what you believe to be true about the way humans should interact with each other, their institutions, and their environment. It is often disturbing because, as you read the thoughts and feelings of writers who hold different views from yours, you may find yourself questioning some of your own beliefs and ideals. The process may be less distressing if you consider that changing an opinion or a belief—or affirming in a new way an old opinion or belief—is an essential part of becoming an educated man or woman. If you pass through college entirely untouched by what you read or hear, you are wasting a great deal of time and money.

6. *Consider the subject matter.* Are certain ideas or emotions routinely associated with the mention of this subject? If so, what does the author do with those associated ideas or emotions? Is this considered a social subject or a personal subject?

USING CRITERIA TO EVALUATE: JOURNAL ENTRIES

Once you have thought about the criteria you are using to evaluate a selection, you need to apply them. Writing journal entries is one way to do this.

An explanation of journal writing and several models of journal entries appear on pages 18–21. While these samples show students' responses rather than evaluations, the process is basically the same. You simply sit down and put on paper the evaluations that come to your mind as you are considering your criteria. In a journal entry, you are not worrying about formal aspects of writing such as organization, style, and mechanics; instead, you are using writing as a way of thinking. Here are two sample journal entries evaluating aspects of Gloria Bonilla's "Leaving El Salvador" (p. 15):

As I read Gloria Bonilla's essay, I noticed that she uses a lot of examples to convince you that the U.S. legal system should have treated her better. As part of her point, she says that she believes she "had good enough reasons to be granted political asylum back in 1981." The thing is that when I looked at her examples closely, most of them had to do with what happened to her after she got here. Only one that I could find really talked about what happened to her in El Salvador and that was that the army broke into her house. She doesn't give enough information for me to be convinced that she should have been given political asylum, and it seems to me that leaving this out weakens the case she is making. How can she say it is as bad here as in El Salvador when she doesn't really show much of what happens there? *Cathy Lively*

What I noticed was that Bonilla uses a lot of comparisons to describe what happened to her. For me, they really make her picture come to life. For instance, she compares herself to a "larva in a cocoon" and you can picture that she stayed in there and then emerged gradually and became the beautiful butterfly who is her current self. She is now well educated and a successful author who has had her essay published in a book. Also she talks about "heartache and homesickness" as though they were diseases and then she says she wrote her own "prescription." This is a comparison that explains how and why she filled her days with work. For me, these comparisons make her story come to life, and I think she uses them effectively to tell about the changes she has lived through. These images remind me of my own feelings when I first came to this country and make me sympathetic with her experience. *Amy Ishigami*

These journal entries look at Bonilla's essay in markedly different ways, yet both make evaluations. Cathy Lively bases her evaluation on the evidence Bonilla offers to support her contention that she should have qualified for political asylum. Amy Ishigami, on the other hand, considers Bonilla's use of language as the main criterion for making a judgment. Lively's entry is somewhat critical of Bonilla's essay while Ishigami's entry indicates approval. Just as there is no single correct response to a reading selection, so there is no single correct evaluation. Evaluations differ according to the criteria used and the way the person doing the evaluating applies those criteria.

USING CRITERIA TO EVALUATE: DISCUSSIONS

Discussing what you have read with others provides another way to explore your responses and develop evaluations. An instructor may ask you to participate in class discussions or small group discussions, or you may form your own group with other students to talk about what you have read. You may also explore ideas through conversations with friends, family members, or co-workers. The great advantage of discussion is that it provides many viewpoints. These different viewpoints help you stay open to revising your original responses and evaluations. That is, you often find yourself developing new ideas or changing old ideas in reaction to what you hear. As an example of the way discussions can help readers discover and explore ideas, consider the following transcript that records the comments and questions of several students who had read and written journal entries responding to Ishmael Reed's "What's American about America?" (p. 12).

FRANK: He's just not realistic—he doesn't—I don't think—he doesn't see the bad side to all this together stuff. To me, this fiesta or festival—whatever—couldn't happen today.

LEE ANN: But that's just one example. He doesn't—well, I don't think he's saying that this happens all the time because here in—in this paragraph here (paragraph 5)—he shows about the "ostracism," as he says, of the white professor. So he does see that conflict and that's realistic, I think.

STAN: He's realistic about the so-called intellectual circle—and you can see they're white—or they're not black, anyway because of paragraph 4, about the "Afro-American intellectuals." But he's not realistic about expecting announcements to be in two languages.

DANYA: Everybody keeps saying "realistic" but what exactly do you mean? Does it have to be something that really happens all the time? Does it have to be something like—what I'm wondering is—like an actual current fact everywhere to be worth reading about it? Is that what it has to be for it to be realistic? I mean it could be like the "I Have a Dream" that they play all the time on Martin Luther King's birthday. Which is something that is what you hope for but it may not be happening everywhere—or maybe it's going to happen in the future.

WILLIAM: But if it's like a dream—so it isn't realistic—then what about all the examples he gives? They're supposed to be real, as far as I can see. I mean, he doesn't—there's no place where he says, "I wish this would happen."

LEE ANN: Well, maybe not a dream like future fantasy or something but like looking at the best possible case—in his opinion that is. So like maybe "idealistic" is the word instead of "realistic" or "dream."

In this short sample discussion, the participants express their own ideas and also listen carefully to what others have to say. Not only do they state opinions, but they also ask questions and indicate an openness to change. For example, they start out working with the idea of realism as a possible way to describe (and perhaps evaluate) the essay. As the discussion moves along, they try the possibility of seeing Reed's ideas as a dream. Then they consider the term *idealistic* as perhaps a better description. The discussion is by no means finished. It's easy to see that there are many different directions it could take. It's also important to note that a discussion like this need not have as its goal finding one "right answer." Groups working together do not always have to agree. In fact, rather than insisting on compromise and decision-making, the most fruitful discussions usually value the way multiple voices open fresh possibilities and raise new questions.

When you discuss what you read with others, keep the following guidelines in mind:

Guidelines: Discussing

1. Before the discussion read thoughtfully and carefully, making notes that record your questions and observations.
2. When you come to the discussion, bring notes, summaries, journal entries—anything you've written that may help ideas flow.
3. Respect your own ideas and come prepared to support them with specific references to what you have read.
4. Respect the ideas of others and listen with full attention. Do not, for example, turn off your hearing because you are planning what you are going to say next.
5. Remember that disagreeing with what someone else says or offering a different viewpoint is a legitimate—and useful—part of discussion.
6. Ask for clarification whenever you are not sure what a person means. (For example, if someone uses a term like *courage, duty,* or *patriotic,* you might want to ask for a definition.)
7. Encourage quiet participants to enter into the conversation—perhaps by asking them their opinion on a specific point.

Exercise 1

Read one of the following selections from Part 2: "Crossing the Border" (p. 76); "I Show a Child What Is Possible" (p. 170); "A Brother's Dreams" (p. 221); "'Real' Men and Women" (p. 279); "Safe Sex and White Lies in the Time of AIDS" (p. 320). As you read, make notes in the margins and then write a journal entry describing an initial response to the selection.

Reread the selection carefully, identifying the main idea and the primary supporting ideas. Then write a summary of no more than two paragraphs showing that you understand the main and supporting ideas.

Return to the selection to see if you can find inferences you might have missed. Remember to "read between the lines." Use the introductory material and the topics that follow the selection to help you think about what you are reading.

Finally, consider ways to evaluate what you have read. If possible, discuss the selection with other students. Then write a journal entry that evaluates some aspect of the selection.

As you do this exercise, keep in mind the following summary of the critical reading process. Remember that these approaches are not locked into place. For example, many readers make inferences as they first read and respond, and most readers develop new responses throughout the reading process, not just when they first encounter a text.

Summary: A Critical Reading Process

1. Initial response
2. Second response (responding to responses)
3. Clarification of meaning (summarizing, making inferences)
4. Evaluation (establishing criteria; forming judgments)

5

A Writing Process

Like reading, writing is a complex activity. People write for many reasons and in many ways. Both active reading and thoughtful writing require many strategies and stages rather than a single rigid approach. For instance, Sections 2 through 4 provide examples of paragraphs written for various purposes. These paragraphs respond to, summarize, or evaluate something that the writer has read. This chapter will look more closely at purposes for writing and at a process for writing papers for any purpose.

WRITING FOR A PURPOSE

Writing takes many different forms, but most forms share the broad purpose of conveying new information to readers. Writers use a variety of approaches that cannot be neatly labeled and are rarely used in isolation. It's helpful, however, to understand some possible ways to present new ideas or offer fresh ways of looking at familiar ideas.

Informing

When writers seek to inform, they are usually concerned mainly with providing facts: offering details, statistics, brief stories, and so on that readers did not know. An essay that is strictly informative almost always tries to be objective. That is, the writer does not offer an opinion about the information but simply provides it, usually ending with a brief summary. Readers then have the chance to draw their own conclusions or determine the implications of the new information. Articles in scientific journals are often written primarily to inform. A set of directions telling someone how to get to a previously unvisited location is one example of informative writing.

Defining

Writers who think about a complex concept may explain their ideas about that concept by developing a detailed, extended definition. Obviously, such essays go far beyond the brief information found in dictionaries. Essays that explain through defining explore complexities and apparent contradictions. They offer examples and details that help the reader see the richness of the subject being discussed.

In "A Question of Language" (p. 142), Gloria Naylor's thoughtful and extended gloss of the word *nigger* shows how definitions of words develop and change.

Analyzing

Analysis means looking at the parts of something to see how they work together to create the whole. To write an analysis, writers look closely at the aspects and qualities that make up such things as a place, a person, an idea, an emotion, a work of literature, or an object of art. Then they focus on those aspects or qualities that seem most significant and explain what they have discovered. It's particularly important to note that the purpose of analysis is not simply to see the parts of a whole. A useful analysis must also see the significance of those parts as they relate to each other.

A practical example of analysis is the process most of us go through when we are trying to fix something that isn't working. Consider, for example, a photocopier that refuses to make clean, clear copies. To solve the problem, we consult the owner's manual. After identifying the parts of the copier, we recognize that the paper tray, the power plug, and the front cover cannot be sources of the problem. However, the instructions tell us to check the glass, the chargers, and the toner box. We consider how these parts should be working together to produce a readable copy. If our analysis is successful, we learn what we need to do to get the whole process working smoothly once again.

Writers who make analyses may look at a complicated principle, a common belief, or, perhaps, a distinguished and unusual person's life. By looking at the parts that make up any of these (or many other) subjects, writers discover new and significant ideas and possibilities. They then explain these ideas and possibilities to the reader. Examples of selections that analyze include "Parish Streets" (p. 85), "Mothers, Sons, and the Gangs" (p. 123), and "The Men We Carry in Our Minds" (p. 286).

Synthesizing

The ability to synthesize information, ideas, and observations is essential for anyone truly interested in learning and growing. This process is particularly important for thinking, reading, and writing across cultures because when you synthesize, you look for connections, contradictions, differences, and similarities. What is more important, you look for the significance of the similarities and contrasts you have observed. Writers who explain through synthesis work to see relationships among apparently different people, places, ideas, concepts, and emotions.

We all use the process of synthesis when we meet a new person who will be significant in our lives (co-worker, roommate, supervisor, in-law). Of course we observe differences between ourselves and these people, and we work to discover how to address those differences. But we also look for similarities and for ways to make connections with those who are important to us.

In "The Myth of the Latin Woman" (p. 272), you can see an excellent example of synthesis. In this essay, Judith Ortiz Cofer explains the many stereotypes of the Latin woman and reveals their absurdity by examining her real experiences and the real experiences of other Latin women she knows.

Evaluating

When writers evaluate, they provide readers with information about a particular person, place, idea, action, or theory. Then they define or imply criteria for judging the subject they are discussing and apply those criteria (see Section 4). Making an evaluation requires writers to form an opinion about the subject and provide evidence to convince the reader that the opinion deserves attention. An evaluation may be as straightforward as judging a book or film. For example, when you recommend a particular movie to a friend and then offer reasons why you think that movie is worth the time, money, and effort required to see it, you are making and expressing an evaluation.

A more complex, yet equally common, way of evaluating is to define a problem and then explain what you see as the significant causes or effects of that problem. An evaluation of a problem may also include suggestions for solving the problem. Selections that provide evaluations include "Mothers, Sons, and the Gangs" (p. 123) and "Just Walk on By: A Black Man Ponders His Power to Alter Public Space" (p. 262).

Persuading

Sometimes, as an extension of explaining, a writer will try to persuade readers. The main goal of such writers is to convince an audience to see a particular point of view as important and valid. As you read persuasive essays, notice the way the writers seek your agreement that their evaluation is worth adopting as your own. Most writers use a combination of facts and opinions that you must think about carefully. In judging the evidence the writer provides, ask yourself the following questions:

1. Has the writer provided sufficient evidence?
2. Has the writer used only evidence that clearly relates to the argument?
3. Has the writer used qualifying words like *some, most,* or *in many cases,* rather than using exaggerated generalizations that often begin with *all, every,* or *each*?
4. Has the writer successfully avoided logical fallacies?

In addition to judging a writer's use of rational appeals, when you read a persuasive essay, you should pay close attention to the way the writer appeals to your emotions.

Emotional appeals cannot be evaluated as easily as rational appeals. Some people believe that any appeal to the emotions is somehow dishonest. Yet as humans, we base most of the decisions in our lives not only on what our minds know to be true but also on what our emotions lead us to see as valid. Most of us agree that a balance between intellect and emotion is a good thing. Few of us would want to live in a world controlled solely by thought or solely by feelings. The problem, then, is to recognize how a writer appeals to our feelings and to reject false manipulation. On the other hand, we do not want to ignore the claims of emotions we see as genuine and worthy of our response.

Examples of persuasive writing include "Give Us Jobs, Not Admiration" (p. 230), "The War on Drinks" (p. 234), and "Surfing's Up and Grades Are Down" (p. 305).

DEVELOPING A WRITING PROCESS

As you think about purposes for writing, you'll recognize that most of your own writing tasks require explanation of one kind or another. For example, professors may ask that you write a review or critique of an article, essay, book, or chapter. Such an assignment calls for evaluating and sometimes for persuading. Many essay exams require you to compare various aspects of the course's subject matter. Although the exam may not directly state that you are to give the significance you see in the similarities and differences, you are usually expected to synthesize the information you have discovered. The instructor expects you to provide a useful conclusion rather than just a list of things that are alike and things that are not alike. Another purpose for writing is to investigate causes and effects. For example, a history instructor may assign a consideration of the causes and effects of the French Revolution or the Great Depression, a writing task that can be accomplished only through analysis. Or a philosophy course that focuses on a semester-long exploration of a concept such as truth or love may require a final paper defining the complexities of the concept.

To write papers that explain requires that you develop a process for exploring ideas, gathering effective data, and formulating a clear thesis (central idea) that will serve as your focus. Whatever approach you take to explaining—informing, defining, analyzing, synthesizing, evaluating, or persuading—you need to keep in mind that your primary purpose is to convey new information or a new way of thinking to your reader. To convince readers that this new information or new way of thinking is worthy of their attention and consideration, you need to provide details, reasons, and examples that show—not just tell—them what you want them to think about. Also remember that when you write to explain, you rarely use one approach exclusively. For instance, a paper that analyzes may also include an extended definition of an important term, and an essay that synthesizes two apparently different ideas may also evaluate the significance the writer sees in newly discovered similarities between these two ideas. And any of these papers might also try to persuade the reader to adopt a new point of view or a new approach to a problem.

A SAMPLE WRITING PROCESS

As an example of a writing process, consider Harue Hashimoto's approach to the following assignment:

> After reading Gary Soto's "Like Mexicans," write an essay that explains a contradiction you have observed or experienced in the relationships between parents and children. As you write, keep in mind that your writing should lead the reader to see the significance you attribute to this contradiction.

(Before you continue, read "Like Mexicans" [p. 113].)

Discovering and Exploring Ideas

FREEWRITING   After reading Soto's essay several times, making notes in the margins, and participating in a discussion of the essay, Harue and her fellow students spent the final ten minutes of class doing a freewriting in response to the topic the instructor suggested.

Freewriting is a process that encourages writers to explore the far corners of their minds by writing without stopping (usually for a given period of time). This process can help writers get past a "blocked" feeling and can lead to new ideas and approaches at any stage in the writing process. For instance, as you begin a writing project, you might use freewriting to discover or narrow a topic; later, you may freewrite again to find details and examples that will successfully develop a weak or thin section of your draft.

Sometimes freewriting begins with whatever thought first pops into the writer's mind; sometimes it begins with a question, observation, or assignment. When you have a specific topic or assignment in mind, the strategy is called **focused freewriting.** Here's part of the focused freewriting Harue worked on as she began thinking about her topic:

So—write about contradiction and do not stop—do not stop—contradict contradict mother says "do not contradict"—father just silent—mother and father I do not understand why mother and father get along—big gap—father simple old Japanese character—shy, vague, conservative—thinks about World War II—"demons"—people who spoke English—mother modern/open-minded—liberal ideas/wanted to study in U.S. Mother wanted English for us—problem with Japanese school system—severe strict—my mother's teaching—feel like a race horse—just being trained to run a race and win for owner—mother-as-owner/but father, too? He wanted the other side—traditional culture/calligraphy/flower arrangement/tea ceremony—confusion—confusion—where am I going here?—keep writing—keep writing—confusion—confusion with English—loved English—radio—American songs—language like rhythmical music—problem with grades/not as good as my older sister—turned away from mother's dream to live through the daughters—father delights to teach Japanese culture/to encourage Japanese womanhood—still no answer—what about these two parts????

As Harue looked at the freewrite, she saw contradictions between her father's and mother's points of view. She decided to sort out and explore these differences by using another discovery strategy called **mapping.**

MAPPING   Mapping is a process similar to freewriting. Mapping encourages a visual picture of your ideas, rather than a strictly verbal exploration. There are no hard-and-fast rules for mapping, but usually you start out with a particular subject, perhaps a word or phrase, in the middle of a blank sheet of paper. From there, you try to come up with several possible subdivisions of that idea. You circle these new possibilities and attach them to the original circled idea with lines. Mapping helps you discover what you know about a topic and organize the information to write a rough draft.

Harue created two maps, one beginning with the word *father* and one beginning with *mother.* You can see these maps on the following page.

After looking back at her freewrite and studying her maps, Harue saw that the purpose of her paper would be to explore the differences she saw between her mother and father and the effects those differences had on her relationship with them. In addition, she was interested in the effects those differences had on the way she understood herself and her goals.

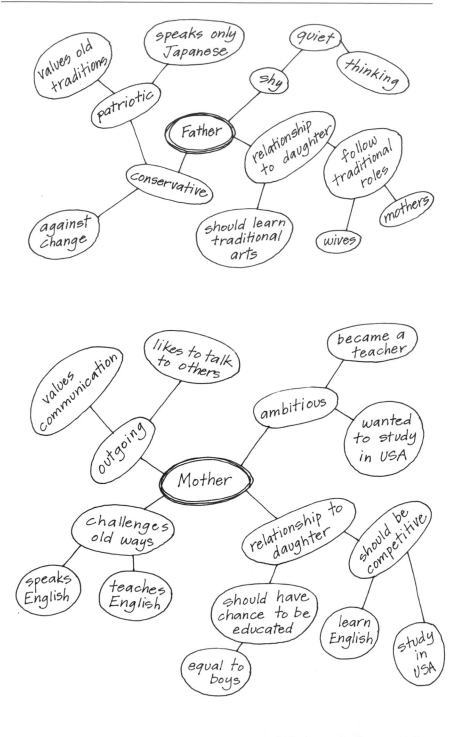

To expand further on what she had learned through freewriting and mapping, Harue used another discovery strategy called **listing.**

LISTING   Harue made two lists: one for her father and one for her mother.

Father

1. shy—values quiet contemplation
2. conservative—does not like change
3. speaks only Japanese—very patriotic
4. thinks daughters (and all girls) should learn Japanese arts—takes traditional approach
5. goal for daughters: to follow traditional roles of Japanese women—wives, mothers

Mother

1. outgoing—values communication, talking to others
2. wanted to study in the United States—ambitious
3. challenges old way of doing things—became a teacher (not a mother who stays at home)
4. speaks English as well as Japanese (teaches English)
5. thinks daughters (and all girls) should have a chance to be completely educated (same subjects as boys)
6. goals for daughters: to be competitive, to learn English perfectly (sister better than I am), to study in the United States

Making these lists allowed Harue to sort out some of her ideas, to discover new points, and to expand on thoughts she had already found through freewriting and mapping. These lists led to a third list, which pointed the way to some of the evaluations she thought she might include in the conclusion of her paper.

Evaluations (Conclusions)

1. First tried to please mother.
2. Then felt like failure in languages.
3. Next tried to please father.
4. Now trying to find my own way.

Planning and Writing a Draft

After making these lists, Harue was still not sure what her thesis would be, but she knew that her purpose would be to explain the contradictions and conflicts she saw between her mother's values and her father's values and to evaluate the effects of these conflicts on her. She decided to write a **discovery draft** (a draft that would explore the ideas she wanted to explain even though those ideas were not yet clearly focused or fully organized).

As she wrote, she knew she needed to keep her audience in mind. Of course, her instructor was part of the audience, but she would also be working in class with other students as peer editors, so she knew she had to consider them too. As she thought about audience, Harue used the following suggestions provided by her instructor:

Suggestions for Thinking about Audience

1. *Keep in mind how much your audience knows about your subject.* Consider what information, explanations, and definitions you need to provide. You do not want to insult readers by telling them things they already know, but you do not want them to be puzzled because your subject matter or approach is entirely unfamiliar.

2. *Keep in mind your readers' values.* You determine your readers' values in many different ways. Sometimes you have talked with your readers, and they have told you that, for instance, they consider getting an education absolutely essential or that they believe practical experience is more important than theories learned in formal schooling. Sometimes you can guess at readers' values if you know such things as their political attitudes or their religious beliefs (or rebellion against religious beliefs). While it's dangerous to make generalizations without recognizing exceptions, you can guess that a group whose motto is "Save the whales" will hold considerably different values from a group who sums up their philosophy with the phrase "Save jobs not owls." If you are writing a paper on environmental issues, knowing that most of your readers belong to one or the other of these groups will certainly affect the way you approach your topic.

   If the values you are explaining are significantly different from those of your readers, consider how you can approach your discussion so that your audience will not immediately become angry or dismiss your ideas because they are looking only at the difference and not at the significance of the difference. You need to help your readers see possible connections with their own values.

3. *Keep in mind that your audience will probably not be a single, easily defined group.* Occasionally you may write for readers who all have nearly the same level of knowledge about your subject and hold similar values relating to your subject. More often, however, you'll be writing for people who, although they may be alike in some

ways, are dramatically different in others. For instance, introductory writing classes often include students whose ages, ethnic background, work experience, and previous education vary widely. When you are writing to such a mixed audience, you have to decide how to meet the needs of as many readers as possible without making your paper a mishmash that fails to communicate clearly because it is trying to be all things to all people.

Harue knew that most people in her class were somewhat familiar with Japanese culture, but she decided that she needed to explain certain aspects of the Japanese education system. She also knew that some students might be uncomfortable with her discussion of her father's views toward his daughters' education and with her own agreement with some of those views. At first she thought about making a detailed explanation of her father's background, including many details about his childhood and his relationship with his parents. After thinking about this possibility, she decided not to take that approach. She made this decision for two reasons: (1) She was afraid it would lead her too far away from her original subject, and (2) she did not want her paper to sound like an apology.

Here is Harue's first draft:

MY FRUSTRATION

I do not understand why my mother and father get along with each   *1*
other because certainly there is big gap between them. My father is a simple old Japanese character, shy, vague and conservative. Because of a long period of isolation from the rest of the world, Japanese have joined together to protect the original race. That is why Japanese think that group harmony is very much more important than the individual opinions, and they are concerned about what people think about them. My father, especially, experienced World War II, and at that time he thought the people who spoke English were demons.

On the other hand, my mother is more open-minded. She has been interested in English since she was a university student. Once she worked at a foreign embassy as an interpreter. In addition, when she was a student, she had a chance to study abroad, but her parents, who are also old type Japanese, opposed it. My mother gave up this chance, but she became an English teacher and still now she teaches junior high school students. She can speak her opinion openly and had very liberal ideas.

My mother began to teach me English when I was in the fourth grade. I was filled with the delight of knowing a language totally different from Japanese. English allowed me to have a bright, new world. I was very happy to share the same thing with my mother. I was excited to learn some English letters and words which were like mathematical signs to me. My mother always listened to the English radio station. I still remember that the sound of English speaking was a kind of rhythmical music to me. When I entered junior high school, I really began to study English. I did very good unexpectedly. So I was so awfully delighted with it. My friends who were around me took it for granted because I was the daughter of an English teacher. In addition, even my mother expected me not to disgrace her occupation. The only thing I had to take care of was to keep good grades in English. It invaded the relationship between my mother and me. English was then becoming a burden for me, because I thought that English alone was the glue to connect between us.

The Japanese educational system is very severe, strict, and competitive, because the academic background decides the way people are valued in society. That is why Japanese parents hope their children will enter a prestigious university. My mother was no exception. Without thinking of their children's feelings, adults compare their children as either better or inferior to others. I studied so as not to disappoint my mother's expectation and to be superior to others in this vehement competition. I was like a racing horse. I lost myself because I was driven by my purpose, but I still did not have any security. My mother began to seem not like a mother to me but like a Japanese woman with an American mask on her face. I now began to hate English.

My older sister has been so smart that she can speak English without 5 difficulty. I thought that my mother loved her more because she was the daughter my mother expected. Before I was aware, my English grades went down. I was very lonely, and in my loneliness, I turned to my father's way of thinking. It is his belief that daughters be educated to the old ways. Thinking about his view, I tried to adopt Japanese traditional cultures such as calligraphy, flower arrangement, and doing tea ceremonies instead of learning English. Through practicing those things, I recognized the Japanese spirit. This isolated island, my homeland, had created such a sensitive race and elegant and refined culture. My father was very delighted to teach me about it.

I can see now that the big gap between my mother and father is that of new ideas versus the old ones. I cannot argue which is better except that there is a large frustration in trying to reconcile them. Right now, as a Japanese woman, I see conflicts because I value my home culture, including the isolation from others, yet I also see how much modern Japan has learned from other cultures all over the world. For instance, although my father still remembers World War II and thinks of the United States as an enemy, my mother points out that behind today's Japanese prosperity, there has been American relief. Also, here I am in

America where my mother often dreamed to go for study. Although I came with some reluctance, I think again that this country is great. It provides me with relief from the frustration I felt in Japan of having to choose between my mother's view and my father's view. From the time I was a young girl, I wanted only to please one parent or to please the other. Now, in this country, I see young people who do what they want to do. Now I understand real liberty means not following someone else's ways. Here I can become educated but also value my traditions. I don't have to be my mother or my father. This is my life and I am me.

Revising

After Harue finished writing her discovery draft, she put it away for several days. When she read it again, she immediately noticed several points of concern. To help in the revision process, she jotted down the following questions and observations to use as she worked with peer editors in class workshop sessions. She also used these revision notes when she visited the campus writing center for tutoring and when she consulted with her professor during office hours.

Revision Notes

1. What is my central idea? Should I focus on contradictions between the Japanese education system and the American education system and way of life?
   On the contradiction between my mother's and father's values?
   On the contradiction between what my mother wants for me and what I want for myself?

2. Do all the paragraphs relate to my general subject of contradiction? (Example: Does paragraph 5 get off topic by talking about my sister?)

3. I talk more about my mother and her ideas than about my father and his ideas, but the aim of the paper is to compare them and the influence of them in my life. Should I talk about both the same amount?

4. Does my conclusion say enough? Does it follow from the stories and examples I have given in the paper?

5. I have the same ideas in different places. Do I repeat too much?

6. Is it all right that I use *I* in this paper? In my English classes before I was told not to, but the essay we read in the textbook ("Like Mexicans" [p. 113]) did use *I*.

7. Do I use *is* and *was* too much? I did this on my last paper. How can I change these words?

8. Do I use apostrophes and commas right? I have problems with this.

9. Do I change the tense of the verbs when this is not necessary?

Harue's revision notes fall into three categories. Her first five questions address **global** issues. These questions look at the content and meaning of her essay. When writers revise, they notice many aspects of their writing. Most experienced writers try to focus on the larger, global issues before they move to issues of **style** (which questions 6 and 7 address) or issues of **grammar** and **mechanics** (which questions 8 and 9 address). As you revise your own work, you may want to consider the following checklist, which suggests global issues as well as issues of style, grammar, and mechanics:

Guidelines: A Revision Checklist

GLOBAL ISSUES

1. Have you focused on a subject that is specific enough to allow full treatment in a paper of the length you've been asked to write?
2. Do you have a clear understanding of the purpose of your paper? Do you communicate the purpose of your paper to your readers? (You can do this through a **thesis statement**—a sentence or two that not only gives your subject but also tells what you intend to say about that subject.)
3. Have you organized the ideas, information, and descriptions you are presenting so that they make sense to your audience?
4. Does each paragraph deal with one main idea, and does each paragraph logically follow the paragraph before it?
5. Does every paragraph offer sufficient information (details, examples, reasons) to support the idea it expresses?
6. Do all the paragraphs relate clearly to the purpose of your paper?
7. Have you analyzed and evaluated your audience, considering their abilities, beliefs, values, opinions, knowledge, and interest? Have you written with your audience analysis in mind?
8. Have you provided an opening paragraph that catches the interest of your audience and makes them want to read further?
9. Have you written a concluding paragraph that provides an original analysis, evaluation, solution, option, or insight? (A strong conclusion usually does more than simply summarize what you've already said.)
10. Does every paragraph in the paper lead logically to the conclusion?

ISSUES OF STYLE

1. Have you used a variety of sentence structures to avoid sounding dull and monotonous?
2. Have you chosen words carefully, considering both **denotation** (the dictionary meaning) and **connotation** (the emotional overtones readers attach to words)?
3. Have you avoided **repetition** (unless, of course, the repetition is used for emphasis)?
4. Have you avoided **passive voice** (sentences in which the subject is acted upon rather than acting)?
   Example: *Passive voice* The map was read by the visitor.
   Active voice The visitor read the map.
5. Have you avoided using long, ornate words when a shorter, more concise word will convey your meaning just as accurately?
6. Have you avoided using unnecessary words (for example, saying "due to the fact that" when you could just as easily say "because")?

ISSUES OF GRAMMAR AND MECHANICS

1. Does each sentence express a complete thought?
2. Have you avoided joining two complete thoughts with no mark of punctuation or with only a comma?
3. Do your **modifiers** (descriptive words or phrases) relate clearly to the word or words they are intended to describe?
4. Do all subjects and verbs agree?
5. Does every pronoun have a clear **antecedent** (a noun to which it refers)?
6. Do all pronouns agree with their antecedents?
7. Is the **tense** (time reference) of verbs consistent throughout the paper except when you intend to indicate a change in time?
8. Are commas, semicolons, and other punctuation marks used correctly?
9. Are possessives formed correctly, using apostrophes with nouns (the girl's book; two girls' books) but not with personal pronouns (the book is hers; its cover is torn)?
10. Are all words spelled correctly?

After Harue talked with other students, with her tutor, and with her instructor, she realized that she did need a clearer focus. Her paper definitely had a purpose—to explain the contrasts she saw between her mother's values and her father's values—but her introduction didn't make clear why Harue saw these conflicting values as important. She realized that although her mother and father were essential to the idea she was explaining, it was her own conflict that was really the subject of the essay. She tried writing a list of several possible thesis statements and finally settled on this one:

> From the time of my earliest memory, I've always tried to understand why I am a person who is determined to go forward yet who always feels drawn back toward the past. Recently, as I was thinking about this question, I realized that the conflict I feel within myself is reflected in my mother and father and the values they hold.

As Harue considered how she would use this idea to focus her paper, she at first thought she would take out references to her sister and to the Japanese education system because they didn't seem to be clearly related to her own conflict. After trying this approach, she realized that she would lose parts of her paper she really liked and that she knew were important to the significance she saw in parents' differences. She then decided not to drop the story of her sister and the evaluation of the Japanese education system. Instead, she would provide transitions that would connect these points more clearly with her central idea.

Harue agreed with her readers that there was no problem with her discussing her mother more than her father because, as her revised conclusion notes, her mother's values are the ones that motivated her most strongly, as well as the ones she most needed to rebel against.

In addition to making the large revisions outlined here, Harue also worked on correcting punctuation and on using more active verbs rather than relying so heavily on forms of the verb *to be*.

After writing several drafts, Harue wrote the following final copy of her paper.

MY FRUSTRATION

From the time of my earliest memory, I've always tried to understand   1
why I am a person who is determined to go forward yet who always feels drawn back toward the past. Recently, as I was thinking about this question, I realized that the conflict I feel within myself reflects the values my mother and father hold. I do not understand why my mother and father get along with each other because certainly a big gap exists between them, which can be represented by the way each one thinks about the English language.

My father is a simple, old Japanese character, shy, vague, and conservative. Like many other Japanese people, he thinks that group harmony is very much more important than individual opinions, and he worries about what other people think about him. He thinks that preserving the old ways is best, and he doesn't try to see things in a new way. For example, he and many of his friends experienced World War II, and at that time they thought the people who spoke English were demons; my father still does not speak English and does not like to hear any of his family speak English.

On the other hand, my mother thinks with a more open mind. She has been interested in English since she was a university student. Once she worked at a foreign embassy as an interpreter. In addition, during her student days, she had a chance to study in the United States, but her parents, who are also old type Japanese, opposed it. To please her parents, my mother gave up this chance, but she became an English teacher, and now she teaches junior high school students. She speaks her opinion openly and has very liberal ideas.

From my early years, I knew my father's beliefs, but my mother was the one who took care of me most of the time. In one way, at least, I was like my father from the beginning: I really cared what other people thought of me. I wanted my mother to think well of me; I wanted to please her. She began to teach me English when I was in the fourth grade, and I was filled with the delight of knowing a language totally different from Japanese. English allowed me to have a bright, new world and to develop an interest I was very happy to share with my mother. I was excited to learn some English letters and words, which were like mathematical signs to me.

During those years, I remember my father often leaving the house while my mother listened to the English radio station. I still can picture myself listening with her. To me the sound of English speaking was a kind of rhythmical music. When I entered junior high school, I really began to study English. Although my mother never said anything directly, I could tell from some hints that she expected me not to disgrace her profession. I started my English class with some dread, but to my delight I did very well with it. As I continued to study, however, I found I lost the pleasure of hearing enjoyable music in the English language. The only thing I had to take care of was to keep good grades. This pressure for high marks invaded the relationship between my mother and me. English was then becoming a burden for me, because I thought that English alone was the glue to connect us.

My mother realized that the Japanese educational system is very severe, strict, and competitive, and she knew that the academic background decides the way people are valued in society. That is why, like other modern Japanese parents, she hoped her children would enter a prestigious university. Without thinking of their children's feelings, my mother and her friends and colleagues compared their children as either better or inferior to others. I studied so as not to disappoint my mother's expectation and to be superior to others in this vehement competition. I was like a racing horse. I lost myself, and my own pleasure in English, because I was driven by my purpose, but I still did not have any security. My mother began to seem not like a mother to me but like a Japanese woman with an American mask on her face. I now began to hate English.

To make things worse, my mother began talking to me more and more about my older sister who was so smart that she learned to speak English without difficulty. As I heard my mother make more and more of these comparisons, I thought that she loved my sister more because she was the daughter my mother expected. Before I was aware, my English grades went down and my mother was very unhappy with me. She did not scold me, but no longer did we share the harmonies of the American radio programs.

One day when she turned on the radio, I was feeling very lonely. In my loneliness, I followed my father out the door as he left to take a walk. For the first time, I listened to him talk about his thoughts about English language. He explained that for a long time Japan was isolated from other countries and that we had to depend on ourselves. Even now, we had to preserve our culture. I saw myself as that isolated island, and I turned to my father's way of thinking. It is his belief that daughters be educated to the old ways so that when they are wives and mothers they may carry on our customs. Thinking about his view, I tried to adopt Japanese traditional cultures such as calligraphy, flower arrangement, and tea ceremonies instead of studying English. Through practicing those things, I recognized the Japanese spirit. I saw that this isolated island, my homeland, had created such a sensitive race and an elegant and refined culture. My father was very delighted to teach me about it.

Now I had my father's approval, but I was still not happy. I saw that I was giving up one important part of myself—studying English—just because I was angry at the pressure my mother put on me. When I told my father I was going to study English again, I could see that he was sad. But I let him know that I was not going to forget all the Japanese culture I had learned. He said he did not see how that was possible, but still when my mother urged me to accept the chance to study in the United States, he did not try to keep me behind.

I can see now that the big gap between my mother and father is that 10 of new ideas versus the old ones. My frustration came from trying always to think which was best. Right now, as a Japanese woman, I see conflicts because I value my home culture, including the isolation from others, yet I also see how much modern Japan has learned from other cultures

Guidelines: Suggestions for a Writing Process

1. As you are prewriting, keep in mind the many purposes for writing: informing, defining, analyzing, synthesizing, evaluating, and persuading.
2. As you explore your ideas, use different discovery strategies such as freewriting, mapping, and listing.
3. As you think about your subject and plan your draft, consider your audience's knowledge, interests, concerns, and values.
4. As you write the opening paragraph, remember that your audience needs to understand your purpose. Readers need to know the subject of your essay as well as what you are going to say about that subject. A standard way to convey this information is in a thesis statement.
5. As you develop your ideas, remember that your purpose is to inform readers of a new idea or a new way of looking at the world. To accomplish this purpose, you'll need to provide plenty of specific details, reasons, and examples. You want to show your readers what you are talking about rather than overwhelming and perhaps confusing them with unsupported generalizations.
6. As you develop your ideas, remember that your audience needs to see clearly how you have organized your thoughts. Readers also need to understand the connections between your thoughts.
7. As you write your conclusion, remember that it should follow logically from the information you have given your reader in the rest of the essay. Remember, too, that the conclusion should do more than summarize. It should provide an original analysis, evaluation, solution, option, or insight.
8. As you consider what you have written, remember the three approaches to revision: global, stylistic, and mechanical grammatical. Use each approach as it is needed.

all over the world. For instance, although my father still remembers World War II and thinks of the United States as an enemy, my mother points out that behind today's Japanese prosperity, there has been American relief. Also, here I am in America where my mother often dreamed to go for study. Although I came with some reluctance, I think that this country is great. Here I find relief from the frustration I felt in Japan of having to choose between my mother's view and my father's view. From the time I was a young girl, I wanted only to please one parent or to please the other. Now, in the United States, I see young people who do what they want to do. Now I understand real liberty means not following someone else's ways. Here I can become educated and study English language but also value my traditions. I don't have to be my mother or my father. This is my life and I am me.

PART 2

Anthology

6
Arrivals, Roots, and Memories

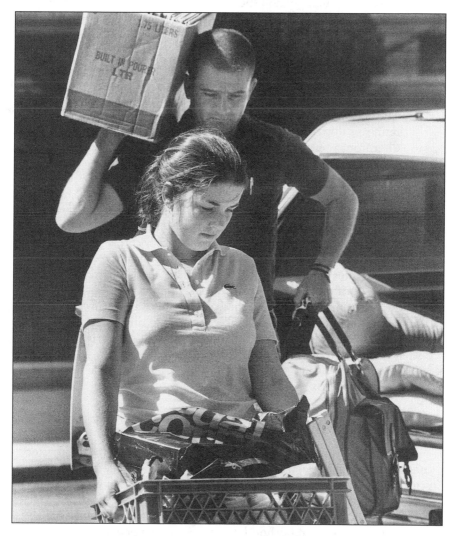

Reading Images

Create a dialogue between the figures in either one of the photographs, bringing to life the actions and emotions of this moment the camera has captured.

MARY ANTIN

The Promised Land

Born to an affluent Russian Jewish family in 1881, Mary Antin saw her family lose their wealth and security to the growing oppression of czarist Russia. This selection shows Antin's optimistic view of the immigrant experience. Neither the journey in steerage nor the difficult living circumstances in her family's crowded Boston apartment dampen her hope for a new and better life. In her 1912 book *The Promised Land*, from which this excerpt is taken, Antin describes her family's move from the Russian ghetto to the "New World." She explains her immigration to the United States as an emergence into a new life, "I was born. I have lived. I have been made over."

Antin was thirteen years old when she boarded the steamer that took her from a restrictive, fear-ridden life in Russia to new possibilities, particularly for education, in the United States. As you read this selection, keep in mind Antin's age when she first arrived, as well as the circumstances of this country in 1912 when, as an adult, she published her highly successful book. At that time, serious doubts were being raised about unlimited immigration policies. The Dillingham Commission to Congress argued in its 1911 report that people entering the United States from eastern and southern Europe constituted a dangerous threat to the country's stability, unlike their earlier predecessors from northern and western European countries. Conservatives pointed to immigrant slums as the basis for social problems such as drug use, organized crime, and joblessness. Into this dismal, fear-ridden atmosphere came Antin's reassuring book, answering with the story of her own optimistic, hardworking, and ultimately successful family the early twentieth-century challenges to the vision of the American Dream.

Pre-Reading and Journal-Writing Suggestions

1. Think back to your earliest memories when life was still full of mystery and magnificence. Describe from this childhood vantage point one specific change and your response to that change. This change should be one that was exciting and positive for you. Include as many details as you can to bring this experience to life for your readers (suggestions: moving to a new neighborhood, taking a trip to a new place, getting a new possession, or being given a new privilege).
2. Describe and explain the significance of a place that may appear ordinary to others but is special to you.

Anybody who knows Boston knows that the West and North Ends are   1
the wrong ends of that city. They form the tenement district, or, in the
newer phrase, the slums of Boston. Anybody who is acquainted with the
slums of any American metropolis knows that that is the quarter where poor
immigrants foregather, to live, for the most part, as unkempt, half-washed,
toiling, unaspiring foreigners; pitiful in the eyes of social missionaries, the
despair of boards of health, the hope of ward politicians, the touchstone of
American democracy. The well-versed metropolitan knows the slums as a
sort of house of detention for poor aliens, where they live on probation till
they can show a certificate of good citizenship.

He may know all this and yet not guess how Wall Street, in the West
End, appears in the eyes of a little immigrant from Polotzk. What would the
sophisticated sight-seer say about Union Place, off Wall Street, where my
new home waited for me? He would say that it is no place at all, but a short
box of an alley. Two rows of three-story tenements are its sides, a stingy strip
of sky is its lid, a littered pavement is the floor, and a narrow mouth its exit.

But I saw a very different picture on my introduction to Union Place. I
saw two imposing rows of brick buildings, loftier than any dwelling I had
ever lived in. Brick was even on the ground for me to tread on, instead of
common earth or boards. Many friendly windows stood open, filled with
uncovered heads of women and children. I thought the people were interested in us, which was very neighborly. I looked up to the topmost row of
windows, and my eyes were filled with the May blue of an American sky!

In our days of affluence in Russia we had been accustomed to uphol-
stered parlors, embroidered linen, silver spoons and candlesticks, goblets of
gold, kitchen shelves shining with copper and brass. We had featherbeds
heaped halfway to the ceiling; we had clothes presses dusky with velvet and
silk and fine woollen. The three small rooms into which my father now
ushered us, up one flight of stairs, contained only the necessary beds, with
lean mattresses; a few wooden chairs; a table or two; a mysterious iron
structure, which later turned out to be a stove; a couple of unornamental
kerosene lamps; and a scanty array of cooking-utensils and crockery. And
yet we were all impressed with our new home and its furniture. It was not
only because we had just passed through our seven lean years, cooking in
earthen vessels, eating black bread on holidays and wearing cotton; it was
chiefly because these wooden chairs and tin pans were American chairs and
pans that they shone glorious in our eyes. And if there was anything lacking
for comfort or decoration we expected it to be presently supplied—at least,
we children did. Perhaps my mother alone, of us newcomers, appreciated
the shabbiness of the little apartment, and realized that for her there was as
yet no laying down of the burden of poverty.

Our initiation into American ways began with the first step on the new   5
soil. My father found occasion to instruct or correct us even on the way

from the pier to Wall Street, which journey we made crowded together in a rickety cab. He told us not to lean out of the windows, not to point, and explained the word "greenhorn." We did not want to be "greenhorns," and gave the strictest attention to my father's instructions. I do not know when my parents found opportunity to review together the history of Polotzk in the three years past, for we children had no patience with the subject; my mother's narrative was constantly interrupted by irrelevant questions, interjections, and explanations.

The first meal was an object lesson of much variety. My father produced several kinds of food, ready to eat, without any cooking, from little tin cans that had printing all over them. He attempted to introduce us to a queer, slippery kind of fruit, which he called "banana," but had to give it up for the time being. After the meal, he had better luck with a curious piece of furniture on runners, which he called "rocking-chair." There were five of us newcomers, and we found five different ways of getting into the American machine of perpetual motion, and as many ways of getting out of it. One born and bred to the use of a rocking-chair cannot imagine how ludicrous people can make themselves when attempting to use it for the first time. We laughed immoderately over our various experiments with the novelty, which was a wholesome way of letting off steam after the unusual excitement of the day.

In our flat we did not think of such a thing as storing the coal in the bathtub. There was no bathtub. So in the evening of the first day my father conducted us to the public baths. As we moved along in a little procession, I was delighted with the illumination of the streets. So many lamps, and they burned until morning, my father said, and so people did not need to carry lanterns. In America, then, everything was free, as we had heard in Russia. Light was free; the streets were as bright as a synagogue on a holy day. Music was free; we had been serenaded, to our gaping delight, by a brass band of many pieces, soon after our installation on Union Place.

Education was free. That subject my father had written about repeatedly, as comprising his chief hope for us children, the essence of American opportunity, the treasure that no thief could touch, not even misfortune or poverty. It was the one thing that he was able to promise us when he sent for us; surer, safer than bread or shelter. On our second day I was thrilled with the realization of what this freedom of education meant. A little girl from across the alley came and offered to conduct us to school. My father was out, but we five between us had a few words of English by this time. We knew the word school. We understood. This child, who had never seen us till yesterday, who could not pronounce our names, who was not much better dressed than we, was able to offer us the freedom of the schools of Boston! No application made, no questions asked, no examinations, rulings, exclusions; no machinations, no fees. The doors stood open for every one of us. The smallest child could show us the way.

This incident impressed me more than anything I had heard in advance of the freedom of education in America. It was a concrete proof—almost the thing itself. One had to experience it to understand it.

It was a great disappointment to be told by my father that we were not to enter upon our school career at once. It was too near the end of the term, he said, and we were going to move to Crescent Beach in a week or so. We had to wait until the opening of the schools in September. What a loss of precious time—from May till September?

Not that the time was really lost. Even the interval on Union Place was crowded with lessons and experiences. We had to visit the stores and be dressed from head to foot in American clothing; we had to learn the mysteries of the iron stove, the washboard, and the speaking-tube; we had to learn to trade with the fruit peddler through the window, and not to be afraid of the policeman; and, above all, we had to learn English.

The kind people who assisted us in these important matters form a group by themselves in the gallery of my friends. If I had never seen them from those early days till now, I should still have remembered them with gratitude. When I enumerate the long list of my American teachers, I must begin with those who came to us on Wall Street and taught us our first steps. To my mother, in her perplexity over the cookstove, the woman who showed her how to make the fire was an angel of deliverance. A fairy godmother to us children was she who led us to a wonderful country called "uptown," where, in a dazzlingly beautiful palace called a "department store," we exchanged our hateful homemade European costumes, which pointed us out as "greenhorns" to the children on the street, for real American machine-made garments, and issued forth glorified in each other's eyes.

With our despised immigrant clothing we shed also our impossible Hebrew names. A committee of our friends, several years ahead of us in American experience, put their heads together and concocted American names for us all. Those of our real names that had no pleasing American equivalents they ruthlessly discarded, content if they retained the initials. My mother, possessing a name that was not easily translatable, was punished with the undignified nickname of Annie. Fetchke, Joseph, and Deborah issued as Frieda, Joseph, and Dora, respectively. As for poor me, I was simply cheated. The name they gave me was hardly new. My Hebrew name being Maryashe in full, Mashke for short, Russianized into Marya (*Mar-ya*), my friends said that it would hold good in English as *Mary:* which was very disappointing, as I longed to possess a strange-sounding American name like the others.

I am forgetting the consolation I had, in this matter of names, from the use of my surname, which I have had no occasion to mention until now. I found on my arrival that my father was "Mr. Antin" on the slightest provocation, and not, as in Polotzk, on state occasions alone. And so I was "Mary Antin," and I felt very important to answer to such a dignified title. It was just like America that even plain people should wear their surnames on week days.

As a family we were so diligent under instruction, so adaptable, and so   15
clever in hiding our deficiencies, that when we made the journey to Crescent Beach, in the wake of our small wagon-load of household goods, my father had very little occasion to admonish us on the way, and I am sure he was not ashamed of us. So much we had achieved toward our Americanization during the two weeks since our landing.

———————

Suggestions for Writing and Discussion
1. In one sentence, how would you describe Antin's experience in this new country?
2. If, as a child, you had had to wait a summer to go to school, would you have regarded the delay as "a loss of precious time"? What is the author's attitude toward education? Why do she and her family consider education a valued gift, a privilege? To what extent do you share her views? How does your own view of education contrast with hers?
3. Antin writes that in the United States even "light was free." List, as quickly as you can, all the things in your daily life that are "free." As far as you know are these things "free" in other countries? Can you think of things that are free in other countries that are not free here?
4. Antin writes that her new Americanized name gives her a "dignified title." Why does this matter to her? Why is it so important that she and her family discard their original names? Have you ever changed your name in any way? Why did you make the change and how did you feel about it? If you have never changed your name, would you consider doing so? Explain.
5. Compare the values of the Antin family with those of modern American families as portrayed on television or in films. What similarities do you see? Differences? As you write your response, imagine that your readers are members of a historical society that is publishing a newsletter focusing on changing family values.

Suggestions for Extended Thinking and Writing
1. Compare the way you saw something as a child to the way you see it today. What do the similarities and differences you see tell you about the ways you have stayed the same and the ways you have changed?
2. Write an essay describing the steps necessary to begin something new. Base this essay on your own experience with a new project. Where did

you start? What obstacles did you face? Where did you find support? What did you have to learn? What did you have to change?

3. Interview someone in your family or someone you know who has experienced a major trip or move. (The move does not have to be to another country; it could be to another state or town or perhaps to a new job or a new school.) Try to uncover the major changes the person encountered and what impact the move had on him or her.

Vocabulary Check

To help ensure that you've understood this selection, and to help you develop a more extensive vocabulary, check the definitions of unfamiliar words in the selection. The words listed below may be new to you, as might others, which you should also identify and define in this exercise.

metropolis (1), foregather (1), interjections (5), perplexity (12), provocation (14)

Using the paragraph numbers in parentheses, which correspond with the numbers in the selection's right margins, locate the words listed above in the reading and develop definitions based on the context in which the words are used (see the guidelines for identifying meaning from context clues on pages 23–24 in Section 3). When you're satisfied with your definitions, use a dictionary to confirm the meaning of each word, and then write your own sentences using these words.

TOSHIO MORI

The Woman Who Makes Swell Doughnuts

Toshio Mori began writing for publication in his late teens, finding time to continue this work even when he became a professional baseball player. He has done extensive research on the Japanese-American experience, conducting many interviews with Japanese-Americans who lived in the United States during the 1930s and 1940s.

Many of his interviews focus on individuals who, like Mori and his family, were interned at a Relocation Center during World War II. These were hastily built, crowded camps where the American government required Americans of Japanese descent to live out the war years. Making the best of this horrifying experience, Mori helped to found a newspaper and served as camp historian during the years he was forced to stay there. His essays have appeared in many journals, magazines, and anthologies, including *Best American Short Stories of 1943*, *Writer's Forum*, and *New Directions*. In addition, he has published several books, including *Yokohama, California* (1949), *The Chauvinist and Other Stories* (1979), and *The Woman from Hiroshima* (1979). Mori's writings are best known for depicting with sensitivity and stunning clarity the ordinary, everyday incidents and people whose lives made up the Japanese-American community in California during the 1930s and 1940s.

Pre-Reading and Journal-Writing Suggestions
1. Write about your favorite food. Aim to write for twenty minutes on this topic, but feel free to go off on any tangents to which the topic leads you.
2. Write about a special childhood memory you have of an older person.
3. What food are you most like? Have some fun as you create this analogy!

There is nothing I like to do better than to go to her house and knock   1
on the door and when she opens the door, to go in. It is one of the experiences I will long remember—perhaps the only immortality that I will ever be lucky to meet in my short life—and when I say experience I do not mean the actual movement, the motor of our lives. I mean by experience the dancing of emotions before our eyes and inside of us, the dance that is still but is the roar and the force capable of stirring the earth and the people.

Of course, she, the woman I visit, is old and of her youthful beauty there is little left. Her face of today is coarse with hard water and there is no question that she has lived her life: given birth to six children, worked side by side with her man for forty years, working in the fields, working in the house, caring for the grandchildren, facing the summers and winters and also the springs and autumns, running the household that is completely her little world. And when I came on the scene, when I discovered her in her little house on Seventh Street, all of her life was behind, all of her task in this world was tabbed, looked into, thoroughly attended, and all that is before her in life and the world, all that could be before her now was to sit and be served; duty done, work done, time clock punched; old-age pension or old-age security; easy chair; soft serene hours till death take her. But this was not of her, not the least bit of her.

When I visit her she takes me to the coziest chair in the living room, where are her magazines and books in Japanese and English. "Sit down," she says. "Make yourself comfortable. I will come back with some hot doughnuts just out of oil."

And before I can turn a page of a magazine she is back with a plateful of hot doughnuts. There is nothing I can do to describe her doughnut; it is in a class by itself, without words, without demonstration. It is a doughnut, just a plain doughnut just out of oil but it is different, unique. Perhaps when I am eating her doughnuts I am really eating her; I have this foolish notion in my head many times and whenever I catch myself doing so I say, that is not so, that is not true. Her doughnuts really taste swell, she is the best cook I have ever known, Oriental dishes or American dishes.

I bow humbly that such a room, such a house exists in my neighbor- 5
hood so I may dash in and out when my spirit wanes, when hell is loose. I sing gratefully that such a simple and common experience becomes an event, an event of necessity and growth. It is an event that is a part of me, an addition to the elements of the earth, water, fire, and air, and I seek the day when it will become a part of everyone.

All her friends, old and young, call her Mama. Everybody calls her Mama. That is not new, it is logical. I suppose there is in every block of every city in America a woman who can be called Mama by her friends and the strangers meeting her. This is commonplace, it is not new and the old sentimentality may be the undoing of the moniker. But what of a woman who isn't a mama but is, and instead of priding in the expansion of her little world, takes her little circle, living out her days in the little circle, perhaps never to be exploited in a biography or on everybody's tongue, but enclosed, shut, excluded from world news and newsreels; just sitting, just moving, just alive, planting the plants in the fields, caring for the children and the grandchildren and baking the tastiest doughnuts this side of the next world.

When I sit with her I do not need to ask deep questions, I do not need to know Plato or The Sacred Books of the East or dancing. I do not need to be on guard. But I am on guard and foot-loose because the room is alive.

"Where are the grandchildren?" I say. "Where are Mickey, Tadao, and Yaeko?"

"They are out in the yard," she says. "I say to them, play, play hard, go out there and play hard. You will be glad later for everything you have done with all your might."

Sometimes we sit many minutes in silence. Silence does not bother her. 10 She says silence is the most beautiful symphony, she says the air breathed in silence is sweeter and sadder. That is about all we talk of. Sometimes I sit and gaze out the window and watch the Southern Pacific trains rumble by and the vehicles whizz with speed. And sometimes she catches me doing this and she nods her head and I know she understands that I think the silence in the room is great, and also the roar and the dust of the outside is great, and when she is nodding I understand that she is saying that this, her little room, her little circle, is a depot, a pause, for the weary traveler, but outside, outside of her little world there is dissonance, hugeness of another kind, and the travel to do. So she has her little house, she bakes the grandest doughnuts, and inside of her she houses a little depot.

Most stories would end with her death, would wait till she is peacefully dead and peacefully at rest but I cannot wait that long. I think she will grow, and her hot doughnuts just out of the oil will grow with softness and touch. And I think it would be a shame to talk of her doughnuts after she is dead, after she is formless.

Instead I take today to talk of her and her wonderful doughnuts when the earth is something to her, when the people from all parts of the earth may drop in and taste the flavor, her flavor, which is everyone's and all flavor; talk to her, sit with her, and also taste the silence of her room and the silence that is herself; and finally go away to hope and keep alive what is alive in her, on earth and in men, expressly myself.

Suggestions for Writing and Discussion

1. What's your initial impression of this piece? Did you like it? Find it boring? Something else?
2. Why are these doughnuts so special to the author? Is he writing this piece to explain how good the doughnuts tasted or for some other reason?
3. In what way might the experience of eating doughnuts be "an event of necessity and growth" (paragraph 5)? Do you feel the author is perhaps exaggerating here? Why or why not?
4. What do you think of Mama? Have you ever known anyone like her? Explain.
5. In paragraph 10, the author indicates that being able to be silent in another person's company is a sign of a special relationship. Using your own experience, do you believe this is true? If so, why, do you think, is it so difficult for people to be comfortable in silence?

6. What do you think the doughnuts "keep alive" (paragraph 12) within the author?

Suggestions for Extended Thinking and Writing
1. Write an essay in which you describe the oldest person you know. Concentrate on physical details and such aspects as voice and actions.
2. In what ways might Mama be described as a teacher? Compare the experiences described here with the experiences Jacques D'Amboise describes in "I Show a Child What Is Possible" (p. 170). To an audience of parents who are anxious to educate their children well, explain what teachers such as Mama and D'Amboise can contribute to a child's growth and development.

Vocabulary Check
   To help ensure that you've understood this selection, and to help you develop a more extensive vocabulary, check the definitions of unfamiliar words in the selection. The words listed below may be new to you, as might others, which you should also identify and define in this exercise.

   immortality (1), wanes (5), exploited (6), depot (10), dissonance (10)

Using the paragraph numbers in parentheses, which correspond with the numbers in the selection's right margins, locate the words listed above in the reading and develop definitions based on the context in which the words are used (see the guidelines for identifying meaning from context clues on pages 23–24 in Section 3). When you're satisfied with your definitions, use a dictionary to confirm the meaning of each word, and then write your own sentences using these words.

JOE KLEIN

The Education of Berenice Belizaire

Born the son of a printer in New York in 1946, Klein has worked as author, editor of *Newsweek,* reporter for WGBH-TV in Boston, and commentator for CBS-TV in Washington, covering such pivotal events as busing in Boston, the Israeli invasion of Lebanon, and every presidential election from 1980 through 1992.

His many journalism awards include the Deems Taylor Award from the American Society of Composers, Authors & Publishers in 1978 for "Notes on a Native Son."

Klein is the author of three books, the best known of which is the controversial *Primary Colors: A Novel of Politics,* published anonymously in 1996.

Pre-Reading and Journal-Writing Suggestions
1. List five qualities that you believe characterize most American high school students. After you've chosen your words, explain which words characterize you and which don't.
2. Be honest—what is more important to you: the grade you receive or the amount of knowledge you receive from a class? Explain your reasons.
3. Looking back on your own high school experience, what advice would you give to someone who is just starting out as a freshman?

When Berenice Belizaire arrived in New York from Haiti with her   1
mother and sister in 1987, she was not very happy. She spoke no English. The family had to live in a cramped Brooklyn apartment, a far cry from the comfortable house they'd had in Haiti. Her mother, a nurse, worked long hours. School was torture. Berenice had always been a good student, but now she was learning a new language while enduring constant taunts from the Americans (both black and white). They cursed her in the cafeteria and threw food at her. Someone hit her sister in the head with a book. "Why can't we go home?" Berenice asked her mother.

Because home was too dangerous. The schools weren't always open anymore, and education—her mother insisted—was the most important thing. Her mother had always pushed her: memorize everything, she ordered. "I have a pretty good memory," Berenice admitted last week. Indeed, the other kids at school began to notice that Berenice always, somehow, knew the answers. "They started coming to me for help," she says. "They never called me a nerd."

Within two years Berenice was speaking English, though not well enough to get into one of New York's elite public high schools. She had to settle for the neighborhood school, James Madison—which is one of the magical American places, the alma mater of Ruth Bader Ginsburg among others, a school with a history of unlikely success stories. "I didn't realize what we had in Berenice at first," says math teacher Judith Khan. "She was good at math, but she was quiet. And the things she didn't know! She applied for a summer program in Buffalo and asked me how to get there on the subway. But she always seemed to ask the right questions. She understood the big ideas. She could think on her feet. She could explain difficult problems so the other kids could understand them. Eventually, I realized: she wasn't just pushing for grades, she was hungry for *knowledge* . . . And you know, it never occurred to me that she was also doing it in English and history, all these other subjects that had to be much tougher for her than math."

She moved from third in her class to first during senior year. She was selected as valedictorian, an honor she almost refused (still shy, she wouldn't allow her picture in the school's yearbook). She gave the speech, after some prodding—a modest address about the importance of hard work and how it's never too late to try hard: an immigrant's valedictory. Last week I caught up with Berenice at the Massachusetts Institute of Technology where she was jump-starting her college career. I asked her what she wanted to be doing in 10 years: "I want to build a famous computer, like IBM," she said. "I want my name to be part of it."

Berenice Belizaire's story is remarkable, but not unusual. The New York   5 City schools are bulging with overachieving immigrants. The burdens they place on a creaky, corroded system are often cited as an argument against liberal immigration policies, but teachers like Judith Khan don't seem to mind. "They're why I love teaching in Brooklyn," she says. "They have a drive in them we no longer seem to have. You see these kids, who aren't prepared academically and can barely speak the language, struggling so hard. They just sop it up. They're like little sponges. You see Berenice, who had none of the usual, preconceived racial barriers in her mind—you see her becoming friendly with the Russian kids, and learning chess from Po Ching [from Taiwan]. It is *so* exciting."

Dreamy hothouse: Indeed, it is possible that immigrant energy reinvigorated not just some schools (and more than a few teachers)—but *the city itself* in the 1980s. "Without them, New York would have been a smaller place, a poorer place, a lot less vital and exciting," says Prof. Emanuel Tobier of New York University. They restored the retail life of the city, starting a raft of small businesses—and doing the sorts of entry-level, bedpan-emptying jobs that nonimmigrants spurn. They added far more to the local economy than they removed; more important, they reminded enlightened

New Yorkers that the city had always worked best as a vast, noisy, dreamy hothouse for the cultivation of new Americans.

The Haitians have followed the classic pattern. They have a significantly higher work-force participation rate than the average in New York. They have a lower rate of poverty. They have a higher rate of new-business formation and a lower rate of welfare dependency. Their median household income, at $28,853, is about $1,000 less than the citywide median (but about $1,000 higher than Chinese immigrants, often seen as a "model" minority). They've also developed a traditional network of fraternal societies, newspapers and neighborhoods with solid—extended, rather than nuclear—families. "A big issue now is whether women who graduate from school should be allowed to live by themselves before they marry," says Lola Poisson, who counsels Haitian immigrants. "There's a lot of tension over that."

Such perverse propriety cannot last long. Immigrants become Americans very quickly. Some lose hope after years of menial labor; others lose discipline, inebriated by freedom. "There's an interesting phenomenon," says Philip Kasinitz of Williams College. "When immigrant kids criticize each other for getting lazy or loose, they say, 'You're becoming American'." (Belizaire said she and the Russians would tease each other that way at Madison.) It's ironic, Kasinitz adds, "Those who work hardest to keep American culture at bay have the best chance of becoming American success stories." If so, we may be fixed on the wrong issue. The question shouldn't be whether immigrants are ruining America, but whether America is ruining the immigrants.

Suggestions for Writing and Discussion

1. Reread any of your pre-reading responses for this essay. In what ways does this essay either confirm or alter your initial response?
2. From the opening paragraph alone, what questions do you have about Berenice's past?
3. Is memorization an important part of any class you are currently taking or have taken in the past? How important do you think it is as far as learning goes?
4. The first four paragraphs of this piece focus on Berenice and her experiences in American public schools. For each paragraph, choose one word that characterizes Berenice and one that characterizes the public schools. What conclusions can you now draw about Berenice and her education based on the words you compiled?
5. The author organizes this piece by first explaining Berenice and her situation and then explaining more general concepts about immigration. How effective do you find this second half of the essay compared

to the first, and what contrasting writing techniques does the author employ?

Suggestions for Extended Thinking and Writing

1. Based on the facts and accounts in this essay, as well as your own personal experiences, what do you think: Is America ruining the immigrants?
2. Implicit in this essay is the message that students from other countries are often more motivated and better learners than their American-born counterparts. Write an essay in which you rely on your own experience to support or undermine this claim.
3. Write an essay in which you describe your own experience as an outsider in a group. Explain the difficulties you encountered and how you coped with this situation.

Vocabulary Check

To help ensure that you've understood this selection, and to help you develop a more extensive vocabulary, check the definitions of unfamiliar words in the selection. The words listed below may be new to you, as might others, which you should also identify and define in this exercise.

elite (3), valedictorian (4), median (7), perverse (8), phenomenon (8)

Using the paragraph numbers in parentheses, which correspond with the numbers in the selection's right margins, locate the words listed above in the reading and develop definitions based on the context in which the words are used (see the guidelines for identifying meaning from context clues on pages 23–24 in Section 3). When you're satisfied with your definitions, use a dictionary to confirm the meaning of each word, and then write your own sentences using these words.

MIGUEL TORRES
Crossing the Border

At the time Miguel Torres told his story to an interpreter, he was twenty years old and was employed in a mushroom plant in California. He told the interviewer that he had entered the United States illegally four times during the past year. His story is representative of the many illegal aliens from various countries who take great risks to find the employment in the United States that they believe will bring them better lives. It is important to note, however, that a survey published by *Time* magazine in November 1993 showed that while 64 percent of Americans believed that most immigrants come into the country illegally, the actual figures demonstrated that 76 percent of immigrants arrive legally; only 24 percent come in illegally.

Pre-Reading and Journal-Writing Suggestions
1. Describe the circumstances under which you would leave your home and your country for a foreign land.
2. In your journal, describe your ideal country. Do any parts of your ideal seem possible in this country? What parts seem improbable?

I was born in a small town in the state of Michoacán in Mexico. When   *1*
I was fifteen, I went to Mexico City with my grandmother and my mother. I worked in a parking lot, a big car lot. People would come in and they'd say, "Well, park my car." And I'd give them a ticket and I'd park the car and I'd be there, you know, watching the cars. I got paid in tips.

But I wanted to come to the United States to work and to earn more money. My uncle was here, and I thought if I could come to him, I could live with him and work and he would help me.

It's not possible to get papers to come over now. So when I decided to come, I went to Tijuana in Mexico. There's a person there that will get in contact with you. They call him the Coyote. He walks around town, and if he sees someone wandering around alone, he says, "Hello, do you have relatives in the United States?" And if you say yes, he says, "Do you want to visit them?" And if you say yes, he says he can arrange it through a friend. It costs $250 or $300.

The Coyote rounded up me and five other guys, and then he got in contact with a guide to take us across the border. We had to go through the hills and the desert, and we had to swim through a river. I was a little scared. Then we come to a highway and a man was there with a van, pretending to fix his motor. Our guide said hello, and the man jumped into the car and we ran and jumped in, too. He began to drive down the highway fast and we knew we were safe in the United States. He took us to San Isidro that night, and the next day he took us all the way here to Watsonville. I had to pay him $250 and then, after I'd been here a month, he came back and I had to give him $50 more. He said I owed him that.

I was here for two months before I started working, and then my uncle   5 got me a job, first in the celery fields picking celery, washing it, packing it, and later picking prunes. Then, all of a sudden, one day the Immigration showed up, and I ran and I hid in a river that was next to the orchard. The man saw me and he questioned me, and he saw I didn't have any papers. So they put me in a van and took me to Salinas, and there was some more illegals there and they put us in buses and took us all the way to Mexicali near the border. We were under guard; the driver and another one that sleeps while one drives. The seats are like hard boards. We'd get up from one side and rub, you know, that side a little bit and then sit on the other side for a while and then rub that side because it's so hard. It was a long trip.

When we arrived in Mexicali, they let us go. We caught a bus to Tijuana, and then at Tijuana, that night, we found the Coyote again and we paid him and we came back the next day. I had to pay $250 again, but this time he knew me and he let me pay $30 then and $30 each week. Because he knew me, you know. He trusted me.

We came through the mountains that time. We had to walk through a train tunnel. It all lasted maybe about three hours, through the tunnel. It was short; for me it was short. We're used to walking, you know. Over in Mexico we have to walk like ten miles to go to work or to go home or to go to school, so we're used to walking. To me it was a short distance to walk for three hours. And after we got out of the tunnel, we got into a car; and from there, from the tunnel, we came all the way into Los Angeles. That was the second time. We didn't see any border patrol either time.

The second time I was here for three months. My uncle managed to get me a job in the mushroom plant. I was working there when the Immigration came. There's this place where they blow air between the walls to make it cool and I hid there. And I was watching. The Immigration was looking around the plant everywhere. There was another illegal there, and he just kept on picking the mushrooms. He'd only been back a couple of days himself. The Immigration walked over there, and that kid turned around and looked at the Immigration and said, "What's the matter? What happened?" And the Immigration looked at him and said, "Oh, nothing," and the kid kept right on picking mushrooms. Yet he was an illegal! He knew how to act, play it cool. If you just sit tight they don't know you're illegal.

Well, the Immigration looked between the walls then and he caught me again. That was the second time. They put handcuffs on me with another guy and we were handcuffed together all the way from California to Mexicali.

Altogether I've been caught three times this year and made the trip over here four times. It's cost me one thousand dollars but it's still better than what I was making in Mexico City.

It's the money. When you come back here you get more money here than you do over there. Right now, the most, the most that I'd be getting in Mexico would be from 25 to 30 pesos a day, which is maybe $2.00, $2.50. And here, with overtime, sometimes I make $150 a week. Things are expensive here, but it's expensive over there, too. And I like the way people live here. All the—what do you call it—all the facilities that you have here, all the things you can get and everything.

The boss at the mushroom factory doesn't ask for papers. He doesn't say anything about it. The last time, he hired me back as soon as I got back here, without any questions.

I learned to hide my money when the Immigration catch me. You know, if you have a lot on you, they take you fifteen or twenty miles from the border in Mexico. But if you have just two dollars or so, they let you go right in Tijuana. Then it's easier to come back. You can just walk right down the street and find the Coyote or someone like him. A man I know was hitchhiking along the road near San Diego and someone picked him up and it was the Immigration man who had just brought him back to Mexico! The Immigration laughed and said, "You got back faster than I did." Of course, he took him back to Mexico again then. But that man is back in Watsonville now, working in the brussels sprouts. It takes a longer time for the Immigration to catch us than it does for us to come back. [*Laughs.*]

I'd like to be able to stay here, to live here and work; but the only way now is to find someone that'll say, "Well, I'll marry you, I'll fix your papers for you." There's a lot of them who do that. I'd be willing to if I could find someone that would do it for me. You pay them, you know. You don't sleep together or even live in the same house, but they marry you. A long time ago you could fix up papers for your nephew or brother, a friend, a cousin. It was real easy then. But now it has to be close relations: mother, father, wife, son, or daughter. My uncle can't do it for me. The only way I could do it would be if I could marry an American citizen.

I'd like to learn English because it would be easier for me. There is a night school here, but I don't like to go because after work I like to go out and mess around and goof off. [*Laughs.*] Maybe I'll go later. If I could just learn a tiny bit of English, you know, I could turn around and tell the Immigration, "What's the matter with you? What do you want?" and I wouldn't be recognized as an illegal.

Suggestions for Writing and Discussion

1. What is your initial reaction to the choices Miguel makes?
2. In paragraph 3, Torres describes a person called "the Coyote." What is the definition of the animal for which this person is named? Consider both denotation and connotation as you explain what the name implies about the way illegal immigrants view the Coyote.
3. Reread the first paragraph of this piece. From the details and language used in these six sentences alone, what would you say Miguel's life was like before he turned fifteen?
4. What would you say are Miguel's personal strengths? What are his weaknesses? Is he someone you would probably have as a friend? Why or why not?
5. Analyze Miguel's reactions for each of the three times he is caught. Do his reactions change over the course of the year? Please explain.
6. Which life do you feel is better for Miguel—life in America with his uncle or life in Mexico City with his mother and grandmother? In a letter to Miguel, explain your point of view.
7. Make a prediction for Miguel's life ten years from the time of this interview. Where might he be living? What might he be doing? Would you see his life as better than his life at the age of fifteen?
8. Is Miguel's presence in America a hindrance or a contribution to this country? Please support your answer with examples and facts from the text itself. You may also offer any personal experiences as support. As you write, keep in mind as your audience a group of United States senators and representatives who are investigating the impact of immigrants on American life today.

Suggestions for Extended Thinking and Writing

1. Rewrite this piece from the immigration officer's point of view.
2. Write an essay in which you describe a time in your life when you felt like an outsider, a stranger in a foreign land.

Vocabulary Check

   To help ensure that you've understood this selection, and to help you develop a more extensive vocabulary, check the definitions of unfamiliar words in the selection. The words listed below may be new to you, as might others, which you should also identify and define in this exercise.

   Immigration (5), border patrol (7), illegal (8), overtime (11), facilities (11)

Using the paragraph numbers in parentheses, which correspond with the numbers in the selection's right margins, locate the words listed above in the reading and develop definitions based on the context in which the words are used (see the guidelines for identifying meaning from context clues on pages 23–24 in Section 3). When you're satisfied with your definitions, use a dictionary to confirm the meaning of each word, and then write your own sentences using these words.

JOHN TARKOV

Fitting In

Born to an immigrant Russian family, John Tarkov is now a writer and editor who lives in Queens, New York. He has written many essays describing his experiences growing up as a Russian American, including the following selection, which first appeared in the *New York Times Sunday Magazine*.

Pre-Reading and Journal-Writing Suggestions
1. Describe your visions of a perfect father and explain how your own father fits into this vision.
2. Explain the topics you and your parents are most comfortable discussing and the ones you seldom, if ever, mention.
3. Explain how your life as a young adult might differ from your parents' lives as young adults.

Not quite two miles and 30 years from the church where these thoughts came to me, is a small, graveled parking lot cut out of the New Jersey pines, behind a restaurant and a dance hall. On road signs, the town is called Cassville. But to the several generations of Russian-Americans whose center of gravity tipped to the Old World, it was known as Roova Farms. I think the acronym stands for Russian Orthodox Outing and Vacation Association. In the summers, the place might as well have been on the Black Sea.

One day during one of those summers, my old man showed up from a job, just off a cargo ship. He made his living that way, in the merchant marine. With him, he had a brittle new baseball glove and a baseball as yet unmarked by human error. We went out to that parking lot and started tossing the ball back and forth; me even at the age of 8 at ease with the motions of this American game, him grabbing at the ball with his bare hands then sending it back with an unpolished stiff-armed heave. It was a very hot day. I remember that clearly. What I can't remember is who put the first scuff mark on the ball. Either I missed it, or he tossed it out of my reach.

I chased it down, I'm sure with American-kid peevishness. I wonder if I said anything. Probably I mouthed off about it.

Last winter, the phone call comes on a Saturday morning. The old man's heart had stopped. They had started it beating again. When I get to the hospital, he's not conscious. They let me in to see him briefly. Then comes an afternoon of drinking coffee and leaning on walls. Around 4 o'clock, two doctors come out of coronary care. One of them puts his hand on my arm and tells me. A nurse takes me behind the closed door.

Two fragments of thought surface. One is primitive and it resonates 5
from somewhere deep: *This all began in Russia long ago.* The other is senti-
mental: *He died near the sea.*

I joined the tips of the first three fingers of my right hand and touch
them to his forehead, then his stomach, then one side of his chest, then the
other. It's what I believe. I pause just briefly, then give him a couple of quick
cuffs on the side of his face, the way men do when they want to express
affection but something stops them from embracing. The nurse takes me
downstairs to sign some forms.

He never did quite get the hang of this country. He never went to the
movies. Didn't watch television on his own. Didn't listen to the radio. Ate a
lot of kielbasa.[1] Read a lot. Read the paper almost cover to cover every day.
He read English well, but when he talked about what he'd read, he'd mis-
pronounce some words and put a heavy accent on them all. The paper was
the window through which he examined a landscape and a people that were
nearly as impenetrable to him as they were known and manageable to me.
For a touch of home, he'd pick up *Soviet Life.* "I'm not a Communist," he
used to tell me. "I'm a Russian." Then he'd catch me up about some new
hydroelectric project on the Dnieper.

And so he vaguely embarrassed me. Who knows how many times, over
the years, this story has repeated itself: the immigrant father and the uneasy
son. This Melting Pot of ours absorbs the second generation over a flame so
high that the first is left encrusted on the rim. In college, I read the
literature—Lenski on the three-generation hypothesis, stuff like that—but
I read it to make my grades, not particularly to understand that I was living it.

When he finally retired from the ocean, he took his first real apartment,
on the Lower East Side, and we saw each other more regularly. We'd sit
there on Saturday or Sunday afternoons, drinking beer and eating Chinese
food. He bought a television set for our diversion, and, depending on the
season, the voices of Keith Jackson and Ara Parseghian or Ralph Kiner and
Lindsey Nelson would overlap with, and sometimes submerge, our own.

After the game, he'd get us a couple more beers, and we would become 10
emissaries: from land and sea, American and ports of destination. We were
never strangers—never that—but we dealt, for the most part, in small talk.
It was a son trying—or maybe trying to try—to share what little he knew
with his father, and flinching privately at his father's foreignness. And it was
a father outspokenly proud of his son, beyond basis in reason, yet at times
openly frustrated that the kid had grown up unlike himself.

---

[1] A type of sausage.

Every father has a vision of what he'd like his son to be. Every son has a vision in kind of his father. Eventually, one of them goes, and the one remaining has little choice but to extinguish the ideal and confront the man of flesh and blood who was. Time and again it happens: The vision shed, the son, once vaguely embarrassed by the father, begins to wear the old man's name and story with pride.

Though he read it daily, the old man hated this newspaper. Sometimes I think he bought it just to make himself angry. He felt the sports editor was trying to suppress the growth of soccer in America. So naturally, I would egg him on. I'd say things like: "Yeah, you're right. It's a conspiracy. The sports editor plus 200 million other Americans." Then we'd start yelling.

But when it came time to put the obituary announcements in the press, after I phoned one in to the Russian-language paper, I started to dial *The Times.* And I remembered. And I put the phone down. And started laughing. "O.K.," I said. "O.K. They won't get any of our business."

So he went out Russian, like he came in. Up on the hill, the church is topped by weathered gold onion domes—sort of like back in the Old Country, but in fact just down the road from his attempt to sneak us both into America through a side door in New Jersey, by tossing a baseball back and forth on a hot, still, bake-in-the-bleachers kind of summer day.

I believe he threw the thing over my head, actually. It *was* a throwing error, the more I think about it. No way I could have caught it. But it was only a baseball, and he was my father, so it's no big deal. I bounced a few off his shins that day myself. Next time, the baseball doesn't touch the ground.

15

Suggestions for Writing and Discussion

1. After reading this piece, what is your initial reaction? Did you like it? Did you feel moved by it? Did you identify with any scene in it?

2. How would you characterize the author's tone in this piece? In other words, how does he come across: as a scholar, a professor, a wise guy, something else?

3. Without rereading this piece, list the images that immediately come to mind of any action, place, or person. Based on your list, what conclusions can you draw about yourself as a reader and about Tarkov as a writer?

4. In what ways does the father educate himself about America and its culture? What do you think? Can he come to a deep understanding of what it means to be an American based on these methods? What would you suggest a parent do to be more "American"?

5. Tarkov writes that "This Melting Pot of ours absorbs the second generation over a flame so high that the first is left encrusted on the rim." Discuss the implications of this metaphor and how effective you find it.

Suggestions for Extended Thinking and Writing
1. Look up and read about Lenski's theory on the generations. Then write a short essay in which you explain how this theory relates or doesn't relate to Tarkov's story.
2. Write an essay in which you describe a particular moment and place where you and a parent were together. Aim to give the details of this place and moment: the time of year, what you did there, how it ended.
3. Imagine you are Tarkov's father and during one night at sea, you reach for your journal and write about the day you and your son played baseball together. From your point of view as the father, what details do you remember? What do you notice? What are your hopes and fears for the future for both you and your son?

Vocabulary Check

To help ensure that you've understood this selection, and to help you develop a more extensive vocabulary, check the definitions of unfamiliar words in the selection. The words listed below may be new to you, as might others, which you should also identify and define in this exercise.

peevishness (3), impenetrable (7), hypothesis (8), emissaries (10), obituary (13)

Using the paragraph numbers in parentheses, which correspond with the numbers in the selection's right margins, locate the words listed above in the reading and develop definitions based on the context in which the words are used (see the guidelines for identifying meaning from context clues on pages 23–24 in Section 3). When you're satisfied with your definitions, use a dictionary to confirm the meaning of each word, and then write your own sentences using these words.

———————

PATRICIA HAMPL

Parish Streets

Born in 1946, Patricia Hampl first won recognition for *A Romantic Education,* her memoir about her Czech heritage, which was awarded a Houghton Mifflin Literary Fellowship in 1981. She has also published two collections of poetry, and in 1987 she published *Spillville,* a meditation about Antonin Dvořák's summer in Iowa. Hampl is now a professor of English at the University of Minnesota. She has written extensively of her early experiences growing up in a Roman Catholic family in the Midwest, and her most recent book is *Virgin Time,* a memoir about her Catholic upbringing and an inquiry into contemplative life. She has also recently edited an anthology of sacred poetry of the West, including poems relating to Islam, Judaism, and Christianity. Speaking about her writing, Hampl once said, "I write about all the things I intended to leave behind, to grow out of, or deny: being a Midwesterner, a Catholic, a woman."

Pre-Reading and Journal-Writing Suggestions
1. Your journal can be a place for private and somewhat complex thoughts. Respond to the words *Religion* and *God* for five to ten minutes. Now reread your responses and write for another ten minutes; respond to your responses!
2. Write about the "holiest" person you have ever known. (You'll need to think about your definition of *holy* as you write.)
3. Write about how your family spent a typical Sunday when you were a child.

Lexington, Oxford, Chatsworth, continuing down Grand Avenue to *1* Milton and Avon, as far as St. Albans—the streets of our neighborhood had an English, even an Anglican, ring to them. But we were Catholic, and the parishes of the diocese, unmarked and ghostly as they were, posted borders more decisive than the street signs we passed on our way to St. Luke's grade school or, later, walking in the other direction to Visitation Convent for high school.

We were like people with dual citizenship. I *lived* on Linwood Avenue, but I *belonged* to St. Luke's. That was the lingo. Mothers spoke of daughters who were going to the junior-senior prom with boys "from Nativity" or "from St. Mark's," as if from fiefdoms across the sea.

"Where you from?" a boy livid with acne asked when we startled each other lurking behind a pillar in the St. Thomas Academy gym at a Friday night freshman mixer.

"Ladies' choice!" one of the mothers cried from a dim corner where a portable hi-fi was set up. She rasped the needle over the vinyl, and Fats Domino came on, insinuating a heavier pleasure than I yet knew: *I found my thrill . . . on Blueberry Hill.*

"I'm from Holy Spirit," the boy said, as if he'd been beamed in to stand 5 by the tepid Cokes and tuna sandwiches and the bowls of sweating potato chips on the refreshments table.

Parish members did not blush to describe themselves as being "from Immaculate Conception." Somewhere north, near the city line, there was even a parish frankly named Maternity of Mary. But then, in those years, the 1950s and early 1960s, breeding was low-grade fever pulsing amongst us unmentioned, like a buzz or hum you get used to and cease to hear. The white noise of matrimonial sex.

On Sundays the gray stone nave of St. Luke's church, big as a warehouse, was packed with families of eight or ten sitting in the honey-colored pews. The fathers wore brown suits. In memory they appear spectrally thin, wraithlike and spent, like trees hollowed of their pulp. The wives were petite and cheerful with helmetlike haircuts. Perkiness was their main trait. But what did they say, these small women, how did they talk? Mrs. Healy, mother of fourteen ("They can afford them," my mother said, as if to excuse her paltry two. "He's a doctor."), never uttered a word, as far as I remember. Even pregnant, she was somehow wiry, as if poised for a tennis match. Maybe these women only wore a *look* of perkiness, and like their lean husbands, they were sapped of personal strength. Maybe they were simply tense.

Not everyone around us was Catholic. Mr. Kirby, a widower who was our next door neighbor, was Methodist—whatever that was. The Nugents across the street behind their cement retaining wall and double row of giant salvia, were Lutheran, more or less. The Williams family, who subscribed to the *New Yorker* and had a living room outfitted with spare Danish furniture, were Episcopalian. They referred to their minister as a priest—a plagiarism that embarrassed me for them because I liked them and their light, airy ways.

As for the Bertrams, our nearest neighbors to the west, it could only be said that Mrs. Bertram, dressed in a narrow suit with a peplum jacket and a hat made of the same heathery wool, went *somewhere* via taxi on Sunday mornings. Mr. Bertram went nowhere—on Sunday or on any other day. He was understood, during my entire girlhood, to be indoors, resting.

Weekdays, Mrs. Bertram took the bus to her job downtown. Mr. Ber- 10 tram stayed home behind their birchwood Venetian blinds in an aquarium half-light, not an invalid (we never thought of him that way), but a man whose occupation it was to rest. Sometimes in the summer he ventured forth with a large wrench-like gadget to root out the masses of dandelions that gave the Bertram lawn a temporary brilliance in June.

I associated him with the Wizard of Oz. He was small and mild-looking, going bald. He gave the impression of extreme pallor except for small, very dark eyes.

It was a firm neighborhood rumor that Mr. Bertram had been a screen-writer in Hollywood. Yes, that pallor was a writer's pallor; those small dark eyes were a writer's eyes. They saw, they noted.

He allowed me to assist him in the rooting-out of his dandelions. I wanted to ask him about Hollywood—had he met Audrey Hepburn? I couldn't bring myself to maneuver for information on such an important subject. But I did feel something serious was called for here. I introduced religion while he plunged the dandelion gadget deep into the lawn.

No, he said, he did not go to church. "But you do believe in God?" I asked, hardly daring to hope he did not. I longed for novelty.

He paused for a moment and looked up at the sky where big, spreading 15 clouds streamed by. "God isn't the problem," he said.

Some ancient fissure split open, a fine crack in reality: So there *was* a problem. Just as I'd always felt. Beneath the family solidity, the claustropho-bia of mother-father-brother-me, past the emphatic certainties of St. Luke's catechism class, there was a problem that would never go away. Mr. Bertram stood amid his dandelions, resigned as a Buddha, looking up at the sky which gave back nothing but drifting white shapes on the blue.

What alarmed me was my feeling of recognition. Of course there was a problem. It wasn't God. Life itself was a problem. Something was not right, would never be right. I'd sensed it all along, some kind of fishy vestigial quiver in the spine. It was bred in the bone, way past thought. Life, deep down, lacked the substantiality that it *seemed* to display. The physical world, full of detail and interest, was a parched topsoil that could be blown away.

This lack, this blankness akin to chronic disappointment, was every-where, under the perkiness, lurking even within my own happiness. "What are you going to do today?" my father said when he saw me digging in the backyard on his way to work at the greenhouse.

"I'm digging to China," I said.

"Well, I'll see you at lunch," he said, "if you're still here."   20

I wouldn't bite. I frowned and went back to work with the bent table-spoon my mother had given me. It wasn't a game. I wanted out. I was on a desperate journey that only looked like play. I couldn't explain.

The blank disappointment, masked as weariness, played on the faces of people on the St. Clair bus. They looked out the windows, coming home from downtown, unseeing: Clearly nothing interested them. What were they thinking of? The passing scene was not beautiful enough—was that it?—to catch their eye. Like the empty clouds Mr. Bertram turned to, their blank looks gave back nothing. There was an unshivered shiver in each of us, a shudder we managed to hold back.

We got off the bus at Oxford where, one spring, in the lime green house behind the catalpa tree on the corner, Mr. Lenart (whom we didn't know well) had slung a pair of tire chains over a rafter in the basement and hanged himself. Such things happened. Only the tight clutch of family life ("The family that prays together stays together.") could keep things rolling along. Step out of the tight, bright circle, and you might find yourself dragging your chains down to the basement.

The perverse insubstantiality of the material world was the problem: Reality refused to be real enough. Nothing could keep you steadfastly happy. That was clear. Some people blamed God. But I sensed that Mr. Bertram was right not to take that tack. *God is not the problem.* The clouds passing in the big sky kept dissipating, changing form. That was the problem—but so what? Such worries resolved nothing and were best left unworried—the unshivered shiver.

There was no one to blame. You could only retire, like Mr. Bertram, 25 stay indoors behind your birchwood blinds, and contemplate the impossibility of things, allowing the Hollywood glitter of reality to fade away and become a vague local rumor.

There were other ways of coping. Mrs. Krueger, several houses down with a big garden rolling with hydrangea bushes, held as her faith a passionate belief in knowledge. She sold *World Book* encyclopedias. After trying Christian Science and a stint with the Unitarians, she had settled down as an agnostic. There seemed to be a lot of reading involved with being an agnostic, pamphlets and books, long citations on cultural anthropology in the *World Book.* It was an abstruse religion, and Mrs. Krueger seemed to belong to some ladies' auxiliary of disbelief.

But it didn't really matter what Mrs. Krueger decided about "the deity-idea," as she called God. No matter what they believed, our neighbors lived not just on Linwood Avenue; they were in St. Luke's parish too, whether they knew it or not. We claimed the territory. And we claimed them—even as we dismissed them. They were all non-Catholics, the term that disposed nicely of all spiritual otherness.

Let the Protestants go their schismatic ways; the Lutherans could splice themselves into synods any which way. Believers, nonbelievers, even Jews (the Kroners on the corner) or a breed as rare as the Greek Orthodox whose church was across the street from St. Luke's—they were all non-Catholics, just so much extraneous spiritual matter orbiting the nethersphere.

Or maybe it was more intimate than that, and we dismissed the rest of the world as we would our own serfs. We saw the Lutherans and Presbyterians, even those snobbish Episcopalians, as rude colonials, non-Catholics all, doing the best they could out there in the bush to imitate the ways of the homeland. *We* were the homeland.

Jimmy Guiliani was a bully. He pulled my hair when he ran by me on   30
Oxford as we all walked home from St. Luke's, the girls like a midget army in navy jumpers and white blouses, the boys with the greater authority of free civilians without uniforms. They all wore pretty much the same thing anyway: corduroy pants worn smooth at the knees and flannel shirts, usually plaid.

I wasn't the only one Jimmy picked on. He pulled Moira Murphy's hair, he punched Tommy Hague. He struck without reason, indiscriminately, so full of violence it may have been pent-up enthusiasm released at random after the long day leashed in school. Catholic kids were alleged, by public school kids, to be mean fighters, dirty fighters.

Jimmy Guiliani was the worst, a terror, hated and feared by Sister Julia's entire third-grade class.

So, it came as a surprise when, after many weeks of his tyranny, I managed to land a sure kick to his groin and he collapsed in a heap and cried real tears. "You shouldn't *do* that to a boy," he said, whimpering. He was almost primly admonishing. "Do you know how that feels?"

It's not correct to say that it was a sure kick. I just kicked. I took no aim and had no idea I'd hit paydirt—or why. Even when the tears started to his eyes and he doubled over clutching himself, I didn't understand.

But I liked it when he asked if I knew how it felt. For a brief, hopeful   35
moment I thought he would tell me, that he would explain. Yes, tell me: How *does* it feel? And what's *there,* anyway? It was the first time the male body imposed itself.

I felt an odd satisfaction. I'd made contact. I wasn't glad I had hurt him, I wasn't even pleased to have taken the group's revenge on the class bully. I hadn't planned to kick him. It all just *happened*—as most physical encounters do. I was more astonished than he that I had succeeded in wounding him, I think. In a simple way, I wanted to say I was sorry. But I liked being taken seriously and could not forfeit that rare pleasure by making an apology.

For a few weeks after I kicked him, I had a crush on Jimmy Guiliani. Not because I'd hurt him. But because he had paused, looked right at me, and implored me to see things from his point of view. *Do you know how it feels?*

I didn't know—and yet I did. As soon as he asked, I realized obscurely that I did know how it felt. I knew what was there between his legs where he hurt. I ceased to be ignorant at that moment. And sex began—with a blow.

The surprise of knowing what I hadn't realized I knew seemed beautifully private, but also illicit. That was a problem. I had no desire to be an outlaw. The way I saw it, you were supposed to know what you had been *taught.* This involved being given segments of knowledge by someone (usu-ally a nun) designated to dole out information in measured drams, like strong medicine.

Children were clean slates others were meant to write on.   40

But here was evidence I was not a blank slate at all. I was scribbled all over with intuitions, premonitions, vague resonances clamoring to give their signals. I had caught Mr. Bertram's skyward look and its implicit promise: Life will be tough. There was no point in blaming God—the Catholic habit. Or even more Catholic, blaming the nuns, which allowed you to blame Mother and God all in one package.

And here was Jimmy Guiliani drawing out of me this other knowledge, bred of empathy and a swift kick to his privates. *Yes, I know how it feels.*

The hierarchy we lived in, a great linked chain of religious being, seemed set to control every entrance and exit to and from the mind and heart. The buff-colored *Baltimore Catechism,* small and square, read like an owner's manual for a very complicated vehicle. There was something pleas-ant, lulling and rhythmic, like heavily rhymed poetry, about the singsong Q-and-A format. Who would not give over heart, if not mind, to the brisk nannyish assurance of the Baltimore prose:

Who made you?
God made me.

Why did God make you?
God made me to know, love and serve Him in this world, in order to be happy with Him forever in the next.

What pleasant lines to commit to memory. And how harmless our Jesuitical discussions about what, exactly, constituted a meatless spaghetti sauce on Friday. Strict constructionists said no meat of any kind should ever, at any time, have made its way into the tomato sauce; easy liberals held with the notion that meatballs could be lurking around in the sauce, as long as you didn't eat them. My brother lobbied valiantly for the meatball *intactus* but present. My mother said nothing doing. They raged for years.

Father Flannery, who owned his own airplane and drove a sports car,   45 had given Peter some ammunition when he'd been asked to rule on the meatball question in the confessional. My mother would hear none of it. "I don't want to know what goes on between you and your confessor," she said, taking the high road.

"A priest, Ma, a *priest,*" my brother cried. "This is an ordained priest saying right there in the sanctity of the confessional that meatballs are OK."

But we were going to heaven my mother's way.

Life was like that—crazy. Full of hair-splitting, and odd rituals. We got our throats blessed on St. Blaise day in February, with the priest holding oversized beeswax candles in an X around our necks, to ward off death by choking on fishbones. There were smudged foreheads on Ash Wednesday and home May altars with plaster statuettes of the Virgin festooned with lilacs. Advent wreaths and nightly family rosary vigils during October (Rosary Month), the entire family on their knees in the living room.

There were snatches of stories about nuns who beat kids with rulers in the coat room; the priest who had a twenty-year affair with a member of the Altar and Rosary Society; the other priest in love with an altar boy—they'd had to send him away. Not St. Luke's stories—oh no, certainly not—but stories, floating, as stories do, from inner ear to inner ear, respecting no parish boundaries. Part of the ether.

And with it all, a relentless xenophobia about other religions. "It's going to be a mixed marriage, I understand," one of my aunts murmured about a friend's daughter who was marrying an Episcopalian. So what if he called himself High Church? What did that change? He was a non-Catholic.

And now, educated out of it all, well climbed into the professions, the Catholics find each other at cocktail parties and get going. The nun stories, the first confession traumas—and a tone of rage and dismay that seems to bewilder even the tellers of these tales.

Nobody says, when asked, "I'm Catholic." It's always, "Yes, I was brought up Catholic." Anything to put it at a distance, to diminish the presence of that grabby heritage that is not racial but acts as if it were. "You never get over it, you know," a fortyish lawyer told me a while ago at a party where we found ourselves huddled by the chips and dip, as if we were at a St. Thomas mixer once again.

He seemed to feel he was speaking to someone with the same hopeless congenital condition. "It's different now, of course." he said. "But when we were growing up back there. . . ." Ah yes, the past isn't a time. It's a place. And it's always there.

He had a very Jimmy Guiliani look to him. A chastened rascal. "I'm divorced," he said. We both smiled: There's no going to hell anymore. "Do they still have mortal sin?" he asked wistfully.

The love-hate lurch of a Catholic upbringing, like having an extra set of parents to contend with. Or an added national allegiance—not to the Vatican, as we were warned that the Baptists thought during John Kennedy's campaign for president. The allegiance was to a different realm. It was the implacable loyalty of faith, that flawless relation between self and existence which we were born into. A strange country where people prayed and believed impossible things.

The nuns who taught us, rigged up in their bold black habits with the big round wimples stiff as frisbees, walked our parish streets; they moved from convent to church in twos or threes, dipping in the side door of the huge church "for a little adoration," as they would say. The roly-poly Irish-born monsignor told us to stand straight and proud when he met us slouching along Summit toward class. And fashionable Father Flannery who, every night, took a gentle, companionable walk with the old Irish pastor, the two of them taking out white handkerchiefs, waving them for safety, as they crossed the busy avenue on the way home in the dark, swallowed in their black suits and cassocks, invisible in the gloom.

But the one I would like to summon up most and to have pass me on Oxford as I head off to St. Luke's in the early morning mist, one of those mid-May weekdays, the lilacs just starting to spill, that one I want most to materialize from "back there"—I don't know her name, where, exactly, she lived, or who she was. We never spoke, in fact. We just passed each other, she coming home from six o'clock daily Mass, I going early to school to practice the piano for an hour before class began.

She was a "parish lady," part of the anonymous population that thickened our world, people who were always there, who were solidly part of us, part of what we were, but who never emerged beyond the bounds of being parishioners to become persons.

We met every morning, just past the Healys' low brick wall. She wore a librarian's cardigan sweater. She must have been about forty-five, and I sensed she was not married. Unlike Dr. and Mrs. Harrigan who walked smartly along Summit holding hands, their bright Irish setter accompanying them as far as the church door where he waited till Mass was over, the lady in the cardigan was always alone.

I saw her coming all the way from Grand where she had to pause for 60 the traffic. She never rushed across the street, zipping past a truck, but waited until the coast was completely clear, and passed across keeping her slow, almost floating pace. A lovely, peaceful gait, no rush to it.

When finally we were close enough to make eye contact, she looked up, straight into my face, and smiled. It was such a *complete* smile, so entire, that it startled me every time, as if I'd heard my name called out on the street of a foreign city.

She was a homely woman, plain and pale, unnoticeable. But I felt— how to put it—that she shed light. The mornings were often frail with mist, the light uncertain and tender. The smile was a brief flood of light. She loved me, I felt.

I knew what it was about. She was praying. Her hand, stuck in her cardigan pocket, held one of the crystal beads of her rosary. I knew this. I'd once seen her take it out of the left pocket and quickly replace it after she had found the handkerchief she needed.

If I had seen a nun mumbling the rosary along Summit (and that did happen), it would not have meant much to me. But here on Oxford, the side street we used as a sleepy corridor to St. Luke's, it was a different thing. The parish lady was not a nun. She was a person who prayed, who prayed alone, for no reason that I understood. But there was no question that she prayed without ceasing, as the strange scriptural line instructed.

She didn't look up to the blank clouds for a response, as Mr. Bertram did in his stoic way. Her head was bowed, quite unconsciously. And when she raised it, keeping her hand in her pocket where the clear beads were, she looked straight into the eyes of the person passing by. It was not an invasive look, but one brimming with a secret which, if only she had words, it was clear she would like to tell. 65

Suggestions for Writing and Discussion

1. After reading this piece, make a list of memories that this piece might have stirred in you. Use the following categories as a guide:

   Church   Neighbors
   Family Rituals   Childhood Questions
   Teachers

2. How would you describe Hampl's childhood? Were the experiences she relates unhappy ones? Magical moments? Something else?

3. Hampl describes her experiences in St. Luke's Church as ritualistic and "crazy" (paragraph 48). Do you think her assessment is exaggerated or slanted in any way? Please explain.

4. What do you think of Mr. Bertram? Why do you think Hampl mentions him here? How about Jimmy Guiliani? Why is he included, too?

5. Toward the end of this reading, we meet a "parish lady." Look back to paragraphs 58–65; perhaps read them out loud. What mood does Hampl create with this character? Why do you think Hampl mentions this nameless character last?

6. In paragraph 50, Hampl notes "a relentless xenophobia about other religions." What does *xenophobia* mean? Explain why you think Hampl's essay either promotes or argues against religious xenophobia.

Suggestions for Extended Thinking and Writing

1. Based on this reading and your own experiences, write an essay in which you persuade your classmates that they should or should not join an organized religion.

2. Hampl introduces us to several "minor" characters in this piece. Choose any one character and write more about the person. Use your imagination to create sensory descriptions and vivid details to make this character come alive.

3. Write about any personal "religious" insight you have had, either recently or in your childhood.

4. Write a piece in which you compare your view of God or religion when you were a child to your viewpoint now.

Vocabulary Check

To help ensure that you've understood this selection, and to help you develop a more extensive vocabulary, check the definitions of unfamiliar words in the selection. The words listed below may be new to you, as might others, which you should also identify and define in this exercise.

lingo (2), matrimonial (6), vestigial (17), schismatic (28), chastened (54)

Using the paragraph numbers in parentheses, which correspond with the numbers in the selection's right margins, locate the words listed above in the reading and develop definitions based on the context in which the words are used (see the guidelines for identifying meaning from context clues on pages 23–24 in Section 3). When you're satisfied with your definitions, use a dictionary to confirm the meaning of each word, and then write your own sentences using these words.

ISAAC BASHEVIS SINGER

The Son from America

This prolific writer, whose genres ranged from novels and short stories to children's books, was born in Poland in 1904, immigrated to the United States at the age of 31, and died in Florida in 1991.

The son of a rabbi, Singer attended Tachkemoni Rabbinical Seminary and received awards for his writing from the Jewish Book Council of America and Hebrew Union College. In 1978 Singer was awarded the Nobel Prize for Literature, and in 1984 he received notable book citations from the *New York Times* and the ALA.

Although he sometimes worked as a translator, Singer chose to write in Yiddish, and his work frequently portrays the Jewish immigrant experience, focused primarily in New York.

Pre-Reading and Journal-Writing Suggestions

1. Describe your vision of a "good life."
2. In your opinion, what are the true sources of happiness in life? Freewrite about them for ten minutes.
3. Given the choice, what would you prefer: to live successfully in a modern city or to live quietly in a remote town as a peasant farmer? Explain.

The village of Lentshin was tiny—a sandy marketplace where the peas-   *1* ants of the area met once a week. It was surrounded by little huts with thatched roofs or shingles green with moss. The chimneys looked like pots. Between the huts there were fields, where the owners planted vegetables or pastured their goats.

In the smallest of these huts lived old Berl, a man in his eighties, and his wife, who was called Berlcha (wife of Berl). Old Berl was one of the Jews who had been driven from their villages in Russia and had settled in Poland. In Lentshin, they mocked the mistakes he made while praying aloud. He spoke with a sharp "r." He was short, broad-shouldered, and had a small white beard, and summer and winter he wore a sheepskin hat, a padded cotton jacket, and stout boots. He walked slowly, shuffling his feet. He had a half acre of field, a cow, a goat, and chickens.

The couple had a son, Samuel, who had gone to America forty years ago. It was said in Lentshin that he became a millionaire there. Every month, the Lentshin letter carrier brought old Berl a money order and a letter that no one could read because many of the words were English. How much money Samuel sent his parents remained a secret. Three times a year, Berl and his wife went on foot to Zakroczym and cashed the money orders there.

But they never seemed to use the money. What for? The garden, the cow, and the goat provided most of their needs. Besides, Berlcha sold chickens and eggs, and from these there was enough to buy flour for bread.

No one cared to know where Berl kept the money that his son sent him. There were no thieves in Lentshin. The hut consisted of one room, which contained all their belongings: the table, the shelf for meat, the shelf for milk foods, the two beds, and the clay oven. Sometimes the chickens roosted in the woodshed and sometimes, when it was cold, in a coop near the oven. The goat, too, found shelter inside when the weather was bad. The more prosperous villages had kerosene lamps, but Berl and his wife did not believe in newfangled gadgets. What was wrong with a wick in a dish of oil? Only for the Sabbath would Berlcha buy three tallow candles at the store. In summer, the couple got up at sunrise and retired with the chickens. In the long winter evenings, Berlcha spun flax at her spinning wheel and Berl sat beside her in the silence of those who enjoy their rest.

Once in a while when Berl came home from the synagogue after evening prayers, he brought news to his wife. In Warsaw there were strikers who demanded that the czar abdicate. A heretic by the name of Dr. Herzl[1] had come up with the idea that Jews should settle again in Palestine. Berlcha listened and shook her bonneted head. Her face was yellowish and wrinkled like a cabbage leaf. There were bluish sacks under her eyes. She was half deaf. Berl had to repeat each word he said to her: She would say, "The things that happen in the big cities!" 5

Here in Lentshin nothing happened except usual events: a cow gave birth to a calf, a young couple had a circumcision party, or a girl was born and there was no party. Occasionally, someone died. Lentshin had no cemetery, and the corpse had to be taken to Zakroczym. Actually, Lentshin had become a village with few young people. The young men left for Zakroczym, for Nowy Dwor, for Warsaw, and sometimes for the United States. Like Samuel's, their letters were illegible, the Yiddish mixed with the languages of the countries where they were now living. They sent photographs in which the men wore top hats and the women fancy dresses like squiresses.

Berl and Berlcha also received such photographs. But their eyes were failing and neither he nor she had glasses. They could barely make out the pictures. Samuel had sons and daughters with gentile names—and grandchildren who had married and had their own offspring. Their names were so strange that Berl and Berlcha could never remember them. But what difference do names make? America was far, far away on the other side of

---

[1] **Dr. Herzl** Theodore Herzl (1860–1904), the founder of Zionism

the ocean, at the edge of the world. A Talmud[2] teacher who came to Lentshin had said that Americans walked with their heads down and their feet up. Berl and Berlcha could not grasp this. How was it possible? But since the teacher said so it must be true. Berlcha pondered for some time and then she said, "One can get accustomed to everything."

And so it remained. From too much thinking—God forbid—one may lose one's wits.

One Friday morning, when Berlcha was kneading the dough for the Sabbath loaves, the door opened and a nobleman entered. He was so tall that he had to bend down to get through the door. He wore a beaver hat and a cloak bordered with fur. He was followed by Chazkel, the coachman from Zakroczym, who carried two leather valises with brass locks. In astonishment Berlcha raised her eyes.

The nobleman looked around and said to the coachman in Yiddish,   *10* "Here it is." He took out a silver ruble and paid him. The coachman tried to hand him change but he said, "You can go now."

When the coachman closed the door, the nobleman said, "Mother, it's me, your son Samuel—Sam."

Berlcha heard the words and her legs grew numb. Her hands, to which pieces of dough were sticking, lost their power. The nobleman hugged her, kissed her forehead, both her cheeks. Berlcha began to cackle like a hen, "My son!" At that moment Berl came in from the woodshed, his arms piled with logs. The goat followed him. When he saw a nobleman kissing his wife, Berl dropped the wood and exclaimed, "What is this?"

The nobleman let go of Berlcha and embraced Berl. "Father!"

For a long time Berl was unable to utter a sound. He wanted to recite holy words that he had read in the Yiddish Bible, but he could remember nothing. Then he asked, "Are you Samuel?"

"Yes, Father, I am Samuel."   *15*

"Well, peace be with you." Berl grasped his son's hand. He was still not sure that he was not being fooled. Samuel wasn't as tall and heavy as this man, but then Berl reminded himself that Samuel was only fifteen years old when he had left home. He must have grown in that faraway country. Berl asked, "Why didn't you let us know that you were coming?"

"Didn't you receive my cable?" Samuel asked.

Berl did not know what a cable was.

Berlcha had scraped the dough from her hands and enfolded her son. He kissed her again and asked, "Mother, didn't you receive a cable?"

---

[2]**Talmud** A collection of ancient writings; the basis of traditional Judaism

"What? If I lived to see this, I am happy to die," Berlcha said, amazed   *20*
by her own words. Berl, too, was amazed. These were just the words he
would have said earlier if he had been able to remember. After a while Berl
came to himself and said, "Pescha, you will have to make a double Sabbath
pudding in addition to the stew."

It was years since Berl had called Berlcha by her given name. When he
wanted to address her, he would say, "Listen," or "Say." It is the young or
those from the big cities who call a wife by her name. Only now did Berlcha
begin to cry. Yellow tears ran from her eyes, and everything became dim.
Then she called out, "It's Friday—I have to prepare for the Sabbath." Yes,
she had to knead the dough and braid the loaves. With such a guest, she had
to make a larger Sabbath stew. The winter day is short and she must hurry.

Her son understood what was worrying her, because he said, "Mother,
I will help you."

Berlcha wanted to laugh, but a choked sob came out. "What are you
saying? God forbid."

The nobleman took off his cloak and jacket and remained in his vest,
on which hung a solid-gold watch chain. He rolled up his sleeves and came
to the trough. "Mother, I was a baker for many years in New York," he said,
and he began to knead the dough.

"What! You are my darling son who will say Kaddish³ for me." She   *25*
wept raspingly. Her strength left her, and she slumped onto the bed.

Berl said, "Women will always be women." And he went to the shed to
get more wood. The goat sat down near the oven; she gazed with surprise
at this strange man—his height and his bizarre clothes.

The neighbors had heard the good news that Berl's son had arrived from
America and they came to greet him. The women began to help Berlcha
prepare for the Sabbath. Some laughed, some cried. The room was full of
people, as at a wedding. They asked Berl's son, "What is new in America?"
And Berl's son answered, "America is all right."

"Do Jews make a living?"

"One eats white bread there on weekdays."

"Do they remain Jews?"   *30*

"I am not a gentile."

After Berlcha blessed the candles, father and son went to the little synagogue across the street. A new snow had fallen. The son took large steps,
but Berl warned him, "Slow down."

In the synagogue the Jews recited "Let Us Exult" and "Come, My
Groom." All the time, the snow outside kept falling. After prayers, when
Berl and Samuel left the Holy Place, the village was unrecognizable. Every-

---

³**Kaddish** The Jewish prayer for the dead

thing was covered in snow. One could see only the contours of the roofs and the candles in the windows. Samuel said, "Nothing has changed here."

Berlcha had prepared gefilte fish, chicken soup with rice, meat, carrot stew. Berl recited the benediction over a glass of ritual wine. The family ate and drank, and when it grew quiet for a while one could hear the chirping of the house cricket. The son talked a lot, but Berl and Berlcha understood little. His Yiddish was different and contained foreign words.

After the final blessing Samuel asked, "Father, what did you do with all 35 the money I sent you?"

Berl raised his white brows. "It's here."

"Didn't you put it in a bank?"

"There is no bank in Lentshin."

"Where do you keep it?"

Berl hesitated. "One is not allowed to touch money on the Sabbath but 40 I will show you." He crouched beside the bed and began to shove something heavy. A boot appeared. Its top was stuffed with straw. Berl removed the straw and the son saw that the boot was full of gold coins. He lifted it.

"Father, this is a treasure!" he called out.

"Well."

"Why didn't you spend it?"

"On what? Thank God, we have everything."

"Why didn't you travel somewhere?" 45

"Where to? This is our home."

The son asked one question after the other, but Berl's answer was always the same: they wanted for nothing. The garden, the cow, the goat, the chickens provided them with all they needed. The son said, "If thieves knew about this, your lives wouldn't be safe."

"There are no thieves here."

"What will happen to the money?"

"You take it." 50

Slowly, Berl and Berlcha grew accustomed to their son and his American Yiddish. Berlcha could hear him better now. She even recognized his voice. He was saying, "Perhaps we should build a larger synagogue."

"The synagogue is big enough," Berl replied.

"Perhaps a home for old people."

"No one sleeps in the street."

The next day after the Sabbath meal was eaten, a gentile from Zakroc- 55 zym brought a paper—it was the cable. Berl and Berlcha lay down for a nap. They soon began to snore. The goat, too, dozed off. The son put on his cloak and his hat and went for a walk. He strode with his long legs across the marketplace. He stretched out a hand and touched a roof. He wanted to smoke a cigar, but he remembered it was forbidden on the Sabbath. He had a desire to talk to someone, but it seemed that the whole of Lentshin was asleep. He entered the synagogue. An old man was sitting there, reciting psalms. Samuel asked, "Are you praying?"

"What else is there to do when one gets old?"

"Do you make a living?"

The old man did not understand the meaning of those words. He smiled, showing his empty gums, and then he said, "If God gives health, one keeps on living."

Samuel returned home. Dusk had fallen. Berl went to the synagogue for the evening prayers and the son remained with his mother. The room was filled with shadows.

Berlcha began to recite in a solemn singsong, "God of Abraham, Isaac, *60* and Jacob, defend the poor people of Israel and Thy name. The Holy Sabbath is departing; the welcome week is coming to us. Let it be one of health, wealth, and good deeds."

"Mother, you don't need to pray for wealth," Samuel said. "You are wealthy already."

Berlcha did not hear—or pretended not to. Her face had turned into a cluster of shadows.

In the twilight Samuel put his hand into his jacket pocket and touched his passport, his checkbook, his letters of credit. He had come here with big plans. He had a valise filled with presents for his parents. He wanted to bestow gifts on the village. He brought not only his own money but funds from the Lentshin Society in New York, which had organized a ball for the benefit of the village. But this village in the hinterland needed nothing. From the synagogue one could hear hoarse chanting. The cricket, silent all day, started again its chirping. Berlcha began to sway and utter holy rhymes inherited from mothers and grandmothers:

> Thy holy sheep
> In mercy keep,
> In Torah[4] good deeds;
> Provide for all their needs,
> Shoes, clothes, and bread
> And the Messiah's tread.

Suggestions for Writing and Discussion
1. If you could design a cover jacket for this piece, what one scene would you highlight? Explain.

---

[4]**Torah** The first five books of the Hebrew Bible

2. What are the major differences between the parents and their son? What do they still have in common?
3. As the Talmud teacher says in this piece, "Americans walk around with their heads down and their feet up." What exactly do you think this means? Do you agree?
4. What questions do you have about the son that this piece fails to answer? What answers do you think are most probable?
5. In the end, the son has changed. What causes him to change, and do you think this change will be permanent? Explain.

Suggestions for Extended Thinking and Writing
1. Compare your perspective as a child on your parents, religion, and home town to how you view them now.
2. In this piece, Berlcha comments that "One can get accustomed to everything." With this thought in mind, write about a modern appliance or luxury that you have come to depend on. Explain the importance of this object in your everyday life and then imagine what your life would be like without this object. How would you cope? How would you change?

Vocabulary Check

To help ensure that you've understood this selection, and to help you develop a more extensive vocabulary, check the definitions of unfamiliar words in the selection. The words listed below may be new to you, as might others, which you should also identify and define in this exercise.

heretic (5), illegible (6), gentile (7), cable (17), valise (63)

Using the paragraph numbers in parentheses, which correspond with the numbers in the selection's right margins, locate the words listed above in the reading and develop definitions based on the context in which the words are used (see the guidelines for identifying meaning from context clues on pages 23–24 in Section 3). When you're satisfied with your definitions, use a dictionary to confirm the meaning of each word, and then write your own sentences using these words.

SUGGESTIONS FOR MAKING CONNECTIONS

1. Many people around the world still view the United States as the land of promise and opportunity. Despite the losses that many immigrants suffered, despite the cruel treatment many received simply because they were viewed as different, why did so many choose to remain in

this country and encourage their relatives to follow? Refer to selections in this section as you write your response, using your own experience and observations as well.

2. Some argue that the concept of America as a melting pot is not entirely accurate. In a melting pot, everything blends together and unites into a new whole. In a short essay, defend this metaphor as accurate, or explain in detail a different metaphor that you believe better represents this country. Feel free to use your own experiences in this piece. In addition, refer to selections in this section that support or refute your own view of the melting-pot metaphor.

3. As Mary Antin's *The Promised Land* shows us, many immigrants came to this country with the intention of becoming part of American society. Other selections attest that many immigrants preferred to hold on to their native culture and values. Explain which approach you would most likely adopt if you were to move to another country. Use your own experiences for support.

4. Several of the writings in this section deal with culture and how it affects the relationships formed between children and their parents or other authority figures. Analyze the inner conflicts, the discoveries, and the resolutions that occur within this framework.

5. Use at least three of the selections in this section to analyze the different processes by which we come to know who we are.

6. To what extent should one's identity, or sense of self, relate to and draw upon the past (including ethnic and religious traditions and beliefs)? In addition to several sources from this section, draw upon your own experiences and observations to answer this question.

7. Consider the differences between being rooted and being uprooted. Examine both the positive and negative aspects of each, and come to some conclusion about how each state of being contributes to what we know and who we are.

8. Analyze the effects of being caught between two identities. Besides using the sources in this section for references, rely on your own experiences and observations. What happens when we are caught in a struggle between who we know we might be and who we used to be or who someone else wants us to be?

9. Write an essay in which you show that loss of one identity is just a natural stage in the evolution of becoming a whole person.

10. Many of the writings in this section deal with the struggle to learn about oneself and one's place in the world. Examine several of these processes and come to some conclusions about the best ways to address such complex issues. What do we need to do? Where do we need to go? Who has the answers? How can we find them?

11. Review the selections in this section. Select the piece that you enjoyed the most, as well as the one that you cared for the least. Now try to analyze why you enjoyed the piece you did. Was it the topic? The theme? The style? The language? Also analyze why you didn't favor the other piece. In other words, what are the major differences between these two pieces as far as you, the reader, are concerned?

12. From all of these readings, choose the person or character you most admired and the character or person you least admired. Compare the two and explain the reasons for your evaluation.

13. List several questions and issues raised by selections in this section. Evaluate these questions and issues and explain which one is the most important to you. Write an essay in which you try to convince others that this issue is of great importance. Use contemporary examples and your own experiences as major support in this essay.

7

Families

Reading Images

Each of these photographs shows families together. In one, the family shares a meal. Identify
the activity in the other photo. What contrasts and comparisons do you see between these
two typical American family activities?

TRAN THI NGA
Letter to My Mother

> Tran Thi Nga, who was born in China in 1927, was a social worker in Vietnam. In addition, she has worked as a journalist in both Asia and the United States. This letter suggests the connections she feels to her mother, as well as the differences she sees between their lives and the places they live.

Pre-Reading and Journal-Writing Suggestions

1. Write a tribute to an older relative in your family. In this tribute, describe what you admire most about this person. What have you learned from observing and hearing about this person's life experiences and everyday values?

2. At this point in your life, what is the greatest sacrifice you have made? What is the greatest sacrifice someone else has made for you? Write a descriptive narrative responding to either of these questions.

3. If you could make one wish for one or both of your parents, what would be your wish? Explain the significance of your response.

Dear Mother,

I do not know if you are receiving my letters, but I will keep writing to you as you are always in my mind.   1

We have been here three years now. I have moved from Greenwich and have a wooden shingled house in Cos Cob. We have a garden in the back where we plant vegetables, flowers in the front the way we used to when we were together. I have a pink dogwood tree that blooms in spring. It looks like the Hoa dai tree, but has no leaves, only flowers.

We worked for months to clear away the poison ivy, a plant that turns your skin red and makes you itch.

We are near a beach, a school and a shopping center. Green lawns go down to the streets and there are many cars and garages. I am even learning to drive.

When we got our new house, people from the church came and took us   5
to "Friendly's" for ice cream. Americans celebrate with ice cream. They have so many kinds—red like watermelon, green for pistachio, orange sherbet like Buddha's robes, mint chocolate chip. You buy it fast and take it away to eat.

Our house is small, but a place to be together and discuss our daily life. At every meal we stare at the dishes you used to fix for us and think about you. We are sorry for you and for ourselves.

If we work hard here, we have everything, but we fear you are hungry and cold and lonesome. Last week we made up a package of clothes. We all tried to figure out how thin you must be now. I do not know if you will ever receive that package wrapped with all our thoughts.

I remember the last days when you encouraged us to leave the country and refused to go yourself. You said you were too old, did not want to leave your home and would be a burden to us. We realize now that you sacrificed yourself for our well-being.

You have a new grandson born in the United States. Thanh looked beautiful at her wedding in a red velvet dress and white veil, a yellow turban in her dark hair. She carried the chrysanthemums you love.

You always loved the fall in Hanoi. You liked the cold. We don't. We have just had the worst winter in a century, snow piled everywhere. I must wear a heavy coat, boots, fur gloves, and a hat. I look like a ball running to the train station. I feel that if I fell down, I could never get up. 10

Your grandson is three, in nursery school. He speaks English so well that we are sad. We made a rule. We must speak Vietnamese at home so that the children will not forget their mother tongue.

We have made an altar to Father. We try to keep up our traditions so that we can look forward to the day we can return to our country, although we do not know when that will be.

Here we are materially well off, but spiritually deprived. We miss our country. Most of all we miss you. Should Buddha exist, we should keep praying to be reunited.

Dear Mother, keep up your mind. Pray to Buddha silently. We will have a future and I hope it will be soon.

We want to swim in our own pond. 15
Clear or stinky, still it is ours.

Your daughter,
Nga

Suggestions for Writing and Discussion

1. How does Tran Thi Nga sound in this letter? Happy? Content? Angry? Something else? Write to a friend who has not read Tran Thi Nga's letter. As you write, refer to specific words and images she uses to explain to your friend how you think Tran Thi Nga feels about the United States and about her homeland.

2. In much of this letter, Nga writes about common, everyday scenes and events. She describes flowers, her neighborhood, ice cream, the clothing she wears, and even the weather. Why do you think she spends so

much time explaining these simple things? How would her story be changed if she omitted these details?

3. Look again at the parts of her life Nga chooses to share with her mother. Can you speculate on parts of her life she does not mention? Why do you think this is?

4. From reading this letter, do you think Nga believes that she will see her mother someday? Do you believe she will return to her homeland? Support your response with specific evidence from the text itself.

5. In her last two lines, Nga writes, "We want to swim in our own pond/ Clear or stinky, still it is ours." Stop and think about this metaphor. What exactly is she comparing to a pond—her old way of life, her homeland, her neighborhood, her yard, or something else? What does the metaphor of the pond imply about her life now?

Suggestions for Extended Thinking and Writing

1. Assume the part of Nga's mother. Write to your daughter responding to the letter from her that you have just read.

2. Imagine that someone close to you (a family member or a good friend) has never seen your present neighborhood. Write a letter to this person in which you selectively describe what your life is like here.

3. Reflect on your response to the first journal suggestion for this piece. Revise this entry now so that you focus on one aspect of this relative: mannerisms, beliefs, appearances, most notable moment, last impression, and so on.

Vocabulary Check

To help ensure that you've understood this selection, and to help you develop a more extensive vocabulary, check the definitions of unfamiliar words in the selection. The words listed below may be new to you, as might others, which you should also identify and define in this exercise.

sacrifice (8), tradition (12), materially (13), spiritually (13), deprived (13)

Using the paragraph numbers in parentheses, which correspond with the numbers in the selection's right margins, locate the words listed above in the reading and develop definitions based on the context in which the words are used (see the guidelines for identifying meaning from context clues on pages 23–24 in Section 3). When you're satisfied with your definitions, use a dictionary to confirm the meaning of each word, and then write your own sentences using these words.

DORIS KEARNS GOODWIN

From Father, with Love

Doris Kearns Goodwin grew up on Long Island in the 1950s, when New York was home to three legendary baseball teams: the New York Yankees, the New York Giants, and the Brooklyn Dodgers. After earning her bachelor's degree at Colby College, she went on to Harvard to earn a doctorate in government. From there she went to Washington as a White House Fellow in 1967, and from 1969 to 1973 she served as special counsel to President Lyndon Johnson. After Johnson left office, she accepted a teaching position at Harvard and also traveled frequently to Texas to help Johnson compile his memoirs. In 1976 she wrote *Lyndon Johnson and the American Dream*. With the help of her husband's contacts as a speechwriter for President John F. Kennedy, she gained access to unpublished Kennedy family papers, which she used as the basis for *The Fitzgeralds and the Kennedys, An American Saga* (1987). Her next book, *No Ordinary Time: Franklin and Eleanor Roosevelt: The Home Front in World War II* (1994) won a Pulitzer Prize in 1995. In 1997, Goodwin returned to her early love of baseball as the unifying theme of *Wait Till Next Year*, a bittersweet memoir of her youth and a history of the 1950s.

Pre-Reading and Journal-Writing Suggestions
1. Write about some of your earliest memories of either your father, the summer, or both combined.
2. Write about a family tradition or passion you hope to preserve for the future.
3. Write about a part of your childhood you wish you could hold on to forever.

The game of baseball has always been linked in my mind with the mystic   1
texture of childhood, with the sounds and smells of summer nights and with the memories of my father.

My love for baseball was born on the first day my father took me to Ebbets Field in Brooklyn. Riding in the trolley car, he seemed as excited as I was, and he never stopped talking; now describing for me the street in Brooklyn where he had grown up, now recalling the first game he had been taken to by his own father, now recapturing for me his favorite memories from the Dodgers of his youth—the Dodgers of Casey Stengel, Zach Wheat, and Jimmy Johnston.

In the evenings, when my dad came home from work, we would sit together on our porch and relive the events of that afternoon's game which I had so carefully preserved in the large, red scorebook I'd been given for my seventh birthday. I can still remember how proud I was to have mastered all those strange and wonderful symbols that permitted me to recapture, in miniature form, the every movement of Jackie Robinson and Pee Wee Reese, Duke Snider and Gil Hodges. But the real power of that scorebook lay in the responsibility it entailed. For all through my childhood, my father kept from me the knowledge that the daily papers printed daily box scores, allowing me to believe that without my personal renderings of all those games he missed while he was at work, he would be unable to follow our team in the only proper way a team should be followed, day by day, inning by inning. In other words, without me, his love for baseball would be forever incomplete.

To be sure, there were risks involved in making a commitment as boundless as mine. For me, as for all too many Brooklyn fans, the presiding memory of "the boys of summer" was the memory of the final playoff game in 1951 against the Giants. Going into the ninth, the Dodgers held a 4–1 lead. Then came two singles and a double, placing the winning run at the plate with Bobby Thomson at bat. As Dressen replaced Erskine with Branca, my older sister, with maddening foresight, predicted the forever famous Thomson homer—a prediction that left me so angry with her, imagining that with her words she had somehow brought it about, that I would not speak to her for days.

So the seasons of my childhood passed until that miserable summer 5 when the Dodgers were taken away to Los Angeles by the unforgivable O'Malley, leaving all our rash hopes and dreams of glory behind. And then came a summer of still deeper sadness when my father died. Suddenly my feelings for baseball seemed an aspect of my departing youth, along with my childhood freckles and my favorite childhood haunts, to be left behind when I went away to college and never came back.

Then one September day, having settled into teaching at Harvard, I agreed, half reluctantly, to go to Fenway Park. There it was again: the cozy ballfield scaled to human dimensions so that every word of encouragement and every scornful yell could be heard on the field; the fervent crowd that could, with equal passion, curse a player for today's failures after cheering his heroics the day before; the team that always seemed to break your heart in the last week of the season. It took only a matter of minutes before I found myself directing all my old intensities toward my new team—the Boston Red Sox.

I am often teased by my women friends about my obsession, but just as often, in the most unexpected places—in academic conferences, in literary discussions, at the most elegant dinner parties—I find other women just as crazily committed to baseball as I am, and the discovery creates an instant bond between us. All at once, we are deep in conversation, mingling together the past and the present, as if the history of the Red Sox had been our history too.

There we stand, one moment recollecting the unparalleled performance of Yaz[1] in '67, the next sharing ideas on how the present lineup should be changed; one moment recapturing the splendid career of "the Splendid Splinter,"[2] the next complaining about the manager's decision to pull the pitcher the night before. And then, invariably, comes the most vivid memory of all, the frozen image of Carlton Fisk as he rounded first in the sixth game of the '75 World Series, an image as intense in its evocation of triumph as the image of Ralph Branca weeping in the dugout is in its portrayal of heartache.

There is another, more personal memory associated with Carlton Fisk, for he was, after all the years I had followed baseball, the first player I actually met in person. Apparently, he had read the biography I had written on Lyndon Johnson and wanted to meet me. Yet when the meeting took place, I found myself reduced to the shyness of childhood. There I was, a professor at Harvard, accustomed to speaking with presidents of the United States, and yet, standing beside this young man in a baseball uniform, I was speechless.

Finally, Fisk said that it must have been an awesome experience to work   10
with a man of such immense power as President Johnson—and with that, I was at last able to stammer out, with a laugh, "Not as awesome as the thought that I am really standing here talking with you."

Perhaps I have circled back to my childhood, but if this is so, I am certain that my journey through time is connected in some fundamental way to the fact that I am now a parent myself, anxious to share with my three sons the same ritual I once shared with my father.

For in this linkage between the generations rests the magic of baseball, a game that has defied the ravages of modern life, a game that is still played today by the same basic rules and at the same pace as it was played one hundred years ago. There is something deeply satisfying in the knowledge of this continuity.

And there is something else as well which I have experienced sitting in Fenway Park with my small boys on a warm summer's day. If I close my eyes against the sun, all at once I am back at Ebbets Field, a young girl once more in the presence of my father, watching the players of my youth on the grassy field below. There is magic in this moment, for when I open my eyes and

---

[1] *Yaz:* Red Sox star Carl Yastrzemski.
[2] *"The Splendid Splinter":* Ted Williams, another famous Red Sox player.

see my sons in the place where my father once sat, I feel an invisible bond between our three generations, an anchor of loyalty linking my sons to the grandfather whose face they never saw but whose person they have already come to know through this most timeless of all sports, the game of baseball.

Suggestions for Writing and Discussion
1. What is your general reaction to this piece? Explain the reasons for this reaction.
2. In one sentence, what is Goodwin's main point in this piece?
3. If you could develop Goodwin's second paragraph with details and dialogue, what would you like to see? What would you like to hear?
4. Explain all the factors that kept Goodwin interested in the game of baseball from her father to the present.
5. What explanation can you offer for the difference between the way that Goodwin reacted when she met Carlton Fisk and her reactions when she met with presidents?

Suggestions for Extended Thinking and Writing
1. In this piece, Goodwin writes that she is often "teased by [her] women friends about [her] obsession" with baseball. Write an essay in which you explain an obsession you have that few of your peers would understand.
2. If you could meet and interview any person living today, who would it be, and why?
3. As an extension to suggestion 2, do some research about the person you would like to meet, and write an essay that reports your findings.

Vocabulary Check
To help ensure that you've understood this selection, and to help you develop a more extensive vocabulary, check the definitions of unfamiliar words in the selection. The words listed below may be new to you, as might others, which you should also identify and define in this exercise.

mystic (1), renderings (3), obsession (7), evocation (8), ravages (12)

Using the paragraph numbers in parentheses, which correspond with the numbers in the selection's right margins, locate the words listed above in the reading and develop definitions based on the context in which the words are used (see the guidelines for identifying meaning from context clues on pages 23–24 in Section 3). When you're satisfied with your definitions, use a dictionary to confirm the meaning of each word, and then write your own sentences using these words.

GARY SOTO

Like Mexicans

Born in California in 1952, Soto toiled as a laborer during his child-hood, and his writing offers a stark, realistic portrait of the lives of Mexican-American workers. Educated at California universities, he subsequently taught at several universities and since 1993 has devoted full-time to his writings.

Recognition of his efforts include National Endowment for the Arts fellowships, the American Book Award, a Before Columbus Foundation grant, an American Library Association Best Book for Young Adults citation, and the Carnegie Medal.

Reviewer Raymund Paredes noted in the *Rocky Mountain Review* that "Soto establishes his acute sense of ethnicity and, simultaneously, his belief that certain emotions, values, and experiences transcend ethnic boundaries and allegiances."

Pre-Reading and Journal-Writing Suggestions

1. When you were little, what did you want to be when you grew up? Who did you want to marry, what work did you want to do, and in what part of the country did you want to live? Thinking back on it now, where do you think these ideas originated?
2. What do you think? Is it better to marry someone who is from your same social class, or doesn't it matter?

My grandmother gave me bad advice and good advice when I was in 1 my early teens. For the bad advice, she said that I should become a barber because they made good money and listened to the radio all day. "Honey, they don't work como burros," she would say every time I visited her. She made the sound of donkeys braying. "Like that, honey!" For the good advice, she said that I should marry a Mexican girl. "No Okies hijo"—she would say—"Look, my son. He marry one and they fight every day about I don't know what and I don't know what." For her, everyone who wasn't Mexican, black, or Asian were Okies. The French were Okies, the Italians in suits were Okies. When I asked about Jews, whom I had read about, she asked for a picture. I rode home on my bicycle and returned with a calendar depicting the important races of the world. "Pues si, son Okies tambien!"[1] she said, nodding her head. She waved the calendar away and we went to

---

[1]Well yes, they're Okies too.

the living room where she lectured me on the virtues of the Mexican girl: first, she could cook and, second, she acted like a woman, not a man, in her husband's home. She said she would tell me about a third when I got a little older.

I asked my mother about it—becoming a barber and marrying Mexican. She was in the kitchen. Steam curled from a pot of boiling beans, the radio was on, looking as squat as a loaf of bread. "Well, if you want to be a barber—they say they make good money." She slapped a round steak with a knife, her glasses slipping down with each strike. She stopped and looked up. "If you find a good Mexican girl, marry her of course." She returned to slapping the meat and I went to the backyard where my brother and David King were sitting on the lawn feeling the inside of their cheeks.

"This is what girls feel like," my brother said, rubbing the inside of his cheek. David put three fingers inside his mouth and scratched. I ignored them and climbed the back fence to see my best friend, Scott, a second-generation Okie. I called him and his mother pointed to the side of the house where his bedroom was a small aluminum trailer, the kind you gawk at when they're flipped over on the freeway, wheels spinning in the air. I went around to find Scott pitching horseshoes.

I picked up a set of rusty ones and joined him. While we played, we talked about school and friends and record albums. The horseshoes scuffed up dirt, sometimes ringing the iron that threw out a meager shadow like a sundial. After three argued-over games, we pulled two oranges apiece from his tree and started down the alley still talking school and friends and record albums. We pulled more oranges from the alley and talked about who we would marry. "No offense, Scott," I said with an orange slice in my mouth, "but I would never marry an Okie." We walked in step, almost touching, with a sled of shadows dragging behind us. "No offense, Gary," Scott said, "but I would *never* marry a Mexican." I looked at him: a fang of orange slice showed from his munching mouth. I didn't think anything of it. He had his girl and I had mine. But our seventh-grade vision was the same: to marry, get jobs, buy cars and maybe a house if we had money left over.

We talked about our future lives until, to our surprise, we were on the   5 downtown mall, two miles from home. We bought a bag of popcorn at Penneys and sat on a bench near the fountain watching Mexican and Okie girls pass. "That one's mine," I pointed with my chin when a girl with eyebrows arched into black rainbows ambled by. "She's cute," Scott said about a girl with yellow hair and a mouthful of gum. We dreamed aloud, our chins busy pointing out girls. We agreed that we couldn't wait to become men and lift them onto our laps.

But the woman I married was not Mexican but Japanese. It was a surprise to me. For years, I went about wide-eyed in my search for the brown girl in a white dress at a dance. I searched the playground at the baseball diamond. When the girls raced for grounders, their hair bounced like something that couldn't be caught. When they sat together in the lunchroom, heads pressed together, I knew they were talking about us Mexican guys. I saw them and dreamed them. I threw my face into my pillow, making up sentences that were good as in the movies.

But when I was twenty, I fell in love with this other girl who worried my mother, who had my grandmother asking once again to see the calendar of the Important Races of the World. I told her I had thrown it away years before. I took a much-glanced-at-snapshot from my wallet. We looked at it together, in silence. Then grandma reclined in her chair, lit a cigarette, and said, "Es pretty." She blew and asked with all her worry pushed up to her forehead: "Chinese?"

I was in love and there was no looking back. She was the one. I told my mother who was slapping hamburger into patties. "Well, sure if you want to marry her," she said. But the more I talked, the more concerned she became. Later I began to worry. Was it all a mistake? "Marry a Mexican girl," I heard my mother say in my mind. I heard it at breakfast. I heard it over math problems, between Western Civilization and cultural geography. But then one afternoon while I was hitchhiking home from school, it struck me like a baseball in the back: my mother wanted me to marry someone of my own social class—a poor girl. I considered my fiancee, Carolyn, and she didn't look poor, though I knew she came from a family of farm workers and pull-yourself-up-by-your-bootstraps ranchers. I asked my brother, who was marrying Mexican poor that fall, if I should marry a poor girl. He screamed "Yeah" above his terrible guitar playing in his bedroom. I considered my sister who had married Mexican. Cousins were dating Mexican. Uncles were remarrying poor women. I asked Scott, who was still my best friend, and he said, "She's too good for you, so you better not."

I was worried about it until Carolyn took me home to meet her parents. We drove in her Plymouth until the houses gave way to farms and ranches and finally her house fifty feet from the highway. When we pulled into the drive, I panicked and begged Carolyn to make a U-turn and go back so we could talk about it over a soda. She pinched my cheek, calling me a "silly boy." I felt better, though, when I got out of the car and saw the house: the chipped paint, a cracked window, boards for a walk to the back door. There were rusting cars near the barn. A tractor with a net of spiderwebs under a mulberry. A field. A bale of barbed wire like children's scribbling leaning against an empty chicken coop. Carolyn took my hand and pulled me to my future mother-in-law who was coming out to greet us.

We had lunch: sandwiches, potato chips, and iced tea. Carolyn and her mother talked mostly about neighbors and the congregation at the Japanese   10

Methodist Church in West Fresno. Her father, who was in khaki work clothes, excused himself with a wave that was almost a salute and went outside. I heard a truck start, a dog bark, and then the truck rattle away.

Carolyn's mother offered another sandwich, but I declined with a shake of my head and a smile. I looked around when I could, when I was not saying over and over that I was a college student, hinting that I could take care of her daughter. I shifted my chair. I saw newspapers piled in corners, dusty cereal boxes and vinegar bottles in corners. The wallpaper was bubbled from rain that had come in from a bad roof. Dust. Dust lay on lamp shades and window sills. These people are just like Mexicans, I thought. Poor people.

Carolyn's mother asked me through Carolyn if I would like a *sushi*. A plate of black and white things were held in front of me. I took one, wide-eyed, and turned it over like a foreign coin. I was biting into one when I saw a kitten crawl up the window screen over the sink. I chewed and the kitten opened its mouth of terror as she crawled higher, wanting in to paw the leftovers from our plates. I looked at Carolyn who said that the cat was just showing off. I looked up in time to see it fall. It crawled up, then fell again.

We talked for an hour and had apple pie and coffee, slowly. Finally, we got up with Carolyn taking my hand. Slightly embarrassed, I tried to pull away but her grip held me. I let her have her way as she led me down the hallway with her mother right behind me. When I opened the door, I was startled by a kitten clinging to the screen door, its mouth screaming "cat food, dog biscuits, *sushi*. . . ." I opened the door and the kitten, still holding on, whined in the language of hungry animals. When I got into Carolyn's car, I looked back: the cat was still clinging. I asked Carolyn if it were possibly hungry, but she said the cat was being silly. She started the car, waved to her mother, and bounced us over the rain-poked drive, patting my thigh for being her lover baby. Carolyn waved again. I looked back, waving, then gawking at a window screen where there were now three kittens clawing and screaming to get in. Like Mexicans, I thought. I remembered the Molinas and how the cats clung to their screens—cats they shot down with squirt guns. On the highway, I felt happy, pleased by it all. I patted Carolyn's thigh. Her people were like Mexicans, only different.

Suggestions for Writing and Discussion
1. Without looking back at this reading, jot down all the images, words, and scenes that you remember from reading this piece. Why do you think you remembered these particular images?
2. What similarities did you find between the experiences in this piece and experiences in your own life? What experiences could you identify with?

3. Although the grandmother and the mother feel the same way about marrying people of the same nationality, they express themselves in different ways. Explain the differences and your reaction to both.
4. Trace the different foods mentioned in this piece and come to some conclusion about why the author took the time to include such details.
5. Why do you think the author wrote this piece? What was his purpose, and what is his message here?
6. Compare Gary's family situation with Carolyn's family situation.

Suggestions for Extended Thinking and Writing
1. Write a narrative essay that reveals how one belief or dream you had in childhood changed as you grew older.
2. Interview three or four different family members from different generations about their opinions on a current social issue. Aim to discover the reasons for the opinions and beliefs they hold, and write an essay that explains these differences.
3. What components make for a successful marriage? Write a research paper that reveals how several experts in the field would answer this question.

Vocabulary Check
   To help ensure that you've understood this selection, and to help you develop a more extensive vocabulary, check the definitions of unfamiliar words in the selection. The words listed below may be new to you, as might others, which you should also identify and define in this exercise.

   meager (4), grounders (6), mulberry (9), congregation (10), gawking (13)

Using the paragraph numbers in parentheses, which correspond with the numbers in the selection's right margins, locate the words listed above in the reading and develop definitions based on the context in which the words are used (see the guidelines for identifying meaning from context clues on pages 23–24 in Section 3). When you're satisfied with your definitions, use a dictionary to confirm the meaning of each word, and then write your own sentences using these words.

LINDSY VAN GELDER

Marriage as a Restricted Club

Lindsy Van Gelder was born in New Jersey in 1944 and earned degrees from Sarah Lawrence College and Northwestern University. She has worked as a reporter for the *New York Post* and WNEW-TV News and has published essays and articles in *Redbook, Esquire,* and *Rolling Stone.* Currently she is a chief writer for *Allure* magazine. With her life partner, Pamela Robin Brandt, she has published the prize-winning gay and lesbian travel book, *Are You Two . . . Together?* (1998) and a collection of interviews with lesbian women, *The Girls Next Door* (1996). The following selection, which suggests that marriage should not be exclusively for heterosexual couples, first appeared in *Ms.* magazine in 1984.

Pre-Reading and Journal-Writing Suggestions
1. Freewrite about what you believe to be the most common reason people choose to get married.
2. What does the word *family* mean to you? Based on your definition, what people would not be considered part of this group?

Several years ago, I stopped going to weddings. In fact, I no longer   1
celebrate the wedding anniversaries or engagements of friends, relatives, or anyone else, although I might wish them lifelong joy in their relationships. My explanation is that the next wedding I attend will be my own—to the woman I've loved and lived with for nearly six years.

Although I've been legally married to a man myself (and come close to marrying two others), I've come, in these last six years with Pamela, to see heterosexual marriage as very much a restricted club. (Nor is this likely to change in the near future, if one can judge by the recent clobbering of what was actually a rather tame proposal to recognize "domestic partnerships" in San Francisco.) Regardless of the *reason* people marry—whether to save on real estate taxes or qualify for married students housing or simply to express love—lesbians and gay men can't obtain the same results should they desire to do so. It seems apparent to me that few friends of Pamela's and mine would even join a club that excluded blacks, Jews, or women, much less assume that they could expect their black, Jewish, or female friends to toast their new status with champagne. But probably no other stand of principle we've ever made in our lives has been so misunderstood, or caused so much bad feeling on both sides.

Several people have reacted with surprise to our views, it never having occurred to them that gay people *can't* legally marry. (Why on earth did they think that none of us had bothered?) The most common reaction, however, is acute embarrassment, followed by a denial of our main point—that the about-to-be-wed person is embarking on a privileged status. (One friend of Pamela's insisted that lesbians are "lucky" not to have to agonize over whether or not to get married.) So wrapped in gauze is the institution of marriage, so ingrained the expectation that brides and grooms can enjoy the world's delighted approval, that it's hard for me not to feel put on the defensive for being so mean-spirited, eccentric, and/or politically rigid as to boycott such a happy event.

Another question we've fielded more than once (usually from our most radical friends, both gay and straight) is why we'd want to get married in the first place. In fact, I have mixed feelings about registering my personal life with the state, but—and this seems to me to be the essence of radical politics—I'd prefer to be the one making the choice. And while feminists in recent years have rightly focused on puncturing the Schlaflyite[1] myth of the legally protected homemaker, it's also true that marriage does confer some very real dollars-and-cents benefits. One example of inequity is our inability to file joint tax returns, although many couples, both gay and straight, go through periods when one partner in the relationship is unemployed or makes considerably less money than the other. At one time in our relationship, Pamela—who is a musician—was between bands and earning next to nothing. I was making a little over $37,000 a year as a newspaper reporter, a salary that put me in the 42 percent tax bracket—about $300 a week taken out of my paycheck. If we had been married, we could have filed a joint tax return and each paid taxes on half my salary, in the 25 or 30 percent bracket. The difference would have been nearly $100 a week in our pockets.

Around the same time, Pamela suffered a months'-long illness which 5 would have been covered by my health insurance if she were my spouse. We were luckier than many; we could afford it. But on top of the worry and expense involved (and despite the fact that intellectually we believe in the ideal of free medical care for everyone), we found it almost impossible to avoid internalizing a sense of personal failure—the knowledge that *because of who we are, we can't take care of each other.* I've heard of other gay people whose lovers were deported because they couldn't marry them and enable them to become citizens; still others who were barred from intensive-care

---

[1]Phyllis Schlafly, a conservative political activist, who opposed the Equal Rights Amendment. [Ed.]

units where their lovers lay stricken because they weren't "immediate family."

I would never begrudge a straight friend who got married to save a lover from deportation or staggering medical bills, but the truth is that I no longer sympathize with most of the less tangible justifications. This includes the oft-heard "for the sake of the children" argument, since (like many gay people, especially women) I *have* children, and I resent the implication that some families are more "legitimate" than others. (It's important to safeguard one's children's rights to their father's property, but a legal contract will do the same thing as marriage.)

But the single most painful and infuriating rationale for marriage, as far as I'm concerned, is the one that goes, "We wanted to stand up and show the world that we've made a *genuine* commitment." When one is gay, such sentiments are labeled "flaunting." My lover and I almost never find ourselves in public settings outside the gay ghetto where we are (a) perceived to be a couple at all (people constantly ask us if we're sisters, although we look nothing like each other), and (b) valued as such. Usually we're forced to choose between being invisible and being despised. "Making a genuine commitment" in this milieu is like walking a high wire without a net— with most of the audience not even watching and a fair segment rooting for you to fall. A disproportionate number of gay couples do.

I think it's difficult for even my closest, most feminist straight women friends to empathize with the intensity of my desire to be recognized as Pamela's partner. (In fact, it may be harder for feminists to understand than for others; I know that when I was straight, I often resented being viewed as one half of a couple. My struggle was for an independent identity, not the cojoined one I now crave.) But we are simply not considered *authentic,* and the reminders are constant. Recently at a party, a man I'd known for years spied me across the room and came over to me, arms outstretched, big happy-to-see-you grin on his face. Pamela had a gig that night and wasn't at the party, my friend's wife was there but in another room, and I hadn't seen her yet. "How's M———?" I asked the man. "Oh, she's fine," he replied, continuing to smile pleasantly. "Are you and Pam still together?"

Our sex life is against the law in many states, of course, and like all lesbians and gay men, we are without many other rights, both large and small. (In Virginia, for instance, it's technically against the law for us to buy liquor.) But as a gay couple, we are also most likely to be labeled and discriminated against in those very settings that, for most heterosexual Americans, constitute the most relaxed and personal parts of life. Virtually every tiny public act of togetherness—from holding hands on the street to renting a hotel room to dancing—requires us constantly to risk humiliation (I think, for example, of the two California women who were recently thrown out of a restaurant that had special romantic tables for couples), sexual harassment (it's astonishing how many men can't resist coming on to a lesbian couple), and even physical assault. A great deal of energy goes into just expecting possible trouble. It's a process which, after six years, has become second nature for me—but occasionally, when I'm in Provincetown or someplace else with a large lesbian population, I experience the *absence* of it as a feeling of virtual weightlessness.

What does all this have to do with my friends' weddings? Obviously, I   10
can't expect my friends to live my life. But I do think that lines are being drawn in this "profamily" Reagan era, and I have no choice about what side I'm placed on. My straight friends do, and at the very least, I expect them to acknowledge that. I certainly expect them to understand why I don't want to be among the rice-throwers and well-wishers at their weddings; beyond that, I would hope that they would commit themselves to fighting for my rights—preferably in personally visible ways, like marching in gay-pride parades. But I also wish they wouldn't get married, period. And if that sounds hard-nosed, I hope I'm only proving my point—that not being able to marry isn't a minor issue.

Not that my life would likely be changed as the result of any individual straight person's symbolic refusal to marry. (Nor, for that matter, do all gay couples want to be wed.) But it's a political reality that heterosexual live-together couples are among our best tactical allies. The movement to repeal the state sodomy laws has profited from the desire of straight people to keep the government out of *their* bedrooms. Similarly, it was a heterosexual New York woman who went to court several years ago to fight her landlord's demand that she either marry her live-in boyfriend or face eviction for violating a lease clause prohibiting "unrelated" tenants—and whose struggle led to the recent passage of a state rent law that had ramifications for thousands of gay couples, including Pamela and me.

The right wing has seized on "homosexual marriage" as its bottom-line scare phrase in much the same way that "Would you want your sister to marry one?" was brandished twenty-five years ago. *They* see marriage as their turf. And so when I see feminists crossing into that territory of respectability and "sinlessness," I feel my buffer zone slipping away. I feel as though my friends are taking off their armbands, leaving me exposed.

Suggestions for Writing and Discussion
1. After reading this piece, what is your overall impression of the author? Choose three to five words that best describe her.
2. What do you suppose the author's main purpose is in writing this piece? Who is she most likely to convince?

3. Which argument do you find the most effective? The least effective?
4. Van Gelder originally wrote this piece in 1984. Have people's views on this subject changed since that time? In what ways?
5. After reading this piece, are you more sympathetic toward homosexuals than you might have been before reading it? Explain why or why not.

Suggestions for Extended Thinking and Writing
1. Write about a cause that you would like your friends to support with you, and explain why this cause is important to you.
2. Write about someone you know who is famous for being a rebel or an outsider.
3. Either in a small group or alone, survey random students on your campus or people in your workplace to see what their feelings are on the issue of homosexuals being allowed to marry. Write up your findings and compare them to the points that Van Gelder makes in this piece.

Vocabulary Check
   To help ensure that you've understood this selection, and to help you develop a more extensive vocabulary, check the definitions of unfamiliar words in the selection. The words listed below may be new to you, as might others, which you should also identify and define in this exercise.

   restricted (2), status (2), eccentric (3), tangible (6), milieu (7)

Using the paragraph numbers in parentheses, which correspond with the numbers in the selection's right margins, locate the words listed above in the reading and develop definitions based on the context in which the words are used (see the guidelines for identifying meaning from context clues on pages 23–24 in Section 3). When you're satisfied with your definitions, use a dictionary to confirm the meaning of each word, and then write your own sentences using these words.

SUE HORTON

Mothers, Sons, and the Gangs

Sue Horton teaches journalism at the University of Southern California. She also publishes widely in a variety of newspapers and magazines, including the *Los Angeles Times Magazine,* where this investigative report first appeared in the October 16, 1988, issue. In her report, Horton focuses on the conflicts and hardships faced by women trying to raise sons in communities where gangs are an everyday fact of life.

Pre-Reading and Journal-Writing Suggestions

1. Write a general description of your neighborhood and the people who live there.
2. Can any parent control how a teenager acts? Explain why or why not.
3. What's your general reaction to or impression of teenagers who join gangs and break the law? Why do you think certain young people join these gangs?

On the side of a market in East Los Angeles is a roughly done mural, painted by gang members from the Lil' Valley Barrio. The untrained artists did the wall to honor homeboys who met violent deaths on the streets. Two blocks away, the same gang painted another mural, this one depicting the mothers of slain gang members. But, when earthquake repairs were made on the small store that held the mural, the painting was covered over. The mothers are forgotten.

To many mothers of gang members, all across Southern California, the obliterated mural could be taken as an appropriate symbol of their lives. They are, they feel, almost invisible, ignored by many of the law-enforcement agencies and institutions set up to deal with their sons. These women feel isolated, frustrated and angry. "I am tired of people assuming I must be a bad person because my son is a Crip," says a mother who lives in South-Central L.A. "I love my son and have cared for him just like any other mother. Maybe I wasn't perfect, but what mother is?"

Lately, however, some of the officials most involved in dealing with local street gangs have come to realize that to blame a gang member's family and upbringing is to grossly oversimplify the problem. "There is no typical profile of a gang parent," says Jim Galipeau, a Los Angeles County probation officer who works exclusively with gang kids and their families in South-Central Los Angeles. "I have one mother who owns a 12-unit complex, and on the other end of the spectrum is a mom who's a cocaine addict and a prostitute. Mostly it's a one-parent family with the mom making the money, but there are working families with nice homes and gardeners. These parents just happen to live where the gangs are a way of life and their kids become involved."

In many parts of Southern California where street gangs flourish, drop-out rates from neighborhood high schools are as high as 35%. A significant proportion of the families in South-Central and East L.A. are living below the poverty level. Drug use and violent crime are rampant. And opportunities for jobs, education and recreation are limited. It's a setting, authorities say, that causes youths to turn to gangs regardless of their upbringing. "For a lot of these kids," says one LAPD officer, "the gang is about the only happening thing in the neighborhood."

Gangs and gang violence have become subjects of great interest and   5 concern for all of Southern California. Law-enforcement agencies are expending enormous resources in their fight against gang-related crime. But, for the mothers of the targets of this law-enforcement effort, the problem is far more immediate than newspaper headlines and stories on TV news. The problem is family.

And now, some police departments are beginning to realize that mothers, instead of being viewed as part of the problem, should be enlisted to help search for solutions.

Capt. Jack Blair of the Pomona Police Department leads weekly gang-truce meetings attended by parents, gang members and local clergy. In the course of his yearlong involvement with the Pomona program, he has become convinced that "parents are the key to [solving] the whole problem." At his meetings, and at other meetings of parents around the county, Blair believes that parents have begun to make a difference. "Once the parents unite and form groups, talking to each other and sharing information, that is threatening to the gang members. They want anonymity. They don't want their tactics or activities talked about with parents of rival gangs. When the moms are saying, 'Hey, don't go over to this neighborhood,' or 'I know that you went over to that neighborhood,' there is a certain amount of sport removed."

"Ours is not a program to turn your kid in. We don't ask parents to be informants on their child. But the moms realize what an effect they can have on the kids," Blair says. "The kids may go out gang-banging at night, but eventually they have to go back home and eat the dinner their mom's prepared. Even though they might exhibit some of the machismo characteristics, there is still concern on how they are impacting their family."

"Just because you shoot someone," Galipeau adds, "it doesn't mean that you don't love your mother."

Still, even as outsiders begin to recognize the contributions they can 10
make, mothers of gang members face constant fear and worry. They feel
overwhelming guilt, asking themselves again and again where they've failed
as parents. And they have to deal with the scorn of a society that holds them
in some measure responsible for the actions of their sons.

Although these mothers of gang members live in divergent parts of the
city and come from a variety of cultures, they share similar pains. These are
some of their stories.

TERESA RODRIGUEZ

Fear: Her Son Lived and the Family Became the Target

Teresa Rodriguez spends her Friday nights cowering in a back bedroom
of the tiny stucco house she shares with her husband and eight children in a
west Pomona barrio. The living room, she knows from experience, is simply
not safe.

During the past two years, most often on Fridays, Rodriguez's home
has been shot up half a dozen times, and one night recently when her
husband came home late from work, someone shot at him. The family's car
and house still bear bullet holes.

The problems all started two years ago, when Rodriguez's youngest son
was 13. Unbeknown to his mother, he had become a member of a small
Pomona gang, Sur 13. One day when he and several other Sur 13 members
were out walking, a car full of rival gang members passed by. "Which barrio
are you from?" the other gang demanded to know. Most of the Sur 13 boys
didn't answer; Rodriguez's son did. Upon hearing the hated neighborhood
name spoken aloud, one of the boys in the car leaned out the window with
a gun and pulled the trigger.

Rodriguez didn't know for several hours that her son had been shot. 15
"His friends took him to the hospital and left him there. They couldn't find
the courage to tell me," she said recently through an interpreter. Finally, one
of the neighborhood kids came to the door and told Rodriguez what had
happened. She was stunned. Having come to the United States from Mexico
in 1973, she was still timid and uncertain about the culture here. "I had no
idea any of my sons was in a gang until that day," she said.

The bullet had lodged near the 13-year-old's heart but hadn't damaged
any internal organs. "The doctor told me we were very, very lucky," Rodriguez recalls. Her son recovered, but Rodriguez's life was irreversibly
changed.

Because the boy claimed his neighborhood with so much bravado on
the day he was shot, he has become a target for the rival gang, which now

sees the boy as Sur 13's most visible member. "Whenever there is a problem, they come after him," his mother says. "The problem is no longer just on him; it is on the house."

Immediately after the shooting, Rodriguez was too grateful that her son was alive to reprimand him. But events soon prompted her to take action. Shortly after the boy returned to school, Rodriguez was summoned by the principal. Four members of the rival gang had been circling the campus all day waiting for her son. The school couldn't take that sort of disruption, so officials were asking the boy to leave and attend continuation school. "My older son told me that if I didn't get [his brother] away from here, he'd be killed," Rodriguez says. "He is looked on as a particular enemy now."

Rodriguez says she knew she would have to talk to the boy, as her husband had always left rearing the children to her. But getting her son to listen proved difficult. "I said to him, 'You're going to get killed,' but he just said, 'I don't care.' He is very rebellious."

This year he is enrolled in a Pomona program for gang members who 20 are at risk in other schools. He continues to dress like and act the part of a Sur 13, although he no longer hangs out on the street. "I finally told him that if he went out, I would send him to live in Mexico," Rodriguez says. "He doesn't want that, so he stays inside."

The shooting, says Rodriguez, has had some positive effects. For one thing, she acknowledged that all three of her older sons were in the gang. "Looking back now, I remember that when they were 9 years old they started wearing khakis and white T-shirts. They started coming home later and later," Rodriguez says. One son had a size 32 waist, but he had his mother buy him size 42 pants. "I didn't know these were gang clothes. Now I do.

"My 16-year-old threw away his *cholo* clothes right when he heard about his brother," she says. "He hasn't been with the gang since then. The two older boys are very repentant, but it is hard to step away from their pasts."

Rodriguez has begun attending meetings of the Pomona chapter of Concerned Parents, a group working to stop gang violence, and is hopeful for the first time that something can be done to prevent recurrences of the kind of gang activity that nearly killed her son. "Communication between parents, police and the church is very important. Together we can solve the problem. We can't do it alone."

Still, Rodriguez dreads Friday nights. On her front door, where a thick board has replaced a window shot out by a gang, she has posted a small picture of Jesus on the cross. "The only thing I can do about the shooting is put it in his hands," she says, gesturing toward the picture. "He's the only one who can take care of me."

MAGGIE GARCIA

Acceptance: Mean Streets, But the Neighborhood Is Still Everything

A few blocks from the Rodriguez house, in another Pomona barrio, 25 Maggie Garcia doesn't really see her youngest son as a gang member. He is just, she says, very loyal to his friends and his neighborhood.

Loyalty to the Cherryville barrio in Pomona where she lives is something Garcia understands completely: "I was raised in the house next door to the one in which I raised my kids. Two of my sisters and one of my brothers live in the neighborhood, too." Maggie Garcia's whole life, she says, is wrapped up in the few blocks radiating from her house. "Here in the neighborhood, it is family."

Garcia realizes that her youngest son has taken his feelings for his barrio a little far on occasion. Last September, when the boy had just turned 14, he got into a fight at school. "He claimed his neighborhood, and the other boy claimed his neighborhood, and all of a sudden they are fighting for two gangs."

After the fight, he was expelled and sent to a local continuation school. "The principal at his old school was upset because my son said, 'I'd die for my neighborhood.' If he'd said, 'I'd die for my country,' the principal probably would have given him a medal."

Garcia worried about her son at the continuation school. Because it drew students from the whole Pomona school district, her son was in constant contact with boys from rival gangs. "One day, two boys from Twelfth Street [another Pomona gang] laid in wait for my son. He came home all bloody and with bruises," Garcia recalls. "I told him you're not going back to school. You could be killed."

Garcia knew that inter-neighborhood conflicts could be deadly in the 30 Pomona barrios: Three nephews and three of her nieces' boyfriends had been killed by rival gang members. She told her son that if he was out late with his cousins, he wasn't to walk home on the streets but should instead cut through neighbors' back yards. When he goes out the door, Garcia blesses him in hopes that God will protect him out on the streets. But there is only so much, she feels, that she can do. "I've tried to talk to him," she says. "Some people think I should forbid him from being with his friends, but that would be like his telling me, 'Mom, I don't want you hanging out with your best friends in this neighborhood.' It's such a small neighborhood, there are only a few boys my son has here. If he didn't hang out with them, he wouldn't have any friends."

"I see it this way," she says. "Nowadays you have to protect yourself as much as possible, and the friends help protect. The Bible says when you are slapped you turn the other cheek, but you don't do that around here because they will shoot you if you're not looking. Children in any neighborhood have to be aware and have eyes in the back of their heads or they will be dead. They are streetwise. I've taught them to be that way. I feel that when a child is running with three or four of his friends it's better than being alone."

So instead of forbidding her son to associate with the gang, Garcia says, she has taken a more moderate line. "I tell him you can live in the fire, but you don't have to let yourself get burned. You've got to learn to live outside, but when you see something about to go down, you have to get out of there."

In early August, it became apparent that Garcia's youngest son hadn't absorbed the lessons his mother was trying to teach him. After coming home late one night, the boy went back out into the neighborhood. What happened next is in dispute, but in the end he was arrested and charged with an armed robbery that took place a few blocks from his house. Garcia insists that her son was simply in the wrong place at the wrong time. After being held at Los Padrinos Juvenile Hall in Downey, he was released into his mother's custody and is attending school through a Pomona program for gang members who are at risk in other schools. His case will be reviewed by a judge in December.

"My older son has gotten very angry at my younger son," Garcia says. "He tells [his brother], 'You know, if they kill you, your friends will go to your Rosary and they'll go to your funeral. Then they'll have a party and forget you.' But my younger son doesn't see it that way. He sort of says, 'Here today, gone tomorrow—so what?' "

GAYLE THOMAS KARY

Death: Just When She Thought She'd Beaten the Odds

Fifteen-year-old Jamee Kary hadn't been active in the Five Deuce 35 Broadway Crips in recent months. But that didn't matter to a car full of the rival Blood gang members who spotted the boy crossing West 27th Street on the night of Sept. 10. The Bloods called the boy to their car. Words were exchanged. The Bloods began to drive off, but then stopped and got out of their car. Jamee tried to run, but he was shot in the face before he could reach cover. He died within minutes.

Gayle Thomas Kary had worried frantically about Jamee, her middle son, for more than two years before his death. His problems, she feels, started four years ago when tight finances forced her to move from Long Beach to a family-owned house in South-Central Los Angeles half a block from the Harbor Freeway. In the old neighborhood, there had been so much for an adolescent boy to do. There were youth centers and year-round organized sports. In the new neighborhood, there was only the gang.

Because Jamee had a slight learning disability, school had always been difficult for him, but he had always had friends. A charming boy with a quick smile and easy affability, Jamee fit right into the new neighborhood. By the time he was 13, he had fit right into the gang.

Kary could tell from her son's style of dress and friends that he had become a gang member. And she was very worried. A data-entry operator with a full-time job and a steady life style, Kary had always believed that if she set a good example and enforced limits, her sons would turn out well. Her oldest son, now 20, had always met his mother's expectations. But Jamee seemed torn. At home he was respectful and loving, but out on the streets, he seemed like a different boy. "He knew that he was loved at home," Kary says, sitting in the immaculate California bungalow she shares with her sons. "But he somehow felt the need to be out there with those boys and not be considered a wimp."

One day during the summer of 1986, when Jamee was 13, his mother found him cutting up soap to look like cocaine. Kary was horrified that the boy found the drug culture so appealing. Within weeks, she sent Jamee off to stay with his father, a Louisiana minister, hoping that a change of environment would divert Jamee from trouble. Three weeks later, his father sent him back, saying he couldn't control the boy.

Later that summer, Jamee stole his mother's car one evening. He was 40 stopped by police for driving the wrong way on a one-way street. But the police just gave the boy a traffic citation and told him to lock up the car and go home. When Kary heard about the incident, she was outraged. She bundled Jamee into the car, drove to the police station, and asked the police there to arrest her son. "I needed help in dealing with my son, but they just said, 'There's nothing we can do,'" Kary says, a bitter sorrow apparent in her voice.

In the months that followed, Jamee was increasingly out of control. Kary had always expected her sons to abide by certain household rules if they wanted to live under her roof. Jamee was required to attend school and do his homework, to keep his room clean, to wash his clothes, to wash dishes on alternate days and to feed the dogs. It was not too much to ask, Kary felt.

Jamee, by the fall of his 14th year, felt differently. "Jamee started seeing these guys out there who were wearing expensive clothes and they didn't have to go to school or do chores or ask their parents for money," Kary recalls. Unwilling to meet his mother's demands, Jamee began running away from home for short periods of time to live with members of the Five Deuce Broadway Crips. By this time, his mother knew from other kids in the neighborhood, her son was also selling drugs.

During his times away from home, Kary tried to keep tabs on him. "I always knew where he was and that he was safe," Kary says. "He'd sneak over and try to get his brothers to get him a clean set of clothes." Eventually, Jamee would tire of life on the streets and return home. "He'd always promise to toe the line," Kary says. "He'd say he had changed. He knew my rules were the same."

When her son was at home, Kary tried to reason with him. "I told him that kind of life could lead to no good," Kary says with tears in her eyes. "I told him that a fast life goes fast." She warned him, she says, that he could be arrested or killed. "He would just tell me he wouldn't get busted because he could run faster than the police. He told me nobody would kill him because he didn't do any bad drug deals."

In the spring of 1987, Jamee was arrested for possession of cocaine with intent to sell. The arrest was a relief for his mother, who hoped that at last her son would be in the hands of people who could help him. But when the time came for Jamee's sentencing, Kary was once again disappointed. "They wanted to give him probation. The conditions were things like he had to be in by 10 and stop associating with gang members. I told them I'd been trying to get him to do those things and he wouldn't. There was no way he was going to do them now, either. I said I wouldn't take him," Kary recalls.

Instead, the court sentenced Jamee to juvenile hall and later to a youth camp. After five months, Jamee returned home. At first he seemed to be less involved with the gang, but he soon returned to his old ways. There was just one difference now: Jamee had been assigned to probation officer Jim Galipeau, who seemed to really care about the boy. Galipeau also listened to Kary's concerns.

"I called Mr. Galipeau and said Jamee was in trouble again. He told me to keep a record of what he was doing and when," Kary recalls. Thankful for something to do, Kary kept detailed notes on her son's transgressions, hoping to build a case for revoking Jamee's probation. But before she could do that, Galipeau had a heart-to-heart talk with her son. "Jamee told Mr. Galipeau he was tired of life on the streets," Kary says. "He got tired of the police swooping up the street and having to run and not knowing where he was going to sleep." At his probation officer's suggestion, Jamee agreed to request placement in a county-run youth facility to get away from his life in Los Angeles.

By last summer, Jamee was doing beautifully. "I knew I still had to take it one day at a time," his mother says, "but he really seemed to have changed. It was like he was the child I used to know. He wouldn't even go up to Broadway [where the gang liked to hang out]. The friends he associated with were not gang members."

Jamee arrived home for his last weekend furlough on Friday, Sept. 9. On Saturday evening, he asked his mother if he could go with a friend to pick up another fellow and get something to eat. She readily agreed. An hour and a half later, a neighbor came to the door with the news that Jamee had been shot on 27th Street.

Kary raced to the scene, where she saw police had cordoned off a large   *50* area. "I saw that yellow police rope, and I knew right then my son was dead," Kary recalls. But police at the scene refused to let her see whether the victim was her son, and after pleading to no avail for information, Kary was finally persuaded to go home and wait. Several hours later, the police called and asked Kary's oldest son to go and identify photographs. Kary finally knew for sure. Her 15-year-old son was dead.

After Jamee's killing, Kary continued to learn what it was like to have a gang member for a son. She wanted to have the funeral service at her own church, but neighbors dissuaded her. "They told me there was a rival gang over there. They said, 'You can't have it there or there'll be troubles,'" Kary says. She also realized with shock that colors, particularly Crip blue, had taken on a new meaning in her life. "All those years that blue stood for boys, and I couldn't let my boy wear blue at his funeral or have the programs printed in blue," Kary says. She had originally planned to wear her nicest dress to the services, but then she realized that it, too, was blue. "A friend told me, 'You can't wear that or you'll be sitting there looking the queen Crip mother,'" Kary says.

Kary worried about how the Five Deuce Broadways would behave at her son's funeral. But that, she says, turned out to be a pleasant surprise. Several days after Jamee's death, some 20 of the gang's members came to Kary's house. While Jamee was alive, she had never allowed gang members in her house, but this once she decided to make an exception.

The young men who gathered in her living room were, she says, very respectful. "They said that even though Jamee wasn't actively involved with them at the time, he was still a member of their family, and they wanted to offer financial support," Kary recalls. The boys contributed about $400 toward funeral costs.

"After they spoke," Kary says, "I said to them, 'I don't like what you do out there on the streets, but I want to tell you something from my heart. You say Jamee was a member of your family. That makes you a member of my family, too, because Jamee was my son. I'm asking you a favor as family members. I don't want any colors at the funeral. I don't want rags, and I don't want trouble.'" To a person, Kary says, the young men honored her requests, and since the funeral they have been eager to help in any way they can.

In the aftermath of Jamee's death, Kary feels lost. Her youngest son, 11-   *55* year-old Lewis, had decided just before his brother's death to go live with his father in Louisiana. "He did not want to be involved on the streets with the gangs and the colors and the drugs. He was scared. He didn't want to go to junior high school here," Kary recalls. While Kary supports Lewis' decision, she is lonely. "I feel so empty inside," she says. "I can't remember when I last felt my heart beat inside my chest. The only thing I can feel in my whole body is my head because it hurts all the time."

In her lowest moments, Kary takes some solace in a poem Jamee wrote for her while he was incarcerated after his cocaine arrest. She included the poem, which Jamee had entitled "If You Only Knew," in the program for Jamee's funeral.

I sit here on my bunk
And don't know what to do
My life just caught up in a mess
Because I was a fool
I sometimes wonder to myself
With my heart just full of pain
Boy when I get out of this place
My life won't be the same
I'm sorry for all the pain I caused
For you as well as them
I promise you, and I'll try my best
To not do wrong again
Every night and every day
I always think of you
I just sit here thinking but
If you only knew

Dedicated to my Mom
I love you

Suggestions for Writing and Discussion
1. Select two or three points that Horton makes or two or three examples that she uses to which you have a strong response. Write a letter to the author explaining your response. Try to convince her that she should consider the points you are making if she writes another article on this topic.
2. In paragraph 8, Horton suggests a relationship between gangs and the concept of machismo. How would you define the term *machismo?* What is the dictionary definition? Do you agree that there is a causal connection between gang activity and machismo? Explain.
3. Without going back to this selection, which one event, character, or phrase stands out in your mind?

4. To what extent, if at all, are parents responsible for how their children turn out? Explain your answer with evidence from the text and from your own life experiences and observations.
5. Comment on the father's role in the three scenarios in this reading.
6. Being an "in" member of one culture often automatically excludes a person from some other cultures. From what cultures are these gang members excluded? To what extent do they choose to be excluded? To what extent is the exclusion forced on them?
7. What do the three gang members described in this selection have in common? In what ways are they different?

Suggestions for Extended Thinking and Writing
1. Write an essay in which you describe the culture to which you belonged as a teenager.
2. Write an essay in which you narrate the outcome of heeding or not heeding your parents' advice.
3. Imagine you have been assigned to counsel one of the parents or one of the gang members from this piece. Write an essay in which you give this person advice both for the present and for the future.

Vocabulary Check

To help ensure that you've understood this selection, and to help you develop a more extensive vocabulary, check the definitions of unfamiliar words in the selection. The words listed below may be new to you, as might others, which you should also identify and define in this exercise.

obliterate (2), flourish (4), anonymity (7), divergent (11), immaculate (38)

Using the paragraph numbers in parentheses, which correspond with the numbers in the selection's right margins, locate the words listed above in the reading and develop definitions based on the context in which the words are used (see the guidelines for identifying meaning from context clues on pages 23–24 in Section 3). When you're satisfied with your definitions, use a dictionary to confirm the meaning of each word, and then write your own sentences using these words.

SEAMUS HEANEY

Midterm Break

Heaney's formative years were emphatically rural and Catholic. The son of a farmer, he was born in 1939 in strife-ridden Northern Ireland and attended Catholic colleges in Derry and Belfast. His works are strongly reflective of his own early experiences. He is popular with readers from all backgrounds, is highly rated by literary critics, and has been honored by membership in the Irish Academy of Letters.

Pre-Reading and Journal-Writing Suggestion
Based on this title alone, what do you imagine this poem will be about? Brainstorm for all the possibilities that come to your mind.

I sat all morning in the college sick bay   1
Counting bells knelling classes to a close.
At two o'clock our neighbors drove me home.

In the porch I met my father crying—
He had always taken funerals in his stride—   5
And Big Jim Evans saying it was a hard blow.

The baby cooed and laughed and rocked the pram
When I came in, and I was embarrassed
By old men standing up to shake my hand

And tell me they were "sorry for my trouble,"   10
Whispers informed strangers I was the eldest,
Away at school, as my mother held my hand

In hers and coughed out angry tearless sighs.
At ten o'clock the ambulance arrived
With the corpse, stanched and bandaged by the nurses,   15

Next morning I went up into the room. Snowdrops
And candles soothed the bedside; I saw him
For the first time in six weeks. Paler now,

Wearing a poppy bruise on his left temple,
He lay in the four foot box as in his cot.   20
No gaudy scars, the bumper knocked him clear.

A four foot box, a foot for every year.

Suggestions for Writing and Discussion
1. Go back and reread the poem, listening to the sounds you hear. In what ways might these sounds connect to the theme of family?

2. Discuss your different reactions to all the people in this poem. To what do you attribute these differences?

Suggestion for Extended Thinking and Writing
Often a poem is a short story in a compact form. Open up this poem and turn it into a short story, giving each stanza its own scene, dialogue, people, and details.

Vocabulary Check
To help ensure that you've understood this selection, and to help you develop a more extensive vocabulary, check the definitions of unfamiliar words in the selection. The words listed below may be new to you, as might others, which you should also identify and define in this exercise.

sick bay (1), knelling (2), pram (7), stanched (15), gaudy (21)

Using the paragraph numbers in parentheses, which correspond with the numbers in the selection's right margins, locate the words listed above in the reading and develop definitions based on the context in which the words are used (see the guidelines for identifying meaning from context clues on pages 23–24 in Section 3). When you're satisfied with your definitions, use a dictionary to confirm the meaning of each word, and then write your own sentences using these words.

SUGGESTIONS FOR MAKING CONNECTIONS

1. Write an essay in which you explain a conflict in your own childhood. Refer to at least three of the selections in this section as you describe the conflict, explaining how your own experiences, challenges, and choices were the same as or different from those described in the readings.
2. What do children contribute to their parents' lives? Refer to at least three selections in this section as you respond to this question.
3. Are parents to blame for the way children turn out? Write an essay that takes a stand on this issue. For support, use your own experience and several selections from this section.
4. Write an essay in which you describe to an "outsider" how it feels to be a member of your main "culture." (Example: As a college student, you write to a parent of a prospective college student or to a high school student who is considering applying to your college. Describe the special aspects of this culture. Further examples: As an art student, you write to a friend of yours in business; as a parent, you write to a friend of yours who does not have children).

8

Questions of Language

Reading Images

Consider these photographs together in light of this chapter's title, "Questions of Language." What relationships do you see between learning a language and having the right to speak freely? What questions do these images raise?

JANICE CASTRO with DAN COOK and CRISTINA GARCIA

Spanglish

Janice Castro is an editor at *Time* magazine, where Dan Cook and Cristina Garcia are staff writers.

Pre-Reading and Journal-Writing Suggestions

1. Either in a small group or with a partner, make a list of current slang terms with which your parents or grandparents would probably not be familiar. Try to figure out where most of these slang terms originated and what they say about your particular culture.
2. Write about your own experience and exposure to the Spanish language and Spanish-speaking cultures. If your exposure is limited, explain why that is. If you have had many experiences with speaking Spanish, explain that too.

In Manhattan a first-grader greets her visiting grandparents, happily exclaiming, "Come here, *siéntate!*" Her bemused grandfather, who does not speak Spanish, nevertheless knows she is asking him to sit down. A Miami personnel officer understands what a job applicant means when he says, "*Quiero un* part time." Nor do drivers miss a beat reading a billboard alongside a Los Angeles street advertising CERVEZA—SIX-PACK!

This free-form blend of Spanish and English, known as Spanglish, is common linguistic currency wherever concentrations of Hispanic Americans are found in the U.S. In Los Angeles, where 55% of the city's 3 million inhabitants speak Spanish, Spanglish is as much a part of daily life as sunglasses. Unlike the broken-English efforts of earlier immigrants from Europe, Asia and other regions, Spanglish has become a widely accepted conversational mode used casually—even playfully—by Spanish-speaking immigrants and native-born Americans alike.

Consisting of one part Hispanicized English, one part Americanized Spanish and more than a little fractured syntax, Spanglish is a bit like a Robin Williams comedy routine: a crackling line of cross-cultural patter straight from the melting pot. Often it enters Anglo homes and families through the children, who pick it up at school or at play with their young Hispanic contemporaries. In other cases, it comes from watching TV; many an Anglo child watching *Sesame Street* has learned *uno dos tres* almost as quickly as one two three.

Spanglish takes a variety of forms, from the Southern California Anglos who bid farewell with the utterly silly "*hasta la* bye-bye" to the Cuban-

American drivers in Miami who *parquean* their *carros.* Some Spanglish sentences are mostly Spanish, with a quick detour for an English word or two. A Latino friend may cut short a conversation by glancing at his watch and excusing himself with the explanation that he must *"ir al* supermarket."

Many of the English words transplanted in this way are simply handier 5 than their Spanish counterparts. No matter how distasteful the subject, for example, it is still easier to say "income tax" than *impuesto sobre la renta.* At the same time, many Spanish-speaking immigrants have adopted such terms as VCR, microwave and dishwasher for what they view as largely American phenomena. Still other English words convey a cultural context that is not implicit in the Spanish. A friend who invites you to *lonche* most likely has in mind the brisk American custom of "doing lunch" rather than the languorous afternoon break traditionally implied by *almuerzo.*

Mainstream Americans exposed to similar hybrids of German, Chinese or Hindi might be mystified. But even Anglos who speak little or no Spanish are somewhat familiar with Spanglish. Living among them, for one thing, are 19 million Hispanics. In addition, more American high school and university students sign up for Spanish than for any other foreign language.

Only in the past ten years, though, has Spanglish begun to turn into a national slang. Its popularity has grown with the explosive increases in U.S. immigration from Latin American countries. English has increasingly collided with Spanish in retail stores, offices and classrooms, in pop music and on street corners. Anglos whose ancestors picked up such Spanish words as *rancho, bronco, tornado* and *incommunicado,* for instance, now freely use such Spanish words as *gracias, bueno, amigo* and *por favor.*

Among Latinos, Spanglish conversations often flow easily from Spanish into several sentences of English and back.

Spanglish is a sort of code for Latinos: the speakers know Spanish, but their hybrid language reflects the American culture in which they live. Many lean to shorter, clipped phrases in place of the longer, more graceful expressions their parents used. Says Leonel de la Cuesta, an assistant professor of modern languages at Florida International University in Miami: "In the U.S., time is money, and that is showing up in Spanish as an economy of language." Conversational examples: *taipiar* (type) and *winshiwiper* (windshield wiper) replace *escribir a máquina* and *limpiaparabrisas.*

Major advertisers, eager to tap the estimated $134 billion in spending 10 power wielded by Spanish-speaking Americans, have ventured into Spanglish to promote their products. In some cases, attempts to sprinkle Spanish through commercials have produced embarrassing gaffes. A Braniff airlines ad that sought to tell Spanish-speaking audiences they could settle back *en* (in) luxuriant *cuero* (leather) seats, for example, inadvertently said they could fly without clothes *(encuero).* A fractured translation of the Miller Lite slogan told readers the beer was "Filling, and less delicious." Similar blunders are often made by Anglos trying to impress Spanish-speaking pals. But if Latinos are amused by mangled Spanglish, they also recognize these goofs as a sort of friendly acceptance. As they might put it, *no problema.*

Suggestions for Writing and Discussion

1. From the opening paragraph alone, what can you guess might be the author's main purpose in writing this essay?
2. What are some of the reasons, according to this article, why Spanglish has come into being?
3. The author writes that Spanglish "is as much a part of daily life as sunglasses" in Los Angeles. Think of other comparisons that might be just as apt.
4. What's your prediction: will Spanglish still be around ten years from now? Why or why not?
5. How would you describe the tone of this essay? In your opinion, how effective do you find it?

Suggestions for Extended Thinking and Writing

1. For a few days or even a week, tune in to the slang and expressions that you hear people using. Pay careful attention to how much Spanish they use. At the end of your observations, write an essay in which you describe and explain your findings.
2. Analyze the original meaning and subsequent alterations of one word in the English language by consulting the Oxford English Dictionary in your library. Write an essay in which you explain how far the meaning has traveled since its birth.
3. Make up your own word, and write an extended definition of it so that readers everywhere will not only understand it but also be anxious to use it.

Vocabulary Check

To help ensure that you've understood this selection, and to help you develop a more extensive vocabulary, check the definitions of unfamiliar words in the selection. The words listed below may be new to you, as might others, which you should also identify and define in this exercise.

linguistic (2), syntax (3), languorous (5), collide (7), gaffe (10)

Using the paragraph numbers in parentheses, which correspond with the numbers in the selection's right margins, locate the words listed above in the reading and develop definitions based on the context in which the words are used (see the guidelines for identifying meaning from context clues on pages 23–24 in Section 3). When you're satisfied with your definitions, use a dictionary to confirm the meaning of each word, and then write your own sentences using these words.

GLORIA NAYLOR

A Question of Language

Born in 1950 in New York City, Gloria Naylor felt, from her grade school years on, "most complete when expressing [herself] through the written word." She notes that, as a child, she "wrote because I had no choice," but she kept her writing private and hidden. After high school, she followed in her mother's footsteps and worked as a telephone operator, continuing to write, but not for publication. In 1968–1975, she traveled in the South as a missionary for the Jehovah's Witnesses. The crucial moment in her life as a writer came when she returned to school (Brooklyn College CUNY) and discovered the works of Toni Morrison. After reading Morrison's *The Bluest Eye* in 1981, Naylor tried her hand at writing a novel, *The Women of Brewster Place,* which was published in 1982 and won an American Book award. Following this early success in the publishing world, she earned a graduate degree in Afro-American studies from Yale University. Her later books include *Linden Hills* (1985) and *Mama Day* (1988). Naylor has worked as a columnist for the *New York Times* and has been visiting professor and writer in residence at Princeton University, New York University, the University of Pennsylvania, Boston University, and Brandeis. "A Question of Language" was first published in the *New York Times* in 1986.

Pre-Reading and Journal-Writing Topics
1. What do you think has had more influence in your life: the spoken word or the written word? Explain by using specific incidents from your past that support your answer.
2. In your household, what topics were or are taboo as far as children are concerned? Explain.

Language is the subject. It is the written form with which I've managed   *1*
to keep the wolf away from the door and, in diaries, to keep my sanity. In spite of this, I consider the written word inferior to the spoken, and much of the frustration experienced by novelists is the awareness that whatever we manage to capture in even the most transcendent passages falls far short of the richness of life. Dialogue achieves its power in the dynamics of a fleeting moment of sight, sound, smell, and touch.

I'm not going to enter the debate here about whether it is language that shapes reality or vice versa. That battle is doomed to be waged whenever we seek intermittent reprieve from the chicken and egg dispute. I will simply take the position that the spoken word, like the written word, amounts to a nonsensical arrangement of sounds or letters without a consensus that assigns "meaning." And building from the meanings of what we hear, we order reality. Words themselves are innocuous; it is the consensus that gives them true power.

I remember the first time I heard the word *nigger*. In my third-grade class, our math tests were being passed down the rows, and as I handed the papers to a little boy in back of me, I remarked that once again he had received a much lower mark than I did. He snatched his test from me and spit out that word. Had he called me a nymphomaniac or a necrophiliac, I couldn't have been more puzzled. I didn't know what a nigger was, but I knew that whatever it meant, it was something he shouldn't have called me. This was verified when I raised my hand, and in a loud voice repeated what he had said and watched the teacher scold him for using a "bad" word. I was later to go home and ask the inevitable question that every black parent must face—"Mommy, what does 'nigger' mean?"

And what exactly did it mean? Thinking back, I realize that this could not have been the first time the word was used in my presence. I was part of a large extended family that had migrated from the rural South after World War II and formed a close-knit network that gravitated around my maternal grandparents. Their ground-floor apartment in one of the buildings they owned in Harlem was a weekend mecca for my immediate family, along with countless aunts, uncles, and cousins who brought along assorted friends. It was a bustling and open house with assorted neighbors and tenants popping in and out to exchange bits of gossip, pick up an old quarrel or referee the ongoing checkers game in which my grandmother cheated shamelessly. They were all there to let down their hair and put up their feet after a week of labor in the factories, laundries, and shipyards of New York.

Amid the clamor, which could reach deafening proportions—two or three conversations going on simultaneously, punctuated by the sound of a baby's crying somewhere in the back rooms or out on the street—there was still a rigid set of rules about what was said and how. Older children were sent out of the living room when it was time to get into the juicy details about "you-know-who" up on the third floor who had gone and gotten herself "p-r-e-g-n-a-n-t!" But my parents, knowing that I could spell well beyond my years, always demanded that I follow the others out to play. Beyond sexual misconduct and death, everything else was considered harmless for our young ears. And so among the anecdotes of the triumphs and disappointments in the various workings of their lives, the word *nigger* was used in my presence, but it was set within contexts and inflections that caused it to register in my mind as something else.

5

In the singular, the word was always applied to a man who had distinguished himself in some situation that brought their approval for his strength, intelligence, or drive:

"Did Johnny really do that?"

"I'm telling you, that nigger pulled in $6,000 of overtime last year. Said he got enough for a down payment on a house."

When used with a possessive adjective by a woman—"my nigger"—it became a term of endearment for husband or boyfriend. But it could be more than just a term applied to a man. In their mouths it became the pure essence of manhood—a disembodied force that channeled their past history of struggle and present survival against the odds into a victorious statement of being: "Yeah, that old foreman found out quick enough—you don't mess with a nigger."

In the plural, it became a description of some group within the community that had overstepped the bounds of decency as my family defined it: Parents who neglected their children, a drunken couple who fought in public, people who simply refused to look for work, those with excessively dirty mouths or unkempt households were all "trifling niggers." This particular circle could forgive hard times, unemployment, the occasional bout of depression—they had gone through all of that themselves—but the unforgivable sin was lack of self-respect.

A woman could never be a *nigger* in the singular, with its connotation of confirming worth. The noun *girl* was its closest equivalent in that sense, but only when used in direct address and regardless of the gender doing the addressing. *Girl* was a token of respect for a woman. The one-syllable word was drawn out to sound like three in recognition of the extra ounce of wit, nerve or daring that the woman had shown in the situation under discussion.

"G-i-r-l, stop. You mean you said that to his face?"

But if the word was used in a third-person reference or shortened so that it almost snapped out of the mouth, it always involved some element of communal disapproval. And age became an important factor in these exchanges. It was only between individuals of the same generation, or from an older person to a younger (but never the other way around), that "girl" would be considered a compliment.

I don't agree with the argument that use of the word *nigger* at this social stratum of the black community was an internalization of racism. The dynamics were the exact opposite: the people in my grandmother's living room took a word that whites used to signify worthlessness or degradation and rendered it impotent. Gathering there together, they transformed *nigger* to signify the varied and complex human beings they knew themselves to be. If the word was to disappear totally from the mouths of even the most liberal of white society, no one in that room was naïve enough to believe it would disappear from white minds. Meeting the word head-on, they proved it had absolutely nothing to do with the way they were determined to live their lives.

So there must have been dozens of times that the word *nigger* was spoken 15 in front of me before I reached the third grade. But I didn't "hear" it until it was said by a small pair of lips that had already learned it could be a way to humiliate me. That was the word I went home and asked my mother about. And since she knew that I had to grow up in America, she took me in her lap and explained.

Suggestions for Writing and Discussion

1. Naylor begins this piece by stating, "Language is the subject." What, then, is the major problem that this subject confronts? Summarize Naylor's main point about this subject.
2. "Words themselves are innocuous; it is the consensus that gives them true power." Explain the words *innocuous* and *consensus* as Naylor uses them here. Do you agree with her claim? Explain.
3. When, according to Naylor, can language be powerfully effective? When can it be powerfully destructive?
4. In your own words, what are the different connotations of the word *nigger* when Naylor heard it used among her own people, in her own household? Why wasn't she puzzled by the meaning of *nigger* at these times in her life?
5. Why does Naylor condone black people using the word *nigger* but find it derogatory when used by others? What gives one group a "right" to a word while the use of it by an outside group is considered wrong? As you write, consider that your audience is a group of college officials who must develop a definition of what comprises acceptable and unacceptable language in public forums on campus.
6. At the end of this piece, when Naylor's mother takes her on her lap to explain what the white boy meant by the term *nigger,* what do you think she says? Consider writing your response in the form of a dialogue between mother and daughter.

Suggestion for Extended Thinking and Writing

Each of the words in the following list contains various levels of meaning. Choose one word from this list and interview fifteen people, asking each for his or her definition of the word. Have those you are interviewing use each word in a sentence to clarify its meaning, and feel free to ask any questions based on the meaning they have assigned to the word. Take careful notes during each interview, and then write an essay in which you synthesize the various meanings people associate with the word.

foreign	polite
dominance	duty
clever	politician
ambition	glamorous
culture	habit
feminist	masculine
feminine	progress

Vocabulary Check

To help ensure that you've understood this selection, and to help you develop a more extensive vocabulary, check the definitions of unfamiliar words in the selection. The words listed below may be new to you, as might others, which you should also identify and define in this exercise.

transcendent (1), reprieve (2), gravitate (4), unkempt (10), naïve (14)

Using the paragraph numbers in parentheses, which correspond with the numbers in the selection's right margins, locate the words listed above in the reading and develop definitions based on the context in which the words are used (see the guidelines for identifying meaning from context clues on pages 23–24 in Section 3). When you're satisfied with your definitions, use a dictionary to confirm the meaning of each word, and then write your own sentences using these words.

_____

BARBARA EHRENREICH
Zipped Lips

Born in 1941, Barbara Ehrenreich is a highly respected journalist who has written reviews, articles, essays, and columns for such publications as the *New York Times, Time* magazine, *Esquire,* and *Harper's.* She is a regular contributor to *The Nation* and wrote the first four of their "Media Matters" columns—a biweekly feature of media analysis. In addition, she has published several books, the most recent of which is *The Snarling Citizen* (1995). A noted public speaker and a frequent radio and TV talk-show guest, Ehrenreich has lectured at many colleges and universities and has appeared on television programs such as *Today, Good Morning America, Nightline,* and *Crossfire.* Known for asking probing social and political questions, Ehrenreich raises the issue of public and private censorship in the following article, which first appeared in *Time* magazine in 1996.

Pre-Reading and Journal-Writing Suggestions
1. Look at your life and determine exactly how free you are.
2. If you had to change something about yourself to work for a company, say, shave a beard or remove your earrings, would you do it? Why or why not?
3. Do you think people should be free to express themselves however, whenever, and wherever they want?

Earlier this month a fellow named Sam Young was fired from his   1
grocery-store job for wearing a Green Bay Packers T-shirt. All right, this was Dallas, and it was a little insensitive to flaunt the enemy team's logo on the weekend of the N.F.C. championship game, but Young was making the common assumption that if you stay away from obscenity, libel, or, perhaps in this case, the subject of groceries, it is a free country, isn't it? Only problem was he had not read the First Amendment carefully enough: It says *government* cannot abridge freedom of expression. Private employers can, on a whim, and they do so every day.

On January 10, for instance, a Peoria, Illinois, man was suspended from his job at Caterpillar Inc. for wearing a T-shirt bearing the words DEFENDING THE AMERICAN DREAM, which happens to have been one of the slogans of the United Auto Workers in their seventeen-month strike against Caterpillar. Since the strike ended in early December, the firm has forbidden incendiary slogans like "Families in Solidarity" and suspended dozens of union employees for infractions as tiny as failing to shake a foreman's hand with sufficient alacrity. A fifty-two-year-old worker who failed to peel union stickers off his toolbox fast enough was threatened with loss of retirement benefits.

It is not just blue-collar employees who are expected to check their freedom of speech at the company door. In mid-December, Boston physician David Himmelstein was fired for going public about the gag clause in his employer's contract with doctors, forbidding them to "make any communication which undermines or could undermine the confidence . . . of the public in U.S. Healthcare . . ." or even revealing that this clause is in their contract.

So where are the guardians of free speech when we need them? For the most part, they are off in the sunny glades of academe, defending professors against the slightest infringement of their presumed right to say anything, at any volume, to anyone. Last fall, for example, history professor Jay Bergman was reprimanded by his employer, Central Connecticut State University, for screaming at a student he found tearing down a flyer he had posted. Now the Anti-Defamation League and the National Association of Scholars are rallying to have the reprimand rescinded. Reprimand, mind you, not firing or suspension.

Or, in 1991, you would have found the New York Civil Liberties   5 Union defending crackpot Afrocentrist professor Leonard Jeffries of New York's City University. Thanks to such support and the fact that CUNY is a public-sector employer, Jeffries still commands a lectern, from which he is free to go on raving about the oppression of blacks by "rich Jews" and how melanin[1] deficiency has warped the white brain.

Most workers, especially in the private sector, have no such protections. Unless their contract says otherwise, they can be fired "for any reason or no reason"—except when the firing can be shown to be discriminatory on the basis of race, sex, or religion. In addition, a few forms of "speech," such as displaying a union logo, are protected by the National Labor Relations Act, and the courts may decide this makes Caterpillar's crackdown illegal. But the general assumption is, any expansion of workers' rights would infringe on the apparently far more precious right of the employer to fire "at will." So the lesson for America's working people is: If you want to talk, be prepared to walk.

Obviously there are reasonable restrictions on an employee's freedom of speech. A switchboard operator should not break into Tourette's-like[2] tor-

---

[1] *melanin:* Dark pigment in skin or hair.
[2] *Tourette's-like:* Reference to Tourette's Syndrome, a neurological disorder that can cause those affected to swear or shout uncontrollably.

rents of profanity; likewise, professors probably *should* be discouraged from screaming at students or presenting their loopier notions as historical fact. But it's hard to see how a Green Bay Packers T-shirt could interfere with the stocking of Pop-Tarts or how a union sticker would slow the tightening of a tractor's axle. When employers are free to make arbitrary and humiliating restrictions, we're saying democracy ends, and dictatorship begins, at the factory gate.

So we seem to have a cynical paradox at the heart of our political culture: "Freedom" is our official national rallying cry, but *un*freedom is, for many people, the price of economic survival. At best this is deeply confusing. In school we're taught that liberty is more precious than life itself—then we're expected to go out and sell that liberty, in eight-hour chunks, in exchange for a livelihood. But if you'd sell your freedom of speech for a few dollars an hour, what else would you sell? Think where we'd be now, as a nation, if Patrick Henry had said, "Give me liberty or give me, uh, how about a few hundred pounds sterling?"

Surely no one really believes productivity would nose-dive if employees were free to wear team logos of their choice or, for that matter, to raise the occasional question about management priorities. In fact, the economy could only benefit from an increase in democracy—and enthusiasm and creativity—on the shop floor. Or does the "free" in "free market" apply just to people on top?

When employers have rights and employees don't, democracy itself is at   *10* risk. It isn't easy to spend the day in a state of servile subjugation and then emerge, at five P.M., as Mr. or Ms. Citizen-Activist. Unfreedom undermines the critical spirit, and suck-ups make lousy citizens.

Suggestions for Writing and Discussion
1. Which example in this piece did you find most convincing? Explain.
2. What similar point is Ehrenreich making about employers and college professors? Do you agree with this point?
3. In a similar vein, what implications does Ehrenreich make about students and employees?
4. How would you characterize the tone of this piece? What specific phrases and words support your claim?
5. Where does Ehrenreich acknowledge the other side of this argument, and how effective do you find it to be?

Suggestions for Extended Thinking and Writing
1. Write about a time where you either spoke out on a controversial issue or chose to remain silent. Explain the consequences of your actions or inactions.

2. Take a stand on a specific issue that addresses an infringement on one's freedom of speech, such as censorship of school newspapers, banning of slogans on T-shirts, or censorship of school reading materials.
3. A wise person once said, "I would rather be sorry for something I said than for something I refused to say." Use personal experiences and observations to examine how true you find this statement to be.

Vocabulary Check

To help ensure that you've understood this selection, and to help you develop a more extensive vocabulary, check the definitions of unfamiliar words in the selection. The words listed below may be new to you, as might others, which you should also identify and define in this exercise.

flaunt (1), alacrity (2), infringement (4), paradox (8), subjugation (10)

Using the paragraph numbers in parentheses, which correspond with the numbers in the selection's right margins, locate the words listed above in the reading and develop definitions based on the context in which the words are used (see the guidelines for identifying meaning from context clues on pages 23–24 in Section 3). When you're satisfied with your definitions, use a dictionary to confirm the meaning of each word, and then write your own sentences using these words.

CHANG-RAE LEE

Mute in an English-Only World

Born in Seoul, South Korea, in 1965, Chang-Rae Lee immigrated with his family to the United States when he was three years old. After earning a BA at Yale University, he pursued graduate studies at the University of Oregon. After completing his MFA at Oregon, he joined the faculty as an assistant professor of creative writing. Currently he is the director of the MFA Program in Creative Writing at Hunter College in New York City. Lee published his first novel, *Native Speaker,* in 1995, and has written another novel, *A Gesture Life,* scheduled to be published during 1999. In the following selection, which first appeared in the *New York Times* in 1996, Lee addresses issues raised by a *Times* feature article describing a town in New Jersey that passed ordinances forbidding Korean shopkeepers from posting signs in Korean, with no English translations.

Pre-Reading and Journal-Writing Suggestions

1. If you were living in a country whose language you didn't know well, how might your life be different?
2. Write about a time you felt like an outsider in a group. What was the main barrier that kept you outside the inner circle?

When I read of the troubles in Palisades Park, N.J., over the proliferation of Korean-language signs along its main commercial strip, I unexpectedly sympathized with the frustrations, resentments, and fears of the longtime residents. They clearly felt alienated and even unwelcome in a vital part of their community. The town, like seven others in New Jersey, has passed laws requiring that half of any commercial sign in a foreign language be in English.

Now I certainly would never tolerate any exclusionary ideas about who could rightfully settle and belong in the town. But having been raised in a Korean immigrant family, I saw every day the exacting price and power of language, especially with my mother, who was an outsider in an English-only world.

In the first years we lived in America, my mother could speak only the most basic English, and she often encountered great difficulty whenever she went out.

We lived in New Rochelle, N.Y., in the early seventies, and most of the local businesses were run by the descendants of immigrants who, generations ago, had come to the suburbs from New York City. Proudly dotting Main

Street and North Avenue were Italian pastry and cheese shops, Jewish tailors
and cleaners, and Polish and German butchers and bakers. If my mother's
marketing couldn't wait until the weekend, when my father had free time,
she would often hold off until I came home from school to buy groceries.

Though I was only six or seven years old, she insisted that I go out   5
shopping with her and my younger sister. I mostly loathed the task, partly
because it meant I couldn't spend the afternoon playing catch with my
friends but also because I knew our errands would inevitably lead to an
awkward scene, and that I would have to speak up to help my mother.

I was just learning the language myself, but I was a quick study, as
children are with new tongues. I had spent kindergarten in almost complete
silence, hearing only the high nasality of my teacher and comprehending
little but the cranky wails and cries of my classmates. But soon, seemingly
mere months later, I had already become a terrible ham and mimic, and I
would crack up my father with impressions of teachers, his friends, and even
himself. My mother scolded me for aping his speech, and the one time I
attempted to make light of hers I rated a roundhouse smack on my bottom.

For her, the English language was not very funny. It usually meant
trouble and a good dose of shame, and sometimes real hurt. Although she
had a good reading knowledge of the language from university classes in
South Korea, she had never practiced actual conversation. So in America
she used English flashcards and phrase books and watched television with us
kids. And she faithfully carried a pocket workbook illustrated with stick-
figure people and compound sentences to be filled in.

But none of it seemed to do her much good. Staying mostly at home to
care for us, she didn't have many chances to try out sundry words and
phrases. When she did, at the window of the post office, her readied speech
would stall, freeze, sometimes altogether collapse.

One day was unusually harrowing. We ventured downtown in the new
Ford Country Squire my father had bought her, an enormous station wagon
that seemed as long—and deft—as an ocean liner. We were shopping for a
special meal for guests visiting that weekend, and my mother had heard that
a particular butcher carried fresh oxtails, which she needed for a traditional
soup.

We'd never been inside the shop, but my mother would pause before its   10
window, which was always lined with whole hams, crown roasts, and ropes
of plump handmade sausages. She greatly esteemed the bounty with her
eyes, and my sister and I did also, but despite our desirous cries she'd turn us
away and instead buy the packaged links at the Finast supermarket, where
she felt comfortable looking them over and could easily spot the price. And,
of course, not have to talk.

But that day she was resolved. The butcher store was crowded, and as
we stepped inside the door jingled a welcome. No one seemed to notice.

We waited for some time, and people who entered after us were now being served. Finally, an old woman nudged my mother and waved a little ticket, which we hadn't taken. We patiently waited again, until one of the beefy men behind the glass display hollered our number.

My mother pulled us forward and began searching the cases, but the oxtails were nowhere to be found. The man, his big arms crossed, sharply said, "Come on, lady, whaddya want?" This unnerved her, and she somehow blurted the Korean word for oxtail, *soggori.*

The butcher looked as if my mother had put something sour in his mouth, and he glanced back at the lighted board and called the next number.

Before I knew it, she had rushed us outside and back in the wagon, which she had double-parked because of the crowd. She was furious, almost vibrating with fear and grief, and I could see she was about to cry.

She wanted to go back inside, but now the driver of the car we were 15 blocking wanted to pull out. She was shooing us away. My mother, who had just earned her driver's license, started furiously working the pedals. But in her haste she must have flooded the engine, for it wouldn't turn over. The driver started honking and then another car began honking as well, and soon it seemed the entire street was shrieking at us.

In the following years, my mother grew steadily more comfortable with English. In Korean, she could be fiery, stern, deeply funny, and ironic; in English, just slightly less so. If she was never quite fluent, she gained enough confidence to make herself clearly known to anyone, and particularly to me.

Five years ago, she died of cancer, and some months after we buried her I found myself in the driveway of my father's house, washing her sedan. I liked taking care of her things; it made me feel close to her. While I was cleaning out the glove compartment, I found her pocket English workbook, the one with the silly illustrations. I hadn't seen it in nearly twenty years. The yellowed pages were brittle and dog-eared. She had fashioned a plain-paper wrapping for it, and I wondered whether she meant to protect the book or hide it.

I don't doubt that she would have appreciated doing the family shopping on the new Broad Avenue of Palisades Park. But I like to think, too, that she would have understood those who now complain about the Korean-only signs.

I wonder what these same people would have done if they had seen my mother studying her English workbook—or lost in a store. Would they have nodded gently at her? Would they have lent a kind word?

Suggestions for Writing and Discussion
1. From reading this piece, what is your general impression of the mother? Of the son?

2. What is the author's overall message about language?
3. Provide some reasons why it may be easier for children to learn a new language than it is for adults.
4. What specific steps did the mother take to learn English? What others could you suggest?
5. Of all the "players" in the butcher shop scene, which one would you be most apt to act like?
6. How would you answer Lee's last two questions?

Suggestions for Extended Thinking and Writing
1. Interview someone you know who is not a native speaker of English. Explain how this person came to learn English and what experiences he or she encountered in this process.
2. Write a letter to the editor of the *Palisades Park Gazette,* stating which side of the issue you support: signs in both languages or signs in Korean? (You may have another solution to offer.)

Vocabulary Check
   To help ensure that you've understood this selection, and to help you develop a more extensive vocabulary, check the definitions of unfamiliar words in the selection. The words listed below may be new to you, as might others, which you should also identify and define in this exercise.

   alienated (1), exclusionary (2), nasality (6), sundry (8), harrowing (9)

Using the paragraph numbers in parentheses, which correspond with the numbers in the selection's right margins, locate the words listed above in the reading and develop definitions based on the context in which the words are used (see the guidelines for identifying meaning from context clues on pages 23–24 in Section 3). When you're satisfied with your definitions, use a dictionary to confirm the meaning of each word, and then write your own sentences using these words.

———————

JOSEPH TELUSHKIN

Words That Hurt, Words That Heal:
How to Choose Words Wisely and Well

Having completed studies at Yeshiva University and become an ordained rabbi, Joseph Telushkin serves at the Synagogue of the Performing Arts in Los Angeles, and pursues a career as a writer. He has written several books on Jewish history, examining such topics as anti-Semitism and Jewish humor. He is perhaps best known for his Rabbi Winter series of mystery novels. In 1996 he published *Words That Hurt, Words That Heal: How to Choose Words Wisely and Well* from which this selection is taken.

Pre-Reading and Journal-Writing Suggestions
1. Write about a time when someone called you a name—a name you cannot forget, no matter how long ago you heard it.
2. What's your connection to the word *gossip?*
3. If you were in charge of deleting any ten words from the English language, which ones would you choose and why?

Over the past decade, whenever I have lectured throughout the country   1
on the powerful, and often negative, impact of words, I have asked audiences if they can go for twenty-four hours without saying any unkind words about, or to, anybody.

Invariably, a minority of listeners raise their hands signifying "yes," some laugh, and quite a large number call out, "no!"

I respond by saying, "Those who can't answer 'yes' must recognize that you have a serious problem. If you cannot go for twenty-four hours without drinking liquor, you are addicted to alcohol. If you cannot go for twenty-four hours without smoking, you are addicted to nicotine. Similarly, if you cannot go for twenty-four hours without saying unkind words about others, then you have lost control over your tongue."

How can I compare the harm done by a bit of gossip or a few unpleasant words to the damage caused by alcohol and smoking? Well, just think about your own life for a minute. Unless you, or someone dear to you, has been the victim of terrible physical violence, chances are the worst pains you have suffered in life have come from words used cruelly—from ego-destroying criticism, excessive anger, sarcasm, public and private humiliation, hurtful nicknames, betrayal of secrets, rumors, and malicious gossip.

TESTING YOUR SPEECH

There is no area of life in which so many of us systematically violate the 5
Golden Rule. Thus if you were about to enter a room and heard the people
inside talking about you, chances are what you would least like to hear them
talking about are your character flaws and the intimate details of your social
life. Yet, when you are with friends and the conversation turns to people
not present, what aspects of their lives are you and your companions most
likely to explore? Is it not their character flaws and the intimate details of
their social lives?

If you do not participate in such talk, congratulations. But before as-
serting this as a definite fact, try monitoring your conversation for two days.
Note on a piece of paper every time you say something negative about
someone who is not present. Also record when others do so, as well as your
reactions when that happens. Do you try to silence the speaker, or do you
ask for more details?

To ensure the test's accuracy, make no effort to change the content of
your conversations throughout the two-day period, and do not try to be
kinder than usual in assessing another's character and actions.

Most of us who take this test are unpleasantly surprised.

Negative comments we make about absent companions is but one way we
wound with words; we also often cruelly hurt those *to whom* we are speaking.
For example, many of us, when enraged, grossly exaggerate the wrong done
by the person who has provoked our ire. If the anger expressed is disproportionate to the provocation (as often occurs when parents rage at children), it
is unfair, often inflicts great hurt and damage, and thus is unethical.

All too often, many of us criticize others with harsh, offensive words, 10
turn disputes into quarrels, belittle or humiliate others, and inflict wounds
that last a lifetime.

THE POWER OF WORDS

One reason that many otherwise "good" people use words irresponsibly
and cruelly is that they regard the injuries inflicted by words as intangible
and therefore minimize the damage they can inflict. For generations, children taunted by playmates have been taught to respond, "Sticks and stones
can break my bones, but words (or names) can never hurt me." But does
anyone really think that a child exposed to such abuse believes it?

An old Jewish teaching compares the tongue to an arrow: "Why not
another weapon—a sword, for example?" one rabbi asks. "Because," he is
told, "if a man unsheathes his sword to kill his friend, and his friend pleads
with him and begs for mercy, the man may be mollified and return the
sword to its scabbard. But an arrow, once it is shot, cannot be returned."

The rabbi's comparison is more than just a useful metaphor. Because words can be used to inflict devastating and irrevocable suffering, Jewish teachings go so far as to compare cruel words to murder. A penitent thief can return the money he has stolen; a murderer, no matter how sincerely he repents, cannot restore his victim to life. Similarly, one who damages another's reputation through malicious gossip or who humiliates another publicly can never fully undo the damage.

Words, quite simply, are very powerful. Indeed, the Bible teaches that God created the world through words. At the beginning of Genesis we learn, "And God said, 'Let there be light,' and there was light." I would submit that human beings, like God, also create with words. Consider the fact that most, if not all, of us have had the experience of reading a novel and being so moved by the fate of a character that we have cried, even though the character who has so moved us doesn't exist. All that happened was that writer took a blank piece of paper, put words on it, and through words alone created a human being so totally real that he or she is capable of evoking our deepest emotions.

Words are powerful enough to lead to love, but they can also lead to 15 hatred and terrible pain. We must be extremely careful how we use them.

A Jewish folktale, set in nineteenth-century Eastern Europe, tells of a man who went through a small community slandering the rabbi. One day, feeling suddenly remorseful, he begged the rabbi for forgiveness and offered to undergo any form of penance to make amends. The rabbi told him to take a feather pillow from his home, cut it open, scatter the feathers to the wind. The man did as he was told and returned to the rabbi. He asked, "Am I now forgiven?"

"Almost," came the response. "You just have to perform one last task: Go and gather all the feathers."

"But that's impossible," the man protested, "for the wind has already scattered them."

"Precisely," the rabbi answered.

The rabbi in this story understands that words define our place in the 20 world. Once our place—in other words, our reputation—is defined, it is very hard to change, particularly if it is negative.

President Andrew Jackson who, along with his wife was the subject of relentless malicious gossip, once noted, "The murderer only takes the life of the parent and leaves his character as a goodly heritage to his children, while the slanderer takes away his goodly reputation and leaves him a living monument to his children's disgrace."

Considerate, fair and civilized use of words is every bit as necessary in the larger society as in one-on-one relationships. Throughout history, words used unfairly have promoted hatred and even murder. African Americans, for example, were long branded with words that depicted them as subhuman.

Those who first described blacks in such terms hoped to enable whites to view them as different and inferior to themselves. This was important because, if whites perceived blacks as fully human, otherwise "decent" people could never have tolerated their persecution, enslavement, or lynching.

Similarly, when the radical Black Panther Party referred to police as "pigs" during the 1960s, its intention was not to hurt policemen's feelings but to dehumanize them and so establish in people's minds that murdering a policeman was really only like killing a dumb animal.

THE BIBLICAL ETHICS OF SPEECH

The biblical ethics of speech derive in large measure from a verse in Leviticus: "You shall not go about as a talebearer among your people" (19:16), which, not coincidentally, appears only two verses before the Bible's most famous law, "Love your neighbor as yourself" (19:18).

Because the commandment is so terse, it is difficult to know exactly 25 what the Bible means by "talebearing." Does this law mean that it is forbidden to talk about any aspect of other people's lives (e.g., telling a friend, "I was at a party at Sam and Sally's house last night. It's absolutely gorgeous what they've done with their kitchen.")? Or does the verse only outlaw damning insinuations (e.g., "When Sam went away on that business trip last month, I saw his wife Sally at a real fancy restaurant with this good-looking guy. She didn't see me, because they were too busy making eyes at each other.")? Is it talebearing, for that matter, to pass on true stories (e.g., "Sally confessed to Betty she's having an affair. Sam ought to know what goes on when he's out of town.")?

The Bible itself never fully answers these questions. But for centuries Jewish teachers have elaborated upon the biblical law and formulated, in ascending order of seriousness, three types of speech that we should decrease or eliminate: nondefamatory and true remarks about others; negative, though true, stories that lower the esteem in which people hold the person being discussed (in Hebrew, *lashon ha-ra*); and slander—that is, lies or rumors that are negative and false (in Hebrew, *motzi shem ra*).

NONDEFAMATORY AND TRUE REMARKS

The comment, "I was at a party at Sam and Sally's house last night. It's absolutely gorgeous what they've done with their kitchen," is nondefamatory and true. What possible reason could there be for discouraging people from exchanging such innocuous, even complimentary, information?

For one thing, the listener might not find the information so innocuous. While one person is describing how wonderful the party was, the other might well wonder, "Why wasn't I invited? I had them over to my house just a month ago."

But the more important reason for discouraging "innocuous" gossip is that it rarely remains so. Suppose I suggest that you and a friend spend twenty minutes talking about a mutual acquaintance. How likely is it that you will devote the entire time to exchanging stories about his or her niceness?

Maybe you will, that is if the person you are discussing is Mother Teresa.   *30* Otherwise the conversation will likely take on a negative tone. For most of us, exchanging critical news and evaluations about others is far more interesting and enjoyable than exchanging accolades. If I were to say to you, "Janet is a wonderful person. There's just *one thing* I can't stand about her," on what aspects of Janet's character do you think the rest of our conversation will most likely focus? The reason is that "Nobody ever gossips about other people's secret virtues," as British philosopher Bertrand Russell once noted. What most interests most people about others are their character flaws and private scandals.

Even if you do not let the discussion shift in a negative direction, becoming an ethical speaker forces you to anticipate the inadvertent harm that your words might cause. For example, although praising a friend might seem like a laudable act, doing so in the presence of someone who dislikes her will probably do your friend's reputation more harm than good. Your words may well provoke her antagonist to voice the reasons for his or her dislike, particularly if you leave soon after making your positive remarks.

Indeed, the danger of praise leading to damage is likely at the root of the Book of Proverbs' rather enigmatic observation: "He who blesses his neighbor in a loud voice in the morning, it will later be thought a curse" (27:14). Bible commentaries understand this to mean that fame and notoriety can ultimately damage a person's good name—or worse.

NEGATIVE TRUTHS

As a rule most people seem to think that there is nothing morally wrong in spreading negative information about another as long as the information is true. But ordinary experience proves otherwise. The Jewish tradition also takes a very different view. Perhaps that is why the Hebrew term *lashon ha-ra* (literally "bad language" or "bad tongue") has no precise equivalent in English. For, unlike slander, which is universally condemned as immoral because it is false, *lashon ha-ra* is true. It is the dissemination of *accurate* information that will lower the status of the person to whom it refers; hence I translate it as "negative truths."

Jewish law forbids spreading negative truths about others unless the person to whom you are speaking needs the information. To do so is a very serious offense, one that has been addressed by many non-Jewish ethicists as well. Two centuries ago, the Swiss theologian and poet Jonathan K. Lavater offered a good guideline concerning the spreading of such news: "Never tell evil of a man if you do not know it for a certainty, and if you know it for a certainty, then ask yourself, 'Why should I tell it?'"

Intention has a great deal to do with the circumstances in which it is 35 prohibited to speak negative truths. The same statement, depending on the context, can constitute a compliment or a mean-spirited attempt to diminish another person's status. For example, if you relate that a person known to have limited funds gave a hundred dollars to a certain charity, you will probably raise the person's stature because people will be impressed at his or her generosity. But, if you say of an individual known to be wealthy that he or she gave a hundred dollars to the same cause, the effect will be to diminish respect for the person; he or she will now be thought of as "cheap."

Unfortunately, this realization does not deter many people from speaking negative truths. Gossip often is so interesting that it impels many of us to violate the Golden Rule to "Do unto others as you would have others do unto you." Although we are likely to acknowledge that we would want embarrassing information about ourselves kept quiet, many of us refuse to be equally discreet concerning others' sensitive secrets.

SLANDER

The most grievous violation of ethical speech is, of course, the spreading of malicious falsehoods, what Jewish law calls *"motzi shem ra,"* or "giving another a bad name." To destroy someone's good name is to commit a kind of murder—that is why it is called "character assassination." Indeed, it has led to literal murder. During Europe's devastating fourteenth-century Black Plague, anti-Semites and others seeking scapegoats spread the lie that Jews had caused the Plague by poisoning village wells. Within a few months, enraged mobs murdered tens of thousands of Jews.

Too often, the victims of slanderous tongues suffer terribly. In Shakespeare's thirty-eight plays, there is no villain more vile than *Othello's* Iago, whose evil is perpetrated almost exclusively through words. At the outset, Iago vows to destroy the Moorish general Othello for bypassing him for promotion. Knowing Othello's jealous nature, Iago convinces him that his new wife, Desdemona, is having an affair with another man. The charge seems preposterous, but Iago repeats the accusation again and again, and he arranges the circumstantial evidence necessary to destroy Desdemona's credibility. Soon, Othello comes to believe the slander, and he murders his beloved, only to learn almost immediately that Iago's words were false. For Othello, "Hell," as an old aphorism teaches, "is truth seen too late."

What if we could share our consciousness of the power of words with many others—even the whole nation? I have proposed an annual "Speak No Evil" Day, starting on May 14, 1996. Senators Connie Mack (R-FL) and Joseph Lieberman (D-CT) have introduced a bipartisan resolution in the U.S. Senate that requires the co-sponsorship of fifty senators. This resolution would establish such a day, requesting that the President issue a proclamation calling on the American people to:

- Eliminate all hurtful and unfair talk for twenty-four hours;
- Transmit negative information only when necessary;
- Monitor and regulate how they speak to others;
- Strive to keep anger under control;
- Argue fairly, and not allow disputes to degenerate into name-calling or other forms of verbal abuse;
- And speak about others with the same kindness and fairness that they wish others to exercise when speaking about them.

A "Speak No Evil" Day would plant the seed of a more permanent shift 40 in our consciousness. It would hopefully touch everyone—from journalists, politicians, activists, teachers, ministers, and businessmen to mothers, fathers, brothers, sisters, sons and daughters.

A rabbi once told me that his grandmother used to say, "It is not within everyone's power to be beautiful, but all of us can make sure that the words that come out of our mouths are." A "Speak No Evil" Day will be a twenty-four hour period of verbal beauty.

It will be a day when a young child frequently teased by his classmates, and called by an ugly nickname, can go to school confident no one will say a cruel word to him.

It will be a day on which an employee with a sharp-tongued boss can go to work without fearing that he or she will be verbally abused.

It will be a day on which that sharp-tongued boss, the type who says, "I don't get ulcers, I give them," might come to understand how vicious such a statement is and will say nothing that will cause pain to another.

It will be a day when a congressional candidate who suffered a nervous 45 breakdown will not have to worry that his opponent will use this painful episode to publicly humiliate him.

It will be a day when a husband who always complains tells his wife what he loves about her.

It will be a day when a person of one race will see beyond the color of another person's skin.

It will be a day when people will use the words that heal others' emotional wounds, not those that inflict them.

Only on such a day will we experience a taste of heaven on earth. A Jewish proverb teaches, "If you will it, it is no fantasy." If we only want it enough, a "Speak No Evil" Day is possible. Let us try.

Suggestions for Writing and Discussion

1. If you had to summarize Telushkin's point in the fewest words possible, what would you write?
2. Why do you think most people tend to remember the hurtful language instead of the positive comments in their lives? Is it something about the words themselves or something about human nature?
3. Write down one statement from this piece with which you agree most strongly and one with which you disagree. Support your opinions with personal examples or observations.
4. Although Telushkin makes a strong case for how harmful language can be, does he adequately prove that in the past decade it has become a persistent problem that warrants an official "Speak No Evil" Day?
5. Go back through this essay and write down the specific references that Telushkin uses for support in this piece. How valid and reliable do you find these sources to be? Based on these sources, how does Telushkin view his audience?
6. Based on this essay, what is the difference between slander and negative truths?

Suggestions for Extended Thinking and Writing

1. Take Telushkin's test, jotting a note anytime you (or others around you) say something negative about another person. After you gather your data, write an essay that explains what surprised or disturbed you about your findings.
2. Telushkin makes a case for having a "Speak No Evil" Day. Write your own proposal for a day that you feel is equally necessary. Like Telushkin, explain the importance of this official day, and then set up a group of rules to go along with this day.
3. Write about a time when language got the better of you—as either the sender or the receiver of the words.

Vocabulary Check

To help ensure that you've understood this selection, and to help you develop a more extensive vocabulary, check the definitions of unfamiliar words in the selection. The words listed below may be new to you, as might others, which you should also identify and define in this exercise.

decade (1), monitor (6), mollified (12), penitent (13), accolade (30)

Using the paragraph numbers in parentheses, which correspond with the numbers in the selection's right margins, locate the words listed above in the reading and develop definitions based on the context in which the words are used (see the guidelines for identifying meaning from context clues on pages 23–24 in Section 3). When you're satisfied with your definitions, use a dictionary to confirm the meaning of each word, and then write your own sentences using these words.

EMILY DICKINSON
Three Poems on Words

Born in Amherst, Massachusetts, in 1830, Emily Dickinson was raised in a highly traditional, rigid, and conservative New England family. Although Dickinson respected her father, she also rebelled against many of the traditions he represented. For example, during the year she spent at Mount Holyoke College (then called the South Hadley Female Seminary), she angered her professors by refusing to acknowledge her religious beliefs publicly. When she returned to Amherst, she did not marry as her family expected but chose the life of a poet, although she did not seek to publish her work. The literary legend depicts Dickinson as an eccentric recluse who dressed only in white; however, recent literary scholarship suggests that she had a number of close friends, including Ben Newton, her father's law apprentice; Thomas Wentworth Higginson, a literary friend of the family; and Helen Hunt Jackson, a respected poet and author of the novel *Ramona*.

Pre-Reading and Journal-Writing Suggestions
1. List twenty of your favorite words. When your list is complete, try to figure out what these words might say about you: what kind of person you are, what you like, what you notice.
2. "Sticks and stones may break my bones, but words will never hurt me." Respond to this childhood verse: Do you agree or disagree with it?

1750

The words the happy say   1
Are paltry melody
But those the silent feel
Are beautiful—

1452

Your thoughts don't have words every day   1
They come a single time
Like signal esoteric sips
Of the communion Wine
Which while you taste so native seems   5
So easy so to be
You cannot comprehend its price
Nor its infrequency

479

She dealt her pretty words like Blades— 1
How glittering they shone—
And every One unbared a Nerve
Or wantoned with a Bone—

She never deemed—she hurt— 5
That—is not Steel's Affair—
A vulgar grimace in the Flesh—
How ill the Creatures bear—

To Ache is human—not polite—
The Film upon the eye 10
Mortality's old Custom—
Just locking up—to Die.

Suggestions for Writing and Discussion

1. In poem 1750, what differences are there between "the happy" and "the silent"? What is the speaker implying here? Do you agree with her?

2. Unravel and extend the central metaphor in poem 1452. In other words, think of every way in which words might be similar to "communion Wine." How is this type of wine different from everyday table wine?

3. In poem 479, the speaker is comparing words to "Blades." What is meant by this comparison? From your reading of this poem, what conclusions can you draw about why someone would use words like blades? How true do you find this to be in your own life?

4. Although all of these poems deal with the same topic—words—in what ways do they differ from one another?

5. If you had to choose to write a response to just one of these poems, which one would you choose and why?

Suggestions for Extended Thinking and Writing

1. Go back to your initial list of twenty favorite words and write a poem in which you use all twenty of them. Experiment with the arrangement of these words, and write a short analysis about putting this poem together and a brief reflection on how it turned out.

2. Find and read three more poems by Emily Dickinson that deal with the same topic, such as death, love, nature, or friendship. Write an essay in which you explain what you think of these poems and how they affect you.

3. Words have the power to heal as well as to destroy. Write a personal narrative in which you show how words spoken either healed a wound or caused an injury.

Vocabulary Check

To help ensure that you've understood this selection, and to help you develop a more extensive vocabulary, check the definitions of unfamiliar words in the selection. The words listed below may be new to you, as might others, which you should also identify and define in this exercise.

paltry (2), signal (3), esoteric (3), comprehend (7), infrequency (8)

Using the paragraph numbers in parentheses, which correspond with the numbers in the selection's right margins, locate the words listed above in the reading and develop definitions based on the context in which the words are used (see the guidelines for identifying meaning from context clues on pages 23–24 in Section 3). When you're satisfied with your definitions, use a dictionary to confirm the meaning of each word, and then write your own sentences using these words.

SUGGESTIONS FOR MAKING CONNECTIONS

1. Write an essay in which you argue that language should belong to the people who speak it. Use the experiences and insights you find in at least three sources in this section to support your argument. You may, of course, use other sources as well.
2. Write an essay in which you argue for or against the following proposition: The rules of standard American English ought to be followed by all writers and speakers in our society. Refer to as many supporting sources in this section as you can.
3. Write a conversation that might take place between two of the authors in this section. The viewpoints do not necessarily have to be contrasting for this conversation to be effective. For example, you could pair up Ehrenreich with Lee and Telushkin with Naylor.
4. Write an essay on sexism or racism in the language of advertising. Use examples from current ads and commercials, as well as the arguments of several authors in this section.
5. Compare the language in three different types of popular music today: perhaps the language of a white female country–western singer, of an urban black rapper, and of a white rock idol. How do the lyrics, messages, and syntax compare with what the authors in this section have told us?

6. Write an extended metaphor that shows how sexist or racist language affects you or someone you know well. You may choose the format of an essay or a poem for this topic.

7. Considering your own observations, as well as what you have discovered from the selections in this section, write a speech in which you try to convince local high school or college students that our language creates and maintains sexist myths. Propose several suggestions that may help change this situation.

8. Write an essay in which you examine the power of a single word, based on the sources in this section.

9. Choose a racial, national, sexist, or religious insult and analyze the possible implications of this slur. See if you can discover where the term originated, and how the term has changed in meaning today.

10. Can people from one culture ever really understand a person from a different culture? Rely on your own experience as well as the information in this section in order to answer this question.

11. Does what we say really reflect what we think? Write an essay in which you explore this question in terms of your own life as well as the lives of the authors you have met in this section.

12. Write a paper in which you examine how television comics and sitcom characters create humor from racial, religious, gender, or age stereotypes. Is the humor harmless? What do you think? What would other authors in this section think?

9

Ways of Learning

Reading Images

Both photographs suggest that the creation and perception of images are significant ways of learning. Look carefully at the mural behind the speaker in the second photograph. What images do you see? What do they suggest to you about the students who created this mural?

JACQUES D'AMBOISE

I Show a Child What Is Possible

Born in 1935, Jacques d'Amboise grew up in the inner city of New York. On the streets, he was surrounded every day by the threat of drugs, zip guns, and gangs. At home, on the other hand, his French Canadian mother read to him about the elegant court life of Versailles, telling tales of nobility and chivalry. Following her dream of beauty and culture, d'Amboise's mother arranged for her daughter to take classical ballet lessons and insisted that her son accompany his sister, hoping that at least for those few hours he would be safe from the dangers and temptations of every neighborhood street corner. After being encouraged by his sister's teacher to join the ballet class, d'Amboise discovered his talent and love for dancing. At the age of fifteen, he joined George Balanchine's New York City Ballet and went on to become one of the finest classical dancers of our time.

Because of his own childhood experiences, d'Amboise developed a strong commitment to bringing dance to other young people whose circumstances were similar to his own. In 1976 he founded the National Dance Institute (NDI), which today has programs in more than thirty public schools in the New York City area. Most NDI dancers come from neighborhoods similar to the one d'Amboise grew up in. Most (80 percent) are black, Hispanic, or Asian. Some are homeless or have handicaps such as visual impairment or hearing loss. To each child, d'Amboise brings his joy of dance and his belief that energy and commitment to dance can bring meaning to all our lives.

Pre-Reading and Journal-Writing Suggestions
1. Everyone is an expert at something. Choose one thing you can do well, and write about it.
2. Fill in the following blanks, and write about this completed statement in your journal.
    "If only someone had taught me to _____, I could be a great _____ right now."
3. Spend the next ten minutes jotting down your immediate response to these questions: Who was the teacher who has most affected your life? Why and how did this teacher affect your life? Do not worry about organizing your thoughts; just write without stopping. If you get stuck, copy the previous sentence until your ideas start flowing again. The point here is to spend ten full minutes actually writing so that you move responses from your mind to the paper in front of you.

When I was 7 years old, I was forced to watch my sister's ballet classes. 1 This was to keep me off the street and away from my pals, who ran with gangs like the ones in *West Side Story*. The class was taught by Madame Seda, a Georgian-Armenian who had a school at 181st Street and St. Nicholas Avenue in New York City. As she taught the little girls, I would sit, fidget and diabolically try to disrupt the class by making irritating little noises.

But she was very wise, Madame Seda. She let me get away with it, ignoring me until the end of the class, when everybody did the big jumps, a series of leaps in place, called *changements*.

At that point, Madame Seda turned and, stabbing a finger at me, said, "All right, little brother, if you've got so much energy, get up and do these jumps. See if you can jump as high as the girls." So I jumped. And loved it. I felt like I was flying. And she said, "Oh, that was wonderful! From now on, if you are quiet during the class, I'll let you join in the *changements*."

After that, I'd sit quietly in the class and wait for the jumps. A few classes later, she said, "You've got to learn how to jump and not make any noise when you come down. You should learn to do the *pliés* [graceful knee bends] that come at the beginning of the class." So I would do *pliés*, then wait respectfully for the end of class to do the jumps.

Finally she said, "You jump high, and you are landing beautifully, but 5 you look awful in the air, flaying your arms about. You've got to take the rest of the class and learn how to do beautiful hands and arms."

I was hooked.

An exceptional teacher got a bored little kid, me, interested in ballet. How? She challenged me to a test, complimented me on my effort and then immediately gave me a new challenge. She set up an environment for the achievement of excellence and cared enough to invite me to be part of it. And, without realizing it fully at the time, I made an important discovery.

Dance is the most immediate and accessible of the arts because it involves your own body. When you learn to move your body on a note of music, it's exciting. You have taken control of your body and, by learning to do that, you discover that you can take control of your life.

I took classes with Madame Seda for six months, once a week, but at the end of spring, in June 1942, she called over my mother, my sister and me and did an unbelievably modest and generous thing. She said, "You and your sister are very talented. You should go to a better teacher." She sent us to George Balanchine's school—the School of American Ballet.

Within a few years, I was performing children's roles. At 15, I became 10 part of a classical ballet company. What an extraordinary thing for a street boy from Washington Heights, with friends in gangs. Half grew up to become policemen and the other half gangsters—and I became a ballet dancer!

I had dreamed of being a doctor or an archaeologist or a priest. But by the time I was 17, I was a principal dancer performing major roles in the ballets, and by the time I was 21, I was doing movies, Broadway shows and choreography. I then married a ballerina from New York City Ballet, Carolyn George, and we were (and still are) blessed with two boys and twin daughters.

It was a joyful career that lasted four decades. That's a long time to be dancing and, inevitably, a time came when I realized that there were not many years left for me as a performer. I wasn't sure what to do next, but then I thought about how I had become a dancer, and the teachers who had graced my life. Perhaps I could engage young children, especially boys, in the magic of the arts—in dance in particular. Not necessarily to prepare them to be professional performers, but to create an awareness by giving them a chance to experience the arts. So I started National Dance Institute.

That was 13 years ago. Since then, with the help of fellow teachers and staff at NDI, I have taught dance to thousands of inner-city children. And in each class, I rediscover why teaching dance to children is so important.

Each time I can use dance to help a child discover that he can control the way he moves, I am filled with joy. At a class I recently taught at P.S. 59 in Brooklyn, there was one boy who couldn't get from his right foot to his left. He was terrified. Everyone was watching. And what he had to do was so simple: take a step with his left foot on a note of music. All his classmates could do it, but he couldn't.

He kept trying, but he kept doing it wrong until finally he was frozen, unable to move at all. I put my arm around him and said, "Let's do it together. We'll do it in slow motion." We did it. I stepped back and said, "Now do it alone, and fast." With his face twisted in concentration, he slammed his left foot down correctly on the note. He did it!   15

The whole class applauded. He was so excited. But I think I was even happier, because I knew what had taken place. He had discovered he could take control of his body, and from that he can learn to take control of his life. If I can open the door to show a child that that is possible, it is wonderful.

Dance is the art to express time and space. That is what our universe is about. We can hardly make a sentence without signifying some expression of distance, place or time: "See you later." "Meet you at the corner in five minutes."

Dance is the art that human beings have developed to express that we live, right now, in a world of movement and varying tempos.

Dance, as an art, has to be taught. However, when teaching, it's important to set up an environment where both the student and teacher can discover together. Never teach something you don't love and believe in. But how to set up that environment?

When I have a new group of young students and I'm starting a class, I 20
use Madame Seda's technique. I say, "Can you do this test? I'm going to
give all 100 of you exactly 10 seconds to get off your seats and be standing
and spread out all over the stage floor. And do it silently. Go!" And I start a
countdown. Naturally, they run, yelling and screaming, and somehow arrive
with several seconds to spare. I say, "Freeze. You all failed. You made noise,
and you got there too soon. I said 'exactly 10 seconds'—not 6 or 8 or 11.
Go back to your seats, and we'll do it again. And if you don't get it, we'll go
back and do it again until you do. And if, at the end of the hour, you still
haven't gotten it, I'm not going to teach you."

They usually get it the second time. Never have I had to do it more
than three.

Demand precision, be clear and absolutely truthful. When they respond—and they will—congratulate them on the extraordinary control
they have just exhibited. Why is that important? Because it's the beginning
of knowing yourself, knowing that you can manage yourself if you want.
And it's the beginning of dance. Once the children see that we are having a
class of precision, order and respect, they are relieved, and we have a great
class.

I've taught dance to Russian children, Australian children, Indian chil-
dren, Chinese children, fat children, skinny children, handicapped children,
groups of Australian triathletes, New York City police, senior citizens and
3-year-olds. The technique is the same everywhere, although there are cultural differences.

For example, when I was in China, I would say to the children, "I want
everybody to come close and watch what I am going to do." But in China
they have had to deal with following a teacher when there are masses of
them. And they discovered that the way to see what the teacher does is not
to move close but to move away. So 100 people moved back to watch the
one—me.

I realized they were right. How did they learn that? Thousands of years 25
of masses of people having to follow one teacher.

There are cultural differences and there are differences among people.
In any group of dancers, there are some who are ready and excel more than
others. There are many reasons—genetic, environment, the teachers they
had. People blossom at different times.

But whatever the differences, someone admiring you, encouraging you,
works so much better than the reverse. "You can do it, you are wonderful,"
works so much better than, "You're no good, the others are better than you,
you've got to try harder." That never works.

I don't think there are any untalented children. But I think there are
those whose talents never get the chance to flower. Perhaps they were never

encouraged. Perhaps no one took the time to find out how to teach them. That is a tragedy.

However, the single most terrible thing we are doing to our children, I believe, is polluting them. I don't mean just with smog and crack, but by not teaching them the civilizing things we have taken millions of years to develop. But you cannot have a dance class without having good manners, without having respect. Dance can teach those things.

I think of each person as a trunk that's up in the attic. What are you   30
going to put in the trunk? Are you going to put in machine guns, loud noises, foul language, dirty books and ignorance? Because, if you do, that's what is going to be left after you, that's what your children are going to have, and that will determine the world of the future. Or are you going to fill that trunk with music, dance, poetry, literature, good manners and loving friends?

I say, fill your trunk with the best that is available to you from the wealth of human culture. Those things will nourish you and your children. You can clean up your own environment and pass it on to the next generation. That's why I teach dance.

Suggestions for Writing and Discussion
1. What aspects of your own life were you thinking about as you read this piece?
2. In paragraph 1, d'Amboise describes himself as "diabolically" trying to disrupt his sister's dance class. How would you define the word *diabolically?* After writing your own definition, based on the context of the sentence in which it appears, look it up in the dictionary. Pay particular attention to the origin of this word. How does understanding the word's origin add to your understanding of the image d'Amboise seeks to convey?
3. What qualities did Madame Seda possess that made her a good teacher? What qualities did the author possess that made him a good pupil? Using the examples of Madame Seda and Jacques d'Amboise, write an extended definition of an ideal teacher-student relationship. As you write, assume that your audience will be college students who are currently training to be teachers.
4. Have you ever had a teacher like Madame Seda or Jacques d'Amboise? Explain.
5. If you were a teacher, what qualities would you like to pass on to the next generation? Explain.
6. In paragraph 22, the author says a teacher should "[d]emand precision, be clear and absolutely truthful." What else should a great teacher do?

Suggestions for Extended Thinking and Writing

1. Write an essay in which you describe a process you went through to learn something new.

2. D'Amboise writes that he thinks of each person "as a trunk that's up in the attic." Write an essay in which you not only explain what this comparison implies, but take it a step further: Devise your own metaphor for the way you see each new person you meet. Explain your reasons for using this metaphor.

Vocabulary Check

To help ensure that you've understood this selection, and to help you develop a more extensive vocabulary, check the definitions of unfamiliar words in the selection. The words listed below may be new to you, as might others, which you should also identify and define in this exercise.

accessible (8), modest (9), choreography (11), tempo (18), nourish (31)

Using the paragraph numbers in parentheses, which correspond with the numbers in the selection's right margins, locate the words listed above in the reading and develop definitions based on the context in which the words are used (see the guidelines for identifying meaning from context clues on pages 23–24 in Section 3). When you're satisfied with your definitions, use a dictionary to confirm the meaning of each word, and then write your own sentences using these words.

ISAAC ASIMOV

What Is Intelligence, Anyway?

Born in the Soviet Union (now Russia) in 1920, Isaac Asimov immigrated to the United States with his parents when he was three. After earning a doctorate at Columbia University, he taught biochemistry at Boston University, but he is best known for his science and science-fiction writing. Before his death in 1992, he had published hundreds of books, including his best-known works *I, Robot* (1950), *The Foundation Trilogy* (1951–53), *The Gods Themselves* (1977), *Isaac Asimov's Guide to Earth and Space* (1992), and *The Exploding Suns: The Secrets of Supernovas* (1996). In addition to his work in biochemistry and his prolific writing, Asimov pursued many interests and avocations. He belonged to the Baker Street Irregulars, a group of avid Sherlock Holmes fans; the Gilbert and Sullivan Society; and the Wodehouse Society, which celebrated the life and works of humorist P. G. Wodehouse. For a while, he belonged to MENSA, the high intelligence organization, but dropped his membership because he believed that some members were arrogant about their high IQs.

Pre-Reading and Journal-Writing Suggestions
1. Define *intelligence*. Based on your definition, how intelligent do you consider yourself?
2. What do you think most people value more: a scholar and intellectual or a highly skilled professional?

What is intelligence, anyway? When I was in the army I received a kind   *1*
of aptitude test that all soldiers took and, against a normal of 100, scored 160. No one at the base had ever seen a figure like that, and for two hours they made a big fuss over me. (It didn't mean anything. The next day I was still a buck private with KP as my highest duty.)

All my life I've been registering scores like that, so that I have the complacent feeling that I'm highly intelligent, and I expect other people to think so, too. Actually, though, don't such scores simply mean that I am very good at answering the type of academic questions that are considered worthy of answers by the people who make up the intelligence tests—people with intellectual bents similar to mine?

For instance, I had an auto-repair man once, who, on these intelligence tests, could not possibly have scored more than 80, by my estimate. I always took it for granted that I was far more intelligent than he was. Yet, when anything went wrong with my car I hastened to him with it, watched him anxiously as he explored its vitals, and listened to his pronouncements as though they were divine oracles—and he always fixed my car.

Well, then, suppose my auto-repair man devised questions for an intelligence test. Or suppose a carpenter did, or a farmer, or, indeed, almost anyone but an academician. By every one of those tests, I'd prove myself a moron. And I'd *be* a moron, too. In a world where I could not use my academic training and my verbal talents but had to do something intricate or hard, working with my hands, I would do poorly. My intelligence, then, is not absolute but is a function of the society I live in and of the fact that a small subsection of that society has managed to foist itself on the rest as an arbiter of such matters.

Consider my auto-repair man, again. He had a habit of telling me jokes   *5* whenever he saw me. One time he raised his head from under the automobile hood to say: "Doc, a deaf-and-dumb guy went into a hardware store to ask for some nails. He put two fingers together on the counter and made hammering motions with the other hand. The clerk brought him a hammer. He shook his head and pointed to the two fingers he was hammering. The clerk brought him nails. He picked out the sizes he wanted, and left. Well, doc, the next guy who came in was a blind man. He wanted scissors. How do you suppose he asked for them?"

Indulgently, I lifted my right hand and made scissoring motions with my first two fingers. Whereupon my auto-repair man laughed raucously and said, "Why, you dumb jerk, he used his voice and asked for them." Then he said, smugly, "I've been trying that on all my customers today." "Did you catch many?" I asked. "Quite a few," he said, "but I knew for sure I'd catch you." "Why is that?" I asked. "Because you're so goddamned educated, doc, I *know* you couldn't be very smart."

And I have an uneasy feeling he had something there.

Suggestions for Writing and Discussion

1. What is Asimov's main point about intelligence? Where in this piece does he state it?

2. What does this piece reveal about the author himself? Is he typical of most "intellectuals" in general?

3. What types of intelligence can people have other than the ones displayed by Asimov and the mechanic?

4. Be honest: What was your response or answer to the mechanic's riddle? What might your response reveal about you?

Suggestions for Extended Thinking and Writing
1. Based on Asimov's distinction between an intelligent person and an educated one, write a piece in which you compare the smartest person you know with one who is better educated.
2. Research Gardner's theory on multiple intelligences and show its relationship both to your own experiences and to Asimov's point.
3. Find another essay written by Asimov, and write a summary and response to it.

Vocabulary Check
To help ensure that you've understood this selection, and to help you develop a more extensive vocabulary, check the definitions of unfamiliar words in the selection. The words listed below may be new to you, as might others, which you should also identify and define in this exercise.

aptitude (1), oracle (3), devise (4), arbiter (4), raucous (6)

Using the paragraph numbers in parentheses, which correspond with the numbers in the selection's right margins, locate the words listed above in the reading and develop definitions based on the context in which the words are used (see the guidelines for identifying meaning from context clues on pages 23–24 in Section 3). When you're satisfied with your definitions, use a dictionary to confirm the meaning of each word, and then write your own sentences using these words.

MAYA ANGELOU
Finishing School

Originally named Marguerita Johnson, Maya Angelou was born in St. Louis in 1928. From the age of three to eight, Angelou and her brother grew up in Stamps, Arkansas, under the watchful, loving eye of the grandmother they called "Momma." Unfortunately her grandmother's boundless energy and affection could not protect Angelou from the pain of poverty, segregated schools, and violence at the hands of both whites and blacks. At age eight, she went to stay with her mother and was raped by her mother's lover; subsequently Angelou refused to talk for more than a year. Shortly after the rape, she returned to her grandmother's home where she began to read voraciously, memorizing extensive passages of writers from Shakespeare to the poets of the Harlem Renaissance. The cadences and rhythms of her early love affair with poetry weave throughout her works. In addition to being a disciplined writer who works each day from 6 a.m. until noon, Angelou is a gifted actress, dancer, and musician. She starred in the European and African road productions of *Porgy and Bess* and has written scores and lyrics for screenplays. In 1973 and 1977 she received Tony award nominations, while in 1972 her book of poems, *Just Give Me a Cool Drink of Water 'fore I Diiie,* was nominated for a Pulitzer Prize. In 1993, as poet laureate of the United States, she wrote and read a poem for the inauguration of President Clinton.

A champion of the narrative as complex, serious art, Angelou sees her work as "stemming from the slave narrative and developing into a new American literary form." In this selection, a chapter from Angelou's highly praised autobiography *I Know Why the Caged Bird Sings* (1969), she tells the story of a painful lesson she learned in a white woman's kitchen that she ironically calls her "finishing school."

Pre-Reading and Journal-Writing Suggestions
1. How do you feel about your name? In other words, if someone calls you something slightly different from your name ("Cathy" instead of "Kate," for instance), does it bother you? How important is your name to you?
2. Write about a significant educational experience you have had *outside* the classroom.

Recently a white woman from Texas, who would quickly describe herself as a liberal, asked me about my hometown. When I told her that in

Stamps my grandmother had owned the only Negro general merchandise store since the turn of the century, she exclaimed, "Why, you were a debutante." Ridiculous and even ludicrous. But Negro girls in small Southern towns, whether poverty-stricken or just munching along on a few of life's necessities, were given as extensive and irrelevant preparations for adulthood as rich white girls shown in magazines. Admittedly the training was not the same. While white girls learned to waltz and sit gracefully with a tea cup balanced on their knees, we were lagging behind, learning the mid-Victorian values with very little money to indulge them. . . .

We were required to embroider and I had trunkfuls of colorful dishtowels, pillowcases, runners and handkerchiefs to my credit. I mastered the art of crocheting and tatting, and there was a life-time's supply of dainty doilies that would never be used in sacheted dresser drawers. It went without saying that all girls could iron and wash, but the finer touches around the home, like setting a table with real silver, baking roasts and cooking vegetables without meat, had to be learned elsewhere. Usually at the source of those habits. During my tenth year, a white woman's kitchen became my finishing school.

Mrs. Viola Cullinan was a plump woman who lived in a three-bedroom house somewhere behind the post office. She was singularly unattractive until she smiled, and then the lines around her eyes and mouth which made her look perpetually dirty disappeared, and her face looked like the mask of an impish elf. She usually rested her smile until late afternoon when her women friends dropped in and Miss Glory, the cook, served them cold drinks on the closed-in porch.

The exactness of her house was inhuman. This glass went here and only here. That cup had its place and it was an act of impudent rebellion to place it anywhere else. At twelve o'clock the table was set. At 12:15 Mrs. Cullinan sat down to dinner (whether her husband had arrived or not). At 12:16 Miss Glory brought out the food.

It took me a week to learn the difference between a salad plate, a bread plate and a dessert plate. 5

Mrs. Cullinan kept up the tradition of her wealthy parents. She was from Virginia. Miss Glory, who was a descendant of slaves that had worked for the Cullinans, told me her history. She had married beneath her (according to Miss Glory). Her husband's family hadn't had their money very long and what they had "didn't 'mount to much."

As ugly as she was, I thought privately, she was lucky to get a husband above or beneath her station. But Miss Glory wouldn't let me say a thing against her mistress. She was very patient with me, however, over the housework. She explained the dishware, silverware and servants' bells. The large round bowl in which soup was served wasn't a soup bowl, it was a tureen.

There were goblets, sherbet glasses, ice-cream glasses, wine glasses, green glass coffee cups with matching saucers, and water glasses. I had a glass to drink from, and it sat with Miss Glory's on a separate shelf from the others. Soup spoons, gravy boat, butter knives, salad forks and carving platter were additions to my vocabulary and in fact almost represented a new language. I was fascinated with the novelty, with the fluttering Mrs. Cullinan and her Alice-in-Wonderland house.

Her husband remains, in my memory, undefined. I lumped him with all the other white men that I had ever seen and tried not to see.

On our way home one evening, Miss Glory told me that Mrs. Cullinan couldn't have children. She said that she was too delicate-boned. It was hard to imagine bones at all under those layers of fat. Miss Glory went on to say that the doctor had taken out all her lady organs. I reasoned that a pig's organs included the lungs, heart and liver, so if Mrs. Cullinan was walking around without those essentials, it explained why she drank alcohol out of unmarked bottles. She was keeping herself embalmed.

When I spoke to Bailey about it, he agreed that I was right, but he also *10* informed me that Mr. Cullinan had two daughters by a colored lady and that I knew them very well. He added that the girls were the spitting image of their father. I was unable to remember what he looked like, although I had just left him a few hours before, but I thought of the Coleman girls. They were very light-skinned and certainly didn't look very much like their mother (no one ever mentioned Mr. Coleman).

My pity for Mrs. Cullinan preceded me the next morning like the Cheshire cat's smile. Those girls, who could have been her daughters, were beautiful. They didn't have to straighten their hair. Even when they were caught in the rain, their braids still hung down straight like tamed snakes. Their mouths were pouty little cupid's bows. Mrs. Cullinan didn't know what she missed. Or maybe she did. Poor Mrs. Cullinan.

For weeks after, I arrived early, left late and tried very hard to make up for her barrenness. If she had her own children, she wouldn't have had to ask me to run a thousand errands from her back door to the back door of her friends. Poor old Mrs. Cullinan.

Then one evening Miss Glory told me to serve the ladies on the porch. After I set the tray down and turned toward the kitchen, one of the women asked, "What's your name, girl?" It was the speckled-faced one. Mrs. Cullinan said, "She doesn't talk much. Her name's Margaret."

"Is she dumb?"

"No. As I understand it, she can talk when she wants to but she's usually *15* quiet as a little mouse. Aren't you, Margaret?"

I smiled at her. Poor thing. No organs and couldn't even pronounce my name correctly.

"She's a sweet little thing, though."

"Well, that may be, but the name's too long. I'd never bother myself. I'd call her Mary if I was you."

I fumed into the kitchen. That horrible woman would never have the chance to call me Mary because if I was starving I'd never work for her. . . .

That evening I decided to write a poem on being white, fat, old and 20 without children. It was going to be a tragic ballad. I would have to watch her carefully to capture the essence of her loneliness and pain.

The very next day, she called me by the wrong name. Miss Glory and I were washing up the lunch dishes when Mrs. Cullinan came to the doorway. "Mary?"

Miss Glory asked, "Who?"

Mrs. Cullinan, sagging a little, knew and I knew. "I want Mary to go down to Mrs. Randall's and take her some soup. She's not been feeling well for a few days."

Miss Glory's face was a wonder to see. "You mean Margaret, ma'am. Her name's Margaret."

"That's too long. She's Mary from now on. Heat that soup from last 25 night and put it in the china tureen and, Mary, I want you to carry it carefully."

Every person I knew had a hellish horror of being "called out of his name." It was a dangerous practice to call a Negro anything that could be loosely construed as insulting because of the centuries of their having been called niggers, jigs, dinges, blackbirds, crows, boots and spooks.

Miss Glory had a fleeting second of feeling sorry for me. Then as she handed me the hot tureen she said, "Don't mind, don't pay that no mind. Sticks and stones may break your bones, but words . . . You know, I been working for her for twenty years."

She held the back door open for me. "Twenty years. I wasn't much older than you. My name used to be Hallelujah. That's what Ma named me, but my mistress give me 'Glory,' and it stuck. I likes it better too."

I was in the little path that ran behind the houses when Miss Glory shouted, "It's shorter too."

For a few seconds it was a tossup over whether I would laugh (imagine 30 being named Hallelujah) or cry (imagine letting some white woman rename you for her convenience). My anger saved me from either outburst. I had to quit the job, but the problem was going to be how to do it. Momma wouldn't allow me to quit for just any reason.

"She's a peach. That woman is a real peach." Mrs. Randall's maid was talking as she took the soup from me, and I wondered what her name used to be and what she answered to now.

For a week I looked into Mrs. Cullinan's face as she called me Mary. She ignored my coming late and leaving early. Miss Glory was a little annoyed because I had begun to leave egg yolk on the dishes and wasn't putting much heart in polishing the silver. I hoped that she would complain to our boss, but she didn't.

Then Bailey solved my dilemma. He had me describe the contents of the cupboard and the particular plates she liked best. Her favorite piece was a casserole shaped like a fish and the green glass coffee cups. I kept his instructions in mind, so on the next day when Miss Glory was hanging out clothes and I had again been told to serve the old biddies on the porch, I dropped the empty serving tray. When I heard Mrs. Cullinan scream, "Mary!" I picked up the casserole and two of the green glass cups in readiness. As she rounded the kitchen door I let them fall on the tiled floor.

I could never absolutely describe to Bailey what happened next, because each time I got to the part where she fell on the floor and screwed up her ugly face to cry, we burst out laughing. She actually wobbled around on the floor and picked up shards of the cups and cried, "Oh, Momma. Oh, dear Gawd. It's Momma's china from Virginia. Oh, Momma, I'm sorry."

Miss Glory came running in from the yard and the women from the 35 porch crowded around. Miss Glory was almost as broken up as her mistress. "You mean to say she broke our Virginia dishes? What we gone do?"

Mrs. Cullinan cried louder, "That clumsy nigger. Clumsy little black nigger."

Old speckled-faced leaned down and asked, "Who did it, Viola? Was it Mary? Who did it?"

Everything was happening so fast I can't remember whether her action preceded her words, but I know that Mrs. Cullinan said, "Her name's Margaret, goddamn it, her name's Margaret." And she threw a wedge of broken plate at me. It could have been the hysteria which put her aim off, but the flying crockery caught Miss Glory right over her ear and she started screaming.

I left the front door wide open so all the neighbors could hear.

Mrs. Cullinan was right about one thing. My name wasn't Mary.   40

Suggestions for Writing and Discussion
1. Write your immediate reaction to this story.
2. In paragraph 12, Angelou speaks of Mrs. Cullinan's *barrenness*. What is the literal meaning of this word? What are its connotations? Cite details from this piece to explain the ways in which Mrs. Cullinan (and her life) can be seen as barren.
3. Why do Miss Glory's cup and Margaret's cup sit on a separate shelf? Can you think of similar distinctions you have seen or experienced? (Example: children eating at tables apart from adults)

4. Angelou writes that she felt sorry for Mrs. Cullinan, so she tried to make up for it by working extra hard. What does this tell you about Angelou's personality and character? When and why does her attitude change toward Mrs. Cullinan?
5. What do you think of Miss Glory? In what ways is she like Margaret? In what ways do they differ? Why do you think Miss Glory has stayed with Mrs. Cullinan for so many years? What do their different decisions suggest about their values? With whom do you more closely identify? Why?
6. Angelou makes several references to *Alice in Wonderland* in this piece. Identify as many references as you can and explain how the *Alice* images connect to the central idea Angelou conveys. As you write your response, consider as your audience a friend who remains, even as an adult, devoted to the *Alice* stories. You are trying to convince this friend to read Angelou's piece.
7. Mrs. Cullinan says that the name Margaret is too long, so she shortens it to Mary. She also does this to Glory's name. Apart from being a convenience, why else does she do this?
8. What do you think of Bailey's solution to Margaret's dilemma? Could she have solved her problem any other way? Explain.

Suggestions for Extended Thinking and Writing
1. Are you a rebel, like Margaret, or a conformist, like Glory? Write an essay in which you explain the causes and effects of an event in your life that shows your approach to challenge and conflict.
2. Margaret says that to really capture someone, you have to watch very carefully. Practice the art of observation yourself. Watch someone very carefully, making notes about what the person does and says. Then write a brief analysis of the person's actions, based on your notes.
3. Time for revenge (and fun). Using precise, vivid description, write an essay highlighting the nastiest, meanest person you've ever met.

Vocabulary Check
To help ensure that you've understood this selection, and to help you develop a more extensive vocabulary, check the definitions of unfamiliar words in the selection. The words listed below may be new to you, as might others, which you should also identify and define in this exercise.

sachet (2), station (7), embalmed (9), essence (20), dilemma (33)

Using the paragraph numbers in parentheses, which correspond with the numbers in the selection's right margins, locate the words listed above in the reading and develop definitions based on the context in which the words are used (see the guidelines for identifying meaning from context clues on pages 23–24 in Section 3). When you're satisfied with your definitions, use a dictionary to confirm the meaning of each word, and then write your own sentences using these words.

NICHOLAS GAGE

The Teacher Who Changed My Life

Born in Greece in 1939, Nicholas Gage has written movingly of the murder in 1948 of his mother, Eleni Gatzoyiannis. During the Greek civil war, when Gage was nine years old, Communist guerrillas arrested, tortured, and executed his mother because she arranged the escape of her five children from their occupied mountain village. Gage grew up and was educated in the United States. As an adult, he became an investigative reporter and, haunted by his mother's death, returned to Greece to track down the story of her final weeks of life. In his best-selling book *Eleni,* he describes the events of this traumatic, terrifying, and astonishingly heroic time.

Following the publication of *Eleni,* Gage wrote another book, *A Place for Us,* from which the following essay is taken. In this autobiography, Gage describes the difficult adjustment he and his sisters faced after arriving in the United States and pays tribute to the teacher he sees as the inspiration and motivating force behind his later success as a writer.

Pre-Reading and Journal-Writing Suggestions
1. Write about someone you see as your mentor, your inspiration.
2. Describe your past experiences with writing, especially in a school environment. How did you learn to write? How do you feel about writing? How would you assess your writing ability at this point in your life?
3. What three characteristics are most important for a good teacher to possess? Explain your answer by describing your own specific experiences with good teachers.

The person who set the course of my life in the new land I entered as a   *1*
young war refugee—who, in fact, nearly dragged me onto the path that would bring all the blessings I've received in America—was a salty-tongued, no-nonsense schoolteacher named Marjorie Hurd. When I entered her classroom in 1953, I had been to six schools in five years, starting in the Greek village where I was born in 1939.

When I stepped off a ship in New York Harbor on a gray March day in 1949, I was an undersized 9-year-old in short pants who had lost his mother and was coming to live with the father he didn't know. My mother, Eleni Gatzoyiannis, had been imprisoned, tortured and shot by Communist guerrillas for sending me and three of my four sisters to freedom. She died so that her children could go to their father in the United States.

The portly, bald, well-dressed man who met me and my sisters seemed a foreign, authoritarian figure. I secretly resented him for not getting the whole family out of Greece early enough to save my mother. Ultimately, I would grow to love him and appreciate how he dealt with becoming a single parent at the age of 56, but at first our relationship was prickly, full of hostility.

As Father drove us to our new home—a tenement in Worcester, Mass.—and pointed out the huge brick building that would be our first school in America, I clutched my Greek notebooks from the refugee camp, hoping that my few years of schooling would impress my teachers in this cold, crowded country. They didn't. When my father led me and my 11-year-old sister to Greendale Elementary School, the grim-faced Yankee principal put the two of us in a class for the mentally retarded. There was no facility in those days for non-English-speaking children.

By the time I met Marjorie Hurd four years later, I had learned English,   5 been placed in a normal, graded class and had even been chosen for the college preparatory track in the Worcester public school system. I was 13 years old when our father moved us yet again, and I entered Chandler Junior High shortly after the beginning of seventh grade. I found myself surrounded by richer, smarter and better-dressed classmates who looked askance at my strange clothes and heavy accent. Shortly after I arrived, we were told to select a hobby to pursue during "club hour" on Fridays. The idea of hobbies and clubs made no sense to my immigrant ears, but I decided to follow the prettiest girl in my class—the blue-eyed daughter of the local Lutheran minister. She led me through the door marked "Newspaper Club" and into the presence of Miss Hurd, the newspaper adviser and English teacher who would become my mentor and my muse.

A formidable, solidly built woman with salt-and-pepper hair, a steely eye and a flat Boston accent, Miss Hurd had no patience with layabouts. "What are all you goof-offs doing here?" she bellowed at the would-be journalists. "This is the Newspaper Club! We're going to put out a *newspaper*. So if there's anybody in this room who doesn't like work, I suggest you go across to the Glee Club now, because you're going to work your tails off here!"

I was soon under Miss Hurd's spell. She did indeed teach us to put out a newspaper, skills I honed during my next 25 years as a journalist. Soon I asked the principal to transfer me to her English class as well. There, she drilled us on grammar until I finally began to understand the logic and structure of the English language. She assigned stories for us to read and discuss; not tales of heroes, like the Greek myths I knew, but stories of underdogs—poor people, even immigrants, who seemed ordinary until a crisis drove them to do something extraordinary. She also introduced us to the literary wealth of Greece—giving me a new perspective on my war-ravaged, impoverished homeland. I began to be proud of my origins.

One day, after discussing how writers should write about what they know, she assigned us to compose an essay from our own experience. Fixing me with a stern look, she added, "Nick, I want you to write about what happened to your family in Greece." I had been trying to put those painful memories behind me and left the assignment until the last moment. Then, on a warm spring afternoon, I sat in my room with a yellow pad and pencil and stared out the window at the buds on the trees. I wrote that the coming of spring always reminded me of the last time I said goodbye to my mother on a green and gold day in 1948.

I kept writing, one line after another, telling how the Communist guerrillas occupied our village, took our home and food, how my mother started planning our escape when she learned that the children were to be sent to re-education camps behind the Iron Curtain and how, at the last moment, she couldn't escape with us because the guerrillas sent her with a group of women to thresh wheat in a distant village. She promised she would try to get away on her own, she told me to be brave and hung a silver cross around my neck, and then she kissed me. I watched the line of women being led down into the ravine and up the other side, until they disappeared around the bend—my mother a tiny brown figure at the end who stopped for an instant to raise her hand in one last farewell.

I wrote about our nighttime escape down the mountain, across the minefields and into the lines of the Nationalist soldiers, who sent us to a refugee camp. It was there that we learned of our mother's execution. I felt very lucky to have come to America, I concluded, but every year, the coming of spring made me feel sad because it reminded me of the last time I saw my mother.

I handed in the essay, hoping never to see it again, but Miss Hurd had it published in the school paper. This mortified me at first, until I saw that my classmates reacted with sympathy and tact to my family's story. Without telling me, Miss Hurd also submitted the essay to a contest sponsored by the Freedoms Foundation at Valley Forge, Pa., and it won a medal. The Worcester paper wrote about the award and quoted my essay at length. My father, by then a "five-and-dime-store chef," as the paper described him, was ecstatic with pride, and the Worcester Greek community celebrated the honor to one of its own.

For the first time I began to understand the power of the written word. A secret ambition took root in me. One day, I vowed, I would go back to Greece, find out the details of my mother's death and write about her life, so her grandchildren would know of her courage. Perhaps I would even track down the men who killed her and write of their crimes. Fulfilling that ambition would take me 30 years.

Meanwhile, I followed the literary path that Miss Hurd had so forcefully set me on. After junior high, I became the editor of my school paper at Classical High School and got a part-time job at the Worcester *Telegram and Gazette*. Although my father could only give me $50 and encouragement toward a college education, I managed to finance four years at Boston University with scholarships and part-time jobs in journalism. During my last year of college, an article I wrote about a friend who had died in the Philippines—the first person to lose his life working for the Peace Corps—led to my winning the Hearst Award for College Journalism. And the plaque was given to me in the White House by President John F. Kennedy.

For a refugee who had never seen a motorized vehicle or indoor plumbing until he was 9, this was an unimaginable honor. When the Worcester paper ran a picture of me standing next to President Kennedy, my father rushed out to buy a new suit in order to be properly dressed to receive the congratulations of the Worcester Greeks. He clipped out the photograph, had it laminated in plastic and carried it in his breast pocket for the rest of his life to show everyone he met. I found the much-worn photo in his pocket on the day he died 20 years later.

In our isolated Greek village, my mother had bribed a cousin to teach her to read, for girls were not supposed to attend school beyond a certain age. She had always dreamed of her children receiving an education. She couldn't be there when I graduated from Boston University, but the person who came with my father and shared our joy was my former teacher, Marjorie Hurd. We celebrated not only my bachelor's degree but also the scholarships that paid my way to Columbia's Graduate School of Journalism. There, I met the woman who would eventually become my wife. At our wedding and at the baptisms of our three children, Marjorie Hurd was always there, dancing alongside the Greeks.

By then, she was Mrs. Rabidou, for she had married a widower when she was in her early 40s. That didn't distract her from her vocation of introducing young minds to English literature, however. She taught for a total of 41 years and continually would make a "project" of some balky student in whom she spied a spark of potential. Often these were students from the most troubled homes, yet she would alternately bully and charm each one with her own special brand of tough love until the spark caught fire. She retired in 1981 at the age of 62 but still avidly follows the lives and careers of former students while overseeing her adult stepchildren and driving her husband on camping trips to New Hampshire.

Miss Hurd was one of the first to call me on Dec. 10, 1987, when President Reagan, in his television address after the summit meeting with Gorbachev, told the nation that Eleni Gatzoyiannis' dying cry, "My children!" had helped inspire him to seek an arms agreement "for all the children of the world."

"I can't imagine a better monument for your mother," Miss Hurd said with an uncharacteristic catch in her voice.

Although a bad hip makes it impossible for her to join in the Greek dancing, Marjorie Hurd Rabidou is still an honored and enthusiastic guest at all family celebrations, including my 50th birthday picnic last summer, where the shish kebab was cooked on spits, clarinets and *bouzoukis* wailed, and costumed dancers led the guests in a serpentine line around our Colonial farmhouse, only 20 minutes from my first home in Worcester.

My sisters and I felt an aching void because my father was not there to 20 lead the line, balancing a glass of wine on his head while he danced, the way he did at every celebration during his 92 years. But Miss Hurd was there, surveying the scene with quiet satisfaction. Although my parents are gone, her presence was a consolation, because I owe her so much.

This is truly the land of opportunity, and I would have enjoyed its bounty even if I hadn't walked into Miss Hurd's classroom in 1953. But she was the one who directed my grief and pain into writing, and if it weren't for her I wouldn't have become an investigative reporter and foreign correspondent, recorded the story of my mother's life and death in *Eleni* and now my father's story in *A Place for Us,* which is also a testament to the country that took us in. She was the catalyst that sent me into journalism and indirectly caused all the good things that came after. But Miss Hurd would probably deny this emphatically.

A few years ago, I answered the telephone and heard my former teacher's voice telling me, in that won't-take-no-for-an-answer tone of hers, that she had decided I was to write and deliver the eulogy at her funeral. I agreed (she didn't leave me any choice), but that's one assignment I never want to do. I hope, Miss Hurd, that you'll accept this remembrance instead.

Suggestions for Writing and Discussion
1. Gage attributes his success in America to his seventh-grade English teacher. After reading this piece, summarize the other factors you see that may have contributed to Gage's success in writing.
2. In paragraph 3, Gage describes his father as "authoritarian." Explain what this means and what it tells the reader about Gage's view of his father.
3. Miss Hurd opens up a new world for Gage, and at the same time she makes him proud of his origins. Think back to your own school days. Did you ever have a teacher who made you feel proud? Describe this teacher as best you can, as well as the incident(s) that encouraged your pride. As you write, imagine that your audience will be other students

who have also been in this teacher's class. Your purpose for writing is to convince your fellow students to join you in planning a celebration on the occasion of this teacher's twenty-fifth year of teaching.

4. What do you think about Miss Hurd's advice—to compose an essay based on one's own experience? Do you think this type of assignment might be particularly effective for seventh graders, or do you think it would be very difficult for most of them? Explain.

5. Gage writes poignantly about how the spring makes him remember the last time he saw his mother. Do you, too, associate a particular season with a powerful memory (either sad or joyful)? If so, write about the season and describe specifically what you see, hear, and smell that triggers thoughts of the past.

6. Miss Hurd succeeded in finding the potential in her students. Have you ever had a teacher who sparked your potential? If so, describe this person and explain what talent or ability this person helped you develop. Explain the process and the effects of discovering this ability.

7. Gage describes Miss Hurd as a catalyst in his life. What does he mean by this metaphor? List other metaphors to describe the good teachers in your own life. Then explain why you chose these metaphors.

Suggestions for Extended Thinking and Writing

1. When Gage's piece was published, he realized how powerful language can be. Consider trying to publish something yourself. Start writing about something that deeply concerns you—perhaps an issue in your school or community. Rewrite this piece as a letter to the editor and send it out to your local or school newspaper.

2. Write an essay that publicly thanks a teacher, that is, a person either in or out of the school system, who has taught you something important. Explain the difference that he or she has made in your life. Consider your audience as you write. You are not addressing only the teacher; you are also trying to convey to others who have never met him or her the profound effect this person has had on you.

Vocabulary Check

To help ensure that you've understood this selection, and to help you develop a more extensive vocabulary, check the definitions of unfamiliar words in the selection. The words listed below may be new to you, as might others, which you should also identify and define in this exercise.

askance (5), hone (7), vocation (16), serpentine (19), eulogy (22)

Using the paragraph numbers in parentheses, which correspond with the numbers in the selection's right margins, locate the words listed above in the reading and develop definitions based on the context in which the words are used (see the guidelines for identifying meaning from context clues on pages 23–24 in Section 3). When you're satisfied with your definitions, use a dictionary to confirm the meaning of each word, and then write your own sentences using these words.

MIKE ROSE
"I Just Wanna Be Average"

Born to immigrant Italian parents in 1944, Mike Rose grew up in South Los Angeles. After beginning school tracked as a "slow learner," Rose went on to graduate from Loyola University of Los Angeles and to earn master's degrees from the University of Southern California and UCLA. He later earned a doctorate in educational psychology from UCLA, where he currently directs the writing program.

Rose is an outstanding scholar and teacher, known especially for his autobiographical book *Lives on the Boundary* (1989), which explains the school experiences of America's students who grow up without privilege or power over their education. "I Just Wanna Be Average," a chapter from that book, shows the terrifying ways students can slip through the cracks in the educational system. Rose also shows, however, that there is hope for the individual lucky enough to encounter a caring teacher and find the motivation to pursue learning both in and out of school.

Pre-Reading and Journal-Writing Suggestions

1. Do you see yourself (or perhaps a close friend or sibling) as having had a label during your school years? For instance, did your teachers or classmates see you (or your friend or sibling) as the class clown, the brain, or the quiet one? In what ways was this label fitting? What might a teacher (or classmates) have missed because of this label?
2. Describe your attitude toward school during your high school years. What interested you? What did school mean to you? What were your best moments? Your worst?
3. If you could go back and change anything about your past educational experiences, what would you change? How? Why?

It took two buses to get to Our Lady of Mercy. The first started deep in 1 South Los Angeles and caught me at midpoint. The second drifted through neighborhoods with trees, parks, big lawns, and lots of flowers. The rides were long but were livened up by a group of South L.A. veterans whose parents also thought that Hope had set up shop in the west end of the country. There was Christy Biggars, who, at sixteen, was dealing and was, according to rumor, a pimp as well. There were Bill Cobb and Johnny Gonzales, grease-pencil artists extraordinaire, who left Nembutal-enhanced swirls of "Cobb" and "Johnny" on the corrugated walls of the bus. And then there was Tyrrell Wilson. Tyrrell was the coolest kid I knew. He ran the dozens like a metric halfback, laid down a rap that outrhymed and outpointed Cobb, whose rap was good but not great—the curse of a moderately soulful kid trapped in white skin. But it was Cobb who would sneak a radio onto the bus, and thus underwrote his patter with Little Richard, Fats Domino, Chuck Berry, the Coasters, and Ernie K. Doe's mother-in-law, an awful woman who was "sent from down below." And so it was that Christy and Cobb and Johnny G. and Tyrrell and I and assorted others picked up along the way passed our days in the back of the bus, a funny mix brought together by geography and parental desire.

Entrance to school brings with it forms and releases and assessments. Mercy relied on a series of tests, mostly the Stanford-Binet, for placement, and somehow the results of my tests got confused with those of another student named Rose. The other Rose apparently didn't do very well, for I was placed in the vocational track, a euphemism for the bottom level. Neither I nor my parents realized what this meant. We had no sense that Business Math, Typing, and English-Level D were dead ends. The current spate of reports on the schools criticizes parents for not involving themselves in the education of their children. But how would someone like Tommy Rose, with his two years of Italian schooling, know what to ask? And what sort of pressure could an exhausted waitress apply? The error went undetected, and I remained in the vocational track for two years. What a place.

My homeroom was supervised by Brother Dill, a troubled and unstable man who also taught freshman English. When his class drifted away from him, which was often, his voice would rise in paranoid accusations, and occasionally he would lose control and shake or smack us. I hadn't been there two months when one of his brisk, face-turning slaps had my glasses sliding down the aisle. Physical education was also pretty harsh. Our teacher was a stubby ex-lineman who had played old-time pro ball in the Midwest. He routinely had us grabbing our ankles to receive his stinging paddle across our butts. He did that, he said, to make men of us. "Rose," he bellowed on our first encounter; me standing geeky in line in my baggy shorts. "'Rose'? What the hell kind of name is that?"

"Italian, sir," I squeaked.

"Italian! Ho. Rose, do you know the sound a bag of shit makes when it   5 hits the wall?"

"No, sir."

"Wop!"

Sophomore English was taught by Mr. Mitropetros. He was a large, bejeweled man who managed the parking lot at the Shrine Auditorium. He would crow and preen and list for us the stars he'd brushed against. We'd ask questions and glance knowingly and snicker, and all that fueled the poor guy to brag some more. Parking cars was his night job. He had little training in English, so his lesson plan for his day work had us reading the district's required text, *Julius Caesar,* aloud for the semester. We'd finish the play way before the twenty weeks was up, so he'd have us switch parts again and again and start again: Dave Snyder, the fastest guy at Mercy, muscling through Caesar to the breathless squeals of Calpurnia, as interpreted by Steve Fusco, a surfer who owned the school's most envied paneled wagon. Week ten and Dave and Steve would take on new roles, as would we all, and render a water-logged Cassius and a Brutus that are beyond my powers of description.

Spanish I—taken in the second year—fell into the hands of a new recruit. Mr. Montez was a tiny man, slight, five foot six at the most, soft-spoken and delicate. Spanish was a particularly rowdy class, and Mr. Montez was as prepared for it as a doily maker at a hammer throw. He would tap his pencil to a room in which Steve Fusco was propelling spitballs from his heavy lips, in which Mike Dweetz was taunting Billy Hawk, a half-Indian, half-Spanish, reed-thin, quietly explosive boy. The vocational track at Our Lady of Mercy mixed kids traveling in from South L.A. with South Bay surfers and a few Slavs and Chicanos from the harbors of San Pedro. This was a dangerous miscellany: surfers and hodads and South Central blacks all ablaze to the metronomic tapping of Hector Montez's pencil.

One day Billy lost it. Out of the corner of my eye I saw him strike out 10 with his right arm and catch Dweetz across the neck. Quick as a spasm, Dweetz was out of his seat, scattering desks, cracking Billy on the side of the head, right behind the eye. Snyder and Fusco and others broke it up, but the room felt hot and close and naked. Mr. Montez's tenuous authority was finally ripped to shreds, and I think everyone felt a little strange about that. The charade was over, and when it came down to it, I don't think any of the kids really wanted it to end this way. They had pushed and pushed and bullied their way into a freedom that both scared and embarrassed them.

Students will float to the mark you set. I and the others in the vocational classes were bobbing in pretty shallow water. Vocational education has aimed at increasing the economic opportunities of students who do not do well in our schools. Some serious programs succeed in doing that, and through exceptional teachers—like Mr. Gross in *Horace's Compromise*—students learn to develop hypotheses and troubleshoot, reason through a problem, and communicate effectively—the true job skills. The vocational track, however, is most often a place for those who are just not making it, a dumping ground for the disaffected. There were a few teachers who worked hard at education; young Brother Slattery, for example, combined a stern voice with weekly quizzes to try to pass along to us a skeletal outline of world history. But mostly the teachers had no idea of how to engage the imaginations of us kids who were scuttling along at the bottom of the pond.

And the teachers would have needed some inventiveness, for none of us was groomed for the classroom. It wasn't just that I didn't know things—

didn't know how to simplify algebraic fractions, couldn't identify different kinds of clauses, bungled Spanish translations—but that I had developed various faulty and inadequate ways of doing algebra and making sense of Spanish. Worse yet, the years of defensive tuning out in elementary school had given me a way to escape quickly while seeming at least half alert. During my time in Voc. Ed., I developed further into a mediocre student and a somnambulant problem solver, and that affected the subjects I did have the wherewithal to handle: I detested Shakespeare; I got bored with history. My attention flitted here and there. I fooled around in class and read my books indifferently—the intellectual equivalent of playing with your food. I did what I had to do to get by, and I did it with half a mind.

But I did learn things about people and eventually came into my own socially. I liked the guys in Voc. Ed. Growing up where I did, I understood and admired physical prowess, and there was an abundance of muscle here. There was Dave Snyder, a sprinter and halfback of true quality. Dave's ability and his quick wit gave him a natural appeal, and he was welcome in any clique, though he always kept a little independent. He enjoyed acting the fool and could care less about studies, but he possessed a certain maturity and never caused the faculty much trouble. It was a testament to his independence that he included me among his friends—I eventually went out for track, but I was no jock. Owing to the Latin alphabet and a dearth of *R*s and *S*s, Snyder sat behind Rose, and we started exchanging one-liners and became friends.

There was Ted Richard, a much-touted Little League pitcher. He was chunky and had a baby face and came to Our Lady of Mercy as a seasoned street fighter. Ted was quick to laugh and he had a loud, jolly laugh, but when he got angry he'd smile a little smile, the kind that simply raises the corner of the mouth a quarter of an inch. For those who knew, it was an eerie signal. Those who didn't found themselves in big trouble, for Ted was very quick. He loved to carry on what we would come to call philosophical discussions: What is courage? Does God exist? He also loved words, enjoyed picking up big ones like *salubrious* and *equivocal* and using them in our conversations—laughing at himself as the word hit a chuckhole rolling off his tongue. Ted didn't do all that well in school—baseball and parties and testing the courage he'd speculated about took up his time. His textbooks were *Argosy* and *Field and Stream,* whatever newspapers he'd find on the bus stop—from the *Daily Worker* to pornography—conversations with uncles or hobos or businessmen he'd meet in a coffee shop, *The Old Man and the Sea.* With hindsight, I can see that Ted was developing into one of those rough-hewn intellectuals whose sources are a mix of the learned and the apocryphal, whose discussions are both assured and sad.

And then there was Ken Harvey. Ken was good-looking in a puffy way 15 and had a full and oily ducktail and was a car enthusiast . . . a hodad. One day in religion class, he said the sentence that turned out to be one of the most memorable of the hundreds of thousands I heard in those Voc. Ed. years. We were talking about the parable of the talents, about achievement, working hard, doing the best you can do, blah-blah-blah, when the teacher called on the restive Ken Harvey for an opinion. Ken thought about it, but just for a second, and said (with studied, minimal affect), "I just wanna be average." That woke me up. Average? Who wants to be average? Then the athletes chimed in with the clichés that make you want to laryngectomize them, and the exchange became a platitudinous melee. At the time, I thought Ken's assertion was stupid, and I wrote him off. But his sentence has stayed with me all these years, and I think I am finally coming to understand it.

Ken Harvey was gasping for air. School can be a tremendously disorienting place. No matter how bad the school, you're going to encounter notions that don't fit with the assumptions and beliefs that you grew up with—maybe you'll hear these dissonant notions from teachers, maybe from the other students, and maybe you'll read them. You'll also be thrown in with all kinds of kids from all kinds of backgrounds, and that can be unsettling—this is especially true in places of rich ethnic and linguistic mix, like the L.A. basin. You'll see a handful of students far excel you in courses that sound exotic and that are only in the curriculum of the elite: French, physics, trigonometry. And all this is happening while you're trying to shape an identity, your body is changing, and your emotions are running wild. If you're a working-class kid in the vocational track, the options you'll have to deal with this will be constrained in certain ways: you're defined by your school as "slow"; you're placed in a curriculum that isn't designed to liberate you but to occupy you, or, if you're lucky, train you, though the training is for work the society does not esteem; other students are picking up the cues from your school and your curriculum and interacting with you in particular ways. If you're a kid like Ted Richard, you turn your back on all this and let your mind roam where it may. But youngsters like Ted are rare. What Ken and so many others do is protect themselves from such suffocating madness by taking on with a vengeance the identity implied in the vocational track. Reject the confusion and frustration by openly defining yourself as the Common Joe. Champion the average. Rely on your own good sense. Fuck this bullshit. Bullshit, of course, is everything you—and the others—fear is beyond you: books, essays, tests, academic scrambling, complexity, scientific reasoning, philosophical inquiry.

The tragedy is that you have to twist the knife in your own gray matter to make this defense work. You'll have to shut down, have to reject intellectual stimuli or diffuse them with sarcasm, have to cultivate stupidity, have to convert boredom from a malady into a way of confronting the world. Keep your vocabulary simple, act stoned when you're not or act more stoned than you are, flaunt ignorance, materialize your dreams. It is a powerful and effective defense—it neutralizes the insult and the frustration of being a vocational kid and, when perfected, it drives teachers up the wall, a delightful secondary effect. But like all strong magic, it exacts a price.

My own deliverance from the Voc. Ed. world began with sophomore biology. Every student, college prep to vocational, had to take biology, and unlike the other courses, the same person taught all sections. When teaching the vocational group, Brother Clint probably slowed down a bit or omitted a little of the fundamental biochemistry, but he used the same book and more or less the same syllabus across the board. If one class got tough, he could get tougher. He was young and powerful and very handsome, and looks and physical strength were high currency. No one gave him any trouble.

I was pretty bad at the dissecting table, but the lectures and the textbook were interesting: plastic overlays that, with each turned page, peeled away skin, then veins and muscle, then organs, down to the very bones that Brother Clint, pointer in hand, would tap out on our hanging skeleton. Dave Snyder was in big trouble, for the study of life—versus the living of it—was sticking in his craw. We worked out a code for our multiple-choice exams. He'd poke me in the back: once for the answer under *A,* twice for *B,* and so on; and when he'd hit the right one, I'd look up to the ceiling as though I were lost in thought. Poke: cytoplasm. Poke, poke: methane. Poke, poke, poke: William Harvey. Poke, poke, poke, poke: islets of Langerhans. This didn't work out perfectly, but Dave passed the course, and I mastered the dreamy look of a guy on a record jacket. And something else happened. Brother Clint puzzled over this Voc. Ed. kid who was racking up 98s and 99s on his tests. He checked the school's records and discovered the error. He recommended that I begin my junior year in the College Prep program. According to all I've read since, such a shift, as one report put it, is virtually impossible. Kids at that level rarely cross tracks. The telling thing is how chancy both my placement into and exit from Voc. Ed. was; neither I nor my parents had anything to do with it. I lived in one world during spring semester, and when I came back to school in the fall, I was living in another.

Switching to College Prep was a mixed blessing. I was an erratic student. 20 I was undisciplined. And I hadn't caught onto the rules of the game: why work hard in a class that didn't grab my fancy? I was also hopelessly behind in math. Chemistry was hard; toying with my chemistry set years before hadn't prepared me for the chemist's equations. Fortunately, the priest who taught both chemistry and second-year algebra was also the school's athletic director. Membership on the track team covered me; I knew I wouldn't get lower than a *C.* U.S. history was taught pretty well, and I did okay. But civics was taken over by a football coach who had trouble reading the textbook aloud—and reading aloud was the centerpiece of his pedagogy. College Prep at Mercy was certainly an improvement over the vocational program—at least it carried some status—but the social science curriculum was weak, and the mathematics and physical sciences were simply beyond me. I had a miserable quantitative background and ended up copying some assignments and finessing the rest as best I could. Let me try to explain how it feels to see again and again material you should once have learned but didn't.

You are given a problem. It requires you to simplify algebraic fractions or to multiply expressions containing square roots. You know this is pretty basic material because you've seen it for years. Once a teacher took some time with you, and you learned how to carry out these operations. Simple versions, anyway. But that was a year or two or more in the past, and these are more complex versions, and now you're not sure. And this, you keep telling yourself, is ninth- or even eighth-grade stuff.

Next it's a word problem. This is also old hat. The basic elements are as familiar as story characters: trains speeding so many miles per hour or shadows of buildings angling so many degrees. Maybe you know enough, have sat through enough explanations, to be able to begin setting up the problem: "If one train is going this fast . . ." or "This shadow is really one line of a triangle . . ." Then: "Let's see . . ." "How did Jones do this?" "Hmmmm." "No." "No, that won't work." Your attention wavers. You wonder about other things: a football game, a dance, that cute new checker at the market. You try to focus on the problem again. You scribble on paper for a while, but the tension wins out and your attention flits elsewhere. You crumple the paper and begin daydreaming to ease the frustration.

The particulars will vary, but in essence this is what a number of students go through, especially those in so-called remedial classes. They open their textbooks and see once again the familiar and impenetrable formulas and diagrams and terms that have stumped them for years. There is no excitement here. *No* excitement. Regardless of what the teacher says, this is not a new challenge. There is, rather, embarrassment and frustration and, not surprisingly, some anger in being reminded once again of long-standing inadequacies. No wonder so many students finally attribute their difficulties to something inborn, organic: "That part of my brain just doesn't work." Given the troubling histories many of these students have, it's miraculous that any of them can lift the shroud of hopelessness sufficiently to make deliverance from these classes possible.

Through this entire period, my father's health was deteriorating with cruel momentum. His arteriosclerosis progressed to the point where a simple nick on his shin wouldn't heal. Eventually it ulcerated and widened. Lou Minton would come by daily to change the dressing. We tried renting an oscillating bed—which we placed in the front room—to force blood through the constricted arteries in my father's legs. The bed hummed through the night, moving in place to ward off the inevitable. The ulcer continued to spread, and the doctors finally had to amputate. My grandfather had lost his leg in a stockyard accident. Now my father too was crippled. His convalescence was slow but steady, and the doctors placed him in the Santa Monica Rehabilitation Center, a sun-bleached building that opened out onto the warm spray of the Pacific. The place gave him some strength and some color and some training in walking with an artificial leg. He did pretty well for a year or so until he slipped and broke his hip. He was confined to a wheelchair after that, and the confinement contributed to the diminishing of his body and spirit.

I am holding a picture of him. He is sitting in his wheelchair and smiling   25 at the camera. The smile appears forced, unsteady, seems to quaver, though it is frozen in silver nitrate. He is in his mid-sixties and looks eighty. Late in my junior year, he had a stroke and never came out of the resulting coma. After that, I would see him only in dreams, and to this day that is how I join him. Sometimes the dreams are sad and grisly and primal: my father lying in a bed soaked with his suppuration, holding me, rocking me. But sometimes the dreams bring him back to me healthy: him talking to me on an empty street, or buying some pictures to decorate our old house, or transformed somehow into someone strong and adept with tools and the physical.

Jack MacFarland couldn't have come into my life at a better time. My father was dead, and I had logged up too many years of scholastic indifference. Mr. MacFarland had a master's degree from Columbia and decided, at twenty-six, to find a little school and teach his heart out. He never took any credentialing courses, couldn't bear to, he said, so he had to find employment in a private system. He ended up at Our Lady of Mercy teaching five sections of senior English. He was a beatnik who was born too late. His teeth were stained, he tucked his sorry tie in between the third and fourth buttons of his shirt, and his pants were chronically wrinkled. At first, we couldn't believe this guy, thought he slept in his car. But within no time, he had us so startled with work that we didn't much worry about where he slept or if he slept at all. We wrote three or four essays a month. We read a book every two to three weeks, starting with the *Iliad* and ending up with Hemingway. He gave us a quiz on the reading every other day. He brought a prep school curriculum to Mercy High.

MacFarland's lectures were crafted, and as he delivered them he would pace the room jiggling a piece of chalk in his cupped hand, using it to scribble on the board the names of all the writers and philosophers and plays and novels he was weaving into his discussion. He asked questions often, raised everything from Zeno's paradox to the repeated last line of Frost's "Stopping by Woods on a Snowy Evening." He slowly and carefully built

up our knowledge of Western intellectual history—with facts, with connections, with speculations. We learned about Greek philosophy, about Dante,
the Elizabethan world view, the Age of Reason, existentialism. He analyzed
poems with us, had us reading sections from John Ciardi's *How Does a Poem
Mean?*, making a potentially difficult book accessible with his own explanations. We gave oral reports on poems Ciardi didn't cover. We imitated the
styles of Conrad, Hemingway, and *Time* magazine. We wrote and talked,
wrote and talked. The man immersed us in language.

Even MacFarland's barbs were literary. If Jim Fitzsimmons, hung over
and irritable, tried to smart-ass him, he'd rejoin with a flourish that would
spark the indomitable Skip Madison—who'd lost his front teeth in a hapless
tackle—to flick his tongue through the gap and opine, "good chop," drawing out the single "o" in stinging indictment. Jack MacFarland, this tobacco-stained intellectual, brandished linguistic weapons of a kind I hadn't
encountered before. Here was this *egghead,* for God's sake, keeping some
pretty difficult people in line. And from what I heard, Mike Dweetz and
Steve Fusco and all the notorious Voc. Ed. crowd settled down as well when
MacFarland took the podium. Though a lot of guys groused in the school-
yard, it just seemed that giving trouble to this particular teacher was a silly
thing to do. Tomfoolery, not to mention assault, had no place in the world
he was trying to create for us, and instinctively everyone knew that. If
nothing else, we all recognized MacFarland's considerable intelligence and
respected the hours he put into his work. It came to this: the troublemaker
would look foolish rather than daring. Even Jim Fitzsimmons was reading
On the Road and turning his incipient alcoholism to literary ends.

There were some lives that were already beyond Jack MacFarland's min-
istrations, but mine was not. I started reading again as I hadn't since elementary school. I would go into our gloomy little bedroom or sit at the dinner
table while, on the television, Danny McShane was paralyzing Mr. Moto
with the atomic drop, and work slowly back through *Heart of Darkness,*
trying to catch the words in Conrad's sentences. I certainly was not Mac-
Farland's best student; most of the other guys in College Prep, even my
fellow slackers, had better backgrounds than I did. But I worked very hard,
for MacFarland had hooked me. He tapped my old interest in reading and
creating stories. He gave me a way to feel special by using my mind. And he
provided a role model that wasn't shaped on physical prowess alone, and
something inside me that I wasn't quite aware of responded to that. Jack
MacFarland established a literacy club, to borrow a phrase of Frank Smith's,
and invited me—invited all of us—to join.

There's been a good deal of research and speculation suggesting that the 30
acknowledgement of school performance with extrinsic rewards—smiling
faces, stars, numbers, grades—diminishes the intrinsic satisfaction children
experience by engaging in reading or writing or problem solving. While it's

certainly true that we've created an educational system that encourages our best and brightest to become cynical grade collectors and, in general, have developed an obsession with evaluation and assessment, I must tell you that venal though it may have been, I loved getting good grades from Mac-Farland. I now know how subjective grades can be, but then they came tucked in the back of essays like bits of scientific data, some sort of spectroscopic readout that said, objectively and publicly, that I had made something of value. I suppose I'd been mediocre for too long and enjoyed a public redefinition. And I suppose the workings of my mind, such as they were, had been private for too long. My linguistic play moved into the world; . . . these papers with their circled, red B-pluses and A-minuses linked my mind to something outside it. I carried them around like a club emblem.

One day in the December of my senior year, Mr. MacFarland asked me where I was going to go to college. I hadn't thought much about it. Many of the students I teach today spent their last year in high school with a physics text in one hand and the Stanford catalog in the other, but I wasn't even aware of what "entrance requirements" were. My folks would say that they wanted me to go to college and be a doctor, but I don't know how seriously I ever took that; it seemed a sweet thing to say, a bit of supportive family chatter, like telling a gangly daughter she's graceful. The reality of higher education wasn't in my scheme of things: no one in the family had gone to college; only two of my uncles had completed high school. I figured I'd get a night job and go to the local junior college because I knew that Snyder and Company were going there to play ball. But I hadn't even prepared for that. When I finally said, "I don't know," MacFarland looked down at me— I was seated in his office—and said, "Listen, you can write."

My grades stank. I had A's in biology and a handful of B's in a few English and social science classes. All the rest were C's—or worse. Mac-Farland said I would do well in his class and laid down the law about doing well in the others. Still, the record for my first three years wouldn't have been acceptable to any four-year school. To nobody's surprise, I was turned down flat by USC and UCLA. But Jack MacFarland was on the case. He had received his bachelor's degree from Loyola University, so he made calls to old professors and talked to somebody in admissions and wrote me a strong letter. Loyola finally accepted me as a probationary student. I would be on trial for the first year, and if I did okay, I would be granted regular status. MacFarland also intervened to get me a loan, for I could never have afforded a private college without it. Four more years of religion classes and four more years of boys at one school, girls at another. But at least I was going to college. Amazing.

In my last semester of high school, I elected a special English course fashioned by Mr. MacFarland, and it was through this elective that there arose at Mercy a fledgling literati. Art Mitz, the editor of the school newspaper and a very smart guy, was the kingpin. He was joined by me and by Mark Dever, a quiet boy who wrote beautifully and who would die before he was forty. MacFarland occasionally invited us to his apartment, and those visits became the high point of our apprenticeship: we'd clamp on our training wheels and drive to his salon.

He lived in a cramped and cluttered place near the airport, tucked away in the kind of building that architectural critic Reyner Banham calls a *dingbat*. Books were all over: stacked, piled, tossed, and crated, underlined and dog eared, well worn and new. Cigarette ashes crusted with coffee in saucers or spilled over the sides of motel ashtrays. The little bedroom had, along two of its walls, bricks and boards loaded with notes, magazines, and oversized books. The kitchen joined the living room, and there was a stack of German newspapers under the sink. I had never seen anything like it: a great flophouse of language furnished by City Lights and Café le Metro. I read every title. I flipped through paperbacks and scanned jackets and memorized names: Gogol, *Finnegans Wake,* Djuna Barnes, Jackson Pollock, *A Coney Island of the Mind,* F. O. Matthiessen's *American Renaissance,* all sorts of Freud, *Troubled Sleep,* Man Ray, *The Education of Henry Adams,* Richard Wright, *Film as Art,* William Butler Yeats, Marguerite Duras, *Redburn, A Season in Hell, Kapital.* On the cover of Alain-Fournier's *The Wanderer* was an Edward Gorey drawing of a young man on a road winding into dark trees. By the hotplate sat a strange Kafka novel called *Amerika,* in which an adolescent hero crosses the Atlantic to find the Nature Theater of Oklahoma. Art and Mark would be talking about a movie or the school newspaper, and I would be consuming my English teacher's library. It was heady stuff. I felt like a Pop Warner athlete on steroids.

Art, Mark, and I would buy stogies and triangulate from MacFarland's apartment to the Cinema, which now shows X-rated films but was then L.A.'s premier art theater, and then to the musty Cherokee Bookstore in Hollywood to hobnob with beatnik homosexuals—smoking, drinking bourbon and coffee, and trying out awkward phrases we'd gleaned from our mentor's bookshelves. I was happy and precocious and a little scared as well, for Hollywood Boulevard was thick with a kind of decadence that was foreign to the South Side. After the Cherokee, we would head back to the security of MacFarland's apartment, slaphappy with hipness.

Let me be the first to admit that there was a good deal of adolescent passion in this embrace of the avant-garde: self-absorption, sexually charged pedantry, an elevation of the odd and abandoned. Still it was a time during which I absorbed an awful lot of information: long lists of titles, images from expressionist paintings, new wave shibboleths, snippets of philosophy, and names that read like Steve Fusco's misspellings—Goethe, Nietzsche, Kierkegaard. Now this is hardly the stuff of deep understanding. But it was an introduction, a phrase book, a Baedeker to a vocabulary of ideas, and it felt good at the time to know all these words. With hindsight I realize how layered and important that knowledge was.

It enabled me to do things in the world. I could browse bohemian bookstores in far-off, mysterious Hollywood; I could go to the Cinema and see events through the lenses of European directors; and, most of all, I could share an evening, talk that talk, with Jack MacFarland, the man I most admired at the time. Knowledge was becoming a bonding agent. Within a year or two, the persona of the disaffected hipster would prove too cynical, too alienated to last. But for a time it was new and exciting: it provided a critical perspective on society, and it allowed me to act as though I were living beyond the limiting boundaries of South Vermont.

Suggestions for Writing and Discussion
1. Respond to this piece. Did you enjoy it? Identify with it? Find it difficult? Boring? Something else? Explain.
2. In paragraph 2, Rose refers to the Stanford-Binet test. From what he says in the rest of the paragraph, what kind of test do you think this is? How can you infer the definition of this test from the details that Rose provides?
3. Rose's experience was based on what is known in education as tracking or homogeneous grouping. Did the schools you attended use this system of grouping? How did grouping (or nongrouping) work out for you? Based on your own experiences, what do you see as the advantages and disadvantages of tracking? Write your response in the form of a report you might send to the school committee, the principal, or the guidance counselors of the secondary school you attended.
4. Rose gives five examples of different teachers in his high school. What are the general characteristics of each teacher?
5. After Brother Clint discovered that Rose was misplaced in his classes, Rose says he hadn't quite "caught onto the rules of the game: why work hard in a class that didn't catch my fancy?" What are the "rules of the game" in education today? What advice would you give to a student who finds a particular (required) class boring?
6. Rose's most influential teacher, Jack MacFarland, "immersed" his class in language. What subjects—if any—have you been immersed in during your educational experience? What subjects were taught to you on a surface, cursory level? What effect did each approach have on you?

Suggestions for Extended Thinking and Writing
1. Write an imaginary letter to your school district's school board in which you describe the positive, as well as the negative, experiences you had during your high school years.

2. Write an essay in which you compare your attitude to learning with Mike Rose's. Use specific episodes from your school experiences and show how they contributed to making your attitude similar to or different from Rose's.

Vocabulary Check

To help ensure that you've understood this selection, and to help you develop a more extensive vocabulary, check the definitions of unfamiliar words in the selection. The words listed below may be new to you, as might others, which you should also identify and define in this exercise.

euphemism (2), hypotheses (11), apocryphal (14), suppuration (25), shibboleth (36)

Using the paragraph numbers in parentheses, which correspond with the numbers in the selection's right margins, locate the words listed above in the reading and develop definitions based on the context in which the words are used (see the guidelines for identifying meaning from context clues on pages 23–24 in Section 3). When you're satisfied with your definitions, use a dictionary to confirm the meaning of each word, and then write your own sentences using these words.

MALCOLM X

Prison Studies

Born in 1925 to Nebraska Baptist minister Earl Little, who was slain by the Ku Klux Klan for promoting black rebellion through his Back-to-Africa movement, Malcolm X worked actively in support of black unity and separatism until his own murder in a Harlem ballroom in 1965.

Although he was an excellent student, Malcolm dropped out of high school after being told by a racist teacher to abandon his aspirations of becoming a lawyer and be "realistic about being a nigger" (*Contemporary Authors,* vol. 125, p. 294).

His subsequent move to Boston led him to criminal associations— gambling, theft, and drug addiction—and ten years of imprisonment. Frequently confined to solitary, he eventually discovered the library and immersed himself in philosophy, politics, and the creed of the Black Muslims' Lost-Found Nation of Islam, which preached the superiority of the black race and depicted the white race as evil and doomed to destruction.

Upon his release from prison, he worked in Elijah Muhammad's Black Muslims sect, but eventually became disillusioned with Muhammad's materialism and sexual harassment and the antagonism of his followers. He left to found his own Organization of Afro-American Unity, using his dynamic and forceful lectures to foster the worldwide unity of blacks and total withdrawal from Western culture.

Malcolm's founding of his rival organization enraged Muhammad and early in 1965 his followers gunned down Malcolm as he was preparing to make one of his famously incendiary speeches.

The crusade of Malcolm X survives in his writings: *The Autobiography of Malcolm X* and several books of lectures and letters.

Pre-Reading and Journal-Writing Suggestions

1. How important is reading in your life? Would your life be significantly different if you could not read? Explain.
2. Write about something you think you could learn on your own. What would you have to do to be successful? Where would you start? How long would it take?
3. Make a list of at least twenty topics you're curious about.

Many who today hear me somewhere in person, or on television, or those who read something I've said, will think I went to school far beyond the eighth grade. This impression is due entirely to my prison studies.

It had really begun back in the Charlestown Prison, when Bimbi first made me feel envy of his stock of knowledge. Bimbi had always taken charge of any conversation he was in, and I had tried to emulate him. But every book I picked up had few sentences which didn't contain anywhere from one to nearly all of the words that might as well have been in Chinese. When I just skipped those words, of course, I really ended up with little idea of what the book said. So I had come to the Norfolk Prison Colony still going through only book-reading motions. Pretty soon, I would have quit even these motions, unless I had received the motivation that I did.

I saw that the best thing I could do was get hold of a dictionary—to study, to learn some words. I was lucky enough to reason also that I should try to improve my penmanship. It was sad. I couldn't even write in a straight line. It was both ideas together that moved me to request a dictionary along with some tablets and pencils from the Norfolk Prison Colony school.

I spent two days just riffling uncertainly through the dictionary's pages. I'd never realized so many words existed! I didn't know which words I needed to learn. Finally, to start some kind of action, I began copying.

In my slow, painstaking, ragged handwriting, I copied into my tablet everything printed on that first page, down to the punctuation marks. 5

I believe it took me a day. Then, aloud, I read back, to myself, everything I'd written on the tablet. Over and over, aloud, to myself, I read my own handwriting.

I woke up the next morning, thinking about those words—immensely proud to realize that not only had I written so much at one time, but I'd written words that I never knew were in the world. Moreover, with a little effort, I also could remember what many of these words meant. I reviewed the words whose meanings I didn't remember. Funny thing, from the dictionary first page right now, that "aardvark" springs to my mind. The dictionary had a picture of it, a long-tailed, long-eared, burrowing African mammal, which lives off termites caught by sticking out its tongue as an anteater does for ants.

I was so fascinated that I went on—I copied the dictionary's next page. And the same experience came when I studied that. With every succeeding page, I also learned of people and places and events from history. Actually the dictionary is like a miniature encyclopedia. Finally the dictionary's A section had filled a whole tablet—and I went on into the B's. That was the way I started copying what eventually became the entire dictionary. It went a lot faster after so much practice helped me to pick up handwriting speed. Between what I wrote in my tablet, and writing letters, during the rest of my time in prison I would guess I wrote a million words.

I suppose it was inevitable that as my word-base broadened, I could for the first time pick up a book and read and now begin to understand what the book was saying. Anyone who has read a great deal can imagine the new world that opened. Let me tell you something; from then until I left that prison, in every free moment I had, if I was not reading in the library, I was reading on my bunk. You couldn't have gotten me out of books with a wedge. Between Mr. Muhammad's teachings, my correspondence, my visitors—usually Ella and Reginald—and my reading of books, months passed without my even thinking about being imprisoned. In fact, up to then, I never had been so truly free in my life. . . .

As you can imagine, especially in a prison where there was heavy em- 10 phasis on rehabilitation, an inmate was smiled upon if he demonstrated an unusually intense interest in books. There was a sizable number of well-read inmates, especially the popular debaters. Some were said by many to be practically walking encyclopedias. They were almost celebrities. No university would ask any student to devour literature as I did when this new world opened to me, of being able to read and *understand.*

I read more in my room than in the library itself. An inmate who was known to read a lot could check out more than the permitted maximum number of books. I preferred reading in the total isolation of my own room.

When I had progressed to really serious reading, every night at about ten P.M. I would be outraged with the "lights out." It always seemed to catch me right in the middle of something engrossing.

Fortunately, right outside my door was a corridor light that cast a glow into my room. The glow was enough to read by, once my eyes adjusted to it. So when "lights out" came, I would sit on the floor where I could continue reading in that glow.

At one-hour intervals the night guards paced past every room. Each time I heard the approaching footsteps, I jumped into bed and feigned sleep. And as soon as the guard passed, I got back out of bed onto the floor area of that light-glow, where I would read for another fifty-eight minutes—until the guard approached again. That went on until three or four every morning. Three or four hours of sleep a night was enough for me. Often in the years in the streets I had slept less than that.

I have often reflected upon the new vistas that reading opened to me. I 15 knew right there in prison that reading had changed forever the course of my life. As I see it today, the ability to read awoke inside me some long dormant craving to be mentally alive. I certainly wasn't seeking any degree, the way a college confers a status symbol upon its students. My homemade education gave me, with every additional book that I read, a little bit more sensitivity to the deafness, dumbness, and blindness that was afflicting the black race in America. Not long ago, an English writer telephoned me from London, asking questions. One was, "What's your alma mater?" I told him, "Books." You will never catch me with a free fifteen minutes in which I'm not studying something I feel might be able to help the black man. . . .

Every time I catch a plane, I have with me a book that I want to read—and that's a lot of books these days. If I weren't out here every day battling the white man, I could spend the rest of my life reading, just satisfying my curiosity—because you can hardly mention anything I'm not curious about. I don't think anybody ever got more out of going to prison than I did. In fact, prison enabled me to study far more intensively than I would have if my life had gone differently and I had attended some college. I imagine that one of the biggest troubles with colleges is there are too many distractions, too much panty-raiding, fraternities, and boola-boola and all of that. Where else but in prison could I have attacked my ignorance by being able to study intensely sometimes as much as fifteen hours a day?

Suggestions for Writing and Discussion
1. In general, what do you think about Malcolm X's approach to learning?
2. What motivated Malcolm to continue in his studies? Why do you think he was motivated at this point in his life when he hadn't been before?
3. What specific audience might Malcolm X have intended for this piece? What message do you think he most wants to impart here?
4. Explain how his purpose for learning changes from the beginning of his learning experience to later when he is a free man.
5. How would you answer his last question?

Suggestions for Extended Thinking and Writing
1. Choose one topic from your curiosity list and then go to three written sources to satisfy your curiosity about this topic. Write a brief report explaining what you learned and what questions and new issues this research process raised.
2. Try Malcolm X's process for learning about words for yourself. Pick one page from a dictionary and copy each word, each definition, each marking on that page. When you are finished, come to some conclusions about what you learned from this exercise.
3. Read a book that's considered a classic that you've always wanted to read. Choose a friend or relative to read this book along with you, and keep a journal of your reading and sharing experience.

Vocabulary Check
To help ensure that you've understood this selection, and to help you develop a more extensive vocabulary, check the definitions of unfamiliar words in the selection. The words listed below may be new to you, as might others, which you should also identify and define in this exercise.

emulate (2), riffling (4), feigned (14), vistas (15), dormant (15)

Using the paragraph numbers in parentheses, which correspond with the numbers in the selection's right margins, locate the words listed above in the reading and develop definitions based on the context in which the words are used (see the guidelines for identifying meaning from context clues on pages 23–24 in Section 3). When you're satisfied with your definitions, use a dictionary to confirm the meaning of each word, and then write your own sentences using these words.

GRACE PALEY
The Loudest Voice

Born into a family of socialist Russian Jews in 1922, Grace Paley spent hours listening to the tales of her parents, uncles, and aunts. Although she earned poor grades in high school (because, she claimed, she was "writing poetry and thinking about boys"), the stories her relatives told, alternately in Russian, English, and Yiddish, inspired Paley to become a writer. Long before Paley was born, these tales originated in the ghettos of eastern Europe as overloaded wagons and crowded trains moved toward the great port cities transporting hundreds of immigrants to steerage compartments in the ships that would carry them to the United States. As she explained in an interview with *Shenandoah* magazine (1981), when she first began writing, Paley found herself too focused on "me—me—me." To get beyond this point, she started listening carefully to "other people's voices" and integrating them into her work by "writing with an accent." In "The Loudest Voice," she offers a fictional picture of a young Jewish girl who learns to listen to the voices around her and to value them all, yet to recognize that her own voice is especially important.

Pre-Reading and Journal-Writing Suggestions
1. What is one ability that makes you feel proud of yourself—something you can do better than most others?
2. If you could play a starring role in any play or film you've seen, which would you choose? Explain.

There is a certain place where dumbwaiters boom, doors slam, dishes   *1*
crash; every window is a mother's mouth bidding the street shut up, go skate somewhere else, come home. My voice is the loudest.

There, my own mother is still as full of breathing as me and the grocer stands up to speak to her. "Mrs. Abramowitz," he says, "people should not be afraid of their children."

"Ah, Mr. Bialik," my mother replies, "if you say to her or her father 'Ssh,' they say, 'In the grave it will be quiet.'"

"From Coney Island to the cemetery," says my papa. "It's the same subway; it's the same fare."

I am right next to the pickle barrel. My pinky is making tiny whirlpools   *5*
in the brine. I stop a moment to announce: "Campbell's Tomato Soup. Campbell's Vegetable Beef Soup. Campbell's S-c-otch Broth . . ."

"Be quiet," the grocer says, "the labels are coming off."

"Please, Shirley, be a little quiet," my mother begs me.

In that place the whole street groans: Be quiet! Be quiet! but steals from the happy chorus of my inside self not a tittle or a jot.

There, too, but just around the corner, is a red brick building that has been old for many years. Every morning the children stand before it in double lines which must be straight. They are not insulted. They are waiting anyway.

I am usually among them. I am, in fact, the first, since I begin with "A."   10

One cold morning the monitor tapped me on the shoulder. "Go to Room 409, Shirley Abramowitz," he said. I did as I was told. I went in a hurry up a down staircase to Room 409, which contained sixth-graders. I had to wait at the desk without wiggling until Mr. Hilton, their teacher, had time to speak.

After five minutes he said, "Shirley?"

"What?" I whispered.

He said, "My! My! Shirley Abramowitz! They told me you had a particularly loud, clear voice and read with lots of expression. Could that be true?"

"Oh, yes," I whispered.   15

"In that case, don't be silly; I might very well be your teacher someday. Speak up, speak up."

"Yes," I shouted.

"More like it," he said. "Now, Shirley, can you put a ribbon in your hair or a bobby pin? It's too messy."

"Yes!" I bawled.

"Now, now, calm down." He turned to the class. "Children, not a   20 sound. Open at page 39. Read till 52. When you finish, start again." He looked me over once more. "Now, Shirley, you know, I suppose, that Christmas is coming. We are preparing a beautiful play. Most of the parts have been given out. But I still need a child with a strong voice, lots of stamina. Do you know what stamina is? You do? Smart kid. You know, I heard you read 'The Lord is my shepherd' in Assembly yesterday. I was very impressed. Wonderful delivery. Mrs. Jordan, your teacher, speaks highly of you. Now listen to me, Shirley Abramowitz, if you want to take the part and be in the play, repeat after me, 'I swear to work harder than I ever did before.'"

I looked to heaven and said at once, "Oh, I swear." I kissed my pinky and looked at God.

"That is an actor's life, my dear," he explained. "Like a soldier's, never tardy or disobedient to his general, the director. Everything," he said, "absolutely everything will depend on you."

That afternoon, all over the building, children scraped and scrubbed the turkeys and the sheaves of corn off the schoolroom windows. Goodbye

Thanksgiving. The next morning a monitor brought red paper and green paper from the office. We made new shapes and hung them on the walls and glued them to the doors.

The teachers became happier and happier. Their heads were ringing like the bells of childhood. My best friend Evie was prone to evil, but she did not get a single demerit for whispering. We learned "Holy Night" without an error. "How wonderful!" said Miss Glacé, the student teacher. "To think that some of you don't even speak the language!" We learned "Deck the Halls" and "Hark! The Herald Angels." . . . They weren't ashamed and we weren't embarrassed.

Oh, but when my mother heard about it all, she said to my father: 25 "Misha, you don't know what's going on there. Cramer is the head of the Tickets Committee."

"Who?" asked my father. "Cramer? Oh yes, an active woman."

"Active? Active has to have a reason. Listen," she said sadly, "I'm surprised to see my neighbors making tra-la-la for Christmas."

My father couldn't think of what to say to that. Then he decided: "You're in America! Clara, you wanted to come here. In Palestine the Arabs would be eating you alive. Europe you had pogroms. Argentina is full of Indians. Here you got Christmas. . . . Some joke, ha?"

"Very funny, Misha. What is becoming of you? If we came to a new country a long time ago to run away from tyrants, and instead we fall into a creeping pogrom, that our children learn a lot of lies, so what's the joke? Ach, Misha, your idealism is going away."

"So is your sense of humor."   30

"That I never had, but idealism you had a lot of."

"I'm the same Misha Abramovitch, I didn't change an iota. Ask anyone."

"Only ask me," says my mama, may she rest in peace. "I got the answer." Meanwhile the neighbors had to think of what to say too.

Marty's father said: "You know, he has a very important part, my boy."   35

"Mine also," said Mr. Sauerfeld.

"Not my boy!" said Mrs. Klieg. "I said to him no. The answer is no. When I say no! I mean no!"

The rabbi's wife said, "It's disgusting!" But no one listened to her. Under the narrow sky of God's great wisdom she wore a strawberry-blond wig.

Every day was noisy and full of experience. I was Right-hand Man. Mr. Hilton said: "How could I get along without you, Shirley?"

He said: "Your mother and father ought to get down on their knees   40 every night and thank God for giving them a child like you."

He also said: "You're absolutely a pleasure to work with, my dear, dear child."

Sometimes he said: "For God's sakes, what did I do with the script? Shirley! Shirley! Find it."

Then I answered quietly: "Here it is, Mr. Hilton."

Once in a while, when he was very tired, he would cry out: "Shirley, I'm just tired of screaming at those kids. Will you tell Ira Pushkov not to come in till Lester points to that star the second time?"

Then I roared: "Ira Pushkov, what's the matter with you? Dope! Mr. 45 Hilton told you five times already, don't come in till Lester points to that star the second time."

"Ach, Clara," my father asked, "what does she do there till six o'clock she can't even put the plates on the table?"

"Christmas," said my mother coldly.

"Ho! Ho!" my father said. "Christmas. What's the harm? After all, history teaches everyone. We learn from reading this is a holiday from pagan times also, candles, lights, even Chanukah. So we learn it's not altogether Christian. So if they think it's a private holiday, they're only ignorant, not patriotic. What belongs to history, belongs to all men. You want to go back to the Middle Ages? Is it better to shave your head with a secondhand razor? Does it hurt Shirley to learn to speak up? It does not. So maybe someday she won't live between the kitchen and the shop. She's not a fool."

I thank you, Papa, for your kindness. It is true about me to this day. I am foolish but I am not a fool.

That night my father kissed me and said with great interest in my career, 50 "Shirley, tomorrow's your big day. Congrats."

"Save it," my mother said. Then she shut all the windows in order to prevent tonsillitis.

In the morning it snowed. On the street corner a tree had been decorated for us by a kind city administration. In order to miss its chilly shadow our neighbors walked three blocks east to buy a loaf of bread. The butcher pulled down black window shades to keep the colored lights from shining on his chickens. Oh, not me. On the way to school, with both my hands I tossed it a kiss of tolerance. Poor thing, it was a stranger in Egypt.

I walked straight into the auditorium past the staring children. "Go ahead, Shirley!" said the monitors. Four boys, big for their age, had already started work as propmen and stagehands.

Mr. Hilton was very nervous. He was not even happy. Whatever he started to say ended in a sideward look of sadness. He sat slumped in the middle of the first row and asked me to help Miss Glacé. I did this, although she thought my voice too resonant and said, "Show-off!"

Parents began to arrive long before we were ready. They wanted to 55 make a good impression. From among the yards of drapes I peeked out at the audience. I saw my embarrassed mother.

Ira, Lester, and Meyer were pasted to their beards by Miss Glacé. She almost forgot to thread the star on its wire, but I reminded her. I coughed a few times to clear my throat. Miss Glacé looked around and saw that everyone was in costume and on line waiting to play his part. She whispered, "All right . . ." Then:

Jackie Sauerfeld, the prettiest boy in first grade, parted the curtains with his skinny elbow and in a high voice sang out:

"Parents dear
We are here
To make a Christmas play in time.
It we give
In narrative
And illustrate with pantomime."

He disappeared.

My voice burst immediately from the wings to the great shock of Ira, Lester, and Meyer, who were waiting for it but were surprised all the same. "I remember, I remember, the house where I was born . . ."

Miss Glacé yanked the curtain open and there it was, the house—an old hayloft, where Celia Kornbluh lay in the straw with Cindy Lou, her favorite doll. Ira, Lester, and Meyer moved slowly from the wings toward her, sometimes pointing to a moving star and sometimes ahead to Cindy Lou.

It was a long story and it was a sad story. I carefully pronounced all the words about my lonesome childhood, while little Eddie Braunstein wandered upstage and down with his shepherd's stick, looking for sheep. I brought up lonesomeness again, and not being understood at all except by some women everybody hated. Eddie was too small for that and Marty Groff took his place, wearing his father's prayer shawl. I announced twelve friends, and half the boys in the fourth grade gathered round Marty, who stood on an orange crate while my voice harangued. Sorrowful and loud, I declaimed about love and God and Man, but because of the terrible deceit of Abie Stock we came suddenly to a famous moment. Marty, whose remembering tongue I was, waited at the foot of the cross. He stared desperately at the audience. I groaned, "My God, my God, why hast thou forsaken me?" The soldiers who were sheiks grabbed poor Marty to pin him up to die, but he wrenched free, turned again to the audience, and spread his arms aloft to show despair and the end. I murmured at the top of my voice, "The rest is silence, but as everyone in this room, in this city—in this world—now knows, I shall have life eternal."

That night Mrs. Kornbluh visited our kitchen for a glass of tea.

"How's the virgin?" asked my father with a look of concern.

"For a man with a daughter, you got a fresh mouth, Abramovitch."   65
"Here," said my father kindly, "have some lemon, it'll sweeten your disposition."

They debated a little in Yiddish, then fell in a puddle of Russian and Polish. What I understood next was my father, who said, "Still and all, it was certainly a beautiful affair, you have to admit, introducing us to the beliefs of a different culture."

"Well, yes," said Mrs. Kornbluh. "The only thing . . . you know Charlie Turner—that cute boy in Celia's class—a couple others? They got very small parts or no part at all. In very bad taste, it seemed to me. After all, it's their religion."

"Ach," explained my mother, "what could Mr. Hilton do? They got very small voices; after all, why should they holler? The English language they know from the beginning by heart. They're blond like angels. You think it's so important they should get in the play? Christmas . . . the whole piece of goods . . . they own it."

I listened and listened until I couldn't listen any more. Too sleepy, I   70
climbed out of bed and kneeled. I made a little church of my hands and said, "Hear, O Israel . . ." Then I called out in Yiddish, "Please, good night, good night. Ssh." My father said, "Ssh yourself," and slammed the kitchen door.

I was happy. I fell asleep at once. I had prayed for everybody: my talking family, cousins far away, passersby, and all the lonesome Christians. I expected to be heard. My voice was certainly the loudest.

Suggestions for Writing and Discussion
1. What kind of person is Shirley Abramowitz? If you were in school with her, do you think you two would be friends? Explain.
2. How do you define the words *conformist* and *nonconformist?* Who would you categorize as a conformist in this story? As a nonconformist? Explain your reasons.
3. Shirley has a reputation for a "loud, clear voice." When you were in school, were you known for any outstanding characteristic? Explain by telling a story that illustrates this characteristic.
4. Mr. Hilton tells Shirley that an actor's life is much like a soldier's: She cannot be late and she must always listen to the general (the director). Create an analogy that explains what your life as a student is like. Develop and explain the comparison you make.
5. Although both are practicing Jews, Shirley's parents find themselves divided on the issue of letting her participate in the Christmas program. Describe each parent's reactions. Do you sympathize equally with each position, or do you find yourself favoring one or the other?

As you write, assume that your audience is a community where the question of celebrating December holidays in public schools has been hotly debated. Your purpose is to argue for the point of view you have developed after reading and thinking about this story.

6. Only Mrs. Klieg won't allow her son to be in the Christmas play. In your opinion, when most parents are under pressure related to a controversial issue, do they give in to please their children? To please the schools? Explain your answer.

7. What does the Christmas tree on the corner symbolize to the Jewish residents who live nearby?

8. Shirley's mother comes to the performance even though she is embarrassed and against her daughter's performing. Why, then, does she come? What does her action say about her?

9. What point does Shirley's mother make when she expresses her concern with the children who got such small parts in the play? How does her view of the selection of the cast differ from Mr. Hilton's? What are his primary concerns as he casts the play?

10. Why, in the end, does Shirley see the Christians as "lonesome"? What is your response to this observation?

Suggestions for Extended Thinking and Writing

1. This story is told from Shirley's point of view. Rewrite any episode in the story through the eyes of another character.

2. If you (or one of your children) were asked to take part in a religious celebration that was contrary to your own religious beliefs, would you do it? Would you allow your child to do it? Why or why not?

3. Describe and explain, to someone outside of your culture, one special observance in which you participate.

Vocabulary Check

To help ensure that you've understood this selection, and to help you develop a more extensive vocabulary, check the definitions of unfamiliar words in the selection. The words listed below may be new to you, as might others, which you should also identify and define in this exercise.

stamina (20), prone (24), pagan (48), resonant (54), harangue (62)

Using the paragraph numbers in parentheses, which correspond with the numbers in the selection's right margins, locate the words listed above in the reading and develop definitions based on the context in which the words are used (see the guidelines for identifying meaning from context clues on pages 23–23 in Section 3). When you're satisfied with your definitions, use a dictionary to confirm the meaning of each word, and then write your own sentences using these words.

SUGGESTIONS FOR MAKING CONNECTIONS

1. Use at least two sources from this section and consider your own educational experiences as you plan and write an essay on this question: What are the most important factors to consider when planning a child's education?
2. Write an essay proposing an ideal grade school. Base your description on your personal educational philosophies and experiences.
3. Define what it means to be an educated person. As you write this definition, use examples from at least three of the selections in this section to illustrate the points you are making.
4. Write an essay exploring one of the following two alternatives to public schooling: private schools and home schooling.
5. Compare the learning experiences of two people whose stories appear in this section. Come to some conclusions about why and how these individuals learn or fail to learn.
6. Write an essay agreeing or disagreeing with the following statement: The trouble with education in the United States today is that it is a guaranteed right, whether or not a student wants to learn. To be effective, education must be a privilege, not a right.
7. Reflecting on your own educational experiences, who or what was most influential as far as your success, or lack of success, was concerned? Refer to at least two of the selections in this section when you explore your own educational experiences.
8. Write an essay in which you categorize three types of teachers. (You may use any teachers in this section as well as those in your past as examples within these categories.)

10

Health: Mind and Body

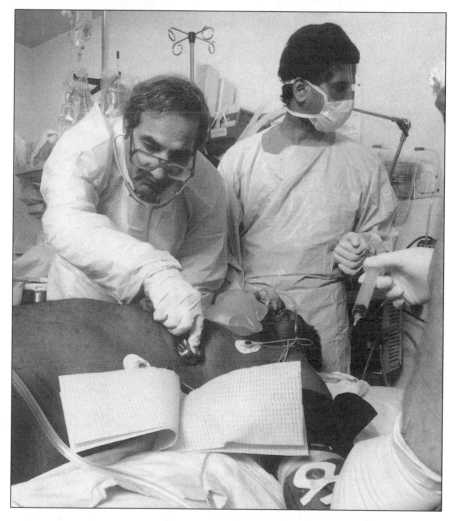

Reading Images

List the differences you see between the photograph above and the one on page 220. Then try to identify any similarities or connections. As you work, keep in mind the theme "Health: Mind and Body."

PAUL ARONOWITZ

A Brother's Dreams

While he was a medical student at Case Western Reserve University, Paul Aronowitz wrote this moving essay, showing the different worlds he and his schizophrenic brother inhabit and describing his own growing understanding of his brother's situation. "A Brother's Dreams" was first published in the *New York Times Magazine*'s weekly "About Men" column.

Pre-Reading and Journal-Writing Suggestions

1. A journal is a place for big dreams. Write about your wildest dreams, your greatest desires.
2. Write about a time you felt uncomfortable or even ashamed to be around someone you knew: a friend, perhaps, or a family member. Or write about a time someone you knew felt ashamed or uncomfortable to be around you.
3. Which handicap do you think you would have a harder time handling: a mental handicap or a physical one? Please explain.

Each time I go home to see my parents at their house near Poughkeepsie, N.Y., my brother, a schizophrenic for almost nine years now, comes to visit from the halfway house where he lives nearby. He owns a car that my parents help him to maintain, and his food and washing are taken care of by the halfway house. Somewhere, somehow along the way, with the support of a good physician, a social worker and my ever-resilient parents, he has managed to carve a niche for himself, to bite off some independence and, with it, elusive dreams that, to any healthy person, might seem trivial.

My brother sits in a chair across from me, chain-smoking cigarettes, trying to take the edge off the medications he'll be on for the rest of his life. Sometimes his tongue hangs loosely from his mouth when he's listening or pops out of his mouth as he speaks—a sign of tardive dyskinesia, an often-irreversible side effect of his medication.

He draws deeply on his cigarette and tells me he can feel his mind healing—cells being replaced, tissue being restored, thought processes returning. He knows this is happening because he dreams of snakes, and hot, acrid places in which he suffocates if he moves too fast. When he wakes, the birds are singing in the trees outside his bedroom window. They imitate people in his halfway house, mocking them and calling their names. The birds are so smart, he tells me, so much smarter than we are.

His face, still handsome despite its puffiness (another side effect of the medications that allow him to function outside the hospital), and warm brown eyes are serious. When I look into his eyes I imagine I can see some of the suffering he has been through. I think of crossed wires, of receptors and neurotransmitters, deficits and surpluses, progress and relapse, and I wonder, once again, what has happened to my brother.

My compassion for him is recent. For many years, holidays, once happy   5
occasions for our family of seven to gather together, were emotional torture sessions. My brother would pace back and forth in the dining room, lecturing us, his voice loud, dominating, crushing all sound but his own, about the end of the world, the depravity of our existences. His speeches were salted with paranoid delusions: our house was bugged by the F.B.I.; my father was Josef Mengele; my mother was selling government secrets to the Russians.

His life was decaying before my eyes, and I couldn't stand to listen to him. My resentment of him grew as his behavior became more disruptive and aggressive. I saw him as being ultimately responsible for his behavior. As my anger increased, I withdrew from him, avoiding him when I came home to visit from college, refusing to discuss the bizarre ideas he brought up over the dinner table. When I talked with my sister or other two brothers about him, our voices always shadowed in whispers, I talked of him as of a young man who had chosen to spend six months of every year in a pleasant, private hospital on the banks of the Hudson River, chosen to alienate his family with threats, chosen to withdraw from the stresses of the world. I hated what he had become. In all those years, I never asked what his diagnosis was.

Around the fifth year of his illness, things finally changed. One hot summer night, he attacked my father. When I came to my father's aid, my brother broke three of my ribs and nearly strangled me. The State Police came and took him away. My father's insurance coverage had run out on my brother, so this time he was taken to a locked ward at the state hospital where heavily sedated patients wandered aimlessly in stockinged feet up and down long hallways. Like awakening from a bad dream, we gradually began talking about his illness. Slowly and painfully, I realized that he wasn't responsible for his disease any more than a cancer patient is for his pain.

As much as I've learned to confront my brother's illness, it frightens me to think that one day, my parents gone from the scene, my siblings and I will be responsible for portions of my brother's emotional and financial support. This element of the future is one we still avoid discussing, much the way we avoided thinking about the nature of his disease and his prognosis. I'm still not capable of thinking about it.

Now I come home and listen to him, trying not to react, trying not to show disapproval. His delusions are harmless and he is, at the very least, communicating. When he asks me about medical school, I answer with a sentence or two—no elaboration, no revelations about the dreams I cradle in my heart.

He talks of his own dreams. He hopes to finish his associate's degree— 10 the same one he has been working on between hospitalizations for almost eight years now—at the local community college. Next spring, with luck, he'll get a job. His boss will be understanding, he tells me, cutting him a little slack when he has his "bad days," letting him have a day off here or there when things aren't going well. He puts out his cigarette and lights another one.

Time stands still. This could be last year, or the year before, or the year before that. I'm within range of becoming a physician, of realizing something I've been working toward for almost five years, while my brother still dreams of having a small job, living in his own apartment and of being well. As the smoke flows from his nose and mouth, I recall an evening some time ago when I drove upstate from Manhattan to tell my parents and my brother that I was getting married (an engagement later severed). My brother's eyes lit up at the news, and then a darkness fell over them.

"What's wrong?" I asked him.

"It's funny," he answered matter-of-factly, "You're getting married, and I've never even had a girlfriend." My mother's eyes filled with tears, and she turned away. She was trying her best to be happy for me, for the dreams I had—for the dreams so many of us take for granted.

"You still have us," I stammered, reaching toward him and touching his arm. All of a sudden my dreams meant nothing; I didn't deserve them and they weren't worth talking about. My brother shrugged his shoulders, smiled and shook my hand, his large, tobacco-stained fingers wrapping around my hand, dwarfing my hand.

Suggestions for Writing and Discussion

1. After reading this piece, what's your initial reaction to the author? What kind of person do you think he is? If you met him, would you like him? Why or why not?

2. Aronowitz writes that during one point in his life, he was resentful of his brother's behavior. What is your response to this reaction? Please explain.

3. After reading this piece, how would you characterize a person who has schizophrenia? As you explain what you have learned, imagine that the members of your audience have heard of schizophrenia but know very little about it. Your purpose is to help them understand the complex issues surrounding this mental illness.

4. What, if anything, did you learn or discover as you read this piece?

5. Go back to Aronowitz's piece and select the one paragraph that you enjoyed the most. Then go back and choose the one line that moved you the most. Briefly explain why you chose these two specific parts of this writing.
6. Paul's brother's schizophrenic behavior set him apart from others who were not suffering from this illness. In varying extremes, we all suffer from moments of feeling different, either because of our life experiences or for some other reason. Write a personal narrative about a time you felt different or misunderstood.

Suggestions for Extended Thinking and Writing
1. Why do some people reach their dreams while others only flounder? Contrast any other selection in this section with Paul's brother's experience as you explore this question.
2. Compare Paul's relationship with his brother with any other family relationship from the Families section (pp. 105–135).

Vocabulary Check
   To help ensure that you've understood this selection, and to help you develop a more extensive vocabulary, check the definitions of unfamiliar words in the selection. The words listed below may be new to you, as might others, which you should also identify and define in this exercise.

schizophrenic (1), resilient (1), elusive (1), relapse (4), delusions (9)

Using the paragraph numbers in parentheses, which correspond with the numbers in the selection's right margins, locate the words listed above in the reading and develop definitions based on the context in which the words are used (see the guidelines for identifying meaning from context clues on pages 23–24 in Section 3). When you're satisfied with your definitions, use a dictionary to confirm the meaning of each word, and then write your own sentences using these words.

FLORIDA SCOTT-MAXWELL

Going Home

Born in Orange Park, Florida, in 1883, Florida Scott-Maxwell completed most of her schooling at home, leaving at age sixteen for a career in the theater. Following five years on the stage, she decided to become a writer and began publishing short stories. In 1910, after marrying John Scott-Maxwell, she returned with him to his native Scotland. In addition to working for the women's suffrage movement, Scott-Maxwell studied with Carl Jung and became a practicing psychologist. She balanced her career in psychology with her career as a writer until her death in 1979.

Pre-Reading and Journal-Writing Suggestions

1. Write about your greatest fears associated with growing old.
2. What are your greatest fears associated with the word *dying*?
3. Write about your general impressions of nursing homes. Are they places you would want to spend the last years of your life? Explain.

April 3rd

I am home, I am home, I am home. I have been home for a week so that it is now natural to be here, but my joy is more than natural. I have life before me, better health, and less pain, less pain; the biggest pain gone for good, only bits of chronic pain left, sharp discomfort say, left to bother me. Not to have pain, even my degree of pain, which was always bearable, is a constant elation which will always be part of me.

When the surgeon looked at me with honest eyes and said I must have an operation, that my age was not against it, that I could not be out of pain with so bad a gall bladder, and that without it I had every chance of normal health, everything became simple and settled. I was given medicine that dulled the pain while I waited for a room in the Nursing Home. My spirits danced. I was gay, gay that I was to lose pain. Everyone was full of concern but I laughed inside. All that time when I had been in pain, when I was a burden to myself, a problem to doctors, and unconvincing to my family and friends, was over. I basked in the respect paid to an operation. People said I was brave. I wasn't brave, I was happy.

Of course I might die, I had heard of the heart giving out under an operation, it was possible, but then I would meet the great mystery. It almost seemed my chance. A mean way of slipping out though, not fair to the surgeon, and I want to be conscious that I am dying. I did not want to die, but I have lived my life—or so I used to feel. Now each extra day is a gift.

An extra day in which I may gain some new understanding, see a beauty, feel love, or know the richness of watching my youngest grandson express his every like and dislike with force and sweetness. But all this is the sentience by which I survive, and who knows, it may matter deeply how we end so mysterious a thing as living.

I had one fear. What if something went wrong, and I became an invalid? What if I became a burden, ceased to be a person and became a problem, a patient, someone who could not die? That was my one fear, but my chances were reasonably good, so all was simple and settled and out of my hands. Being ill in a nursing home became my next task, a sombre dance in which I knew some of the steps. I must conform. I must be correct. I must be meek, obedient and grateful, on no account must I be surprising. If I deviated by the breadth of a toothbrush I would be in the wrong.

A book of poems I had ordered weeks before arrived as I left for the   5
Nursing Home, and they occupied me during that long evening when I lay waiting for time to pass. Finally the night began when my body belonged to brisk strangers. The ugliness of my age was exposed to trim, fresh women. I was at last sent to have a bath at five in the morning, and then more drugs, and the strangeness of knowing less and less until knowing ceased.

Next day I was told that all was over and all had gone well. I was lost in pain and drugs and that was the only truly bad day. I thought I was screaming with pain, I could feel the screams in my throat, but days later I asked Sister and she said I had not made a sound, that few did. So it was part of the fog I was in. By the third day a sense of achievement came for I was doing my task well, no mistakes so far, and already there was that sense that came six years before when I had a fractured femur. Then I had felt so frail and weary of life that it seemed as though I had met defeat. To learn to walk again seemed beyond me. Then strength arrived and forced me to recognize that just because this accident had happened I was stronger. Where the strength and the will to use it had come from I could not imagine, but who understands the ebb and flow of energy? At first I did not believe in this new strength, but it was there, vital, mine. Now after the operation some new life was near. I must use it carefully, rest on it, test it. There was not enough yet to feel anything but hope, yet it was in the offing, I recognised it, I must do my work of being a patient with care. This was work that one did by lying still, remembering, judging. Deciding when your discomfort justified asking for help, and when it was the youness of you. I made some mistakes and then I was contrite and very reasonable. Patients must like and dislike as little as possible.

On the fourth, or was it the fifth day I saw the great wound healed for most of its length. If my body could do that then surely I could do all my body wanted of me. Then I began to feel so well that I knew I was in danger of breaking rules. I must not. I must remember that this new vitality was partly the strength that comes to me when needed, and partly sheer exhilaration, always my undoing. I must be quiet. I would woo each nurse so that rules would slacken a little, and then I would know them as woman to woman. The goodness of most of the nurses was real; some radiated goodness, one had beauty, two used professional virtue to cover bitterness, but bit by bit we blent civility with humanity and liked each other.

Then the rage I knew so well rose in me and threatened all. I heard the animal growl in me when they did all the things it is my precious privacy and independence to do for myself. I hated them while I breathed, "Thank you, nurse". At last I was allowed a bath in a tub, though with a nurse to direct my every move, and in a burst of naturalness I told her that being ill made me bad tempered, and while they were being kind and caring for me I wanted to say, "Let me alone, I'll do it myself", and oh my relief when the dear woman laughed and said, "You're the kind that get well quickly. Some want everything done for them, just won't take themselves on at all".

More and more I belonged to myself. I hopped from my bed and watered my flowers, careful not to leave a petal where it should not be. On perhaps the seventh or eighth morning I could see that the sun was shining, even the black silk bandage I wore over my eyes showed that, and before anyone had come in, at what seemed an early hour—though I had accepted that time in a Nursing Home was different from other time—I got up, threw back the curtains, opened all four windows—they would not open very wide—and expanded into the blue sky. Or so my whole heart longed to do. I wanted to be out of my body, without limit, I was rejuvenated, young, I wanted a future. I was still eighty-two, they had done nothing about that, and I wanted to scale the sky.

I remembered that yesterday four aircraft had flown in repeating circles, 10 crossing and recrossing, and I knew that would satisfy me. A moment more of joy, and I drew the curtains, resumed my black bandage, and sleepily greeted nurse when she entered with the crisp cheer of someone who has been on night duty. Later I noticed the little window in the door through which nurses assure themselves that all is well.

I was strong enough on the twelfth day to go to a non-surgical Nursing Home, and there I could look at the sea, the coast, the cliffs, and take two short walks a day. I felt so well that I thought it was the air that was curing me, for now I did everything for myself, even making my bed. Then it seemed the quiet of the scene that steadied me—the cliffs, the sea; I spent hours with a book in my hand but watching gulls and clouds. I was told that the immutable land was always moving, sliding, falling, even the caves rich in fossils almost lost now; so the land was movement, the water was movement, and the wind, mist, sunshine, rain were change, nothing was still.

I took a day or two to realize that most of the patients were too old to leave their rooms. One still strong enough to tidy her room daily was a hundred and two. She longed to die, had given up eating as the one permissible way, but became so hungry that she had to begin eating again. I was among people who could not die. How many longed to? Who should? Who can say? We cannot know what dying is. Is there a right moment for each of us? If we have hardly lived at all, it may be much harder to die. We may have to learn that we failed to live our lives. Looking at the old from outside I think—"Let them go, there is no one there. They have already gone, and left their bodies behind. Make a law that is impossible to abuse, and allow release". But inside the old, who makes the final decision? They are mysteries like everything else.

The nursing was good, homely and warm, natural compassion from country girls and kindly women. One sister was simple virtue, complete as a pearl. I asked, I had to know, was nursing the old depressing; could nurses do it only for short periods as no cure was possible? They seemed surprised and said that old people were dears, and needed help so much that everyone liked nursing them. I had seen with what grace and gentleness the nurses behaved, so here was a good that life would be poorer without, and my rational reaction was an ugly thing beside it.

Suggestions for Writing and Discussion
1. After reading this piece, what three words would you choose to characterize the speaker?
2. What are Maxwell's reactions to dying? Where do you find this information in the text?
3. Discuss the factors that contribute to her recovery, and decide which one you feel is most crucial. Explain why.
4. How does Maxwell characterize the nurse-patient relationship, and what conclusions can you draw about what a patient most needs from a nurse?
5. What do you think Maxwell means by "If we have hardly lived at all, it may be much harder to die"? Explain anyone you know who might support this statement.
6. What are Maxwell's feelings or beliefs on euthanasia? Do you agree or disagree with her?

Suggestions for Extended Thinking and Writing
1. Write a character description about the oldest person you know, and explain what this person has taught you about living and, perhaps, dying.

2. Visit a local nursing home and make observations about the setting, the people who work there, and the residents. Come to some conclusions about these three areas.

3. Conduct an interview with an elderly person with whom you feel comfortable discussing living and dying. (This project could also be done in a small group, with all group members pooling their interview information to come to some conclusions about what the elderly feel about their lives as they approach the end.)

Vocabulary Check

To help ensure that you've understood this selection, and to help you develop a more extensive vocabulary, check the definitions of unfamiliar words in the selection. The words listed below may be new to you, as might others, which you should also identify and define in this exercise.

sentience (2), sombre (3), ebb (6), offing (6), immutable (11)

Using the paragraph numbers in parentheses, which correspond with the numbers in the selection's right margins, locate the words listed above in the reading and develop definitions based on the context in which the words are used (see the guidelines for identifying meaning from context clues on pages 23–24 in Section 3). When you're satisfied with your definitions, use a dictionary to confirm the meaning of each word, and then write your own sentences using these words.

ERIC BIGLER

Give Us Jobs, Not Admiration

Born in Ohio in 1958, Eric Bigler was paralyzed from the chest down by a high-school diving accident. He later attended Wright State University in Dayton, Ohio, earning degrees in social work and business and industrial counseling management. Bigler's primary commitment is to developing computer programs for those with disabilities.

Pre-Reading and Journal-Writing Suggestions
1. Write about the first time you applied for a job. What were your hopes and fears as you went through the application process? What was the outcome?
2. What are your personal career goals? Can you foresee any factors that might prevent you from attaining these goals?
3. Write two portraits of yourself, one from your own point of view and the other from an outsider's viewpoint. After writing these two pieces, explain to the outsider what he or she cannot possibly know just by looking at you.

Tuesday I have another job interview. Like most I have had so far, it will probably end with the all-too-familiar words, "We'll let you know of our decision in a few days."

Many college graduates searching for their first career job might simply accept that response as, "Sorry, we're not interested in you," and blame the rejection on inexperience or bad chemistry. For myself and other disabled people, however, this response often seems to indicate something more worrisome: a reluctance to hire the handicapped even when they're qualified. I have been confined to a wheelchair since 1974, when a high-school diving accident left me paralyzed from the chest down. But that didn't prevent me from earning a bachelor's in social work in 1983, and I am now finishing up a master's degree in business and industrial management, specializing in employee relations and human-resource development.

Our government spends a great deal of money to help the handicapped, but it does not necessarily spend it all wisely. For example, in 1985 Ohio's Bureau of Vocational Rehabilitation (BVR) spent more than $4 million in tuition and other expenses so that disabled students could obtain a college education. BVR's philosophy is that the amount of money spent educating students will be repaid in disabled employees' taxes. The agency assists graduates by offering workshops on résumé writing and interviewing techniques, skills many already learned in college. BVR also maintains files of résumés that are matched with help-wanted notices from local companies and employs placement specialists to work directly with graduates during their job search.

Even with all this assistance, however, graduates still have trouble getting hired. Such programs might do better if they concentrated on the perceptions of employers as well as the skills of applicants. More important, improving contacts with prospective employers might encourage them to actively recruit the disabled.

Often, projects that *do* show promise don't get the chance to thrive. I   5 was both a client and an informal consultant to one program, Careers for the Disabled in Dayton, which asked local executives to make a commitment to hire disabled applicants whenever possible. I found this strategy to be on target, since support for a project is more likely when it is ordered from the top. The program also offered free training seminars to corporations on how they can work effectively with the disabled candidate. In April of 1986—less than a year after it was started and after only three disabled people were placed—the program was discontinued because, according to the director, they had "no luck at getting [enough] corporations to join the program."

Corporations need to take a more independent and active part in hiring qualified handicapped persons. Today's companies try to show a willingness to innovate, and hiring people like myself would enhance that image. Madison Avenue has finally recognized that the disabled are also consumers; more and more often, commercials include them. But advertisers could break down even more stereotypes. I would like to see one of those Hewlett-Packard commercials, for instance, show an employee racing down the sidewalk in his wheelchair, pulling alongside a pay phone and calling a colleague to ask "What if . . . ?"

Corporate recruiters also need to be better prepared for meeting with disabled applicants. They should be ready to answer queries about any barriers that their building's design may pose, and they should be forthright about asking their own questions. It's understandable that employers are afraid to mention matters that are highly personal and may prove embarrassing—or, even worse, discriminatory. There's nothing wrong, however, with an employer reassuring him- or herself about whether an applicant will be able to reach files, operate computers or even get into the bathroom. Until interviewers change their style, disabled applicants need to initiate discussion of disability-related issues.

Government has tried to improve hiring for the disabled through Affirmative Action programs. The Rehabilitation Act of 1973 says institutions or programs receiving substantial amounts of federal money can't discriminate on the basis of handicap. Yet I was saddened and surprised to discover how many companies spend much time and money writing great affirmative-action and equal-opportunity guidelines but little time following them. Then there are the cosmetic acts, such as the annual National Employ the Handicapped Week every October. If President Reagan (or anyone else) wants to help the disabled with proclamations, more media exposure is necessary. I found out about the last occasion in 1985 from a brief article on the back of a campus newspaper—a week after it had happened.

As if other problems were not enough, the disabled who search unsuccessfully for employment often face a loss of self-esteem and worth. In college, many disabled people I have talked to worked hard toward a degree so they would be prepared for jobs after graduation. Now they look back on their four or more years as wasted time. For these individuals, the days of earning good grades and accomplishing tough tasks fade away, leaving only frustrating memories. Today's job market is competitive enough without prejudice adding more "handicaps."

About that interview . . . five minutes into it, I could feel the atmo-   10
sphere chill. The interviewer gave me general information instead of trying to find out if I was right for the job. I've been there before. Then the session closed with a handshake, and those same old words: "We'll let you know." They said I should be so proud of myself for doing what I am doing. That's what they always say. I'm tired of hearing how courageous I am. So are other disabled people. We need jobs, and we want to work like anyone else.

But still, I remain an optimist. I know someday soon a company will be smart enough to realize how much I have to offer them in both my head and my heart.

Maybe then I'll hear the words so many of us really want to hear: "You're hired."

Suggestions for Writing and Discussion
1. In paragraph 1, Bigler mentions a job interview. He concludes with the outcome of the interview. Summarize the events of the interview and explain how he uses this interview to express his main idea.
2. In paragraph 3, Bigler refers to "Vocational Rehabilitation." Explain the meaning of this phrase.
3. What's your initial reaction to the author after reading this piece? Do you feel sorry for him? Indifferent toward him? Angry? Something else? Please explain.
4. After reading this piece, how would you characterize the author? Does he sound intelligent? Angry? Lazy? Sincere? Honest? Point to three places in this writing that support your response.
5. Why do you think some employers might be reluctant to hire a handicapped worker? For every reason you give, try to provide a counterargument. Imagine that you are writing a proposal for an organization

of business and industry executives who are in the process of developing a policy for hiring (or not hiring) handicapped workers. Your purpose is to provide them with many possible ways of looking at this issue.

6. What do you see as Bigler's main purpose in writing this piece? What might he hope to accomplish?

7. Reflect on the career goals you wrote about in your journal before reading this piece. Imagine, now, that you still have these same goals but that you are confined to a wheelchair. Write a letter to an employer who has just refused you this job, despite your qualifications.

Suggestions for Extended Thinking and Writing

1. Using this essay, as well as any two other sources from this text, write an extended definition paper in which you expand on the meaning of the word *right* or the word *responsibility*. Feel free to use your own experiences as illustrations as you develop this definition.

2. Write an essay in which you explain the differences between a right and a privilege. Refer to examples from this selection, as well as from your own experiences, as you explain the distinction.

Vocabulary Check

To help ensure that you've understood this selection, and to help you develop a more extensive vocabulary, check the definitions of unfamiliar words in the selection. The words listed below may be new to you, as might others, which you should also identify and define in this exercise.

reluctance (2), recruit (4), strategy (5), stereotype (6), forthright (7)

Using the paragraph numbers in parentheses, which correspond with the numbers in the selection's right margins, locate the words listed above in the reading and develop definitions based on the context in which the words are used (see the guidelines for identifying meaning from context clues on pages 23–24 in Section 3). When you're satisfied with your definitions, use a dictionary to confirm the meaning of each word, and then write your own sentences using these words.

ANNA QUINDLEN
The War on Drinks

Born in Philadelphia in 1953, Anna Quindlen was one of three children of an upper-middle-class Roman Catholic family.

Best known as a reporter and columnist for the *New York Post* and *New York Times,* her columns were targeted at women and rooted in the concerns of day-to-day life placed in the perspective of wider issues. The names she chose for her columns are indicative of her subject matter: "Home," "Life in the 30s," and "Public & Private."

Her best-selling novel, *Object Lessons,* depicts a large Irish-Catholic family in suburban New York coping with adolescent rebellion and subsequent cohesion in the mid-1960s. Another novel, *One True Thing,* deals with a daughter who postpones a high-powered career to care for her dying mother.

Quindlen's columns won honors from the Associated Press and Women in Communications, and in 1992 she was awarded the Pulitzer Prize for commentary.

Pre-Reading and Journal-Writing Suggestions
1. Write about any memories you have of personal or observed experiences with alcohol.
2. Imagine a country where alcohol and other drugs do not exist. What is it like, and how does it differ from our country today?
3. Do you feel that alcohol is dangerous in and of itself? Explain.

When she was in fourth grade the girl wrote, "What do you think   1
it does to somebody to live with a lot of pressure?" Starting at age 8 she had been cashing the public assistance check each month, buying money orders, paying the bills and doing the grocery shopping. One little brother she walked to school; the other she dressed and fed before leaving him at home.

Their mother drank.

"The pressure she was talking about wasn't even the pressure of running an entire household," said Virginia Connelly, who oversees substance abuse services in schools in New York City. "She didn't know there was anything strange about that. The pressure she was talking about was the pressure of leaving her younger brother at home."

Surgeon General Antonia Novello has opened fire on the alcohol industry, complaining that too much beer and wine advertising is aimed at young people. Her predecessor, C. Everett Koop, did the same in 1988, and you can see how radically things have changed: Spuds MacKenzie is out and the Swedish bikini team is in. There's a move afoot to have warning labels on ads for beer, wine and liquor, much like the ones on cigarettes. Dr. Novello didn't mention that; she said she would be taking a meeting with the big guys in the liquor industry. That's not enough.

There's no doubt that beer ads, with their cool beaches, cool women   5 and cool parties, are designed to make you feel you're cool if you drink, milking a concern that peaks in most human beings somewhat shy of the legal drinking age. And those sneaky little wine coolers are designed to look like something healthy and fruit-juicy; kids will tell you they're sort of like alcohol, but not really. This has joined "it's only beer" as a great kid drinking myth.

(I've got a press release here from an organization called the Beer Drinkers of America that notes that "many of the Founding Fathers were private brewers" and goes on to rail against "special interests" that would interfere with the right to a cold one. Isn't it amazing how much time people have on their hands?)

But Dr. Novello should take note of what many counselors discover: that the drinking problem that damages kids most is the one that belongs to their parents. The father who gets drunk and violent, the mother who drinks when she's depressed, the parents whose personality shifts with the movements of the sun and the bottle. The enormous family secret.

"An Elephant in the Living Room" is the title of one book for kids whose parents drink. "When I was about ten years old, I started to realize that my dad had a drinking problem," it begins. "Sometimes he drank too much. Then he would talk loudly and make jokes that weren't funny. He would say unkind things to my mom in front of the neighbors and my friends. I felt embarrassed."

That's the voice of an adult who has perspective on her past. This is the voice of a 12-year-old at a school in the kind of neighborhood where we talk, talk, talk about crack though the abuse of alcohol is much more widespread. She is talking about her father, who drinks: "I hate him. He should just stay in his room like a big dog." This would make a good commercial—the moment when your own kid thinks of you as an animal.

The folks who sell alcohol will say most people use it responsibly, but   10 the fact remains that many people die in car accidents because of it, many wind up in the hospital because of it, and many families are destroyed because of it. Dr. Novello is right to excoriate the commercials; it is not just that they make drinking seem cool, but that they make it seem inevitable, as though parties would not take place, Christmas never come, success be elusive without a bottle. It's got to be confusing to see vodka as the stuff of which family gatherings are made and then watch your mother pass out in the living room.

This is the drug that has been handed down from generation to generation, that most kids learn to use and abuse at home. I'd love to see warning labels, about fetal alcohol syndrome and liver damage and addiction. But it's time for a change, not just in the ads, but in the atmosphere that assumes a substance is innocuous because it's not illegal. For most of our children, the most powerful advertisement for alcohol may be sitting at the kitchen table. Or sleeping it off in the bedroom.

Suggestions for Writing and Discussion
1. What do you feel worked best in this essay? Explain why.
2. According to this short article, what factors contribute to alcohol abuse? What other ones might the author have mentioned?
3. If children are so traumatized by seeing their parents abuse alcohol, as Quindlen claims, then why do you think that the alcohol problem continues to be handed down "from generation to generation"?
4. How would you characterize Quindlen's style in this piece? Is it one that appeals to you personally? Explain.
5. Do you agree or disagree with Quindlen when she calls alcohol a "drug"? Explain your reasons.

Suggestions for Extended Thinking and Writing
1. Write an essay in which you categorize at least five different types of people who drink alcohol. Base your categories on people you know as well as those you have heard about.
2. Is alcoholism a disease? Write an essay in which you explore both sides of this question.
3. If you feel strongly, as Quindlen does, that advertisers are much to blame for alcohol abuse, write a letter to a specific company voicing your concerns.
4. Is alcohol abuse a problem on your campus? Conduct an interview in which you survey a variety of students at your college to come to some conclusion to this question. (Recommended as a small group project.)

Vocabulary Check
To help ensure that you've understood this selection, and to help you develop a more extensive vocabulary, check the definitions of unfamiliar words in the selection. The words listed below may be new to you, as might others, which you should also identify and define in this exercise.

predecessor (4), milking (5), perspective (9), excoriate (10), inevitable (10)

Using the paragraph numbers in parentheses, which correspond with the numbers in the selection's right margins, locate the words listed above in the reading and develop definitions based on the context in which the words are used (see the guidelines for identifying meaning from context clues on pages 23–24 in Section 3). When you're satisfied with your definitions, use a dictionary to confirm the meaning of each word, and then write your own sentences using these words.

RICHARD SELZER

The Discus Thrower

Born in upstate New York in 1928, Richard Selzer knew from early childhood that he wanted to follow in the footsteps of his physician father. After earning his MD at Albany Medical College and completing postdoctoral study at Yale, he established a private practice in general surgery, taught surgery at Yale Medical School, and served in the U.S. Army from 1955 to 1957.

Selzer combined his medical experiences with a talent for writing, publishing short stories, essays, and memoirs vividly describing the gruesome and bloody details, as well as the humanistic rewards, of a career in medicine.

In recognition of his achievements, Selzer received the National Magazine Award from Columbia University School of Journalism and honorary degrees from four colleges.

Pre-Reading and Journal-Writing Suggestions
1. From the title alone, make predictions about this piece. Where might it take place, and what might the main character be like? What message or messages might the author present?
2. Imagine that you are alone in a hospital room. You are dying, you have no one to visit you, and you are confined to your bed. Predict how you might feel and react in this situation.
3. How would you react or what would you do if you were in charge of caring for an elderly patient who was abusive?

I spy on my patients. Ought not a doctor to observe his patients by any   1
means and from any stance, that he might the more fully assemble evidence? So I stand in the doorways of hospital rooms and gaze. Oh, it is not all that furtive an act. Those in bed need only look up to discover me. But they never do.

From the doorway of Room 542 the man in the bed seems deeply tanned. Blue eyes and close-cropped white hair give him the appearance of vigor and good health. But I know that his skin is not brown from the sun. It is rusted, rather, in the last stage of containing the vile repose within. And the blue eyes are frosted, looking inward like the windows of a snowbound cottage. This man is blind. This man is also legless—the right leg missing from midthigh down, the left from just below the knee. It gives him the look of a bonsai, roots and branches pruned into the dwarfed facsimile of a great tree.

Propped on pillows, he cups his right thigh in both hands. Now and then he shakes his head as though acknowledging the intensity of his suffering. In all of this he makes no sound. Is he mute as well as blind?

The room in which he dwells is empty of all possessions—no get-well cards, small, private caches of food, day-old flowers, slippers, all the usual kick-shaws of the sickroom. There is only the bed, a chair, a nightstand, and a tray on wheels that can be swung across his lap for meals.

"What time is it?" he asks.   5

"Three o'clock."

"Morning or afternoon?"

"Afternoon."

He is silent. There is nothing else he wants to know.

"How are you?" I say.   10

"Who is it?" he asks.

"It's the doctor. How do you feel?"

He does not answer right away.

"Feel?" he says.

"I hope you feel better," I say.   15

I press the button at the side of the bed.

"Down you go," I say.

"Yes, down," he says.

He falls back upon the bed awkwardly. His stumps, unweighted by legs and feet, rise in the air, presenting themselves. I unwrap the bandages from the stumps, and begin to cut away the black scabs and the dead, glazed fat with scissors and forceps. A shard of white bone comes loose. I pick it away. I wash the wounds with disinfectant and redress the stumps. All this while, he does not speak. What is he thinking behind those lids that do not blink? Is he remembering a time when he was whole? Does he dream of feet? Of when his body was not a rotting log?

He lies solid and inert. In spite of everything, he remains impressive, as   20
though he were a sailor athwart a slanting deck.

"Anything more I can do for you?" I ask.

For a long moment he is silent.

"Yes," he says at last and without the least irony. "You can bring me a pair of shoes."

In the corridor, the head nurse is waiting for me.

"We have to do something about him," she says. "Every morning he   25
orders scrambled eggs for breakfast, and, instead of eating them, he picks up the plate and throws it against the wall."

"Throws his plate?"

"Nasty. That's what he is. No wonder his family doesn't come to visit. They probably can't stand him any more than we can."

She is waiting for me to do something.

"Well?"

"We'll see," I say.   30

The next morning I am waiting in the corridor when the kitchen delivers his breakfast. I watch the aide place the tray on the stand and swing it across his lap. She presses the button to raise the head of the bed. Then she leaves.

In time the man reaches to find the rim of the tray, then on to find the dome of the covered dish. He lifts off the cover and places it on the stand. He fingers across the plate until he probes the eggs. He lifts the plate in both hands, sets it on the palm of his right hand, centers it, balances it. He hefts it up and down slightly, getting the feel of it. Abruptly, he draws back his right arm as far as he can.

There is the crack of the plate breaking against the wall at the foot of his bed and the small wet sound of the scrambled eggs dropping to the floor.

And then he laughs. It is a sound you have never heard. It is something new under the sun. It could cure cancer.

Out in the corridor, the eyes of the head nurse narrow.   35

"Laughed, did he?"

She writes something down on her clipboard.

A second aide arrives, brings a second breakfast tray, puts it on the nightstand, out of his reach. She looks over at me shaking her head and making her mouth go. I see that we are to be accomplices.

"I've got to feed you," she says to the man.

"Oh, no you don't," the man says.   40

"Oh, yes I do," the aide says, "after the way you just did. Nurse says so."

"Get me my shoes," the man says.

"Here's oatmeal," the aide says. "Open." And she touches the spoon to his lower lip.

"I ordered scrambled eggs," says the man.

"That's right," the aide says.   45

I step forward.

"Is there anything I can do?" I say.

"Who are you?" the man asks.

In the evening I go once more to that ward to make my rounds. The head nurse reports to me that Room 542 is deceased. She has discovered this quite by accident, she says. No, there had been no sound. Nothing. It's a blessing, she says.

I go into his room, a spy looking for secrets. He is still there in his bed.   50
His face is relaxed, grave, dignified. After a while, I turn to leave. My gaze sweeps the wall at the foot of the bed, and I see the place where it has been repeatedly washed, where the wall looks very clean and very white.

Suggestions for Writing and Discussion

1. What do you find most disturbing about this piece: the behavior of the patient, the treatment given by the nurses, the reaction of the doctor, or the situation and setting? Explain.
2. Reread paragraph 19. What conclusions can you draw about what the doctor is thinking or feeling as he examines the patient's infected stump?
3. The author could have written an essay describing the scene. Instead, he chose to depend a great deal on dialogue here. How effective do you find this technique, and what does it do for the writing itself?
4. What does the word *accomplices* imply (paragraph 38)?
5. What is your reaction to the patient throwing his dish against the wall? What might he be thinking? Why might he be doing this?
6. In the end, what do you think the author's purpose was in writing this piece? What is his message, and what audience does he want to hear it?

Suggestions for Extended Thinking and Writing

1. Write an essay in which you discuss the three most important traits of a good doctor.
2. Interview several friends and family members to discover what their experiences have been with illness and the medical profession. Present your findings in a short essay.
3. Research the work of a hospice in your town or city. Write about the philosophy and work of hospice volunteers.

Vocabulary Check

To help ensure that you've understood this selection, and to help you develop a more extensive vocabulary, check the definitions of unfamiliar words in the selection. The words listed below may be new to you, as might others, which you should also identify and define in this exercise.

stance (1), vigor (2), intensity (3), forceps (19), athwart (20)

Using the paragraph numbers in parentheses, which correspond with the numbers in the selection's right margins, locate the words listed above in the reading and develop definitions based on the context in which the words are used (see the guidelines for identifying meaning from context clues on pages 23–24 in Section 3). When you're satisfied with your definitions, use a dictionary to confirm the meaning of each word, and then write your own sentences using these words.

JACQUELINE NAVARRA RHOADS

Nurses in Vietnam

Born in 1948, in Albion, New York, Jacqueline Navarra Rhoads moved to the Southwest where she has been part of the teaching faculty in the school of nursing at the University of New Mexico. From 1970 to 1971, she was attached to the 18th Surgical Hospital in Quang Tri, Vietnam, as an army nurse.

Pre-Reading and Journal-Writing Suggestions
1. Write down all the images and questions that come to your mind when you hear the phrase "Vietnam War."
2. Is nursing something you think you could ever do as a career? Explain why or why not.
3. In what ways can a person's formal education not train him or her for life in the real world?

We arrived in Vietnam on April 26, 1970, right in the middle of a   1
rocket attack. We were ordered off the plane and everyone was supposed to lay down on the ground. So here I am with my dress uniform, stockings, shoes, and skirt, and suddenly I'm lying down on a cement pavement at Tan Son Nhut wondering, "My God, what did I get myself into?" The noise was so deafening. The heat—I remember how hot it was. We eventually got inside this terminal building where there were all these guys waiting to get on the plane to go home. They were whooping it up, running around with signs saying things like: "Only one hour and thirty-five minutes left!" They saw us coming and one of them said, "Cheer up, the worst is yet to come." We stayed there sixteen hours before we could get out. When we got on the bus, all the windows were screened. I learned from the bus driver that this was to prevent the Vietnamese from throwing grenades in through the windows. I said, "But I thought the enemy was up north somewhere." He told me, "No, the enemy is all around you here. You never know who you're fighting."

My first assignment was in Phu Bai. I was there for thirty days because they needed some emergency room nurses there. Then I was transferred to the 18th Surgical Hospital in Quang Tri, just a few miles from the DMZ. They had just put a MUST (Medical Unit Self-Transportable) unit in there from Camp Evans and they needed operating and emergency room nurses right away. I was there the remainder of my tour.

I was a very young twenty-one. At St. Mary's School of Nursing in Rochester (New York), I kept these Army recruiting posters all over my room. There was a big push at that time for nurses, and we had recruiters coming to the school constantly from the time I started in 1966. I don't know what it was, I loved nursing so much. I always thought—I know it sounds crazy—but I wanted to do something for my country. I just had a feeling that being a nurse in the Army was what I wanted to do. And of course my uncles were all in the Army in World War II. There were nine brothers in my mother's family, and they all went into the Army within six months of each other.

Everyone thought I was crazy. I remember my mother saying, "Jacque, do you know what you're getting yourself into?" Of course, when you're young you have no fear.

I did basic training at Fort Sam Houston in San Antonio. My main   5
memory of that time is the parties, big parties. I never took basic training very seriously. It was only later I realized that I should have. What to do in case of a nuclear attack, what to do for chemical warfare, how to handle a weapon—these were things we laughed at. We went out to Camp Bullis and shot weapons, but as nurses we never thought that shooting a weapon was something we needed to know. True, we never had to fire weapons, but we had wounded who came in with weapons as splints, and they were loaded weapons. When that happened, I thought, "Why didn't I listen when they taught us how to take this weapon apart?" You know, an M-16 with a full magazine. We had a young guy come in, he had a grenade with the pin pulled wrapped in a handkerchief and stuffed into his fatigue pocket, a live grenade! I thought, "Gosh, if only I had listened."

I think the practice village out where we trained at Camp Bullis is still in existence. The bamboo sticks smeared with excrement, they were authentic. There was an instructor in black pajamas, camouflage makeup on his face. Well, we kind of laughed. We didn't take it seriously until we started seeing these kinds of injuries in Vietnam.

My first real exposure to the war came five days after I landed. It was at Phu Bai. We received twenty-five body bags in on this giant Chinook helicopter. You know, the Chinook is this great big helicopter, this two-blade deal that can carry one hundred to one hundred and fifty people. And this Chinook came in with twenty-five body bags aboard. One of the nurses' responsibilities was to look inside these body bags to determine cause of death. Of course, they couldn't release the doctors for such trivial work. What you had to do was open the bag, look inside and see what possibly could have killed this person, and then write down on the tag what you felt the cause of death was. It was so obvious most of the time. That's something I still have flashbacks about—unzipping these bags. It was my first exposure to maggots, something I had never seen before in my life.

One was a young guy who had had his face blown away, with hundreds of maggots eating away where his face used to be. Another one, he had his eyes wide open. He was staring up at me. I remember he had a large hole in his chest and I knew it was a gunshot wound or a grenade injury. It had blown his heart, his lungs, everything to shreds. He had nothing left but a rib cage. Evidently, they had lain out on the ground awhile before someone could get to them. The corpsmen were told to take care of the wounded first, instead of spending time getting the dead in the bags. There were GIs exposed to flame throwers or gas explosions. We used to call them "crispy critters" to keep from getting depressed. They'd come in and there would be nothing more than this shell of a person. That was a little easier to take, they didn't have a face. It could have been an animal's carcass for all you knew. But to have to go looking for dog tags, to find the dog tags on a person, that bothered me. I remember the first time I looked in a body bag I shook so badly. One of the doctors was kind enough to help me through it, saying, "Come on, it's your duty and you're going to have to do this. It's just something that I'm going to help you through. It's just a dead person." It was such a close-knit group. We were considered the most beautiful women in the world. The guys treated us special. You could have been the ugliest woman in the world, but still you were treated special.

The mass-cal, that's mass-casualty situation, traditionally was anything more than ten or fifteen wounded. It was mass chaos, bordering on panic. There'd be a corpsman walking around saying, "Dust off just called and they're bringing in twenty-five wounded. Everybody get going." So we'd pull out all our supplies. The nurses would put extra tourniquets around their necks to get ready to clamp off blood vessels. The stretchers were all prepared, and we'd go down each row hanging IVs all plugged and ready to go. It was mass production. You'd start the IVs on those people when the doctor was able to say, "This one is saved, this one is saved." We put them in triage categories. The expectant ones were the ones who required too much care. We'd make them comfortable and allow them to die. I guess it was making us comfortable too.

I remember this guy named Cliff, a triple amputee we once had. He 10 came in with mast-trousers on. Mast-trousers is an apparatus you inflate that puts pressure on the lower half of your body to allow adequate blood flow to your heart and brain. When Cliff came in, he was conscious, which was amazing. He looked like a stage dummy who'd been thrown haphazardly in a pile. One of his legs was up underneath his chin so that he was able to look down at the underside of his foot. His left arm was twisted behind his head in a horrible way. We couldn't even locate his second leg. He had stepped on a land mine. With his legs that bad, we knew there probably wasn't much backbone left. He was alive because of these trousers. The corpsman must have been right there when he got wounded. He had put him in this bag and inflated it. Cliff should have been dead.

It was really funny because he looked at two of us nurses there and said, "God, I think I've died and gone to heaven . . . a round-eye, an American, you look so beautiful." He was so concerned about the way he looked because of us standing there, "Gee, I must look a mess." But he was alert, he knew where he was. "Doc, take good care of me. I know my leg is pretty bad because I can see it, but take good care of me, doc." The docs couldn't put him in the expectant category and give him morphine to make him comfortable, because he was too alert. The docs had trouble letting go. So one of them finally said, "Well, let's get him into the operating room, deflate the bag, and let's get in there and see if we can't do something."

Well, we knew just by looking at him in that condition that he wasn't going to last, that as soon as we deflated the bag he'd bleed to death in a matter of seconds. Somehow, he knew it too. I remember I was getting blood prepared for him. He called me from across the room, "Jacque, come here quick." I went over to him and said, "What's the matter Cliff, what's wrong?" He said, "Just hold my hand and don't leave me." I said, "Why, Cliff? Are you in pain?" We always worried about pain, alleviating pain. We'd do anything to alleviate pain. He said, "I think I'm going to die and I don't want to be alone." So I stood there crying, with him holding my hand. And when we deflated the trousers, we lost him in seconds. We found no backbone, no lower part of his body. Really, he had been cut in half.

The leg that was folded underneath his neck was completely severed from his body. It was just there. The corpsmen had evidently bundled him together into the bag hoping maybe something would be there that was salvageable. And he just died. I remember he had blond hair, blue eyes— cute as a button. I had to take his body myself to graves registration. I just couldn't let him go alone. I just couldn't do that. I had to pry my hand away from his hand, because he had held on to my hand so tightly. I had to follow him to graves registration and put him in the bag myself. I couldn't let go of him. It was something I had to do.

Usually the expectants had massive head injuries. They were practically gone, they couldn't communicate with you. You were supposed to clean them up, call the chaplain. You did all that stuff, I guess, to make you feel as though you were helping them. To preserve their lives, you would've had to put them on a respirator and evac them to a neuro facility, which in our case would have been all the way to Da Nang, which was hours, miles away. I was an operating room nurse, but when there was a mass-cal, since there were only twelve of us, we'd be called into triage to work there. After that, I'd follow them into the operating room and help do the surgery. A lot of the shrapnel extractions we'd do ourselves, and a lot of the closures too. The docs would say, "Why don't you close? I got this next case in the next room." You didn't have to worry about it too much, if you got into trouble he'd be right there next door.

We wanted to save everyone. We had a lot of ARVNs (Army of the 15
Republic of Vietnam), we called them "Marvin the ARVN." We tried to
take care of the Americans first, but we also had to take care of whoever
needed care—period, whether he was a Vietnamese, a POW, or whatever.
In fact, when we tried to save Cliff, they brought in the Vietnamese who
had laid the mine. He had an amputation. He was bleeding badly and had
to be treated right away. And we saved him. I guess in my heart I felt angry
about what happened.

We were short on anesthesia and supplies. And we were giving anesthesia to this POW, which made me angry because I thought, "What if—what
happens if someone comes in like Cliff and we don't have any anesthesia left
because we gave it all to this POW?" Again, because I was very strongly
Catholic, as soon as I heard myself thinking this, I thought, "God, how can
you think that? The tables could be turned, and what if it was Cliff in the
POW's place, and how would I feel if he received no anesthesia simply
because he was an enemy?" First of all, it shocked me and embarrassed me.
It made me think, "Gosh, I'm losing my values, what's happened to me?" I
had been taught in nursing school to save everybody regardless of race,
creed, color, ethnic background, whatever. Life is life. But suddenly I wasn't
thinking that anymore. I was thinking, "I'm American, and they're the
enemy. Kill the enemy and save the American."

Before I went to Vietnam, I was kind of bubbly, excited about life. I
haven't changed that much really, I'm still that way. But back then, suddenly,
I began quesioning things, wondering about what we were doing there. I
remember talking with the chaplain, saying, "What are we doing? For what
purpose are we here?" We were training Vietnamese helicopter pilots to go
out and pick up their wounded and take them to their hospitals. And we
treated plenty of them at our hospitals, too. Yet when we'd call up and say,
"We got a wounded soldier in Timbuktu," they'd say, "It's five o'clock and
we don't fly at night." We had soldiers in the hospital shot by ten-year-old
boys and girls. We had women who'd invite GIs to dinner—nice women—
and they'd have someone come out from behind a curtain and shoot them
all down dead. I mean, what kind of war was this?

The chaplain told me, "Hey Jacque, you can't condemn the American government. We can't say the American government is wrong to put
us in this position here. We can't say, because there is so much we don't
know." It was good advice at the time, it really helped me. I was thinking, "Here I am judging, and I'm saying what the heck are we doing here,
look at all these lives lost, all these young boys and for what? And who am
I to judge that? There has to be a reason." I guess I'm still trying to hold
on to that belief, even though people laugh at me when I say it. They
think I'm living in a dream world because I'm hoping there was a good
reason.

I didn't really have much time to worry about right and wrong back then, because during these mass-cals we'd be up for thirty-six hours at a stretch. Nobody wanted to quit until the last surgery case was stabilized. By that time, we were emotionally and physically numb. You couldn't see clearly, you couldn't react. Sounds were distant. We kind of policed each other. When we saw each other reacting strangely or slowly, we'd say, "Hey, Jacque, get some sleep, someone will cover, go get some sleep." That's how close we were. That's how we coped with stress.

You didn't have time to think about how unhappy you were. It was afterwards, when you couldn't go to sleep . . . here you were without sleep for thirty-six hours, lying in your bed expecting sleep to overwhelm you, but you couldn't fall asleep because you were so tensed and stressed from what you saw. I knew I had a problem the day I was with a nurse I was training who was going to replace someone else. I remember I had completed this amputation and I had the soldier's leg under my arm. I was holding the leg because I had to dress it up and give it to graves registration. They'd handle all the severed limbs in a respectful manner. They wouldn't just throw them in the garbage pile and burn them. They were specially labeled and handled the good old government way.

I remember this nurse came in and she was scheduled to take the place of another nurse. When she saw me, I went to greet her and I had this leg under my arm. She collapsed on the ground in a dead faint. I thought, "What could possibly be wrong with her?" There I was trying to figure out what's wrong with her, not realizing that here I had this leg with a combat boot still on and half this man's combat fatigue still on, blood dripping over the exposed end. And I had no idea this might bother her.

We had a lot of big parties, too. The Army had all these rules about fraternization, how officers couldn't fraternize with enlisted. In Quang Tri, we were just one big family. You didn't worry about who had an E-2 stripe or who had the colonel's insignia. I'm not saying we didn't have problems with officers and enlisted people or things like insubordination. But everybody partied together.

I never had a sexual relationship over there. You have to remember how Catholic I was. Dating, well, you'd walk around bunkers and talk about home. Every hooch had a bunker, so you'd bring a bottle of wine and he'd bring glasses and—this sounds gross, I guess—you'd sit and watch the B-52s bomb across the DMZ. It produced this northern lights effect. The sky would light up in different colors and you'd sit and watch the fireworks. I know it sounds strange, watching somebody's village get blown up. We didn't want to think about the lives being lost.

The grunts always knew where the female nurses were. They all knew that at the hospital there was a good chance of seeing a "round-eye." Once, during monsoon season, we received a dust off call saying there'd been a truck convoy ambush involving forty or fifty guys. They were in bad shape but not far from the hospital, maybe seven or eight miles. We could stand on the tops of our bunkers and see flashes of light from where they were fighting the VC. One of these deuce-and-a-half trucks with a load of wounded came barreling up right into our triage area. Like I said, they all knew where the hospital was. The truck's canvas and wood back part were all on fire. Evidently they had just thrown the wounded in back and driven straight for us.

We were concerned about the truck, about getting it out of the way, but we were also trying to get to the wounded. There were two guys in the back, standing up. There was a third guy we couldn't see, and the first two were carrying him and shrieking at the top of their lungs. One was holding the upper part of his torso, under the arms, and the other held the legs. Their eyes were wild and they were screaming. I couldn't see what was wrong with the guy they were carrying. Everyone else on the truck was jumping off. We were shouting to these guys to get off too, that the truck was about to explode. We were screaming, "You're OK, you're at the hospital."

Two of the corpsmen got up in the truck, grabbing them to let go and get moving. The corpsmen literally had to pick them up and throw them off the truck. Once they were off, they sat down in a heap, still shrieking. It wasn't until then that I got a look at the wounded one. He didn't have a head. He must have been a buddy of theirs. The buddy system was very strong, and these two evidently weren't going to leave without their friend. We brought them to the docs and had them sedated. We didn't have any psychiatric facilities, so we got them evac'd to Da Nang. We never heard what happened to them.

After awhile in Vietnam, I guess I wasn't so young anymore. I was seeing things, doing things that I never imagined could happen to anyone. I had to do a lot of things on my own, making snap decisions that could end up saving someone or costing him his life. Like once, when I'd been there about seven months, they brought in this guy who'd been shot square in the face. It was the middle of the night and I was on duty with a medical corpsman, no doctors around at all. They were sleeping, saving their strength. We got the call from dust off that this guy was coming in. Apparently he'd been shot by a sniper. Amazingly enough, he was conscious when they brought him in. As a matter of fact, he was sitting up on the stretcher. It was incredible.

His face was a huge hole, covered with blood. You couldn't see his eyes, his nose, or his mouth. There was no support for his jaw and his tongue was just hanging. You could hear the sound of blood gurgling as he took a breath, which meant he was taking blood into his lungs. We were afraid he'd aspirate. The corpsman was this older guy, over 40 anyway, an experienced sergeant. I took a look at this guy and knew we'd have to do a trach on him pretty fast. He couldn't hear us and we couldn't get him to lie down.

I told the sergeant, "We gotta call the doc in." He told me we didn't have time for that. We had to stabilize him with a trach and ship him out to Da Nang. I told the corpsman that the only time I'd ever done a trach was on a goat back in basic training at Fort Sam Houston. The corpsman said, "If you don't do it, he'll die." So he put my gloves on for me, and handed me the scalpel. I was shaking so badly I thought I'd cut his throat. I remember making the incision, and hearing him cough. The blood came out of the hole, he was coughing out everything he was breathing in. The drops flew into my eyes, spotting my contact lenses. After the blood finished spurting out, we slid the tube in. He laid back and I worried, "What's going on?"

But he was breathing. He didn't have to fight or struggle for breath 30 anymore. I could see the air was escaping from the trach, just like it was supposed to. It was a beautiful feeling, believe me. We packed his face with four-by-fours and roller gauze to stop the bleeding. We told him what we were doing and he nodded his head. When they finally loaded him up for the trip to Da Nang, I was shaking pretty badly. The whole thing had taken less than forty-five minutes, from the time dust off landed to the time we packed him off. We never did get his name.

But three months later, I was sitting in the mess hall in Da Nang, waiting to take a C-130 to Hong Kong for R&R. I'd been in country ten months by then, and I was in the mess hall alone, drinking coffee and eating lunch, still in my fatigues. Somebody tapped me on the shoulder. I remember turning around. You have to remember, I was used to guys being friendly. I saw this guy standing there in hospital pajamas, the green-gray kind with the medical corps insignia on it. He had blond hair on the sides, bald on top. His face was a mass of scars, and you could see the outline of a jaw and chin. He had lips and a mouth, but no teeth. He looked like he had been badly burned, with a lot of scar tissue. You couldn't really tell where his lips began and the scar tissue ended.

The rest of his body was fine, and he could talk. "Do you remember me?" I was used to that, too, people coming up to me and saying, "Hey, I drove that tank by you the other day. . . ." Then he pointed to his trach scar and I said, "You can't be the same guy." He said something like, "I'll never forget you." I asked him how he knew who I was, because, I mean, there had been nothing left of his face. Apparently, the shot had flipped this skin flap up over his eyes so he could still see through the corners. I couldn't believe it. They called my flight right then, so I started saying a hasty goodbye. He mumbled something about how they had taken his ribs from his ribcage and artificially made a jawbone, and reconstructed portions of his face, taking skin from the lower legs, the buttocks.

Well, they began calling my name over the loud speaker. I remember giving him a big hug, saying I wished I had more time to talk to him. I wanted to learn his name, but I don't think he ever said it. I wanted to go back to the hospital and tell the others, "Hey, you remember what's-his-name? He's from Arkansas and he's doing fine." We always wanted to put names to faces, but we rarely got a chance to do it. You kept believing that everyone who left the hospital actually lived. When you found out someone actually had survived, it helped staff morale.

I came back home on a Friday, on a Pan American flight that landed in Seattle. I remember how we were told not to wear our uniforms, not to go out into the streets with our uniforms on. That made us feel worthless. There was no welcome home, not even from the Army people who processed your papers to terminate your time in the service. That was something. I felt like I had just lost my best friend. I decided to fly home to upstate New York in my uniform anyway. Nobody said anything. There were no dirty looks or comments. I was kind of excited. I wanted to say to people, "I just got back from Vietnam." Nobody cared. When I got home, my parents had a big banner strung up across the garage, "Welcome Home, Jacque." But that was about it. My parents were proud of me, of course. But other civilians? "Oh, you were in Vietnam? That's right, I remember reading something in the newspaper about you going there. That's nice." And then they'd go on talking about something else.

You were hungry to talk about it. You wanted so badly to say, "Gee, don't you want to hear about what's going on there, and what we did, and how proud you should be of your soldiers and your nurses and your doctors?" I expected them to be waiting there, waving the flag. I remember all those films of World War II, with the tape that flew from the buildings in New York City, the motorcades. Of course, I had my mother. My mom was always willing to listen, but of course she couldn't understand it when I started talking about "frag wounds" or "claymore mines." There was no way she could. The first six months at home, I just wanted to go back to Vietnam. I wanted to go back to where I was needed, where I felt important. The first job I took was in San Francisco. It was awful. Nobody cared who I was. I remember the trouble I got into because I was doing more than a nurse was supposed to do. I got in trouble because I was a "minidoctor." They kept saying, "You're acting like you're a doctor! You're doing all these things a doctor is supposed to do. What's the big idea? You're a nurse, not a doctor." And I thought, how can I forget all the stuff I learned—putting in chest tubes, doing trachs. True, doctors only do that, but how do you prevent yourself from doing things that came automatically to you for eighteen months? How do you stop the wheels, and become the kind of nurse you were before you left?

I was completely different. Even my parents didn't recognize me as the immature little girl who left Albion, New York, just out of nursing school. San Francisco was a bomb, and there wasn't an Army post for miles around Albion. So that's why I came back to San Antonio. All my friends were back in and around Fort Sam Houston, so I just naturally gravitated back toward my network. I came to San Antonio in 1974 to get my B.S. in nursing from Incarnate Word College. The best thing I did was to get into the reserve unit there. That's where I met my husband. It gave me a chance to share my feelings with other Vietnam veterans. It kept me in touch with Army life, the good things and the bad. It was like a family.

On weekends at North Fort Hood, we really do sit around the campfire and talk about 'Nam, about what we as reservists can do to be better prepared than we were back there. If there is another Vietnam-type war, God forbid, I just know I'd want to be part of it. I couldn't sit on the sidelines. We usually just talk about these things among ourselves. I think the reason a lot of people are hesitant to talk about it is that they don't know anyone who wants to listen. A lot of people don't want to hear those kinds of stories. A lot of people just want to forget that time altogether. I don't know why. I guess I'm just not like that.

I'm not saying you don't pay a price for your memories. Last year, I had an intense flashback while flying on a Huey (helicopter) around North Fort Hood. It was the last day of this reserve unit exercise and I was invited on this tour of the area. We were flying a dust off, a medevac helicopter, just like the ones we had back then. It was my first time up in a helicopter since. I thought "Gee, this is going to be great." One of the other nurses said to me, "Are you sure you want to do this? You're pretty tired." I brushed her aside, "No problem." We sat in back in seats strapped in next to where they held the litters. I was sitting in the seat, the helicopter was revving up . . . I don't know how to describe it. It was like a slide show, one of the old-fashioned kind where you go through this quick sequence . . . flick, flick, flick . . . now I know where they got the term flashback.

At first, it was as though I was daydreaming. What scared me to death 40 was that I couldn't turn it off. I couldn't control my mind. The cow grazing in the field became a water buffalo. Fields marked off and cross-sectioned became cemeteries. We flew over this tent, it was the 114th (reserve hospital unit) and suddenly it became the 18th surg. I was scared. All I could do was grasp the hand of this friend of mine. We couldn't talk above the helicopter roar. I just started to cry, I couldn't control myself. I saw blood coming down onto the windshield and the wiper blades swishing over it. There was blood on the floor, all over the passenger area where we were sitting. The stretchers clicked into place had bodies on top of them. I was crying. The nurse next to me kept shouting about whether I was all right. My contacts were swimming around, I wanted the ride to end. I could see why GIs felt scared . . . I couldn't just turn around and open up to the nurse sitting next to me. How could you explain something like that?

I had had a flashback or two before, but the difference was I could control them. Even when the nurse started shaking me, I couldn't turn it off. I just looked past her toward the racks in the helicopter, with bodies on stretchers, body bags on the floor, blood everywhere. When we landed, everyone saw I was visibly upset. The pilot came over to see if I was OK. The only thing I could say was, "It brought back a lot of memories." How could I explain my feelings to these people at North Fort Hood. A lot of them were too young to remember Vietnam as anything more than some dim kind of image on the nightly news. I was scared to death, because all these feelings were brought back that I never knew I had.

I still try to think of the good memories from Vietnam, the people we were able to save. A flashback has certain negative connotations. It's a flashback when they can't think of another way of explaining it. I guess I'm lucky it took fourteen years for it to hit me like that. The one positive thing I can say about it is that it felt awfully good to come back and hover down to that red cross on the top of the tent. It felt good to come home.

Suggestions for Writing and Discussion
1. From the opening three paragraphs, how would you characterize the author? What are her strengths and weaknesses?
2. After reading this entire piece, what one scene is most vivid in your mind?
3. What is your reaction to the graphic images in paragraph 8, and to what extent do you think they contribute to or detract from this piece of writing?
4. What does the example of Cliff reflect about the war, the patient, and the nurse in this piece?
5. What role, if any, does faith play in this piece? What role does humor play?
6. Does the author use either understatement or exaggeration as a writing technique in this piece? Support your answer with specific passages.
7. Is there any part that the author could have omitted and still stayed true to her point? What do you think?

Suggestions for Extended Thinking and Writing
1. Go back through this piece, isolate the most powerful images, and create a poem based on these images. Revise the poem several times to make order, rhythm, character, and theme apparent and effective.
2. Interview someone who has actually been in a war, and encourage them to tell you their stories. Write an essay in which you retell these

stories either from a first-person point of view or from the perspective of an objective reporter.

3. Write a series of "portraits" in which you use extended metaphor to explain the following concepts: war, compassion, dying, helplessness, power.

Vocabulary Check

To help ensure that you've understood this selection, and to help you develop a more extensive vocabulary, check the definitions of unfamiliar words in the selection. The words listed below may be new to you, as might others, which you should also identify and define in this exercise.

trivial (7), triage (9), stabilize (19), aspirate (28), morale (33)

Using the paragraph numbers in parentheses, which correspond with the numbers in the selection's right margins, locate the words listed above in the reading and develop definitions based on the context in which the words are used (see the guidelines for identifying meaning from context clues on pages 23–24 in Section 3). When you're satisfied with your definitions, use a dictionary to confirm the meaning of each word, and then write your own sentences using these words.

WILLIAM CARLOS WILLIAMS

The Use of Force

Williams was born into a middle-class family in Rutherford, New Jersey, in 1883. He died in the same town 80 years later after spending most of his life there in private medical practice.

Williams always loved literature, especially such poets as Keats and Whitman, but his taste underwent a radical change when he formed a friendship with Ezra Pound while studying medicine at the University of Pennsylvania. Thereafter, Williams' writing was unleashed from the rigid romanticism of the era, and he became an imaginative innovator, creating fresh and vigorous poetry. He wrote in many genres and was acclaimed as poet, playwright, novelist, and essayist. He won the Pulitzer Prize in 1963 for his volume of poems *Pictures from Brueghel*. In much of his work, Williams drew on his experiences as a rural physician for his characters and images.

Pre-Reading and Journal-Writing Suggestions
1. List all the situations you can think of in which the use of force is justified.
2. On a scale from 1 to 10 (1 being least, 10 being most), how comfortable do you feel when you go to the doctor, either for a well checkup or for a sick visit? Explain your answer.
3. Write about a time when you were quite ill. Who helped you more than anyone else?

They were new patients to me, all I had was the name, Olson. Please come down as soon as you can, my daughter is very sick.

When I arrived I was met by the mother, a big startled looking woman, very clean and apologetic who merely said, Is this the doctor? and let me in. In the back, she added. You must excuse us, doctor, we have her in the kitchen where it is warm. It is very damp here sometimes.

The child was fully dressed and sitting on her father's lap near the kitchen table. He tried to get up, but I motioned for him not to bother, took off my overcoat and started to look things over. I could see that they were all very nervous, eyeing me up and down distrustfully. As often, in such cases, they weren't telling me more than they had to, it was up to me to tell them; that's why they were spending three dollars on me.

The child was fairly eating me up with her cold, steady eyes, and no expression to her face whatever. She did not move and seemed, inwardly, quiet; an unusually attractive little thing, and as strong as a heifer in appearance. But her face was flushed, she was breathing rapidly, and I realized that she had a high fever. She had magnificent blonde hair, in profusion. One of those picture children often reproduced in advertising leaflets and the photogravure sections of the Sunday papers.

She's had a fever for three days, began the father, and we don't know $_5$ what it comes from. My wife has given her things, you know, like people do, but it don't do no good. And there's been a lot of sickness around. So we tho't you'd better look her over and tell us what is the matter.

As doctors often do I took a trial shot at it as a point of departure. Has she had a sore throat?

Both parents answered me together, No . . . No, she says her throat don't hurt her.

Does your throat hurt you? added the mother to the child. But the little girl's expression didn't change, nor did she move her eyes from my face.

Have you looked?

I tried to, said the mother, but I couldn't see. $_{10}$

As it happens, we had been having a number of cases of diphtheria in the school to which this child went during that month and we were all, quite apparently, thinking of that, though no one had as yet spoken of the thing.

Well, I said, suppose we take a look at the throat first. I smiled in my best professional manner and asking for the child's first name I said, come on, Mathilda, open your mouth and let's take a look at your throat.

Nothing doing.

Aw, come on, I coaxed, just open your mouth wide and let me take a look. Look, I said opening both hands wide, I haven't anything in my hands. Just open up and let me see.

Such a nice man, put in the mother. Look how kind he is to you. Come $_{15}$ on, do what he tells you to. He won't hurt you.

At that I ground my teeth in disgust. If only they wouldn't use the word "hurt" I might be able to get somewhere. But I did not allow myself to be hurried or disturbed, but speaking quietly and slowly I approached the child again.

As I moved my chair a little nearer, suddenly with one catlike movement both her hands clawed instinctively for my eyes and she almost reached them too. In fact she knocked my glasses flying and they fell, though unbroken, several feet away from me on the kitchen floor.

Both the mother and father almost turned themselves inside out in embarrassment and apology. You bad girl, said the mother, taking her and shaking her by one arm. Look what you've done. The nice man. . . .

For heaven's sake, I broke in. Don't call me a nice man to her. I'm here to look at her throat on the chance that she might have diphtheria and possibly die of it. But that's nothing to her. Look here, I said to the child, we're going to look at your throat. You're old enough to understand what I'm saying. Will you open it now by yourself or shall we have to open it for you? Not a move. Even her expression hadn't changed. Her breaths however 20 were coming faster and faster. Then the battle began. I had to do it. I had to have a throat culture for her own protection. But first I told the parents that it was entirely up to them. I explained the danger but said that I would not insist on a throat examination so long as they would take the responsibility.

If you don't do what the doctor says you'll have to go to the hospital, the mother admonished her severely.

Oh yeah? I had to smile to myself. After all, I had already fallen in love with the savage brat, the parents were contemptible to me. In the ensuing struggle they grew more and more abject, crushed, exhausted while she surely rose to magnificent heights of insane fury of effort bred of her terror of me.

The father tried his best, and he was a big man but the fact that she was his daughter, his shame at her behavior and his dread of hurting her made him release her just at the critical moment several times when I had almost achieved success, till I wanted to kill him. But his dread also that she might have diphtheria made him tell me to go on, go on though he himself was almost fainting, while the mother moved back and forth behind us raising and lowering her hands in an agony of apprehension.

Put her in front of you on your lap, I ordered, and hold both her wrists.

But as soon as he did the child let out a scream. Don't, you're hurting 25 me. Let go of my hands. Let them go I tell you. Then she shrieked terrifyingly, hysterically. Stop it! Stop it! You're killing me!

Do you think she can stand it, doctor! said the mother.

You get out, said the husband to his wife. Do you want her to die of diphtheria?

Come on now, hold her, I said.

Then I grasped the child's head with my left hand and tried to get the wooden tongue depressor between her teeth. She fought, with clenched teeth, desperately! But now I also had grown furious—at a child. I tried to hold myself down but I couldn't. I know how to expose a throat for inspection. And I did my best. When finally I got the wooden spatula behind the last teeth and just the point of it into the mouth cavity, she opened up for an instant but before I could see anything she came down again and gripping the wooden blade between her molars she reduced it to splinters before I could get it out again.

Aren't you ashamed, the mother yelled at her. Aren't you ashamed to 30 act like that in front of the doctor?

Get me a smooth-handled spoon of some sort, I told the mother. We're going through with this. The child's mouth was already bleeding. Her tongue was cut and she was screaming in wild hysterical shrieks. Perhaps I should have desisted and come back in an hour or more. No doubt it would have been better. But I have seen at least two children lying dead in bed of neglect in such cases, and feeling that I must get a diagnosis now or never I went at it again. But the worst of it was that I too had got beyond reason. I could have torn the child apart in my own fury and enjoyed it. It was a pleasure to attack her. My face was burning with it.

The damned little brat must be protected against her own idiocy, one says to one's self at such times. Others must be protected against her. It is social necessity. And all these things are true. But a blind fury, a feeling of adult shame, bred of a longing for muscular release are the operatives. One goes on to the end.

In a final unreasoning assault I overpowered the child's neck and jaws. I forced the heavy silver spoon back of her teeth and down her throat till she gagged. And there it was—both tonsils covered with membrane. She had fought valiantly to keep me from knowing her secret. She had been hiding that sore throat for three days at least and lying to her parents in order to escape just such an outcome as this.

Now truly she was furious. She had been on the defensive before but now she attacked. Tried to get off her father's lap and fly at me while tears of defeat blinded her eyes.

Suggestions for Writing and Discussion
1. What is your initial response to the characters in this story? With whom do you sympathize the most? Explain.
2. What impression do you have of this doctor? What specifics from the text lead you to this impression?
3. Go back through the piece and comment on the specific details the doctor notices about the family. What conclusions can you draw from his observations?
4. Isolate the verbs in paragraphs 29, 31, and 33. With what actions do you associate most of these words?
5. Would it make any difference if the doctor in this piece were female? If the child were a boy? Explain.

Suggestions for Extended Thinking and Writing
1. Argue for or against the following: The doctor's use of force in this situation was justified.
2. Creative option: Write this piece from another character's point of view or a neutral reporter's point of view. How does your version compare to the original? What is lost, and what is gained?

3. Imagine you are a counselor giving advice to everyone in this piece on what he or she could do to help resolve this conflict. Write an essay in which you analyze the present behaviors of each player and suggest alternative strategies to ease the conflict.

Vocabulary Check

To help ensure that you've understood this selection, and to help you develop a more extensive vocabulary, check the definitions of unfamiliar words in the selection. The words listed below may be new to you, as might others, which you should also identify and define in this exercise.

heifer (4), profusion (4), diphtheria (11), contemptible (22), desist (31)

Using the paragraph numbers in parentheses, which correspond with the numbers in the selection's right margins, locate the words listed above in the reading and develop definitions based on the context in which the words are used (see the guidelines for identifying meaning from context clues on pages 23–24 in Section 3). When you're satisfied with your definitions, use a dictionary to confirm the meaning of each word, and then write your own sentences using these words.

SUGGESTIONS FOR MAKING CONNECTIONS

1. In an essay, compare and contrast the experiences, attitudes, and outcomes of any two patients in this section.
2. Write a speech to an audience of interns and nursing students in which you explain what it is like to be a patient and what a patient needs most from a doctor or nurse. Use your own experience as well as the experiences of the characters in this section to write your speech.
3. Pay close attention to television commercials and magazine ads that glamorize alcohol. Analyze the various means by which these manufacturers attract their customers, and come to some conclusions about who might be most affected by these appeals.
4. Research current statistics on alcohol consumption in this country as well as one social problem associated with alcohol, such as car accidents, violence, addiction, abuse, and use with other drugs. Write a report in which you detail your findings and come to some conclusions about the role alcohol plays in this country.
5. Take action: If any of the topics in this section affected you deeply, write a letter to make your views known. You could address your letter to the director of a nursing home, a hospital, or a company that makes alcoholic beverages. To be fair-minded in your approach, you need to

know your subject well before writing. Personal experience and observations are prerequisites to the actual writing.

6. Aim to understand one of the cultures mentioned in this section by interviewing a subject at length. Possibilities include nurses, doctors, patients, the elderly, nursing home staff, Vietnam veterans, alcoholics, children of alcoholics.

7. Research and write about another health issue not mentioned in this section. Share your report and findings with the class.

8. Watch a current popular television drama that deals with health issues. Analyze the behavior and attitudes of doctors, patients, and family members. Based on the readings in this section and your own experience, come to some conclusions about how true the television portrayal is compared to real life.

9. What is your stance on euthanasia? Write an essay in which you argue for or against this controversial issue.

11
Men and Women

Reading Images

The theme of this section is "Women and Men." Would you use those words to describe the individuals in these photographs? Why? As you work on this topic, consider your definition of "man" and "woman"—would you apply either term to yourself? Or would you more comfortably describe yourself as a "girl" or "boy"? Explain.

BRENT STAPLES

Just Walk on By: A Black Man Ponders
His Power to Alter Public Space

Educated at Widener University and the University of Chicago, where he earned a Ph.D. in psychology in 1982, Brent Staples has served on the editorial board of the *New York Times* since 1990. Staples has also been an editor of the *New York Times Book Review* and an assistant metropolitan editor. A prolific writer, he has been published in such magazines and journals as *Down Beat, Harper's, New York Woman,* and the *New York Times Magazine.* "Just Walk on By" was first published in *Ms.* magazine in 1986. Most recently Staples has written a memoir, *Parallel Time* (Pantheon Books, 1994), which examines the contrast between his current life as a highly acclaimed writer and that of his blue-collar family in Chester, Pennsylvania.

In describing his own growing consciousness of what it means to be a black writer and scholar in America today, Staples recounts an episode that happened when he was a graduate student at the University of Chicago. A professor told him he had been admitted to a seminar only because, "We've been so mean to black people, we've got to make it up." Staples notes that he felt profoundly humiliated by the professor's condescension: "My grades were absolutely at the top of my class. I knew then I was going to be judged as black no matter what" (*GQ,* March 1992).

Pre-Reading and Journal-Writing Suggestions
1. To people who don't know you, in what ways is your personal appearance misleading about the person deep inside, the person you really are?
2. Write about a time in which your initial impression of someone else was wrong. On what facts did you make your initial judgment? What caused you to change your mind? What, if anything, did you learn from this event?
3. If you are walking all alone at night and a black man in jeans and a beard is following close behind you, what thought might go through your head? If you are alone at night and a black man in a conservative suit is walking behind you, do you have the same thoughts? What if each of these men were white? What if each were a black woman (minus the beard, of course)? A white woman? Explain the differences and similarities in the responses you describe.

My first victim was a woman—white, well dressed, probably in her early   *1*
twenties. I came upon her late one evening on a deserted street in Hyde
Park, a relatively affluent neighborhood in an otherwise mean, impoverished section of Chicago. As I swung onto the avenue behind her, there
seemed to be a discreet, uninflammatory distance between us. Not so. She
cast back a worried glance. To her, the youngish black man—a broad six
feet two inches with a beard and billowing hair, both hands shoved into the
pockets of a bulky military jacket—seemed menacingly close. After a few
more quick glimpses, she picked up her pace and was soon running in
earnest. Within seconds she disappeared into a cross street.

That was more than a decade ago. I was twenty-two years old, a graduate student newly arrived at the University of Chicago. It was in the echo of
that terrified woman's footfalls that I first began to know the unwieldy
inheritance I'd come into—the ability to alter public space in ugly ways. It
was clear that she thought herself the quarry of a mugger, a rapist, or worse.
Suffering a bout of insomnia, however, I was stalking sleep, not defenseless
wayfarers. As a softy who is scarcely able to take a knife to a raw chicken—
let alone hold it to a person's throat—I was surprised, embarrassed, and
dismayed all at once. Her flight made me feel like an accomplice in tyranny.
It also made it clear that I was indistinguishable from the muggers who
occasionally seeped into the area from the surrounding ghetto. That first
encounter, and those that followed, signified that a vast, unnerving gulf lay
between nighttime pedestrians—particularly women—and me. And I soon
gathered that being perceived as dangerous is a hazard in itself. I only needed
to turn a corner into a dicey situation, or crowd some frightened, armed
person in a foyer somewhere, or make an errant move after being pulled
over by a policeman. Where fear and weapons meet—and they often do in
urban America—there is always the possibility of death.

In that first year, my first away from my hometown, I was to become
thoroughly familiar with the language of fear. At dark, shadowy intersec-
tions in Chicago, I could cross in front of a car stopped at a traffic light and
elicit the *thunk, thunk, thunk, thunk* of the driver—black, white, male, or
female—hammering down the door locks. On less traveled streets after dark,
I grew accustomed to but never comfortable with people who crossed to
the other side of the street rather than pass me. Then there were the standard
unpleasantries with police, doormen, bouncers, cabdrivers, and others whose
business is to screen out troublesome individuals *before* there is any nastiness.

I moved to New York nearly two years ago and I have remained an avid
night walker. In central Manhattan, the near-constant crowd cover mini-
mizes tense one-on-one street encounters. Elsewhere—visiting friends in
SoHo, where sidewalks are narrow and tightly spaced buildings shut out the
sky—things can get very taut indeed.

Black men have a firm place in New York mugging literature. Norman 5
Podhoretz in his famed (or infamous) 1963 essay, "My Negro Problem—
And Ours," recalls growing up in terror of black males; they "were tougher
than we were, more ruthless," he writes—and as an adult on the Upper West
Side of Manhattan, he continues, he cannot constrain his nervousness when
he meets black men on certain streets. Similarly, a decade later, the essayist
and novelist Edward Hoagland extols a New York where once "Negro
bitterness bore down mainly on other Negroes." Where some see mere
panhandlers, Hoagland sees "a mugger who is clearly screwing up his nerve
to do more than just *ask* for money." But Hoagland has "the New Yorker's
quick-hunch posture for broken-field maneuvering," and the bad guy
swerves away.

I often witness that "hunch posture," from women after dark on the
warrenlike streets of Brooklyn where I live. They seem to set their faces on
neutral and, with their purse straps strung across their chests bandolier style,
they forge ahead as though bracing themselves against being tackled. I understand, of course, that the danger they perceive is not a hallucination.
Women are particularly vulnerable to street violence, and young black males
are drastically overrepresented among the perpetrators of that violence. Yet
these truths are no solace against the kind of alienation that comes of being
ever the suspect, against being set apart, a fearsome entity with whom pedestrians avoid making eye contact.

It is not altogether clear to me how I reached the ripe old age of twenty-
two without being conscious of the lethality nighttime pedestrians attributed to me. Perhaps it was because in Chester, Pennsylvania, the small, angry
industrial town where I came of age in the 1960s, I was scarcely noticeable
against a backdrop of gang warfare, street knifings, and murders. I grew up
one of the good boys, had perhaps a half-dozen fistfights. In retrospect, my
shyness of combat has clear sources.

Many things go into the making of a young thug. One of those things
is the consummation of the male romance with the power to intimidate. An
infant discovers that random flailings send the baby bottle flying out of the
crib and crashing to the floor. Delighted, the joyful babe repeats those
motions again and again, seeking to duplicate the feat. Just so, I recall the
points at which some of my boyhood friends were finally seduced by the
perception of themselves as tough guys. When a mark cowered and surren-
dered his money without resistance, myth and reality merged—and paid off.
It is, after all, only manly to embrace the power to frighten and intimidate.
We, as men, are not supposed to give an inch of our lane on the highway;
we are to seize the fighter's edge in work and in play and even in love; we
are to be valiant in the face of hostile forces.

Unfortunately, poor and powerless young men seem to take all this
nonsense literally. As a boy, I saw countless tough guys locked away; I have

since buried several, too. They were babies, really—a teenage cousin, a brother of twenty-two, a childhood friend in his midtwenties—all gone down in episodes of bravado played out in the streets. I came to doubt the virtues of intimidation early on. I chose, perhaps even unconsciously, to remain a shadow—timid, but a survivor.

The fearsomeness mistakenly attributed to me in public places often has 10 a perilous flavor. The most frightening of these confusions occurred in the late 1970s and early 1980s when I worked as a journalist in Chicago. One day, rushing into the office of a magazine I was writing for with a deadline story in hand, I was mistaken for a burglar. The office manager called security and, with an ad hoc posse, pursued me through the labyrinthine halls, nearly to my editor's door. I had no way of proving who I was. I could only move briskly toward the company of someone who knew me.

Another time I was on assignment for a local paper and killing time before an interview. I entered a jewelry store on the city's affluent Near North Side. The proprietor excused herself and returned with an enormous red Doberman pinscher straining at the end of a leash. She stood, the dog extended toward me, silent to my questions, her eyes bulging nearly out of her head. I took a cursory look around, nodded, and bade her good night. Relatively speaking, however, I never fared as badly as another black male journalist. He went to nearby Waukegan, Illinois, a couple of summers ago to work on a story about a murderer who was born there. Mistaking the reporter for the killer, police hauled him from his car at gunpoint and but for his press credentials would probably have tried to book him. Such episodes are not uncommon. Black men trade tales like this all the time.

In "My Negro Problem—And Ours," Podhoretz writes that the hatred he feels for blacks makes itself known to him through a variety of avenues—one being his discomfort with that "special brand of paranoid touchiness" to which he says blacks are prone. No doubt he is speaking here of black men. In time, I learned to smother the rage I felt at so often being taken for a criminal. Not to do so would surely have led to madness—via that special "paranoid touchiness" that so annoyed Podhoretz at the time he wrote the essay.

I began to take precautions to make myself less threatening. I move about with care, particularly late in the evening. I give a wide berth to nervous people on subway platforms during the wee hours, particularly when I have exchanged business clothes for jeans. If I happen to be entering a building behind some people who appear skittish, I may walk by, letting them clear the lobby before I return, so as not to seem to be following them. I have been calm and extremely congenial on those rare occasions when I've been pulled over by the police.

And on late-evening constitutionals along streets less traveled by, I employ what has proved to be an excellent tension-reducing measure: I whistle

melodies from Beethoven and Vivaldi and the more popular classical composers. Even steely New Yorkers hunching toward nighttime destinations
seem to relax, and occasionally they even join in the tune. Virtually everybody seems to sense that a mugger wouldn't be warbling bright, sunny
selections from Vivaldi's *Four Seasons.* It is my equivalent of the cowbell that
hikers wear when they know they are in bear country.

Suggestions for Writing and Discussion

1. In his opening paragraph, Staples describes a woman who was so nervous because a black man was walking behind her that she began running. Do you think her reaction is a common one? Is it justified?
   Explain your answers.
2. Why, at the age of twenty-two, is Staples, a black man, surprised at the
   reaction that people have toward him on his nightly walks? Besides the
   reaction of surprise, what other feelings might he have when people
   avoid him or hurry away from him, simply because he is a black man?
3. In paragraph 5, Staples cites two pieces of literature that convey the
   image of black man as mugger. When people fear someone because he
   is a black male, does this fear usually occur because, like Norman Podhoretz, they have been mugged by a black man? If not, where does their
   concept of "black as dangerous" come from?
4. Staples admits that women are "particularly vulnerable to street violence
   and young black males are overly represented among perpetrators of
   that violence." So what is his point in this essay? Does he seek to place
   blame or analyze causes? Something else?
5. According to Staples, in what ways do the concepts of being male and
   having power connect? Do you agree with his point that men are supposed to be tough? Write this piece for an audience that is (a) all male
   or (b) all female. When you finish your final draft, on a separate piece of
   paper write a paragraph describing briefly what you think you might
   have done differently if you were writing for an audience other than the
   one you chose.
6. Briefly summarize Staples' solution to avoid frightening others while he
   takes walks. Explain why this tactic apparently works to ease a stranger's
   fear. What is your response to his solution?

Suggestions for Extended Thinking and Writing

1. Watch prime-time television for several weeks. Notice how many
   shows and commercials include black male characters, and note the
   types of roles these characters play. Based on your observations, what
   categories do these characters fall into? Are any of the roles stereotypes?

Are any of the characters "real" people? Come to some conclusion about how black men are portrayed on television.

2. Staples explains why he did not get pulled into the life of a street mugger. Drawing on your own experiences with peer pressure as well as on your reading or viewing of television documentaries, explain why you think young people are attracted to gangs or to other negative behaviors. In addition, explain how you think young people can be convinced not to be influenced by negative peer pressure. Use specific examples to illustrate your points.

Vocabulary Check

To help ensure that you've understood this selection, and to help you develop a more extensive vocabulary, check the definitions of unfamiliar words in the selection. The words listed below may be new to you, as might others, which you should also identify and define in this exercise.

quarry (2), seep (2), avid (4), solace (6), cursory (11)

Using the paragraph numbers in parentheses, which correspond with the numbers in the selection's right margins, locate the words listed above in the reading and develop definitions based on the context in which the words are used (see the guidelines for identifying meaning from context clues on pages 23–24 in Section 3). When you're satisfied with your definitions, use a dictionary to confirm the meaning of each word, and then write your own sentences using these words.

JON KATZ
How Boys Become Men

Jon Katz, who was born in 1947, has worked as a reporter and editor for several newspapers, including the *Boston Globe,* the *Philadelphia Inquirer,* and the *Washington Post.* His interest in the media and its impact on society has led him to work as media critic for *Rolling Stone* and *New York* magazines and to an editorial position at *Wired.* His book *Virtual Reality* addresses issues related to the media and values. In the selection that follows, which first appeared in *Glamour* magazine in 1993, Katz examines the experiences that he believes shape the personalities of young men.

Pre-Reading and Journal-Writing Suggestions
1. What are little boys made of? What are little girls made of?
2. According to society (and, according to you), what Ten Commandments might boys have to follow to fit in with their peers?

Two nine-year-old boys, neighbors and friends, were walking home   1
from school. The one in the bright blue windbreaker was laughing and swinging a heavy-looking book bag toward the head of his friend, who kept ducking and stepping back. "What's the matter?" asked the kid with the bag, whooshing it over his head. "You chicken?"

His friend stopped, stood still and braced himself. The bag slammed into the side of his face, the thump audible all the way across the street where I stood watching. The impact knocked him to the ground, where he lay mildly stunned for a second. Then he struggled up, rubbing the side of his head. "See?" he said proudly. "I'm no chicken."

No. A chicken would probably have had the sense to get out of the way. This boy was already well on the road to becoming a *man,* having learned one of the central ethics of his gender. Experience pain rather than show fear.

Women tend to see men as a giant problem in need of solution. They tell us that we're remote and uncommunicative, that we need to demonstrate less machismo and more commitment, more humanity. But if you don't understand something about boys, you can't understand why men are the way we are, why we find it so difficult to make friends or to acknowledge our fears and problems.

Boys live in a world with its own Code of Conduct, a set of ruthless,   5
unspoken, and unyielding rules:

Don't be a goody-goody.

Never rat. If your parents ask about bruises, shrug.

Never admit fear. Ride the roller coaster, join the fistfight, do what you have to do. Asking for help is for sissies.

Empathy is for nerds. You can help your best buddy, under certain circumstances. Everyone else is on his own.

Never discuss anything of substance with anybody. Grunt, shrug, dump on teachers, laugh at wimps, talk about comic books. Anything else is risky.

Boys are rewarded for throwing hard. Most other activities—reading, befriending girls, or just thinking—are considered weird. And if there's one thing boys don't want to be, it's weird.

More than anything else, boys are supposed to learn how to handle themselves. I remember the bitter fifth-grade conflict I touched off by elbowing aside a bigger boy named Barry and seizing the cafeteria's last carton of chocolate milk. Teased for getting aced out by a wimp, he had to reclaim his place in the pack. Our fistfight, at recess, ended with my knees buckling and my lip bleeding while my friends, sympathetic but out of range, watched resignedly.

When I got home, my mother took one look at my swollen face and screamed. I wouldn't tell her anything, but when my father got home I cracked and confessed, pleading with them to do nothing. Instead, they called Barry's parents, who restricted his television for a week.

The following morning, Barry and six of his pals stepped out from behind a stand of trees. "It's the rat," said Barry.

I bled a little more. *Rat* was scrawled in crayon across my desk.   10

They were waiting for me after school for a number of afternoons to follow. I tried varying my routes and avoiding bushes and hedges. It usually didn't work.

I was as ashamed for telling as I was frightened. "You did ask for it," said my best friend. Frontier Justice has nothing on Boy Justice.

In panic, I appealed to a cousin who was several years older. He followed me home from school, and when Barry's gang surrounded me, he came barreling toward us. "Stay away from my cousin," he shouted, "or I'll kill you."

After they were gone, however, my cousin could barely stop laughing. "You were afraid of *them*?" he howled. "They barely came up to my waist."

Men remember receiving little mercy as boys; maybe that's why it's   15 sometimes difficult for them to show any.

"I know lots of men who had happy childhoods, but none who have happy memories of the way other boys treated them," says a friend. "It's a macho marathon from third grade up, when you start butting each other in the stomach."

"The thing is," adds another friend, "you learn early on to hide what you feel. It's never safe to say, 'I'm scared.' My girlfriend asks me why I don't talk more about what I'm feeling. I've gotten better at it, but it will *never* come naturally."

You don't need to be a shrink to see how the lessons boys learn affect their behavior as men. Men are being asked, more and more, to show sensitivity, but they dread the very word. They struggle to build their increasingly uncertain work lives but will deny they're in trouble. They want love, affection, and support but don't know how to ask for them. They hide their weaknesses and fears from all, even those they care for. They've learned to be wary of intervening when they see others in trouble. They often still balk at being stigmatized as weird.

Some men get shocked into sensitivity—when they lose their jobs, their wives, or their lovers. Others learn it through a strong marriage, or through their own children.

It may be a long while, however, before male culture evolves to the 20 point that boys can learn more from one another than how to hit curve balls. Last month, walking my dog past the playground near my house, I saw three boys encircling a fourth, laughing and pushing him. He was skinny and rumpled, and he looked frightened. One boy knelt behind him while another pushed him from the front, a trick familiar to any former boy. He fell backward.

When the others ran off, he brushed the dirt off his elbows and walked toward the swings. His eyes were moist and he was struggling for control.

"Hi," I said through the chain-link fence. "How ya doing?"

"Fine," he said quickly, kicking his legs out and beginning his swing.

Suggestions for Writing and Discussion
1. In general, do you agree with Katz's portrayal of boyhood experiences? On what do you base your opinion?
2. In what ways did you react to the scenes in which Katz is bullied and beaten up? What, if anything, could his parents have done differently to help him through this time?
3. Imagine you, too, are a player in the above scenes. How do you see yourself: as the tormented or the tormentor?
4. Other than "weird," what other stigmas might boys today fear? What stigmas might girls fear?
5. How do your initial "commandments" compare to Katz's Code of Conduct?
6. From this piece, what do you think Katz's point is about American boyhood (and manhood) in general?

Suggestions for Extended Thinking and Writing
1. Observe a group of grade school boys in an informal setting (not an organized sports event). Write an essay in which you compare your observations with Katz's assertions in this piece.
2. Interview three different males from three different age groups about their boyhoods, and compare your findings with Katz's piece.
3. Either collaboratively or alone, write a parody to this piece entitled "How Girls Become Women."

Vocabulary Check

To help ensure that you've understood this selection, and to help you develop a more extensive vocabulary, check the definitions of unfamiliar words in the selection. The words listed below may be new to you, as might others, which you should also identify and define in this exercise.

audible (2), ruthless (5), empathy (5), marathon (16), wary (18)

Using the paragraph numbers in parentheses, which correspond with the numbers in the selection's right margins, locate the words listed above in the reading and develop definitions based on the context in which the words are used (see the guidelines for identifying meaning from context clues on pages 23–24 in Section 3). When you're satisfied with your definitions, use a dictionary to confirm the meaning of each word, and then write your own sentences using these words.

JUDITH ORTIZ COFER

The Myth of the Latin Woman:
I Just Met a Girl Named María

In 1956 when she was four years old, Cofer immigrated to the
United States from Puerto Rico to join her father, who was in the U.S.
Navy.

After acquiring bachelor's and master's degrees, she taught bilingual
classes, English, and Spanish in public schools, community colleges,
and colleges in Florida and Georgia. Concurrently she was producing
chapbooks, plays, poems, a personal essay, and a novel. In 1983 and
1984 she was on the administrative staff of Bread Loaf Writers'
Conference.

The main themes of her poetry reflect her own family, and her first
novel, *Line of the Sun,* gives a vivid picture of life in a poor Puerto
Rican village. Cofer herself sees her work as a study of the "process of
change, assimilation, and transformation" (*Contemporary Authors,* New
Revision Series, vol. 32, p. 89).

Pre-Reading and Journal-Writing Suggestions
1. If someone observed you walking down the street, what conclusions
   would they draw about you based on your looks, your clothes, your
   hairstyle, your walk, the things you carry with you? How accurate
   would these judgments be?
2. List all the famous Hispanic people or characters you've heard of: authors, actors, politicians, world leaders, singers, artists. Based on this list,
   what conclusions can you draw about your breadth of knowledge and
   exposure to Hispanic culture?
3. What cultures have most influenced your identity?

On a bus trip to London from Oxford University where I was earning   1
some graduate credits one summer, a young man, obviously fresh from a
pub, spotted me and as if struck by inspiration went down on his knees in
the aisle. With both hands over his heart he broke into an Irish tenor's
rendition of "María" from *West Side Story.* My politely amused fellow passengers gave his lovely voice the round of gentle applause it deserved.
Though I was not quite as amused, I managed my version of an English
smile: no show of teeth, no extreme contortions of the facial muscles—I
was at this time of my life practicing reserve and cool. Oh, that British
control, how I coveted it. But María had followed me to London, reminding
me of a prime fact of my life: you can leave the Island, master the English

language, and travel as far as you can, but if you are a Latina, especially one like me who so obviously belongs to Rita Moreno's gene pool, the Island travels with you. This is sometimes a very good thing—it may win you that extra minute of someone's attention. But with some people, the same things can make *you* an island—not so much a tropical paradise as an Alcatraz, a place nobody wants to visit. As a Puerto Rican girl growing up in the United States and wanting like most children to "belong," I resented the stereotype that my Hispanic appearance called forth from many people I met.

Our family lived in a large urban center in New Jersey during the sixties, where life was designed as a microcosm of my parents' casas on the island. We spoke in Spanish, we ate Puerto Rican food bought at the bodega, and we practiced strict Catholicism complete with Saturday confession and Sunday mass at a church where our parents were accommodated into a one-hour Spanish mass slot, performed by a Chinese priest trained as a missionary for Latin America.

As a girl I was kept under strict surveillance, since virtue and modesty were, by cultural equation, the same as family honor. As a teenager I was instructed on how to behave as a proper señorita. But it was a conflicting message girls got, since the Puerto Rican mothers also encouraged their daughters to look and act like women and to dress in clothes our Anglo friends and their mothers found too "mature" for our age. It was, and is, cultural, yet I often felt humiliated when I appeared at an American friend's party wearing a dress more suitable to a semiformal than to a playroom birthday celebration. At Puerto Rican festivities, neither the music nor the colors we wore could be too loud. I still experience a vague sense of letdown when I'm invited to a "party" and it turns out to be a marathon conversation in hushed tones rather than a fiesta with salsa, laughter, and dancing—the kind of celebration I remember from my childhood.

I remember Career Day in our high school, when teachers told us to 5 come dressed as if for a job interview. It quickly became obvious that to the barrio girls, "dressing up" sometimes meant wearing ornate jewelry and clothing that would be more appropriate (by mainstream standards) for the company Christmas party than as daily office attire. That morning I had agonized in front of my closet, trying to figure out what a "career girl" would wear because, essentially, except for Marlo Thomas on TV, I had no models on which to base my decision. I knew how to dress for school: at the Catholic school I attended we all wore uniforms; I knew how to dress for Sunday mass, and I knew what dresses to wear for parties at my relatives' homes. Though I do not recall the precise details of my Career Day outfit, it must have been a composite of the above choices. But I remember a comment my friend (an Italian-American) made in later years that coalesced my impressions of that day. She said that at the business school she was attending the Puerto Rican girls always stood out for wearing "everything at once." She meant, of course, too much jewelry, too many accessories. On that day at school, we were simply made the negative models by the nuns who were themselves not credible fashion experts to any of us. But it was painfully obvious to me that to the others, in their tailored skirts and silk blouses, we must have seemed "hopeless" and "vulgar." Though I now know that most adolescents feel out of step much of the time, I also know that for the Puerto Rican girls of my generation that sense was intensified. The way our teachers and classmates looked at us that day in school was just a taste of the culture clash that awaited us in the real world, where prospective employers and men on the street would often misinterpret our tight skirts and jingling bracelets as a come-on.

Mixed cultural signals have perpetuated certain stereotypes—for example, that of the Hispanic woman as the "Hot Tamale" or sexual firebrand. It is a one-dimensional view that the media have found easy to promote. In their special vocabulary, advertisers have designated "sizzling" and "smoldering" as the adjectives of choice for describing not only the foods but also the women of Latin America. From conversations in my house I recall hearing about the harassment that Puerto Rican women endured in factories where the "boss men" talked to them as if sexual innuendo was all they understood and, worse, often gave them the choice of submitting to advances or being fired.

It is custom, however, not chromosomes, that leads us to choose scarlet over pale pink. As young girls, we were influenced in our decisions about clothes and colors by the women—older sisters and mothers who had grown up on a tropical island where the natural environment was a riot of primary colors, where showing your skin was one way to keep cool as well as to look sexy. Most important of all, on the island, women perhaps felt freer to dress and move more provocatively, since, in most cases, they were protected by the traditions, mores, and laws of a Spanish/Catholic system of morality and machismo whose main rule was: *You may look at my sister, but if you touch her I will kill you.* The extended family and church structure could provide a young woman with a circle of safety in her small pueblo on the island; if a man "wronged" a girl, everyone would close in to save her family honor.

This is what I have gleaned from my discussions as an adult with older Puerto Rican women. They have told me about dressing in their best party clothes on Saturday nights and going to the town's plaza to promenade with their girlfriends in front of the boys they liked. The males were thus given an opportunity to admire the women and to express their admiration in the form of *piropos:* erotically charged street poems they composed on the spot. I have been subjected to a few piropos while visiting the Island, and they can be outrageous, although custom dictates that they must never cross into obscenity. This ritual, as I understand it, also entails a show of studied indifference on the woman's part; if she is "decent," she must not acknowledge the man's impassioned words. So I do understand how things can be lost in translation. When a Puerto Rican girl dressed in her idea of what is attractive meets a man from the mainstream culture who has been trained to react to certain types of clothing as a sexual signal, a clash is likely to take place. The line I first heard based on this aspect of the myth happened when the boy who took me to my first formal dance leaned over to plant a sloppy over-eager kiss painfully on my mouth, and when I didn't respond with sufficient passion said in a resentful tone: "I thought you Latin girls were supposed to mature early"—my first instance of being thought of as a fruit or vegetable— I was supposed to *ripen,* not just grow into womanhood like other girls.

It is surprising to some of my professional friends that some people, including those who should know better, still put others "in their place." Though rarer, these incidents are still commonplace in my life. It happened to me most recently during a stay at a very classy metropolitan hotel favored by young professional couples for their weddings. Late one evening after the theater, as I walked toward my room with my colleague (a woman with whom I was coordinating an arts program), a middle-aged man in a tuxedo, a young girl in satin and lace on his arm, stepped directly into our path. With his champagne glass extended toward me, he exclaimed, "Evita!"

Our way blocked, my companion and I listened as the man half-recited, *10* half-bellowed "Don't Cry for Me, Argentina." When he finished, the young girl said: "How about a round of applause for my daddy?" We complied, hoping this would bring the silly spectacle to a close. I was becoming aware that our little group was attracting the attention of the other guests. "Daddy" must have perceived this too, and he once more barred the way as we tried to walk past him. He began to shout-sing a ditty to the tune of "La Bamba"—except the lyrics were about a girl named María whose exploits all rhymed with her name and gonorrhea. The girl kept saying "Oh, Daddy" and looking at me with pleading eyes. She wanted me to laugh along with the others. My companion and I stood silently waiting for the man to end his offensive song. When he finished, I looked not at him but at his daughter. I advised her calmly never to ask her father what he had done in the army. Then I walked between them and to my room. My friend complimented me on my cool handling of the situation. I confessed to her that I really had wanted to push the jerk into the swimming pool. I knew that this same man—probably a corporate executive, well educated, even worldly by most standards—would not have been likely to regale a white woman with a dirty song in public. He would perhaps have checked his impulse by assuming that she could be somebody's wife or mother, or at least *somebody* who might take offense. But to him, I was just an Evita or a María: merely a character in his cartoon-populated universe.

Because of my education and my proficiency with the English language, I have acquired many mechanisms for dealing with the anger I experience. This was not true for my parents, nor is it true for the many Latin women working at menial jobs who must put up with stereotypes about our ethnic group such as: "They make good domestics." This is another facet of the myth of the Latin woman in the United States. Its origin is simple to deduce. Work as domestics, waitressing, and factory jobs are all that's available to women with little English and few skills. The myth of the Hispanic menial has been sustained by the same media phenomenon that made "Mammy" from *Gone with the Wind* America's idea of the black woman for generations; María, the housemaid or counter girl, is now indelibly etched into the national psyche. The big and the little screens have presented us with the picture of the funny Hispanic maid, mispronouncing words and cooking up a spicy storm in a shiny California kitchen.

This media-engendered image of the Latina in the United States has been documented by feminist Hispanic scholars, who claim that such portrayals are partially responsible for the denial of opportunities for upward mobility among Latinas in the professions. I have a Chicana friend working on a Ph.D. in philosophy at a major university. She says her doctor still shakes his head in puzzled amazement at all the "big words" she uses. Since I do not wear my diplomas around my neck for all to see, I too have on occasion been sent to that "kitchen," where some think I obviously belong.

One such incident that has stayed with me, though I recognize it as a minor offense, happened on the day of my first public poetry reading. It took place in Miami in a boat-restaurant where we were having lunch before the event. I was nervous and excited as I walked in with my notebook in my hand. An older woman motioned me to her table. Thinking (foolish me) that she wanted me to autograph a copy of my brand new slender volume of verse, I went over. She ordered a cup of coffee from me, assuming that I was the waitress. Easy enough to mistake my poems for menus, I suppose. I know that it wasn't an intentional act of cruelty, yet of all the good things that happened that day, I remember that scene most clearly, because it reminded me of what I had to overcome before anyone would take me seriously. In retrospect I understand that my anger gave my reading fire, that I have almost always taken doubts in my abilities as a challenge— and that the result is, most times, a feeling of satisfaction at having won a convert when I see the cold, appraising eyes warm to my words, the body language change, the smile that indicates that I have opened some avenue for communication. That day I read to that woman and her lowered eyes told me that she was embarrassed at her little faux pas, and when I willed her to look up at me, it was my victory, and she graciously allowed me to punish her with my full attention. We shook hands at the end of the reading, and I never saw her again. She has probably forgotten the whole thing but maybe not.

Yet I am one of the lucky ones. My parents made it possible for me to acquire a stronger footing in the mainstream culture by giving me the chance at an education. And books and art have saved me from the harsher forms of ethnic and racial prejudice that many of my Hispanic *compañeras* have had to endure. I travel a lot around the United States, reading from my books of poetry and my novel, and the reception I most often receive is one of positive interest by people who want to know more about my culture. There are, however, thousands of Latinas without the privilege of an education or the entrée into society that I have. For them life is a struggle against the misconceptions perpetuated by the myth of the Latina as whore, domestic, or criminal. We cannot change this by legislating the way people look at us. The transformation, as I see it, has to occur at a much more individual level. My personal goal in my public life is to try to replace the old pervasive stereotypes and myths about Latinas with a much more interesting set of realities. Every time I give a reading, I hope the stories I tell, the dreams and fears I examine in my work, can achieve some universal truth which will get my audience past the particulars of my skin color, my accent, or my clothes.

I once wrote a poem in which I called us Latinas "God's brown daugh- 15
ters." This poem is really a prayer of sorts, offered upward, but also, through the human-to-human channel of art, outward. It is a prayer for communication, and for respect. In it, Latin women pray "in Spanish to an Anglo God / with a Jewish heritage," and they are "fervently hoping / that if not omnipotent, / at least He be bilingual."

Suggestions for Writing and Discussion

1. Describe the writer's attitude toward her culture and her self, as well as the larger, more dominant culture outside her Hispanic roots.
2. With what specific incidents could you identify, and what experiences were totally foreign to you?
3. Summarize the basic differences between the Hispanic culture and the mainstream American culture. How divisive do you find these differences to be really?
4. In paragraph 13, the author says that the incident she's about to reveal is "minor." Do you agree with her assessment here? Why do you think she includes it?
5. In as few words as possible, state the author's main point.
6. After reading this piece, would you be more or less likely to read any of Cofer's other writings, such as her books and her poems? Explain.

Suggestions for Extended Thinking and Writing
1. Read a collection of poems or a novel by a noted Hispanic writer. Keep a journal of your reading experience, and write an essay that explains what you learned from the readings you chose and how they changed you.
2. Research a famous Hispanic person who is living today. Aim to discover the effect that his or her culture had on this person.
3. For one week, pay attention to the number of Hispanics you notice in the media: television, radio, newspapers, magazines, movies. Write an essay in which you analyze the ways that the Hispanic culture is portrayed.

Vocabulary Check
   To help ensure that you've understood this selection, and to help you develop a more extensive vocabulary, check the definitions of unfamiliar words in the selection. The words listed below may be new to you, as might others, which you should also identify and define in this exercise.

   contortions (1), surveillance (4), innuendo (6), exploits (10), menial (11)

Using the paragraph numbers in parentheses, which correspond with the numbers in the selection's right margins, locate the words listed above in the reading and develop definitions based on the context in which the words are used (see the guidelines for identifying meaning from context clues on pages 23–24 in Section 3). When you're satisfied with your definitions, use a dictionary to confirm the meaning of each word, and then write your own sentences using these words.

_____

CHARLES OSGOOD

"Real" Men and Women

Born in New York City in 1933, Charles Osgood grew up fascinated with the radio programs that were part of his daily life. After graduating from Fordham University, he began working as program director and general manager at small radio and television stations and eventually moved to anchor at WCBS TV in New York City, later becoming correspondent and host of "News Week" and "The Osgood Files" at CBS.

While Osgood covered catastrophies and tragic events, he preferred the upbeat, humorous side of the news. His view can be summed up by the title of one of his collections of poems, *Nothing Could Be Finer Than a Crisis That Is Minor in the Morning.*

Pre-Reading and Journal-Writing Suggestions

1. Imagine you have been assigned to write about either one of these topics: What is a real man? What is a real woman? First of all, consider your reaction to this assignment. What difficulties might you encounter? How would you approach this writing assignment?

2. Freewrite for ten minutes on the word *man*. Now do the same for the word *woman*. Looking over your two entries, what conclusions can you draw?

Helene, a young friend of mine, has been assigned a theme in English   *1*
composition class. She can take her choice: "What is a *real* man?" or if she wishes, "What is a *real* woman?" Seems the instructor has some strong ideas on these subjects. Helene says she doesn't know which choice to make. "I could go the women's-lib route," she says, "but I don't think he'd like that. I started in on that one once in a class, and it didn't go over too well." So, what is a real man and what is a real woman?

"As opposed to what?" I asked.

"I don't know, as opposed to unreal men and women, I suppose. Got any ideas?"

Yes, it just so happens I do. Let's start with the assumption that reality is that which is, as opposed to that which somebody would like, or something that is imagined or idealized. Let's assume that all human beings who are alive, therefore, are real human beings, who can be divided into two categories: real men and real women. A man who exists is a real man. His reality is in no way lessened by his race, his nationality, political affiliation, financial status, religious persuasion, or personal proclivities. All men are real men. All women are real women.

The first thing you do if you want to destroy somebody is rob him of 5 his humanity. If you can persuade yourself that someone is a gook and therefore not a real person, you can kill him rather more easily, burn down his home, separate him from his family. If you can persuade yourself that someone is not really a person but a spade, a Wasp, a kike, a wop, a mick, a fag, a dike, and therefore not a real man or woman, you can more easily hate and hurt him.

People who go around making rules, setting standards that other people are supposed to meet in order to qualify as real, are real pains in the neck— and worse, they are real threats to the rest of us. They use their own definitions of real and unreal to filter out unpleasant facts. To them, things like crime, drugs, decay, pollution, slums, et cetera, are not the real America. In the same way, they can look at a man and say he is not a real man because he doesn't give a hang about pro football and would rather chase butterflies than a golfball; or they can look at a woman and say she is not a real woman because she drives a cab or would rather change the world than change diapers.

To say that someone is not a real man or woman is to say that they are something less than, and therefore not entitled to the same consideration as, real people. Therefore, Helene, contained within the questions "What is a real man?" and "What is a real woman?" are the seeds of discrimination and of murders, big and little. Each of us has his own reality, and nobody has the right to limit or qualify that—not even English composition instructors.

Suggestions for Writing and Discussion
1. In this piece, the author says he has an idea for approaching this assignment. In your own words, summarize the advice he would give to someone who is approaching the same assignment.
2. What is the author's interpretation of the word *real?* What other interpretations can you think of for this word?
3. In paragraph 5, the author lists terms that degrade different nationalities and groups. Why do you think he uses these specific terms? What effect does his choosing to use these words have on you as a reader?
4. Consider your own definitions of *real man* and *real woman.* How do your views compare to the stereotypes Osgood describes in paragraph 6?
5. What is your response to Osgood's last line? What is he saying? Do you agree with him? Please explain.
6. The newspaper in your university or college community has asked you to write a paper describing the "real" college man or the "real" college woman of the 1990s. What is your response?

Suggestions for Extended Thinking and Writing

1. Try this assignment out on several of your acquaintances (fellow students, co-workers, family, friends). Ask both men and women the question "What is a real man?" Then ask the same people, "What is a real woman?" After collecting your data, write a paper in which you discuss your findings.
2. Select several advertisements from the same magazine and write an essay in which you analyze these ads and infer what they suggest about "real" men and women.

Vocabulary Check

To help ensure that you've understood this selection, and to help you develop a more extensive vocabulary, check the definitions of unfamiliar words in the selection. The words listed below may be new to you, as might others, which you should also identify and define in this exercise.

theme (1), assumption (4), affiliation (4), proclivity (4), filter (6)

Using the paragraph numbers in parentheses, which correspond with the numbers in the selection's right margins, locate the words listed above in the reading and develop definitions based on the context in which the words are used (see the guidelines for identifying meaning from context clues on pages 23–24 in Section 3). When you're satisfied with your definitions, use a dictionary to confirm the meaning of each word, and then write your own sentences using these words.

SUSAN JACOBY
Unfair Game

Born in 1946, Susan Jacoby is a writer with two particularly strong interests: women's issues and Russian culture. She lived in Moscow for several years and has written many highly acclaimed books and articles reflecting on her experiences during those years. These works include *Moscow Conversations* (1972), *Ten Russian Encounters* (1972), and *Inside Soviet Schools* (1974). In 1992, she coauthored, with Yelena Khanga, *Soul to Soul: The Story of a Black Russian American Family*. In addition, she has been the author of the "Hers" column in the *New York Times* and has published a collection of these columns, *The Possible She* (1979). In an essay for the *New York Times Book Review*, Ellen Goodman noted that Jacoby's greatest strength as a writer comes from "the connection she has maintained with all the strands of her rich personal experience."

Pre-Reading and Journal-Writing Suggestions
1. Who do you think is most vulnerable to being "picked up"—a single man or a single woman? Explain why.
2. When you're out alone, what type of person are you—one who enjoys talking with strangers or one who prefers being left alone? Explain.

My friend and I, two women obviously engrossed in conversation, are   1
sitting at a corner table in the crowded Oak Room of the Plaza at ten o'clock on a Tuesday night. A man materializes and interrupts us with the snappy opening line, "A good woman is hard to find."

We say nothing, hoping he will disappear back into his bottle. But he fancies himself as our genie and asks, "Are you visiting?" Still we say nothing. Finally my friend looks up and says, "We live here." She and I look at each other, the thread of our conversation snapped, our thoughts focused on how to get rid of this intruder. In a minute, if something isn't done, he will scrunch down next to me on the banquette and start offering to buy us drinks.

"Would you leave us alone, please," I say in a loud but reasonably polite voice. He looks slightly offended but goes on with his bright social patter. I become more explicit. "We don't want to talk to you, we didn't ask you over here, and we want to be alone. Go away." This time he directs his full attention to me—and he is mad. "All right, all right, *excuse me*." He pushes up the corners of his mouth in a Howdy Doody smile. "You ought to try smiling. You might even be pretty if you smiled once in a while."

At last the man leaves. He goes back to his buddy at the bar. I watch
them out of the corner of my eye, and he gestures angrily at me for at least
fifteen minutes. When he passes our table on the way out of the room, this
well-dressed, obviously affluent man mutters, "Good-bye, bitch," under his
breath.

Why is this man calling me names? Because I have asserted my right to   5
sit at a table in a public place without being drawn into a sexual flirtation.
Because he has been told, in no uncertain terms, that two attractive women
prefer each other's company to his.

This sort of experience is an old story to any woman who travels, eats,
or drinks—for business or pleasure—without a male escort. In Holiday Inns
and at the Plaza, on buses and airplanes, in tourist and first class, a woman is
always thought to be looking for a man in addition to whatever else she may
be doing. The man who barged in on us at the bar would never have broken
into the conversation of two men, and it goes without saying that he
wouldn't have imposed himself on a man and a woman who were having a
drink. But two women at a table are an entirely different matter. Fair game.

This might be viewed as a relatively small flaw in the order of the
universe— something in a class with an airline losing luggage or a computer
fouling up a bank statement. Except a computer doesn't foul up your bank
account every month and an airline doesn't lose your suitcase every time
you fly. But if you are an independent woman, you have to spend a certain
amount of energy, day in and day out, in order to go about your business
without being bothered by strange men.

On airplanes, I am a close-mouthed traveler. As soon as the "No Smoking" sign is turned off, I usually pull some papers out of my briefcase and
start working. Work helps me forget that I am scared of flying. When I am
sitting next to a woman, she quickly realizes from my monosyllabic replies
that I don't want to chat during the flight. Most men, though, are not
content to be ignored.

Once I was flying from New York to San Antonio on a plane that was
scheduled to stop in Dallas. My seatmate was an advertising executive who
kept questioning me about what I was doing and who remained undiscour-
aged by my terse replies until I ostentatiously covered myself with a blanket
and shut my eyes. When the plane started its descent into Dallas, he made
his move.

"You don't really have to get to San Antonio today, do you?"   10
"Yes."

"Come on, change your ticket. Spend the evening with me here. I'm
staying at a wonderful hotel, with a pool, we could go dancing . . ."

"No."

"Well, you can't blame a man for trying."

I do blame a man for trying in this situation—for suggesting that a 15
woman change her work and travel plans to spend a night with a perfect
stranger in whom she had displayed no personal interest. The "no personal
interest" is crucial; I wouldn't have blamed the man for trying if I had been
stroking his cheek and complaining about my dull social life.

There is a nice postscript to this story. Several months later, I was walking my dog in Carl Schurz Park when I ran into my erstwhile seatmate, who
was taking a stroll with his wife and children. He recognized me, all right,
and was trying to avoid me when I went over and courteously reintroduced
myself. I reminded him that we had been on the same flight to Dallas. "Oh
yes," he said. "As I recall you were going on to somewhere else." "San
Antonio," I said. "I was in a hurry that day."

The code of feminine politeness, instilled in girlhood, is no help in
dealing with the unwanted approaches of strange men. Our mothers didn't
teach us to tell a man to get lost; they told us to smile and hint that we'd be
just delighted to spend time with the gentleman if we didn't have other
commitments. The man in the Oak Room bar would not be put off by a
demure lowering of eyelids; he had to be told, roughly and loudly, that his
presence was a nuisance.

Not that I am necessarily against men and women picking each other
up in public places. In most instances, a modicum of sensitivity will tell a
woman or a man whether someone is open to approaches.

Mistakes can easily be corrected by the kind of courtesy so many people
have abandoned since the "sexual revolution." One summer evening, I was
whiling away a half hour in the outdoor bar of the Stanhope Hotel. I was
alone, dressed up, having a drink before going on to meet someone in a
restaurant. A man at the next table asked, "If you're not busy, would you
like to have a drink with me?" I told him I was sorry but I would be leaving
shortly. "Excuse me for disturbing you," he said, turning back to his own
drink. Simple courtesy. No insults and no hurt feelings.

One friend suggested that I might have avoided the incident in the Oak 20
Room by going to the Palm Court instead. It's true that the Palm Court is
a traditional meeting place for unescorted ladies. But I don't like violins
when I want to talk. And I wanted to sit in a large, comfortable leather
chair. Why should I have to hide among the potted palms to avoid men who
think I'm looking for something else?

Suggestions for Writing and Discussion
1. Explain your reaction to the man in the opening scene. Explain your
   reaction to the woman. In what ways are your reactions similar?
   Different?

2. How would you describe the tone of this piece?
3. What is the author's implied point about the relationship between men and women? Do you agree or disagree with this point? Please explain.
4. The author develops this essay with three different encounters. Compare the similarities and differences within each example, and show how the outcomes in each could have changed, depending on one of the character's actions.
5. What specific audience might be most receptive to this essay? What group of people might be most resistant? Explain.

Vocabulary Check

To help ensure that you've understood this selection, and to help you develop a more extensive vocabulary, check the definitions of unfamiliar words in the selection. The words listed below may be new to you, as might others, which you should also identify and define in this exercise.

genie (2), banquette (2), flaw (7), terse (9), modicum (18)

Using the paragraph numbers in parentheses, which correspond with the numbers in the selection's right margins, locate the words listed above in the reading and develop definitions based on the context in which the words are used (see the guidelines for identifying meaning from context clues on pages 23–24 in Section 3). When you're satisfied with your definitions, use a dictionary to confirm the meaning of each word, and then write your own sentences using these words.

SCOTT RUSSELL SANDERS

The Men We Carry in Our Minds . . . and How They
Differ from the Real Lives of Most Men

From his boyhood in Memphis, Tennessee, where he was born in
1945, Sanders consistently evinced an interest in nature, the environment, and the adaptations of humans to their place in the universe. His
youthful pursuits took him into unpeopled areas as he biked and hiked,
savoring the wildflowers and nature's bounty.

Much of his writing is about the lives of marginalized people—the
elderly, the outcasts, country people, children. He was active in oppos-
ing the Vietnam War and nuclear weapons. His books and essays
clearly reveal his deep concern for the preservation of the wilderness
environment and for the future of our planet.

Pre-Reading and Journal-Writing Suggestions

1. Reflecting on your own childhood, who do you think had a harder
   time of it in your family: the men or the women? Explain.
2. Imagine that for one day you can get under the skin and walk in the
   shoes of the opposite sex. Describe how a day might go for you under
   these circumstances. In the end, come to some conclusion: How was
   the imagined experience?
3. Describe your ideal man or woman.

"This must be a hard time for women," I say to my friend Anneke.   *1*
"They have so many paths to choose from, and so many voices calling
them."

"I think it's a lot harder for men," she replies.

"How do you figure that?"

"The women I know feel excited, innocent, like crusaders in a just
cause. The men I know are eaten up with guilt."

"Women feel such pressure to be everything, do everything," I say.   *5*
"Career, kids, art, politics. Have their babies and get back to the office a
week later. It's as if they're trying to overcome a million years' worth of
evolution in one lifetime."

"But we help one another. And we have this deep-down sense that
we're in the *right*—we've been held back, passed over, used—while men
feel they're in the wrong. Men are the ones who've been discredited, who
have to search their souls."

I search my soul. I discover guilty feelings aplenty—toward the poor,
the Vietnamese, Native Americans, the whales, an endless list of debts. But

toward women I feel something more confused, a snarl of shame, envy, wary tenderness, and amazement. This muddle troubles me. To hide my unease I say, "You're right, it's tough being a man these days."

"Don't laugh," Anneke frowns at me. "I wouldn't be a man for anything. It's much easier being the victim. All the victim has to do is break free. The persecutor has to live with his past."

How deep is that past? I find myself wondering. How much of an inheritance do I have to throw off?

When I was a boy growing up on the back roads of Tennessee and 10 Ohio, the men I knew labored with their bodies. They were marginal farmers, just scraping by, or welders, steelworkers, carpenters; they swept floors, dug ditches, mined coal, or drove trucks, their forearms ropy with muscle; they trained horses, stoked furnaces, made tires, stood on assembly lines wrestling parts onto cars and refrigerators. They got up before light, worked all day long whatever the weather, and when they came home at night they looked as though somebody had been whipping them. In the evenings and on weekends they worked on their own places, tilling gardens that were lumpy with clay, fixing broken-down cars, hammering on houses that were always too drafty, too leaky, too small.

The bodies of the men I knew were twisted and maimed in ways visible and invisible. The nails of their hands were black and split, the hands tattooed with scars. Some had lost fingers. Heavy lifting had given many of them finicky backs and guts weak from hernias. Racing against conveyor belts had given them ulcers. Their ankles and knees ached from years of standing on concrete. Anyone who had worked for long around machines was hard of hearing. They squinted, and the skin of their faces was creased like the leather of old work gloves. There were times, studying them, when I dreaded growing up. Most of them coughed, from dust or cigarettes, and most of them drank cheap wine or whiskey, so their eyes looked bloodshot and bruised. The fathers of my friends always seemed older than the mothers. Men wore out sooner. Only women lived into old age.

As a boy I also knew another sort of men, who did not sweat and break down like mules. They were soldiers, and so far as I could tell they scarcely worked at all. But when the shooting started, many of them would die. This was what soldiers were *for,* just as a hammer was for driving nails.

Warriors and toilers: these seemed, in my boyhood vision, to be the chief destinies for men. They weren't the only destinies, as I learned from having a few male teachers, from reading books, and from watching television. But the men on television—the politicians, the astronauts, the generals, the savvy lawyers, the philosophical doctors, the bosses who gave orders to both soldiers and laborers—seemed as remote and unreal to me as the figures in Renaissance tapestries. I could no more imagine growing up to become one of these cool, potent creatures than I could imagine becoming a prince.

A nearer and more hopeful example was that of my father, who had escaped from a red-dirt farm to a tire factory, and from the assembly line to the front office. Eventually he dressed in a white shirt and tie. He carried himself as if he had been born to work with his mind. But his body, remembering the earlier years of slogging work, began to give out on him in his fifties, and it quit on him entirely before he turned 65.

A scholarship enabled me not only to attend college, a rare enough feat *15* in my circle, but even to study in a university meant for the children of the rich. Here I met for the first time young men who had assumed from birth that they would lead lives of comfort and power. And for the first time I met women who told me that men were guilty of having kept all the joys and privileges of the earth for themselves. I was baffled. What privileges? What joys? I thought about the maimed, dismal lives of most of the men back home. What had they stolen from their wives and daughters? The right to go five days a week, 12 months a year, for 30 or 40 years to a steel mill or a coal mine? The right to drop bombs and die in war? The right to feel every leak in the roof, every gap in the fence, every cough in the engine as a wound they must mend? The right to feel, when the layoff comes or the plant shuts down, not only afraid but ashamed?

I was slow to understand the deep grievances of women. This was because, as a boy, I had envied them. Before college, the only people I had ever known who were interested in art or music or literature, the only ones who read books, the only ones who ever seemed to enjoy a sense of ease and grace were the mothers and daughters. Like the menfolk, they fretted about money, they scrimped and made do. But, when the pay stopped coming in, they were not the ones who had failed. Nor did they have to go to war, and that seemed to me a blessed fact. By comparison with the narrow, ironclad days of fathers, there was an expansiveness, I thought, in the days of mothers. They went to see neighbors, to shop in town, to run errands at school, at the library, at church. No doubt, had I looked harder at their lives, I would have envied them less. It was not my fate to become a woman, so it was easier for me to see the graces. I didn't see, then, what a prison a house could be, since houses seemed to me brighter, handsomer places than any factory. I did not realize—because such things were never spoken of—how often women suffered from men's bullying. Even then I could see how exhausting it was for a mother to cater all day to the needs of young children. But if I had been asked, as a boy, to choose between tending a baby and tending a machine, I think I would have chosen the baby. (Having now tended both, I know I would choose the baby.)

So I was baffled when the women at college accused me and my sex of having cornered the world's pleasures. I think something like my bafflement has been felt by other boys (and by girls as well) who grew up in dirt-poor farm country, in mining country, in black ghettos, in Hispanic barrios, in the shadows of factories, in Third World nations—any place where the fate of men is just as grim and bleak as the fate of women.

When the women I met at college thought about the joys and privileges of men, they did not carry in their minds the sort of men I had known in my childhood. They thought of their fathers, who were bankers, physicians, architects, stockbrokers, the big wheels of the big cities. They were never laid off, never short of cash at month's end, never lined up for welfare. These fathers made decisions that mattered. They ran the world.

The daughters of such men wanted to share in this power, this glory. So did I. They yearned for a say over their future, for jobs worthy of their abilities, for the right to live at peace, unmolested, whole. Yes, I thought, yes yes. The difference between me and these daughters was that they saw me, because of my sex, as destined from birth to become like their fathers, and therefore as an enemy to their desires. But I knew better. I wasn't an enemy, in fact or in feeling. I was an ally. If I had known, then, how to tell them so, would they have believed me? Would they now?

Suggestions for Writing and Discussion
1. What does the opening scene of this essay show you about the author and the conflict going on here?
2. Explore the connotations of the words *victim* and *persecutor* (paragraph 8). How appropriate do you find these terms in the context of men and women?
3. In what ways could the men who the author says affected him the most claim they are victims?
4. What scene or image in this piece do you find most powerful? Explain.
5. What purpose does the final question serve? How effective do you find it?

Suggestions for Extended Thinking and Writing
1. Looking at your own family tree, your own family experiences, analyze the ways in which male and female roles have changed.
2. Conduct a survey on your local college campus to find out what others think about this question: Whose lives are harder today—men's or women's?
3. Research current statistics to find out what jobs are most popular for men and for women today. Compare these facts with statistics available 10, 20, 30, 40, and 50 years ago. Write a report documenting your findings.

Vocabulary Check
   To help ensure that you've understood this selection, and to help you develop a more extensive vocabulary, check the definitions of unfamiliar

words in the selection. The words listed below may be new to you, as might others, which you should also identify and define in this exercise.

muddle (7), tilling (10), tapestry (13), dismal (15), cater (16)

Using the paragraph numbers in parentheses, which correspond with the numbers in the selection's right margins, locate the words listed above in the reading and develop definitions based on the context in which the words are used (see the guidelines for identifying meaning from context clues on pages 23–24 in Section 3). When you're satisfied with your definitions, use a dictionary to confirm the meaning of each word, and then write your own sentences using these words.

KATE CHOPIN

The Storm

Chopin's place in American feminist literature must be viewed within the context of the times in which she lived. She was born in 1851 in St. Louis, Missouri, at the height of the Victorian era. Her mother was prominent in the aristocratic French-Creole community, while her father was an Irish immigrant who became a successful merchant and a founder of the Pacific Railroad. When Chopin was a young child, he was a passenger on the train's inaugural run and drowned when the train plunged into a river from a broken bridge.

Her childhood was spent with her mother and great-grandmother, who filled her mind with tales of the French settlers. Her imagination was further fueled by reading fairy tales, religious allegories, poetry, and novels by Scott and Dickens.

In her early adult life she participated in St. Louis's high society, played the piano, attended operas and symphonies, and presided over a salon of intellectuals and celebrities.

She came to question the view that favored male domination and the submission of women. Her radical depictions of love, sex, and marriage were considered scandalous, and her first novel, *The Awakening,* was severely censured, as were her collections of short stories denouncing marriage and advocating self-determination for women.

In today's more enlightened climate, *The Awakening* has been hailed as a masterpiece, and Chopin has gained stature as a pioneer in American feminist literature.

Pre-Reading and Journal-Writing Suggestions
1. What are your feelings on the topic of adultery? Explore them.
2. What is the purpose of the institution of marriage? Explain your thoughts.
3. If "love" were a character, what would he or she look like? Likewise, if "passion" were a character, what would he or she look like?

1

The leaves were so still that even Bibi thought it was going to rain. *1* Bobinôt, who was accustomed to converse on terms of perfect equality with his little son, called the child's attention to certain sombre clouds that were rolling with sinister intention from the west, accompanied by a sullen, threatening roar. They were at Friedheimer's store and decided to remain there till the storm had passed. They sat within the door on two empty kegs. Bibi was four years old and looked very wise.

"Mama'll be 'fraid, yes," he suggested with blinking eyes.

"She'll shut the house. Maybe she got Sylvie helpin' her this evenin'," Bobinôt responded reassuringly.

"No; she ent got Sylvie. Sylvie was helpin' her yistiday," piped Bibi.

Bobinôt arose and going across to the counter purchased a can of ⁵ shrimps, of which Calixta was very fond. Then he returned to his perch on the keg and sat stolidly holding the can of shrimps while the storm burst. It shook the wooden store and seemed to be ripping great furrows in the distant field. Bibi laid his little hand on his father's knee and was not afraid.

2

Calixta, at home, felt no uneasiness for their safety. She sat at a side window sewing furiously on a sewing machine. She was greatly occupied and did not notice the approaching storm. But she felt very warm and often stopped to mop her face on which the perspiration gathered in beads. She unfastened her white sacque at the throat. It began to grow dark, and suddenly realizing the situation she got up hurriedly and went about closing windows and doors.

Out on the small front gallery she had hung Bobinôt's Sunday clothes to air and she hastened out to gather them before the rain fell. As she stepped outside, Alcée Laballière rode in at the gate. She had not seen him very often since her marriage, and never alone. She stood there with Bobinôt's coat in her hands, and the big rain drops began to fall. Alcée rode his horse under the shelter of a side projection where the chickens had huddled and there were plows and a harrow piled up in the corner.

"May I come and wait on your gallery till the storm is over, Calixta?" he asked.

"Come 'long in, M'sieur Alcée."

His voice and her own startled her as if from a trance, and she seized ¹⁰ Bobinôt's vest. Alcée, mounting to the porch, grabbed the trousers and snatched Bibi's braided jacket that was about to be carried away by a sudden gust of wind. He expressed an intention to remain outside, but it was soon apparent that he might as well have been out in the open: the water beat in upon the boards in driving sheets, and he went inside, closing the door after him. It was even necessary to put something beneath the door to keep the water out.

"My! what a rain! It's good two years sence it rain' like that," exclaimed Calixta as she rolled up a piece of bagging and Alcée helped her to thrust it beneath the crack.

She was a little fuller of figure than five years before when she married; but she had lost nothing of her vivacity. Her blue eyes still retained their melting quality; and her yellow hair, dishevelled by the wind and rain, kinked more stubbornly than ever about her ears and temples.

The rain beat upon the low, shingled roof with a force and clatter that threatened to break an entrance and deluge them there. They were in the dining room—the sitting room—the general utility room. Adjoining was her bed room, with Bibi's couch along side her own. The door stood open, and the room with its white, monumental bed, its closed shutters, looked dim and mysterious.

Alcée flung himself into a rocker and Calixta nervously began to gather up from the floor the lengths of a cotton sheet which she had been sewing.

"If this keeps up, *Dieu sait** if the levees goin' to stan' it!" she exclaimed. *15*

"What have you got to do with the levees?"

"I got enough to do! An' there's Bobinôt with Bibi out in that storm— if he only didn't left Friedheimer's!"

"Let us hope, Calixta, that Bobinôt's got sense enough to come in out of a cyclone."

She went and stood at the window with a greatly disturbed look on her face. She wiped the frame that was clouded with moisture. It was stiflingly hot. Alcée got up and joined her at the window, looking over her shoulder. The rain was coming down in sheets obscuring the view of far-off cabins and enveloping the distant wood in a gray mist. The playing of the lightning was incessant. A bolt struck a tall chinaberry tree at the edge of the field. It filled all visible space with a blinding glare and the crash seemed to invade the very boards they stood upon.

Calixta put her hands to her eyes, and with a cry, staggered backward. *20* Alcée's arm encircled her, and for an instant he drew her close and spasmodically to him.

"*Bonté!*"† she cried, releasing herself from his encircling arm and retreating from the window, "the house'll go next! If I only knew w'ere Bibi was!" She would not compose herself; she would not be seated. Alcée clasped her shoulders and looked into her face. The contact of her warm, palpitating body when he had unthinkingly drawn her into his arms, had aroused all the old-time infatuation and desire for her flesh.

"Calixta," he said, "don't be frightened. Nothing can happen. The house is too low to be struck, with so many tall trees standing about. There! aren't you going to be quiet? say, aren't you?" He pushed her hair back from her face that was warm and steaming. Her lips were as red and moist as

---

**Dieu sait:* God knows.
†*Bonté!:* My goodness!

pomegranate seed. Her white neck and a glimpse of her full, firm bosom disturbed him powerfully. As she glanced up at him the fear in her liquid blue eyes had given place to a drowsy gleam that unconsciously betrayed a sensuous desire. He looked down into her eyes and there was nothing for him to do but to gather her lips in a kiss. It reminded him of Assumption.

"Do you remember—in Assumption, Calixta?" he asked in a low voice broken by passion. Oh! she remembered; for in Assumption he had kissed her and kissed and kissed her; until his senses would well nigh fail, and to save her he would resort to a desperate flight. If she was not an immaculate dove in those days, she was still inviolate; a passionate creature whose very defenselessness had made her defense, against which his honor forbade him to prevail. Now—well, now—her lips seemed in a manner free to be tasted, as well as her round, white throat and her whiter breasts.

They did not heed the crashing torrents, and the roar of the elements made her laugh as she lay in his arms. She was a revelation in that dim, mysterious chamber; as white as the couch she lay upon. Her firm, elastic flesh that was knowing for the first time its birthright, was like a creamy lily that the sun invites to contribute its breath and perfume to the undying life of the world.

The generous abundance of her passion, without guile or trickery, was 25 like a white flame which penetrated and found response in depths of his own sensuous nature that had never yet been reached.

When he touched her breasts they gave themselves up in quivering ecstasy, inviting his lips. Her mouth was a fountain of delight. And when he possessed her, they seemed to swoon together at the very borderland of life's mystery.

He stayed cushioned upon her, breathless, dazed, enervated, with his heart beating like a hammer upon her. With one hand she clasped his head, her lips lightly touching his forehead. The other hand stroked with a soothing rhythm his muscular shoulders.

The growl of the thunder was distant and passing away. The rain beat softly upon the shingles, inviting them to drowsiness and sleep. But they dared not yield.

The rain was over; and the sun was turning the glistening green world into a palace of gems. Calixta, on the gallery, watched Alcée ride away. He turned and smiled at her with a beaming face; and she lifted her pretty chin in the air and laughed aloud.

3

Bobinôt and Bibi, trudging home, stopped without at the cistern to 30 make themselves presentable.

"My! Bibi, w'at will yo' mama say! You ought to be ashame'. You oughtn' put on those good pants. Look at 'em! An' that mud on yo' collar! How you got that mud on yo' collar, Bibi? I never saw such a boy!" Bibi was the picture of pathetic resignation. Bobinôt was the embodiment of serious solicitude as he strove to remove from his own person and his son's the signs of their tramp over heavy roads and through wet fields. He scraped the mud off Bibi's bare legs and feet with a stick and carefully removed all traces from his heavy brogans. Then, prepared for the worst—the meeting with an over-scrupulous housewife, they entered cautiously at the back door.

Calixta was preparing supper. She had set the table and was dripping coffee at the hearth. She sprang up as they came in.

"Oh, Bobinôt! You back! My! but I was uneasy. W'ere you been during the rain? An' Bibi? he ain't wet? he ain't hurt?" She had clasped Bibi and was kissing him effusively. Bobinôt's explanations and apologies which he had been composing all along the way, died on his lips as Calixta felt him to see if he were dry, and seemed to express nothing but satisfaction at their safe return.

"I brought you some shrimps, Calixta," offered Bobinôt, hauling the can from his ample side pocket and laying it on the table.

"Shrimps! Oh, Bobinôt! you too good fo' anything!" and she gave him a smacking kiss on the cheek that resounded. "*J'vous reponds,** we'll have a feas' to-night! umph-umph!" 35

Bobinôt and Bibi began to relax and enjoy themselves, and when the three seated themselves at table they laughed much and so loud that anyone might have heard them as far away as Laballière's.

4

Alcée Laballière wrote to his wife, Clarisse, that night. It was a loving letter, full of tender solicitude. He told her not to hurry back, but if she and the babies liked it at Biloxi, to stay a month longer. He was getting on nicely; and though he missed them, he was willing to bear the separation a while longer—realizing that their health and pleasure were the first things to be considered.

5

As for Clarisse, she was charmed upon receiving her husband's letter. She and the babies were doing well. The society was agreeable; many of her

*J'vous reponds: I assure you.

old friends and acquaintances were at the bay. And the first free breath since her marriage seemed to restore the pleasant liberty of her maiden days. Devoted as she was to her husband, their intimate conjugal life was something which she was more than willing to forego for a while.

So the storm passed and everyone was happy.

Suggestions for Writing and Discussion
1. Analyze the role that the storm plays in this story.
2. What is your initial reaction to this piece? Do you like it or not? Give a few reasons for your answer.
3. Without rereading the story, what images and details stand out most clearly in your mind?
4. Which character do you like the most in this piece? The least? Explain.
5. Do you think that Calixta and Bobinôt's marriage will survive the "storm"? Will Alcée and Clarisse's? Explain.
6. What might the author's purpose be in writing this story? Examine several possibilities and then settle on the one you find most plausible.

Suggestions for Extended Thinking and Writing
1. Write an argument defending or criticizing Calixta and Alcée's actions. As you plan your essay, consider the final line of the story: "So the storm passed and everyone was happy." Do you agree?
2. Go back to the pre-reading response you gave in which you created metaphors for the concepts of "love" and "passion." Write an essay in which you compare these two concepts based on your metaphors as well as the images and characters in Chopin's short story.
3. What is love? Write an essay in which you define it without ever naming it.

Vocabulary Check
To help ensure that you've understood this selection, and to help you develop a more extensive vocabulary, check the definitions of unfamiliar words in the selection. The words listed below may be new to you, as might others, which you should also identify and define in this exercise.

converse (1), harrow (7), vivacity (12), drowsy (22), conjugal (8)

Using the paragraph numbers in parentheses, which correspond with the numbers in the selection's right margins, locate the words listed above in the reading and develop definitions based on the context in which the words are used (see the guidelines for identifying meaning from context clues on pages 23–24 in Section 3). When you're satisfied with your definitions, use a dictionary to confirm the meaning of each word, and then write your own sentences using these words.

SUGGESTIONS FOR MAKING CONNECTIONS

1. Watch a few popular sitcoms on television today, noting especially the roles that men and women play. After several observations, compare these media roles to those mentioned in any two essays in this section. Do the media portrayals support the conflicts mentioned in either one of the essays? As far as your own experience is concerned, which portrayal is most true?
2. Write an essay in which you analyze the relationships between men and women according to several sources in this section. Feel free to include your own personal knowledge about this topic as well.
3. Which sex really has the upper hand in America today? Write an essay in which you argue effectively for either the men or the women. Refer to selections in this section as you respond.
4. In what ways does a black man's life differ from a white man's life? Write an essay in which you compare these two groups and draw some conclusions about what traits these men share, as well as what, if anything, keeps them distinct and apart.
5. In what ways do you see white women's lives in the United States as different from the lives of minority women? Write an essay in which you analyze these two groups to find the similarities and the differences among women, according to their culture.
6. "Am I really my brother's or sister's keeper?" Write an essay in which you explore whether each human has a moral responsibility to aid fellow humans. Here, you will explore your own philosophy on this question as well as referring to several sources in this section.
7. Working as a group with several other students in your class, design a questionnaire that raises questions about how men view women or women view men on your college campus. Distribute the questionnaire among faculty, staff, and students. After studying the data you gather, write an essay in which you draw conclusions based on the information you received and on the discussions with your group about these data. Do your conclusions coincide with or contradict any of the writers in this section?
8. Compare the power that men have with the power that women possess. Are these two groups equally "strong," or does one group have an advantage over the other? Document your findings with sources from this section as well as any outside sources you care to consult.

9. You have the choice of being born a white male, a black male, a white woman, or a black woman. Based on the opinions and facts offered in this section, make a decision. Support your answer not from a personal standpoint, but from the standpoint that you are "unborn" and have only these sources to guide you.

10. Working with a group of your fellow students, interview professional women to discover how the feminist movement has affected their careers, their roles, and the quality of their lives. Interview professional men for the same purpose. Write a report explaining and evaluating your findings. Do these findings contradict or confirm any author's beliefs in this section? Do they contradict or confirm your own?

12
Choices, Actions, and the Future

Reading Images

Do the concerns suggested by the details of the photograph above and the one on page 300 seem typical to you of the choices and actions that will be required of you? Explain why or why not.

CHARLES KRAUTHAMMER

Of Headless Mice . . . and Men

Charles Krauthammer was born in New York City in 1950. In his early childhood, his family moved to Canada, where he later attended McGill University. After earning his BA at McGill, Krauthammer studied at Harvard Medical School, earning his MD in 1975. After working for several years as a psychiatrist at Massachusetts General Hospital, he accepted the invitation of President Carter to become a science adviser. In addition, he became a speechwriter for Vice President Walter Mondale. Krauthammer has worked as a reporter for the *New Republic* and as a columnist for the *Washington Post* and *Time* magazine. The following essay first appeared in *Time* in 1998.

Pre-Reading and Journal-Writing Suggestions
1. What's your gut reaction to cloning?
2. In general, how do you view modern technology: as a gift or a danger?

Last year Dolly the cloned sheep was received with wonder, titters and   1
some vague apprehension. Last week the announcement by a Chicago physicist that he is assembling a team to produce the first human clone occasioned yet another wave of Brave New World anxiety. But the scariest news of all—and largely overlooked—comes from two obscure labs, at the University of Texas and at the University of Bath. During the past four years, one group created headless mice; the other, headless tadpoles.

For sheer Frankenstein wattage, the purposeful creation of these animal monsters has no equal. Take the mice. Researchers found the gene that tells the embryo to produce the head. They deleted it. They did this in a thousand mice embryos, four of which were born. I use the term loosely. Having no way to breathe, the mice died instantly.

Why then create them? The Texas researchers want to learn how genes determine embryo development. But you don't have to be a genius to see the true utility of manufacturing headless creatures: for their organs—fully formed, perfectly useful, ripe for plundering.

Why should you be panicked? Because humans are next. "It would almost certainly be possible to produce human bodies without a forebrain," Princeton biologist Lee Silver told the London *Sunday Times*. "These human bodies without any semblance of consciousness would not be considered persons, and thus it would be perfectly legal to keep them 'alive' as a future source of organs."

"Alive." Never have a pair of quotation marks loomed so ominously. 5 Take the mouse-frog technology, apply it to humans, combine it with cloning, and you are become a god: with a single cell taken from, say, your finger, you produce a headless replica of yourself, a mutant twin, arguably lifeless, that becomes your own personal, precisely tissue-matched organ farm.

There are, of course, technical hurdles along the way. Suppressing the equivalent "head" gene in man. Incubating tiny infant organs to grow into larger ones that adults could use. And creating artificial wombs (as per Aldous Huxley),[1] given that it might be difficult to recruit sane women to carry headless fetuses to their birth/death.

It won't be long, however, before these technical barriers are breached. The ethical barriers are already cracking. Lewis Wolpert, professor of biology at University College, London, finds producing headless humans "personally distasteful" but, given the shortage of organs, does not think distaste is sufficient reason not to go ahead with something that would save lives. And Professor Silver not only sees "nothing wrong, philosophically or rationally," with producing headless humans for organ harvesting, he wants to convince a skeptical public that it is perfectly O.K.

When prominent scientists are prepared to acquiesce in—or indeed encourage—the deliberate creation of deformed and dying quasi-human life, you know we are facing a bioethical abyss. Human beings are ends, not means. There is no grosser corruption of biotechnology than creating a human mutant and disemboweling it at our pleasure for spare parts.

The prospect of headless human clones should put the whole debate about "normal" cloning in a new light. Normal cloning is less a treatment for infertility than a treatment for vanity. It is a way to produce an exact genetic replica of yourself that will walk the earth years after you're gone.

But there is a problem with a clone. It is not really you. It is but a twin, 10 a perfect John Doe Jr., but still a junior. With its own independent consciousness, it is, alas, just a facsimile of you.

The headless clone solves the facsimile problem. It is a gateway to the ultimate vanity: immortality. If you create a real clone, you cannot transfer your consciousness into it to truly live on. But if you create a headless clone of just your body, you have created a ready source of replacement parts to keep you—your consciousness—going indefinitely.

Which is why one form of cloning will inevitably lead to the other. Cloning is the technology of narcissism, and nothing satisfies narcissism like immortality. Headlessness will be cloning's crowning achievement.

---

[1]Aldous Huxley (1894–1963) was a British writer. His novel *Brave New World* (1932) satirizes a technological society where human embryos are developed in bottles. [Editor's note.]

The time to put a stop to this is now. Dolly moved President Clinton to create a commission that recommended a temporary ban on human cloning. But with physicist Richard Seed threatening to clone humans, and with headless animals already here, we are past the time for toothless commissions and meaningless bans.

Clinton banned federal funding of human-cloning research, of which there is none anyway. He then proposed a five-year ban on cloning. This is not enough. Congress should ban human cloning now. Totally. And regarding one particular form, it should be draconian: the deliberate creation of headless humans must be made a crime, indeed a capital crime. If we flinch in the face of this high-tech barbarity, we'll deserve to live in the hell it heralds.

Suggestions for Writing and Discussion

1. Either alone or in small groups, skim through each paragraph and jot down one or two of the most powerful words you find. Based on this list, what initial conclusions can you draw about the author's stance on cloning?

2. Krauthammer uses the word *headless* ten times. What purpose does he achieve in doing so?

3. How fair do you find Krauthammer's argument in this piece? Would you accuse him of exaggeration? If so, point to examples to prove your point.

4. How possible is it, do you believe, that cloning could be a reality for the immediate future?

5. What comparison might Krauthammer want his readers to make when he uses the phrase "spare parts"?

6. If you have read Steinbeck's novel, *Of Mice and Men,* provide some connections between that book and the title of this piece.

Suggestions for Extended Thinking and Writing

1. Write Krauthammer a letter in which you either reinforce or disagree with several of the points he is making about cloning.

2. Locate a current journal article or newspaper feature about the topic of cloning and write a summary and response to the piece.

3. Write an essay in which you persuade an audience of your peers about the dangers of another present use of technology.

Vocabulary Check

To help ensure that you've understood this selection, and to help you develop a more extensive vocabulary, check the definitions of unfamiliar words in the selection. The words listed below may be new to you, as might others, which you should also identify and define in this exercise.

clone (1), replica (5), abyss (8), narcissism (12), draconian (14)

Using the paragraph numbers in parentheses, which correspond with the numbers in the selection's right margins, locate the words listed above in the reading and develop definitions based on the context in which the words are used (see the guidelines for identifying meaning from context clues on pages 23–24 in Section 3). When you're satisfied with your definitions, use a dictionary to confirm the meaning of each word, and then write your own sentences using these words.

RENE SANCHEZ

Surfing's Up and Grades Are Down

Born in 1965, Rene Sanchez graduated from Loyola University of the South and then became an intern for the *Washington Post.* She currently works as a reporter for the *Post,* covering national events and issues related to education and the schools. The following article first appeared in the *Washington Post National Weekly Edition* in 1996.

Pre-Reading and Journal-Writing Suggestions
1. Imagine the world without computers. What difference does it make to your life?
2. In general, how do you use your "free" time? What activity or hobby occupies most of this "free" time?

A new campus support group called "Caught in the Web" is being   *1*
formed at the University of Maryland to counsel students spending too much time on computers.

At the Massachusetts Institute of Technology, students unable to break their addiction to playing computer games on campus terminals have new help. At their request, the university will deny them access whenever they try to sign on.

Faculty studying the freshman dropout rate at Alfred University in New York have just found that nearly half the students who quit last semester had been logging marathon, late-night time on the Internet.

Nationwide, as colleges charge into the digital age with high-tech libraries, wired dormitories, and computerized course work, faculty and campus counselors are discovering a troubling side effect: A growing number of students are letting computers overwhelm their lives.

It is hardly a crisis on any campus—yet. Some college officials say it is   *5*
merely a fad, and not nearly as harmful as other bad habits students often fall prey to on campuses—such as binge drinking of alcohol. But concern over the issue is spreading.

Some universities now are imposing limits on the time students spend each day, or each week, on campus computers. Other colleges are debating whether to monitor the time students spend on computer games and chat rooms, then program a warning to appear on their screens when it gets excessive.

Some college counselors are creating workshops on the subject and planning to include them in freshman orientation programs. Others already are urging students not to plunge into on-line relationships with strangers.

"More and more students are losing themselves in this," says Judith Klavans, the director of Columbia University's Center for Research on Information Access. "It's very accessible on campuses, and students have time on their hands. We're seeing some of them really drift off into this world at the expense of practically everything else."

Campus officials say that communicating on the Internet or roaming the huge universe of information on the World Wide Web holds an especially powerful lure for many college students because it takes them into a vast new realm of learning and research, usually at no cost. But for students having trouble establishing social ties at large universities, or who are on their own, unsupervised, and facing adult pressures for the first time, it also poses an array of new risks.

At the University of California's Berkeley campus, counselors say they 10 are dealing with a small but increasing number of student cases linked to excessive computer use. Some students, they say, are putting too much emphasis on electronic relationships, are neglecting course work, and, in a few instances, are even being swindled out of money by e-mail strangers they have come to trust.

"There can be a real sense of isolation on a large campus, and for young students or new students, this seems like a safe, easy way to form relationships," says Jeff Prince, the associate director of counseling at UC-Berkeley. "But some go overboard. It becomes their only way to connect to the world. One of the things we're really working on now is helping students balance how many social needs they try to have fulfilled by computers."

Linda Tipton, a counselor at the University of Maryland, which limits students to forty hours a week on campus terminals, says she began noticing some of the same problems arise last year in individual and group therapy sessions.

Some of them, she says, spoke of spending more than six hours a day on-line and considered a computerized forum the only setting in which they could express themselves or relate well to others. A few students told her of dropping or flunking courses partly because they were so preoccupied with the Internet. Others confessed to trying to get multiple computer accounts with the university to circumvent its forty-hour-a-week rule.

"Obviously, this is a wonderful tool, and for many students it's perfectly fine," says Tipton, who is trying to form a campus support group and develop a workshop on Internet addiction. "But for others it's becoming a tremendous escape from the pressures of college life. Students can become whomever they want, for as long as they want, and many other things in their lives, like classes, start to suffer."

Nathaniel Cordova, a graduate student at Maryland, says his problems 15 are not that severe—but he is nevertheless heeding Tipton's advice and trying to cut back on the time he spends on computers. And he says he routinely talks to other students on campus also trying to break habits like his. "I don't think I'm an addict," Cordova says. "But I admit, sometimes I'll be in my office at eight o'clock at night, and then the next thing I know it's three A.M., and I realize I forgot to eat. It's so easy to get drawn in, and not just in research, but talking to people. You tell yourself, 'Okay, just one more link-up.' But you keep going."

Other college officials, however, say the concern seems exaggerated.

Some say they see few signs of trouble, and others say student interest in computer games or the Web is often intense at first, then fades. One of the venerable rites of college, they contend, is for students to find distractions from their academic burdens. They say this one is much safer than many others causing campus problems.

"There will always be something like this on college campuses," says Richard Wiggins, who manages information systems and teaches computer courses at Michigan State University. "In my day, in the 1970s, it was pinball. We played that all the time to get rid of stress. Usually things like this are not that harmful."

"For some people, it's just a great new way to waste time," says Jeff 20 Boulier, a senior at George Washington University who spends several hours a day on the Internet. "And college students have always been quite dedicated to wasting time."

At MIT, Patrick McCormick, an undergraduate who helps administer computer game systems for the university, says he sees both sides of the trend. A few students in his residence hall dropped classes, or saw their grades sink, after they lapsed into intensive computer use. "But others stay up all night with this stuff and still get 4.0s," he says. "It's very easy to get sucked in, but it isn't always bad."

Still, McCormick notes one problem he spots consistently: Classmates who trust virtually everyone they meet, or everything they read, on-line. "Some people think if it's on a computer screen, it must be true, and they get burned," he says. "You hear them talking about flying their dream lover up, and of course they never show."

This spring, Alfred University in upstate New York decided to examine what the students who dropped out last semester had in common. What prompted the inquiry was that twice as many students as usual—seventy-five, mostly freshmen—did not return for classes there this spring.

Every student at Alfred receives a campus computer account, which is free. So Connie Beckman, the director of Alfred's computer center, decided to check the account records of all the students who had dropped out. She found that half of them had been logging as much as six hours a day on computer games or the Web, usually late at night. "It was the only thing that correlated among so many of them," Beckman says.

University officials say they doubt that is the only, or even the primary, 25 reason many of those students quit. But the discovery has led to several new policies.

Next fall, for the first time, freshmen at Alfred will be told about the dangers of heavy computer use as soon as they arrive on campus. Residence halls, all of which have computer rooms, also will each have a full-time, professional counselor to keep a close eye on late-night computer addicts. Other campuses are studying similar moves.

"We've dealt with alcohol and drugs; we've dealt with TV and video games. Now this looks like the latest pitfall for college students," Beckman says. "They're doing this all night instead of doing their homework, or eating, or sleeping. When they're up until five A.M. playing around on the Web, they're not going to make their eight A.M. classes."

Suggestions for Writing and Discussion
1. Overall, does Sanchez's article convince you that there is a problem with college students and their overuse of computers? Explain.
2. What examples or quotes in this piece do you find most convincing? Least convincing?
3. To what does Sanchez attribute this addiction: the nature of the individual, the allure of computers, or the atmosphere on college campuses?
4. Explore the reasons why some students today may find computers their "only way to connect with the world" (paragraph 11).
5. What do you think of this claim: "College students have always been dedicated to wasting time"? (paragraph 20). On what do you base your response?

Suggestions for Extended Thinking and Writing
1. Explain, in either a serious or a humorous manner, an "addiction" you have experienced. Try to express how this addiction changed you and how it got started.
2. Write an essay in which you compare your own experiences with college students and computer use to Sanchez's observations and claims.
3. Write a letter to your college newspaper in which you take a strong stance on one side of this issue: Colleges should regulate computer use by their students.

Vocabulary Check
To help ensure that you've understood this selection, and to help you develop a more extensive vocabulary, check the definitions of unfamiliar words in the selection. The words listed below may be new to you, as might others, which you should also identify and define in this exercise.

prey (5), lure (9), forum (13), venerable (18), lapsed (21)

Using the paragraph numbers in parentheses, which correspond with the numbers in the selection's right margins, locate the words listed above in the reading and develop definitions based on the context in which the words are used (see the guidelines for identifying meaning from context clues on pages 23–24 in Section 3). When you're satisfied with your definitions, use a dictionary to confirm the meaning of each word, and then write your own sentences using these words.

LORE SEGAL

Modern Courtesy

Lore Segal was born in Austria and emigrated to New York. She is widely known for her children's books such as *Tell Me a Mitzi, Tell Me a Trudi,* and *The Story of Mrs. Lovewright and Purrless Her Cat,* as well as for her adult novels, including *Her First American.* Her articles and fiction have appeared in such periodicals as the *New Yorker,* the *New Republic,* and the *Saturday Evening Post.* The following essay, which comments on the way manners and courtesies change with each generation, first appeared in 1987 in the *New York Times.*

Pre-Reading and Journal-Writing Suggestions
1. List five words that come to your mind when you think of today's teenagers and young adults. Now go back and briefly explain the reasons for these choices.
2. What are you most apt to do when you're in the presence of someone you find totally annoying: smile and be polite, ignore them outright, or tell them what you really think of them? Explain your reasons for acting in this manner.

My son and I were having one of our rare quarrels. Jacob is a formidable   1
person and our difference was on a matter of substance—modern manners versus the old courtesies. Signor Giuseppe, an elderly neighbor from the Old World, had complained that Jacob didn't say good morning when he got on the elevator and that he answered Signor Giuseppe's questions reluctantly.

My son said Signor Giuseppe's questions were phonies. Signor Giuseppe did not give a hoot about how many inches my son had grown and couldn't care less what subjects he was taking in school. My son said these were questions that didn't deserve answers.

I argued that it is the business of courtesy to cover up the terrible truth that we don't give a hoot about the other person in the elevator.

"Why is that terrible and why cover it up?" my son asked sensibly.

Jacob belongs to the generation that says "Me and Joe are going out,"   5
and whichever walks through the door first trusts the other to take care its back swing doesn't catch him in the head. My generation says "Signor Giuseppe and I are going out," and Signor Giuseppe opens the door and holds it for me.

Jacob said: "Why? You can open it for yourself."

This is true. It is also true that "me and Joe" is the formulation that corresponds to my experience. It's my own passage through the door that occupies my mind. It's because Signor Giuseppe might, in the press of the things on *his* mind, forget that I'm coming behind, that courtesy tells him to let me go ahead. Courtesy makes me pass him the cookies, keeping me artificially aware of his hunger, which I don't experience. My own appetite can be trusted to take care of *my* cookies.

Signor Giuseppe and I reach the corner. His anachronistic hand under my forearm presumes that a lady cannot step off the curb without a supporting gentleman—a presumption for which modern men have been hit across the head with umbrellas. That is why my graduate student, who chats amusingly as we walk down the corridor, does *not* open the door for me.

"Why should he?" Jacob asked.

"Because I'm carrying two packages in my right hand, my books in my   *10* left, and my handbag and umbrella under my armpit," I said.

If my son or my graduate student were boors, we would not be addressing this matter. A boor is a boor and was always a boor. But I can tell that the muscles of my graduate student's back are readying to bend and pick up the book and umbrella I have dropped. He struggles between his natural courtesy and the learned inhibition that *I* have taught him: My being a woman is no reason for him to pick my things up for me. I crawl on the floor retrieving my property. He remains standing.

My son is not only formidable, he is a person of good will. He said: "That's stupid! If you see someone is in trouble you go and help them out. What's it got to do with courtesy?"

This is what it has to do with it: Having thrown out the old, dead, hypocritical rules about napkins, knives, and how to address the ladies, it is Jacob's and it is my graduate student's business to recover the essential baby that went down the drain as well. They must invent their own rules for eating so they don't look and sound nasty, and my student must count my packages to see if I need his help. When Jacob enters the elevator, he is required to perform a complex act of the imagination: Is Signor Giuseppe a plain pain in the neck or does he have trouble?

"His trouble is he's a pain in the neck," Jacob said.

"And your business is to keep him from finding it out."   *15*

"Why?" Jacob shouted.

"Because once Signor Giuseppe understands that he's too great a pain to chat with for the time the elevator takes to descend from the 12th to the ground floor, he will understand that he will die alone."

My son guffawed. He is not required to join me in this leap: The old courtesy was in the essential business of the cover-up. It was the contract by which I agreed to pretend to find your concerns of paramount interest, in return for which you took care not to let on that you did not care a hoot about mine.

Jacob said he still thought one should say what one meant and talk to the people one liked. But he said next time he got in the elevator with Signor Giuseppe, he was going to tell him good morning.

Suggestions for Writing and Discussion
1. Summarize Segal's main point and find where it is implied or stated most dramatically in this essay.
2. What differences are most apparent among the three generations in this piece? Which one do you find yourself sympathizing with most? What reasons can you give for this response?
3. What are your general impressions of the son, Jacob? How does he compare to the list you made in the pre-reading exercise?
4. Do you agree with Segal when she writes that her son and the graduate student are not "boors"? Does she convince you that her son is "a person of good will"? Why or why not?
5. Who "wins" the "rare quarrel" in this piece? Explain.

Suggestions for Extended Thinking and Writing
1. Compare and contrast the beliefs, manners, or actions between two members of your family who represent two different generations.
2. Observe the manners of college students in one specific setting, such as the classroom, dorm rooms, cafeteria, library, or a sports event. Compare your findings to Segal's.
3. Read a few chapters from Emily Post's book on manners. Analyze the relevance of or adherence to three or four specific manners as they relate to young people today.

Vocabulary Check
   To help ensure that you've understood this selection, and to help you develop a more extensive vocabulary, check the definitions of unfamiliar words in the selection. The words listed below may be new to you, as might others, which you should also identify and define in this exercise.

   reluctantly (1), formulation (7), anachronistic (8), formidable (12), paramount (18)

Using the paragraph numbers in parentheses, which correspond with the numbers in the selection's right margins, locate the words listed above in the reading and develop definitions based on the context in which the words are used (see the guidelines for identifying meaning from context clues on pages 23–24 in Section 3). When you're satisfied with your definitions, use a dictionary to confirm the meaning of each word, and then write your own sentences using these words.

SAMUEL FRANCIS

Illegal Motives

Born in Tennessee in 1947, Samuel Francis earned a B.A. from Johns Hopkins University and a Ph.D. in modern history from the University of North Carolina at Chapel Hill. From 1977 to 1981, he was a policy analyst at the Heritage Foundation in Washington, D.C., specializing in foreign affairs, terrorism, and intelligence and internal security issues. From 1981 to 1986, he was legislative assistant for national security affairs to Senator John P. East (Republican, North Carolina) and worked closely with the Senate Judiciary Committee's Subcommittee on Security and Terrorism. From 1986 to 1995, Francis held several editorial positions at the Washington *Times*. He is the author of several articles and studies on international and domestic terrorism.

Pre-Reading and Journal-Writing Suggestions
1. How would you define the word *hate?* As you consider your definition, think of examples to illustrate it.
2. Think of an image or a symbol that you believe represents the concept of hate. Describe the image or symbol and explain why you see it as representing *hate.*

The *Economist,* a British-based but globally circulated news magazine of the proper progressive tint, is not exactly a hate-sheet of the racialist right, but even it is having problems with the very concept of "hate crimes." . . . Acknowledging that the murder in Jasper—where three white men, ex-convicts, tied a black man to the bumper of their pickup truck and dragged him to death, dismembering his body—was one of particular "horror," the editorial nevertheless proceeds to argue that "the notion of 'hate crimes' is flawed."

Had the black victim in Jasper, James Byrd, been white and had he been killed in the same way by the same men, the magazine asks, would the crime have been any less a horror? Had the killers been motivated by perverse sexual drives, by psychopathic delusions, or simply by mercenary reasons, to swipe the change in Mr. Byrd's pockets, would the killing merit the additional punishment that state and federal law reserve only for crimes motivated by race?

Put in that context, the answer ought to be obvious. Murder is murder, and to say that some are motivated by "hate" and others aren't strikes most normal folk as at best a bizarre usage of the word. Sadists who dismember children for pleasure and jilted husbands who beat their wives to a pulp are at least as driven by "hate" in any normal usage as white hoodlums who murder a black man for the fun of it. Yet, the editorial concludes, hate crime laws imply that murders for other motives are "less awful" than those motivated by race.

It also notes that "Once race—or religion, or gender—is introduced into the equation, this naturally colours the motive for the crime in the eyes of the criminal justice system." In effect, the law criminalizes the motives, as it does not do for any other kind of crime.

But the "white supremacist" opinions and the Nazi paraphernalia supposedly left at the scene of the crime are not in themselves against the law. Hence, "The notion of 'hate crime' may be, in effect, an extra penalty imposed on people whose views are offensive, as well as their actions. Ironically, it makes the justice system pick on them simply because they are different." 5

The editorial implies an important point, namely, that hate crime laws come very close to outlawing certain opinions, ideas and attitudes simply because they're offensive to most people. On the same grounds, the law could plausibly penalize perverse sexuality and even jealousy and greed at least as much as it currently punishes "hate."

Yet the editorial could go a bit further. Anglo-American law does not traditionally criminalize motive, no matter how offensive, and the distinction between "motive" and "intent" (which is criminalized in law) used to be quite clear.

If I rob a bank to help my family and my accomplice robs the bank to pad his pockets, we each have a different motive—but we both had the same intent: to rob the bank. "In law," found a leading court case on the issue, People v. Weiss, "there is a clear distinction between" "motive" and "intent." "'Motive' is the moving power which impels to action for a definite result. Intent is the purpose to use a particular means to effect such result."

"Intent," of course, is the element in law that creates the crime itself. A homicide without intent is not murder but manslaughter, and carries a lesser penalty. "Motive," on the other hand, is largely irrelevant to the criminal act and to the punishment the act receives.

No one seems to doubt that the suspects in Jasper "intended" to commit 10 murder, and if the prosecution can prove that intent, their road to the death house will be expedited. But if their crime is tried as one of "hate," not only their intent to kill but also their reasons for killing will have to be proved in court.

That may or may not add to the burdens of the prosecution, but there's no reason to think it will enhance whatever justice is eventually dispensed—and there's every reason to believe that other ideas and the motives they create sooner or later may also become criminal acts.

Suggestions for Writing and Discussion

1. Read paragraph 2; briefly state how Francis defines the phrase "hate crimes." Now read paragraph 4; how does the quotation Francis uses expand the definition he gives in paragraph 2?
2. In paragraph 2, Francis asks two questions. After reading the article and considering the topic, how would you answer those questions?
3. Paragraph 5 raises the issue of First Amendment rights, that is, the right of United States citizens to hold and to express opinions that may not be held by the majority of citizens or by the government. How far do you think First Amendment rights should be extended? Should expressions of hate toward minority groups be protected by the First Amendment?
4. In the final paragraph, Francis notes that there is a difference between "motive" and "intent" in the way laws in the United States are written and interpreted. Check the definitions of both words and explain the distinction Francis is making.
5. Do you see the problem of hate crimes as a major issue facing the United States as we move into the twenty-first century? Explain.

Suggestions for Extended Thinking and Writing

1. Using the *New York Times Index,* or a similar index of current magazines and journals, find at least two articles related to hate crimes. After reading these articles, explain how the information you have discovered leads you to agree or disagree with the ideas expressed by Samuel Francis.
2. Consider the concept of hate crimes as it might apply to wars. For example, do you consider a war that involves the hate crime of "ethnic cleansing," such as that undertaken in Germany before and during World War II or, more recently, in Bosnia, to be more morally repulsive than a war fought over an issue such as one country's desire to take over the land of another country? Explain.
3. Make a study of graffiti within ten miles of your campus. Do you find any evidence that the graffiti you observed reflects concepts that might be related to "hate crimes"? Explain.

Vocabulary Check

   To help ensure that you've understood this selection, and to help you develop a more extensive vocabulary, check the definitions of unfamiliar words in the selection. The words listed below may be new to you, as might others, which you should also identify and define in this exercise.

   tint (1), mercenary (2), plausibly (6), irrelevant (9), enhance (11)

Using the paragraph numbers in parentheses, which correspond with the numbers in the selection's right margins, locate the words listed above in the reading and develop definitions based on the context in which the words are used (see the guidelines for identifying meaning from context clues on pages 23–24 in Section 3). When you're satisfied with your definitions, use a dictionary to confirm the meaning of each word, and then write your own sentences using these words.

LINDA CHAVEZ
There's No Future in Lady Luck

> Linda Chavez, who was born in 1947, served as executive director of the U.S. Commission on Civil Rights during the Reagan administration (1983–85). Her writing focuses on politics and the role of Hispanics from a conservative point of view. She has published articles in the *New Republic,* the *Los Angeles Times,* and the *Wall Street Journal.* In addition, she is the author of *Out of the Barrio: Toward a New Politics of Hispanic Assimilation* (1991). Chavez currently is the president of the Center for Equal Opportunity, based in Washington, D.C. She is writing a book addressing the impact of feminism on social policy. In the article that follows, which was first published in *USA Today* (1991), she challenges readers to consider the implications of choices made by those who participate in legalized gambling.

Pre-Reading and Journal-Writing Suggestions

1. In general, how do you think most people get rich? Explain your response based on your own observations and experiences.
2. Are you one who buys lottery tickets and fills out mailings in the hope of one day winning a huge amount of money? Explain why or why not.

Remember when the American dream meant becoming a millionaire   *1* through talent, hard work, and thrift?

No longer.

Now it's hitting the lottery, with state governments spending millions of dollars a year to promote luck as the key to success.

In 1995, New York expanded the frontier of legalized gambling by offering a new, casino-style game called Quick Draw. Now, instead of a daily lottery, the state draws winning numbers every five minutes, thirteen hours a day, in bars and restaurants around the state.

It's a constant adrenaline rush for compulsive gamblers.   *5*

As one woman explained to the *New York Times,* "I play the daily number, but you have to wait until 7:30 P.M. to know. This is quicker—five minutes—it's like being in Atlantic City."

This same woman, interviewed at a Staten Island, N.Y., shopping center, had come into the place to buy milk and diapers. She won $1 in half an hour—and lost $7. "I have no more money for the diapers and the milk but I had fun," she said in the interview.

Yeah, well what about her baby? What fun will Junior have sitting in wet diapers all day, crying from hunger?

This woman isn't alone—in fact, she's typical of state lottery players.

If you doubt it, spend some time in any convenience store in an inner 10 city in one of the thirty-seven states or the District of Columbia that sell state lottery tickets. The lines of men and women waiting to play their lucky numbers are filled with poor people, many of them no doubt refunding to the state cash from welfare checks paid out for the care of dependent children.

In 1994, states sold $34 billion in lottery tickets. Lottery defenders— most prominently the state officials who oversee the games—claim this money brings in needed revenue for everything from education to health care.

But the fact is, the money is conned from the least educated, most gullible segment of the population.

Joshua Wolf Shenk, writing in the *Washington Monthly* magazine, notes that state lotteries clearly target the poor as their best customers. He quotes an Iowa lottery media plan "to target our message demographically against those that we know to be heavy users."

According to several studies on the subject, that means blacks, Hispanics, and poor whites.

It's bad enough that the state sponsors lotteries, but what is worse is the 15 huge state investment in promoting ticket sales. New York spends $30 million a year in advertising.

And lottery ads are slick.

Virginia's Lady Luck commercials are among the most appealing on television. But their message is no different from all the other lottery ads. You've got to play to win, which means playing every week, every day— or, as now in New York, every hour.

And adults who are legally permitted to buy tickets aren't the only targets of the ad campaigns. Kids are tomorrow's customers.

Recently, I went riding in Potomac, Md., with a little boy who visits me each summer from New York where he lives in a housing project. He had never seen houses like the huge homes that dot the affluent Washington suburb.

"Is that where people who win the lottery live?" he asked. No, I ex- 20 plained, most of the people in those houses are lawyers, doctors, or other professionals who had studied hard, gone to college, and worked many years before they could buy such homes.

Of course, my little New Yorker isn't likely to ever buy a house such as the ones he saw—nor am I, for that matter.

But his chances of owning any house are certainly improved if he heeds my message rather than his own state government's.

Suggestions for Writing and Discussion

1. After reading this selection, what conclusions can you draw about the author's point, purpose, and intended audience?
2. What principles might be at the root of Chavez's obvious disdain for state lotteries?
3. Go back through this piece and find specific facts and examples that Chavez uses to support her claims about lotteries in general. How valid do you find her support to be?
4. Besides working hard, what other advantages might the "doctors, lawyers, and other professionals" have had over Chavez's little friend from New York? Explain.
5. What is your response to Chavez's message at the end? Do you find it realistic? Motivating? True?

Suggestions for Extended Thinking and Writing

1. Write a letter to your local newspaper in which you argue for or against the selling of lottery tickets.
2. Write about yourself or someone you know who has a habit of playing the lottery. In order to present a fair impression, you may want to interview the person about whom you are writing.
3. Spend some time observing the people who buy lottery tickets from a local store in your town. Aim to record dialogue as well as descriptions to draw some conclusions about those who buy tickets. If you feel comfortable, you may also ask these consumers why they are buying the tickets. Compare your findings to Chavez's observations.

Vocabulary Check

To help ensure that you've understood this selection, and to help you develop a more extensive vocabulary, check the definitions of unfamiliar words in the selection. The words listed below may be new to you, as might others, which you should also identify and define in this exercise.

frontier (4), adrenaline (5), gullible (12), demographically (13), heed (22)

Using the paragraph numbers in parentheses, which correspond with the numbers in the selection's right margins, locate the words listed above in the reading and develop definitions based on the context in which the words are used (see the guidelines for identifying meaning from context clues on pages 23–24 in Section 3). When you're satisfied with your definitions, use a dictionary to confirm the meaning of each word, and then write you own sentences using these words.

MEGHAN DAUM

Safe Sex and White Lies in the Time of AIDS

Born in 1970, Meghan Daum completed her undergraduate studies at Vassar in 1992 and earned a master's degree in nonfiction writing at Columbia in 1996. Daum has published articles in the *New York Times* and *GQ* and has worked at Columbia University Press as an assistant editor. In "Safe Sex and White Lies in the Time of AIDS," which was first published in the *New York Times Magazine* (1996), she raises questions about sexual decisions and the language used to define sexual choices and actions.

Pre-Reading and Journal-Writing Suggestions
1. Write a one-page reaction to the acronym AIDS.
2. Write a one-page response to the phrase "safe sex."

I have been tested for HIV three times; the opportunities for testing were there, so I took them, forgetting, each time, the fear and nausea that always ensues before the results come back, those minutes spent in a publicly funded waiting room staring at a video loop about "living with" this thing that kills you. I've been negative each time, which is not surprising in retrospect, since I am not a member of a "high risk group." Yet I continue to go into relationships with the safest of intentions and often discard precaution at some random and tacitly agreed-upon juncture. Perhaps this is a shocking admission, but my hunch is that I'm not the only one doing this. My suspicion is, in fact, that very few of us—"us" being the demographic frequently charged with thinking we're immortal, the population accused of being cynical and lazy and weak for lack of a war draft and altogether unworthy of the label "adult"—have really responded to the AIDS crisis in the way the federal government and the educational system would like to think. My guess is that we're all but ignoring it and that almost anyone who claims otherwise is lying.

It's not that we're reckless. It's more that we're grasping at straws, trying like hell to feel good in a time when half of us seem to be on Prozac and the rest of us have probably been told that we need it. When it comes down to it, it's hard to use condoms. Even as a woman, I know this. Maybe the risk is a substitute for thrills we're missing in other areas of life. Maybe there's something secretly energizing about flirting with death for a night and then ˍhecking six months later to see if we've survived. This, at least, constitutes ˍtensity of experience, a real, tangible interaction with raw fear. It's so ˍ•ch more than what we get most of the time, subject as we are to the largely protected, government approved, safety first-ness of American society. For my peers and myself, it's generally safe to assume that our homes will not be bombed while we sleep, that our flight will not crash, that we will make the daily round trip from our beds to the office and back again without deadly intervention somewhere in between. We live in the land of side impact air bags, childproof caps on vitamins, "do not ingest" warnings on deodorant bottles. We don't intend to die in childbirth. Even for those of us, like myself, who live in cities, who read in *USA Today* polls that we'll probably get mugged eventually, who vaguely mull over the fact that the person shot on the corner last week could have been us, fear continues to exist in the abstract. We've had it pretty cushy. We've been shielded from most forms of undoing by parents and educational institutions and health insurance. But AIDS is housed in its own strange caveat of intimate conversations among friends and those occasional sleepless nights when it occurs to us to wonder about it, upon which that dark paranoia sets in and those catalogs of who we've done it with and who they might have done it with and oh-my-god-I'll-surely-die seem to project themselves onto the ceiling the way fanged monsters did when we were kids. But we fall asleep and then we wake up. And nothing's changed except our willingness to forget about it, which is, in fact, almost everything.

I experience these nights every so often. The last one occurred after listening to a call-in radio show called Love Phones, in which barely articulate yet shockingly precocious teenagers call up a hip, throaty-voiced psychologist and ask questions ranging from prom dates to the latest bondage techniques. One night a 15-year-old girl called and said she'd just been told that a former lover, with whom she'd engaged in unprotected sex, had recently tested HIV positive, and that she herself had so far learned she had chlamydia and was awaiting her own HIV results. The psychologist, Dr. Judy, who usually steers her answers in the direction of promoting her recent book, *Generation Sex,* actually encouraged the audience to pray. I thought this was a curious and unnerving response, especially coming from a shrewd, cutting-edge therapist who had counseled a previous female caller to "go for it" in terms of pursuing a lesbian threesome with two cheerleading squad mates from Floral Park. Over the FM waves that night, Dr. Judy sounded on the brink of tears, and I lay under my covers, horribly concerned, but mostly regretting that I had listened to Love Phones that night, because I wasn't in the mood to face one of these fearful falling asleep sessions. Like witnessing a car accident in which someone's bleeding or screaming, I wish I had taken another road. I wish I hadn't heard that call. I had to be up early the next morning.

And in the morning I did feel better because I convinced myself the caller must be someone living in an altogether different world from and the guy was probably either some 25-year-old junkie she'd picke a dance club in Queens or a bisexual pretty boy of the sort whose effeminacy is enticing to 15-year-olds for its apparent safety and that Love Phones had probably never before received such a call and its producers had patched her through as a way of shaking up the audience and proving to the sponsors that the show was not only entertainment but something *essential*. These were the reasons that I could go on with my life, that plus the fact that I really had no other choice anyway.

But even when we turn off the radio, the media makes it hard for us to   5
go on. A few days after hearing the caller on Love Phones, I saw a movie called *Kids,* photographer Larry Clark's cinema verité foray into the drug-ridden world of a group of unsupervised New York City teenagers. In the film we watch blond, waif-like Chloe get back a positive HIV test result, try unsuccessfully to call her unavailable mother, and then wind her way through the barbaric, trash talking landscape of her "friends" in an effort to seek out Telly, the barely pubescent, sex obsessed marauder who deflowered her and gave her the virus. He, in the meantime, has spent his day soiling another naïf, stealing money from his mother, and viciously attacking someone who looked sideways at his skater buddies before wooing another virgin to his poisoned loins. *Kids,* with its apocalyptic heavy-handedness, tells us that life has surely gone down the tubes. We're goaded into believing that today's youth is so removed from compassion, so alienated from joy, that even the most intimate acts have become as routine as flicking a cigarette, the ashes of which are likely to land in a bed of chemically treated dry leaves that will ignite and burn down the whole block.

Much of the discourse surrounding AIDS in the early 1990s was informed by a male homosexual community, which, in the interests of prevention, assumed an alarmist position about prevention. In a *Village Voice* review of two books about the AIDS crisis and gay men, writer Michael Warner described HIV negative status as "living around, under, and next to crisis for that indefinite, rest-of-your-life blank stretch of time." And even though he is speaking largely of the crisis as it relates to gay men, he points out that for homosexuals and heterosexuals alike, "negative status is always in jeopardy and has to be preserved through effort." These sorts of statements are, in many ways, a legitimate tactic for HIV prevention in the gay community, which has been devastated by the disease in staggering proportions. But when words like "crisis" and "effort" are aimed at the heterosexual population, a lot of us tend to stop listening. What constitutes strenuous effort for one person may be routine behavior for another. For better or worse, guidelines for HIV prevention among straight people are often a matter of interpretation. *Kids* insinuates that it's scarcely possible to make it through a day without exposing oneself to the virus, especially if one is young, trusting, and vulnerable to the smooth talk of boys like Telly, whose slurred lines like

"I think about you all the time" are enough to make 13-year-olds lead him to their ruffled beds. The message here is a troubling one: that AIDS exposes itself to those who expose in themselves some kind of emotional neediness, who possess some semblance of romanticism (even in its uniquely post-modern form of fifteen minutes of sweet talk).

The message is that trusting anyone is itself an irresponsible act, that having faith in an intimate partner, particularly women in relation to men, is a symptom of such profound naiveté that we're obviously not mature enough to be having sex anyway. That this reasoning runs counter to almost any feminist ideology—the ideology that told us, at least back in the 70s, that women should feel free to ask men on dates and wear jeans and have orgasms—is an admission that few AIDS-concerned citizens are willing to make. Two decades after *The Joy of Sex* made sexual pleasure accessible to both genders and the pill put a government approved stamp on premarital sex, we're still being told not to trust each other. Women are being told that if they believe a man who claims he's healthy, they're just plain stupid. Men are wary of any woman who seems one or more steps away from virginhood. Twenty years after the sexual revolution, we seem to be in a sleepier, sadder time than the 1950s. We've entered a period where mistrust equals responsibility, where paranoia signifies health.

Since I spent all of the 1970s under the age of ten, I've never known a significantly different sexual and social climate. Supposedly this makes it easier. Health educators and AIDS activists like to think that people of my generation can be made to unlearn what we never knew, to break the reckless habits we didn't actually form. But what we have learned thoroughly is how not to enjoy ourselves. Just like our mothers, whose adolescences were haunted by the abstract taboo of "nice" girls versus some other kind of girl, my contemporaries and I are again discouraged from doing what feels good. As it was with our mothers, the onus falls largely on the women. We know that it's much easier for women to contract HIV from a man than the other way around. We know that an "unsafe" man generally means someone who's shot drugs or slept with other men, or possibly slept with prostitutes. We find ourselves wondering about these things over dinner dates. We look for any hints of homosexual tendencies, any references to a hypodermic moment. We try to catch him in the lie we've been told he'll tell.

What could be sadder? When I was a young teenager, around the age of Chloe and Telly, I looked forward to growing up and being able to do what I wanted, to live without a curfew, to talk on the phone as long as wanted, and even to find people whom I could love and trust. But trust out of vogue. We're not allowed to believe anyone anymore. And the r we're not isn't because of AIDS but because of the lack of specifi the anxiety that ripples around the disease. The information about AIDS that was formerly known as "awareness" has been subsumed into the unfortunate—and far less effective—incarnation of "style." As in *Kids,* where violence and ignorance are shown so relentlessly that we don't notice it by the end, AIDS awareness has become so much a part of the pop culture that not only is it barely noticeable, it is ineffectual. MTV runs programs about safe sex that are virtually identical to episodes of "The Real World." Madonna pays self-righteous lip service to safe sex despite basketball star Dennis Rodman's claim that she refused to let him wear a condom during their tryst. A print advertisement for the Benetton clothing company features a collage of hundreds of tiny photographs of young people, some of whom are shaded and have the word AIDS written across their faces. Many are white and blond and have the tousled, moneyed look common to more traditional fashion spreads or even yearbooks from colleges like the one I attended. There is no text other than the company's slogan. There is no explanation of how these faces were chosen, no public statement of whether these people actually have the disease or not. I called Benetton for clarification and was told that the photographs were supposed to represent people from all over the world and that no one shown was known to be HIV positive. Just as I suspected, the advertisement was essentially a work of art, which meant I could interpret the image any way I liked. This is how the deliverers of the safer sex message shoot themselves in the foot. By choosing a hard sell over actual information, people like me are going to believe what we want to believe, which, of course, is the thing that isn't so scary. So, I turn the page.

I personally don't know any white female with AIDS. Nor have I ever 10 heard of a man who contracted the virus from a woman. And because of this there have been some situations where I haven't taken precautions and I don't necessarily think I was unwise. This is a difficult admission and it may be stupid logic, but it is the truth. For me and many of my peers, we're simply not seeing AIDS in our community. We're not going to sacrifice the thing we believe we deserve, the experiences we waited for, because of a Chloe or a caller on Love Phones.

This is where I get called a racist, an elitist, an idiot. This is where my college alumni association, chagrined that I didn't absorb all the free information the institution dispensed, removes me from the mailing list. However, I'm speaking for my community, which does make me an elitist in that my community is white, middle-class, educated, and generally prefers to gain some semblance of "relationship" before leaping unshielded on to the scene. I'm speaking for myself, who is not promiscuous, who has said no on more than one occasion, who has been careful on other occasions, but who lies awake at night and wonders if I'll die.

But the inconsistent behavior continues, as do the hushed confessionals among friends and the lies to health care providers during routine exams because we just can't bear the terrifying lectures that ensue when we confess to not always protecting ourselves. Life in one's twenties is fraught not only with the financial and professional uncertainty that is often implicit in the pursuit of one's dreams, but with the specter of death that floats above the pursuit of a sex life. And there is no solution, only the conclusion that invariably finishes the hushed conversations: the whole thing simply "sucks." It's a bummer on a grand scale.

Heterosexuals are being sent vague signals. We're being told that if we are sufficiently vigilant, we'll probably be all right. We're told to assume the worst and not to invite disaster by hoping for the best. We're encouraged to keep our fantasies on tight reigns, otherwise we'll lose control of the whole buggy, and no one will be able to say we weren't warned.

But I've been warned over and over again and there's still no visible cautionary tale. Since I'm as provincial and self-absorbed as the next person, I probably won't truly begin to take the AIDS crisis personally until I see either someone like me succumb to it or concrete statistics that show that we are. Until then, my peers and I are left with generalized anxiety, a low grade fear and anger that resides at the core of everything we do. Our attitudes have been affected by the disease in that we're scared, but our behavior has stayed largely the same. The result of this is a corrosion of the soul, a chronic dishonesty and fear of ourselves that will, for us, likely do more damage than the disease itself. In this world, peace of mind is a utopian concept.

Suggestions for Writing and Discussion

1. Compare your pre-reading responses to the author's views on AIDS and "safe sex." What do your responses have in common with hers? How do they differ?

2. How would you describe the basic tone of this essay, and based on this, what are your impressions of the writer?

3. Explain your understanding of the author's basic message. In general, do you agree or disagree with her? Explain.

4. Without looking back at this piece, what images or scenes come to mind? What conclusions can you draw based on these visuals?

5. Daum describes the film *Kids* and states that such films suggest that young people today are "alienated from joy" and that "even the most intimate acts have become as routine as flicking a cigarette." Do you believe that these descriptions of young people are generally accurate? Explain.

Suggestions for Extended Thinking and Writing
1. Either alone or working collaboratively, distribute a survey on your college campus about how students view AIDS and sex today. Report your findings in a scientific and unbiased manner.
2. Write a letter to the author in which you address several of the points she makes in this piece.
3. Analyze one commercial or ad today that deals with the issue of AIDS.

Vocabulary Check

To help ensure that you've understood this selection, and to help you develop a more extensive vocabulary, check the definitions of unfamiliar words in the selection. The words listed below may be new to you, as might others, which you should also identify and define in this exercise.

tangible (2), abstract (2), effeminacy (4), tryst (9), corrosion (14)

Using the paragraph numbers in parentheses, which correspond with the numbers in the selection's right margins, locate the words listed above in the reading and develop definitions based on the context in which the words are used (see the guidelines for identifying meaning from context clues on pages 23–24 in Section 3). When you're satisfied with your definitions, use a dictionary to confirm the meaning of each word, and then write your own sentences using these words.

———————

KURT VONNEGUT

Harrison Bergeron

Born in 1922 in Indianapolis, Indiana, Kurt Vonnegut is an American novelist noted for his ironic wit and dark humor. Many of his novels have elements of science fiction, which he uses to probe and question what he sees as alarming social and political trends of modern times. For example, in *Slaughterhouse-Five* (1969) he draws heavily on his memories of being a prisoner during the World War II firebombing of Dresden, Germany, while *Player Piano* (1952) satirizes the tyranny of automation, and *Cat's Cradle* (1963) provides a fantasy about the end of the world. In the following selection, written in 1961, he imagines a future where everyone is equal and it is a crime for anyone to excel at anything.

Pre-Reading and Journal-Writing Suggestions

1. Write about the one modern appliance on which you are most dependent. How would your life be different without it? How would you be different without it?
2. What have we lost and what have we gained because of modern technology?
3. Do you tend to go along with the majority, or do you risk rejection by going against the crowd? Explain.

The year was 2081, and everybody was finally equal. They weren't only equal before God and the law. They were equal every which way. Nobody was smarter than anybody else. Nobody was better looking than anybody else. Nobody was stronger or quicker than anybody else. All this equality was due to the 211th, 212th, and 213th Amendments to the Constitution, and to the unceasing vigilance of agents of the United States Handicapper General.

Some things about living still weren't quite right, though. April, for instance, still drove people crazy by not being springtime. And it was in that clammy month that the H-G men took George and Hazel Bergeron's fourteen-year-old son, Harrison, away.

It was tragic, all right, but George and Hazel couldn't think about it very hard. Hazel had a perfectly average intelligence, which meant she couldn't think about anything except in short bursts. And George, while his intelligence was way above normal, had a little mental handicap radio in his ear. He was required by law to wear it at all times. It was tuned to a government transmitter. Every twenty seconds or so, the transmitter would out some sharp noise to keep people like George from taking unfair advantage of their brains.

George and Hazel were watching television. There were tears on Hazel's cheeks, but she'd forgotten for the moment what they were about. On the television screen were ballerinas.   5

A buzzer sounded in George's head. His thoughts fled in panic, like bandits from a burglar alarm.

"That was a real pretty dance, that dance they just did," said Hazel.

"Huh?" said George.

"That dance—it was nice," said Hazel.

"Yup," said George. He tried to think a little about the ballerinas. They   10
weren't really very good—no better than anybody else would have been, anyway. They were burdened with sashweights and bags of birdshot, and their faces were masked, so that no one, seeing a free and graceful gesture or a pretty face, would feel like something the cat drug in. George was toying with the vague notion that maybe dancers shouldn't be handicapped. But he didn't get very far with it before another noise in his ear radio scattered his thoughts.

George winced. So did two out of the eight ballerinas.

Hazel saw him wince. Having no mental handicap herself, she had to ask George what the latest sound had been.

"Sounded like somebody hitting a milk bottle with a ball peen hammer," said George.

"I'd think it would be real interesting, hearing all the different sounds," said Hazel, a little envious. "All the things they think up."

"Um," said George.   15

"Only, if I was Handicapper General, you know what I would do?" said Hazel. Hazel, as a matter of fact, bore a strong resemblance to the Handicapper General, a woman named Diana Moon Glampers. "If I was Diana Moon Glampers," said Hazel, "I'd have chimes on Sunday—just chimes. Kind of in honor of religion."

"I could think, if it was just chimes," said George.

"Well—maybe make 'em real loud," said Hazel. "I think I'd make a good Handicapper General."

"Good as anybody else," said George.

"Who knows better'n I do what normal is?" said Hazel.   20

"Right," said George. He began to think glimmeringly about his abnormal son who was now in jail, about Harrison, but a twenty-one-gun salute in his head stopped that.

"Boy!" said Hazel, "that was a doozy, wasn't it?"

It was such a doozy that George was white and trembling, and tears stood on the rims of his red eyes. Two of the eight ballerinas had collapsed studio floor, were holding their temples.

"All of a sudden you look so tired," said Hazel. "Why don't you stretch out on the sofa, so's you can rest your handicap bag on the pillows, honeybunch." She was referring to the forty-seven pounds of birdshot in a canvas bag, which was padlocked around George's neck. "Go on and rest the bag for a little while," she said. "I don't care if you're not equal to me for a while."

George weighed the bag with his hands. "I don't mind it," he said. "I don't notice it any more. It's just a part of me."

"You been so tired lately—kind of wore out," said Hazel. "If there was just some way we could make a little hole in the bottom of the bag, and just take out a few of them lead balls. Just a few."

"Two years in prison and two thousand dollars fine for every ball I took out," said George. "I don't call that a bargain."

"If you could just take a few out when you came home from work," said Hazel. "I mean—you don't compete with anybody around here. You just set around."

"If I tried to get away with it," said George, "then other people'd get away with it—and pretty soon we'd be right back to the dark ages again, with everybody competing against everybody else. You wouldn't like that, would you?"

"I'd hate it," said Hazel.

"There you are," said George. "The minute people start cheating on laws, what do you think happens to society?"

If Hazel hadn't been able to come up with an answer to this question, George couldn't have supplied one. A siren was going off in his head.

"Reckon it'd fall all apart," said Hazel.

"What would?" said George blankly.

"Society," said Hazel uncertainly. "Wasn't that what you just said?"

"Who knows?" said George.

The television program was suddenly interrupted for a news bulletin. It wasn't clear at first as to what the bulletin was about, since the announcer, like all announcers, had a serious speech impediment. For about half a minute, and in a state of high excitement, the announcer tried to say, "Ladies and gentlemen—"

He finally gave up, handed the bulletin to a ballerina to read.

"That's all right—" Hazel said of the announcer, "he tried. That's the big thing. He tried to do the best he could with what God gave him. He should get a nice raise for trying so hard."

"Ladies and gentlemen—" said the ballerina, reading the bulletin. She must have been extraordinarily beautiful, because the mask she wore was hideous. And it was easy to see that she was the strongest and most graceful of all the dancers, for her handicap bags were big as those worn by hundred-pound men.

And she had to apologize at once for her voice, which was a very unfair voice for a woman to use. Her voice was a warm, luminous, timeless melody. "Excuse me——" she said, and she began again, making her voice absolutely uncompetitive.

"Harrison Bergeron, age fourteen," she said in a grackle squawk, "has just escaped from jail, where he was held on suspicion of plotting to overthrow the government. He is a genius and an athlete, is under-handicapped, and should be regarded as extremely dangerous."

A police photograph of Harrison Bergeron was flashed on the screen upside down, then sideways, upside down again, then right side up. The picture showed the full length of Harrison against a background calibrated in feet and inches. He was exactly seven feet tall.

The rest of Harrison's appearance was Halloween and hardware. Nobody had ever borne heavier handicaps. He had outgrown hindrances faster than the H-G men could think them up. Instead of a little ear radio for a mental handicap, he wore a tremendous pair of earphones, and spectacles with thick wavy lenses. The spectacles were intended to make him not only half blind, but to give him whanging headaches besides.

Scrap metal was hung all over him. Ordinarily, there was a certain symmetry, a military neatness to the handicaps issued to strong people, but Harrison looked like a walking junkyard. In the race of life, Harrison carried three hundred pounds. 45

And to offset his good looks, the H-G men required that he wear at all times a red rubber ball for a nose, keep his eyebrows shaved off, and cover his even white teeth with black caps at snaggle-tooth random.

"If you see this boy," said the ballerina, "do not—I repeat, do not—try to reason with him."

There was the shriek of a door being torn from its hinges.

Screams and barking cries of consternation came from the television set. The photograph of Harrison Bergeron on the screen jumped again and again, as though dancing to the tune of an earthquake.

George Bergeron correctly identified the earthquake, and well he might have—for many was the time his own home had danced to the same crashing tune. "My God——" said George, "that must be Harrison!" 50

The realization was blasted from his mind instantly by the sound of an automobile collision in his head.

When George could open his eyes again, the photograph of Harrison was gone. A living, breathing Harrison filled the screen.

Clanking, clownish, and huge, Harrison stood in the center of the ⹀dio. The knob of the uprooted studio door was still in his hand. Balle-⹀s, technicians, musicians, and announcers cowered on their knees before ⹀expecting to die.

"I am the Emperor!" cried Harrison. "Do you hear? I am the Emperor! Everybody must do what I say at once!" He stamped his foot and the studio shook.

"Even as I stand here—" he bellowed, "crippled, hobbled, sickened—I am a greater ruler than any man who ever lived! Now watch me become what I *can* become!"   55

Harrison tore the straps of his handicap harness like wet tissue paper, tore straps guaranteed to support five thousand pounds.

Harrison's scrap-iron handicaps crashed to the floor.

Harrison thrust his thumbs under the bar of the padlock that secured his head harness. The bar snapped like celery. Harrison smashed his headphones and spectacles against the wall.

He flung away his rubber-ball nose, revealed a man that would have awed Thor, the god of thunder.

"I shall now select my Empress!" he said, looking down on the cowering people. "Let the first woman who dares rise to her feet claim her mate and her throne!"   60

A moment passed, and then a ballerina arose, swaying like a willow.

Harrison plucked the mental handicap from her ear, snapped off her physical handicaps with marvelous delicacy. Last of all, he removed her mask.

She was blindingly beautiful.

"Now—" said Harrison, taking her hand, "shall we show the people the meaning of the word dance? Music!" he commanded.

The musicians scrambled back into their chairs, and Harrison stripped them of their handicaps, too. "Play your best," he told them, "and I'll make you barons and dukes and earls."   65

The music began. It was normal at first—cheap, silly, false. But Harrison snatched two musicians from their chairs, waved them like batons as he sang the music as he wanted it played. He slammed them back into their chairs.

The music began again and was much improved.

Harrison and his Empress merely listened to the music for a while— listened gravely, as though synchronizing their heartbeats with it.

They shifted their weights to their toes.

Harrison placed his big hands on the girl's tiny waist, letting her sense the weightlessness that would soon be hers.   70

And then, in an explosion of joy and grace, into the air they sprang!

Not only were the laws of the land abandoned, but the law of gravity and the laws of motion as well.

They reeled, whirled, swiveled, flounced, capered, gamboled, and spu

They leaped like deer on the moon.

The studio ceiling was thirty feet high, but each leap brought the d ers nearer to it.

It became their obvious intention to kiss the ceiling. They kissed it.

And then, neutralizing gravity with love and pure will, they remained suspended in air inches below the ceiling, and they kissed each other for a long, long time.

It was then that Diana Moon Glampers, the Handicapper General, came into the studio with a double-barreled ten-gauge shotgun. She fired twice, and the Emperor and the Empress were dead before they hit the floor.

Diana Moon Glampers loaded the gun again. She aimed it at the musi- 80 cians and told them they had ten seconds to get their handicaps back on.

It was then that the Bergerons' television tube burned out.

Hazel turned to comment about the blackout to George. But George had gone out into the kitchen for a can of beer.

George came back in with the beer, paused while a handicap signal shook him up. And then he sat down again. "You been crying?" he said to Hazel.

"Yup," she said.

"What about?" he said.   85

"I forget," she said. "Something real sad on television."

"What was it?" he said.

"It's all kind of mixed up in my mind," said Hazel.

"Forget sad things," said George.

"I always do," said Hazel.

"That's my girl," said George. He winced. There was the sound of a rivetting gun in his head.

"Gee—I could tell that one was a doozy," said Hazel.

"You can say that again," said George.

"Gee—" said Hazel, "I could tell that one was a doozy."

Suggestions for Writing and Discussion
1. What messages might Vonnegut be trying to convey in this piece?
2. What modern appliances might keep people from thinking on their own?
3. Is this piece far-fetched fiction or a realistic warning? Explain your answer.
4. What might be the author's underlying purpose in writing this piece?
5. What character do you identify with most in this piece? Explain.

gestions for Extended Thinking and Writing
  With the intent to persuade a specific audience to your way of thinking,
  rite about the dangers or benefits of a modern appliance today.

2. Write a letter to your college newspaper about a specific issue or problem on campus that you'd like to see changed.

Vocabulary Check

To help ensure that you've understood this selection, and to help you develop a more extensive vocabulary, check the definitions of unfamiliar words in the selection. The words listed below may be new to you, as might others, which you should also identify and define in this exercise.

clammy (2), temples (23), luminous (41), consternation (49), gambol (73)

Using the paragraph numbers in parentheses, which correspond with the numbers in the selection's right margins, locate the words listed above in the reading and develop definitions based on the context in which the words are used (see the guidelines for identifying meaning from context clues on pages 23–24 in Section 3). When you're satisfied with your definitions, use a dictionary to confirm the meaning of each word, and then write your own sentences using these words.

SUGGESTIONS FOR MAKING CONNECTIONS

1. Choose any three authors (or characters) from this section to engage in a lively discussion of the following statement: "We don't need any laws in this country, and we don't need the constitution. All we need to do is treat people with respect."
2. Choose three pieces from this section and compare their views of the role of the individual in modern American society.
3. Initiate a discussion among Krauthammer, Sanchez, and Daum about a person's basic rights and the limits on those rights.
4. What makes an effective argument? To answer this question, choose the piece in this section that made the greatest impact on you. Analyze what specific elements in the writing created this effect.
5. Compare and contrast the values and beliefs inherent in two different generations from two different pieces represented in this section.
6. Using three selections from this section, write an essay in which you make a prediction about America fifty years from now.
7. Using three selections from this section, write an essay in which you argue either that America is a nation of individuals who make up a melting pot of beliefs and possibilities or that it is a nation of followers who no longer value individualism.

Acknowledgments

Text Credits

MAYA ANGELOU, "Finishing School," from *I Know Why the Caged Bird Sings* by Maya Angelou. Copyright © 1969 and renewed 1997 by Maya Angelou. Reprinted by permission of Random House, Inc.

PAUL ARONOWITZ, "A Brother's Dreams," from *The New York Times*, January 24, 1988. Copyright © 1988 by The New York Times Company. Reprinted by permission.

ISAAC ASIMOV, "What Is Intelligence, Anyway?" Published by permission of the Estate of Isaac Asimov, c/o Ralph M. Vicinanza, Ltd.

ERIC BIGLER, "Give Us Jobs, Not Admiration," originally published in *Newsweek*. Reprinted by permission of the author.

GLORIA BONILLA, "Leaving El Salvador," from *You Can't Drown the Fire: Latin American Women Writing in Exile*, ed. by Alicia Portnoy, 1988. Reprinted by permission of Cleis Press.

JANICE CASTRO WITH DAN COOK AND CRISTINA GARCIA, "Spanglish," from *Time*, July 11, 1998. © 1998 Time, Inc. Reprinted by permission.

LINDA CHAVEZ, "There's No Future in Lady Luck." © 1997 by Linda Chavez. Reprinted by permission from Linda Chavez.

KATE CHOPIN, "The Storm," from *The Complete Works of Kate Chopin* edited by Per Seyersted. Copyright © 1969 by Louisiana State University Press. Reprinted by permission of Louisiana State University Press.

JUDITH ORTIZ COFER, "The Myth of the Latin Woman: I Just Met a Girl Named María," from *The Latin Deli: Prose and Poetry*. Copyright © 1993 by Judith Ortiz Cofer. Reprinted by permission from the University of Georgia Press.

JOHN COLEMAN, excerpt from *Blue Collar Journal*. Copyright © 1974 by John R. Coleman. With permission of Collier Associates, P.O. Box 20149, West Palm Beach, FL 33416.

JACQUES D'AMBOISE, "I Show a Child What Is Possible," from *Parade*, August 6, 1989. Copyright © 1989 Parade Magazine. Reprinted with permission from Parade and the author.

MEGHAN DAUM, "Safe Sex and White Lies in the Time of AIDS." Reprinted by permission from the author and from International Creative Management.

EMILY DICKINSON, from *The Poems of Emily Dickinson*, ed. by Ralph W. Franklin. Reprinted by permission of the publishers and Trustees of Amherst College,

GRACE PALEY, "The Loudest Voice," from *The Little Disturbances of Man*. Copyright © 1959, 1994 by Grace Paley. All rights reserved. Reprinted by permission of Grace Paley.

ANNA QUINDLEN, "The War on Drinks," from *The New York Times*, November 6, 1991. Copyright © 1991 by The New York Times Company. Reprinted by permission.

ISHMAEL REED, excerpt from *Writin' Is Fightin'.* Copyright © 1988 by Ishmael Reed. Published by Atheneum Publishers. Reprinted by permission from Lowenstein Associates, Inc.

JACQUELINE NAVARRA RHOADS, "Nurses in Vietnam," from *Nurses in Vietnam: The Forgotten Veterans* by Dan Freedman and Jacqueline Navarra Rhoads. Reprinted by permission from Dan Freedman.

MIKE ROSE, "I Just Wanna Be Average," from *Lives on the Boundary: The Struggles and Achievements of America's Underprepared*. Copyright © 1989 by Mike Rose. Reprinted with the permission of The Free Press, a Division of Simon & Schuster, Inc.

RENE SANCHEZ, "Surfing's Up and Grades Are Down." Copyright © 1996 The Washington Post. Reprinted with permission.

SCOTT RUSSELL SANDERS, "The Men We Carry in Our Minds . . . and How They Differ from the Real Lives of Most Men," from *The Paradise of Bombs*. Copyright © 1984 by Scott Russell Sanders; first appeared in Milkweed Chronicle. Reprinted by permission of the author and the Virginia Kidd Agency, Inc.

FLORIDA SCOTT-MAXWELL, "Going Home," from *The Measure of My Days*. Copyright © 1968 by Florida Scott-Maxwell. Reprinted by permission of Alfred A. Knopf, Inc.

LORE SEGAL, "Modern Courtesy," from *The New York Times*, November 19, 1987. Copyright © 1987 by The New York Times Company. Reprinted by permission.

RICHARD SELZER, "The Discus Thrower," from *Confessions of a Knife*, William Morrow, 1979. Copyright © 1979 by David Goldman and Janet Selzer, Trustees. Reprinted by permission of George Borchardt, Inc. for the author.

ISAAC BASHEVIS SINGER, "The Son from America," from *A Crown of Feathers*. Copyright © 1973 by Isaac Bashevis Singer. Reprinted by permission of Farrar, Straus & Giroux, Inc.

GARY SOTO, "Like Mexicans," from *Small Faces*. Text copyright © 1986 by Gary Soto. Used with permission of the author and BookStop Literary Agency. All rights reserved.

BRENT STAPLES, "Just Walk On By: A Black Man Ponders His Power to Alter Public Space." Copyright © 1986 by Brent Staples. Reprinted by permission of the author.

JOHN TARKOV, "Fitting In," from *The New York Times*, July 7, 1985. Copyright © 1985 by The New York Times Company. Reprinted by permission.

JOSEPH TELUSHKIN, "Words That Hurt, Words That Heal: How to Choose Words Wisely and Well," *Imprimis*, 1996 issue. Reprinted by permission from Imprimis and Hillsdale College Press.

MIGUEL TORRES, "Crossing the Border," from *American Mosaic: The Immigrant Experience in the Words of Those Who Lived It*, ed. by Joan Morrison and Charlotte Fox Zabusky. Copyright © 1980, 1982, 1992 by Joan Morrison and Charlotte Fox Zabusky. Reprinted with permission from John A. Ware Literary Agency.

LINDSY VAN GELDER, "Marriage as a Restricted Club," originally appeared in *Ms.* Magazine in 1984. Reprinted by permission of Lindsy Van Gelder.

KURT VONNEGUT, JR., "Harrison Bergeron," from *Welcome to the Monkey House.* Copyright © 1961 by Kurt Vonnegut, Jr. Used by permission of Delacorte Press/ Seymour Lawrence, a division of Random House, Inc.

WILLIAM CARLOS WILLIAMS, "Use of Force," from *The Collected Stories of William Carlos Williams.* Copyright © 1938 by William Carlos Williams. Reprinted by permission of New Directions Publishing Corp.

Photo Credits

Page 60, © Topham/The Image Works; page 61, © Stock Boston; page 104, © H. Armstrong Roberts; page 105, © The Image Works; page 136, © Stock Boston; page 137, © Joel Gordon Photography; page 168, Charles Harbutt/Actuality, Inc.; page 169, © Stock Boston; page 219, © Joel Gordon Photography; page 220 © Jerry Speier, Joel Gordon Photography; page 260, © Stock Boston; page 261, © Jane Scherr/ Jeroboam, Inc.; page 299, © Stock Boston; page 300, © Jennings/The Image Works.

Index